MEDIÆVAL PLAYS IN SCOTLAND

Excerpt from the Minutes of the Faculty of Arts
of St Andrews University, 1514.

See p. 284.

MEDIÆVAL PLAYS IN SCOTLAND

BY

ANNA JEAN MILL

BENJAMIN BLOM  New York/London

ST ANDREWS UNIVERSITY PUBLICATIONS

No. XXIV.

First Published 1924
Reissued 1969 by
Benjamin Blom, Inc., Bronx, New York 10452
and 56 Doughty Street, London, W.C. 1

Library of Congress Catalog Card Number 68-56497

Printed in the United States of America

PREFATORY NOTE.

THIS investigation was carried out mainly during my
tenure of a Carnegie Trust scholarship and research grant,
and its publication has been made possible by a generous
guarantee against loss promised by the Carnegie Trust.

In carrying out a piece of work which involved the
examination of original records in many different parts of
the country, I have incurred numerous debts. For per-
mission to examine manuscripts in their custody I have
to thank the Town Clerks of Aberdeen, Arbroath, Ayr,
Crail, Cupar, Dumfries, Dundee, Dunfermline, Edinburgh,
Elgin, Forres, Haddington, Inverness, Lanark, Linlithgow,
Montrose, Newburgh, North Berwick, Perth, Selkirk, and
St Andrews; the Session Clerk of Perth; the Presbytery
Clerks of Dalkeith, Edinburgh, Kelso, and Stirling; the
Deans of Guild of Dundee, Edinburgh, and Perth; the Clerks
to the Incorporations of Tailors, Wrights, Glovers, and
Hammermen of Perth, and to the Incorporation of Wrights
and Masons of Edinburgh; and all the local officials who
have answered my inquiries regarding records. I acknow-
ledge with gratitude the way in which my heavy demands
have been met in the various libraries where I have worked,
and, in particular, in St Andrews University Library,
Dundee Public Library, the Advocates' Library, Edinburgh
University Library, the British Museum, and Harvard

University Library, as well as in Register House, Edinburgh, and the Public Record Office, London. For help on special points I have to thank Professor Craigie, Dr Maitland Anderson, Professor J. D. Mackie, and Mr G. M. Shirley. Professor W. I. Zeitler kindly lightened my task of proof-reading. Through the courtesy of Mr A. O. Anderson I am permitted to reproduce the photograph which appears in this book. Finally, my thanks are due to Professor Blyth Webster, at whose suggestion this investigation was begun, and without whose encouragement at each step of its progress it would never have been completed.

With the exception of a few minor alterations, this volume represents the thesis presented by me for the degree of Doctor of Philosophy of St Andrews. Owing to the scattered nature of my sources and to my absence abroad, it has been impossible in all cases to collate my proofs with the original manuscripts. I can only hope that the possibility of serious error has been eliminated by a rigorous process of checking and rechecking at an earlier stage.

A. J. M.

Aug. 1927.

CONTENTS.

LIST OF AUTHORITIES.

A.P.S. The Acts of the Parliaments of Scotland. Edited by Thomas Thomson and Cosmo Innes, 1844, etc.

Bain. Calendar of Documents relating to Scotland, preserved in Her Majesty's Public Record Office, London, 1108-1509. Edited by Joseph Bain. 4 vols. 1881-88.

Bain and Boyd. Calendar of State Papers relating to Scotland and Mary, Queen of Scots, 1547-1603, preserved in the Public Record Office, the British Museum, and elsewhere in England. Edited by J. Bain and W. K. Boyd, 1898, etc.

Bann. Club. Bannatyne Club publications. Edinburgh, 1823-61.

Buchanan, George. Opera, 1725. Rerum Scoticarum Historia. 1762.

B.U.K. The Booke of the Universall Kirk of Scotland. Acts and Proceedings of the General Assemblies of the Kirk of Scotland, from the year MDLX. Mait. Club. 3 vols. 1839.

Calderwood. History of the Kirk of Scotland. By Mr David Calderwood. Edited by Thomas Thomson. Wodrow Society. 8 vols. 1842-49.

C.H.L. The Cambridge History of English Literature. Edited by A. W. Ward and A. R. Waller, 1907, etc.

Chambers, E. K. The Mediæval Stage. 2 vols. 1903.
The Elizabethan Stage. 4 vols. 1923.

Creizenach, W. Geschichte des neueren Dramas. 4 vols. 1893-1909.

D'Ancona, A. Origini del teatro italiano. 2 vols. 1891.

Dibdin, J. C. Annals of the Edinburgh Stage. 1888.

D.R.O. A diurnal of remarkable occurrents that have passed within the country of Scotland since the death of King James the Fourth till the year MDLXXV. Bannatyne Club. 1833.

Dunbar, William. Poems. Scottish Text Society. 3 vols. 1893.

E.R. Rotuli scaccarii regum Scotorum. The Exchequer Rolls of Scotland, 1264-1600. Edited by John Stuart and others. 23 vols. 1878-1908.

Frazer, J. G. The Golden Bough. Abridged edition. 1922.

Herford, C. H. The Literary Relations of England and Germany in the Sixteenth Century. 1886.

Irving, D. History of Scotish Poetry. Edited by J. A. Carlyle, 1861.

Keith. History of the Affairs of Church and State in Scotland, from the beginning of the Reformation to the year 1568, by the Right Rev. Robert Keith. Spottiswoode Society. 3 vols. 1844-50.

Knox. Works of John Knox. Wodrow Society. 6 vols. 1846-64.

Lesley, Bishop John. De Origine Moribus et Rebus Gestis Scotorum 1578, 1675. The Historie of Scotland (1436-1561). Bannatyne Club. 1830. The Historie of Scotland wrytten first in Latin by the most reuerend and worthy Jhone Leslie, Bishop of Rosse, and translated into Scottish by Father James Dalrymple, etc. Scottish Text Society. 1888-95.

L.H.T.A. Compota thesaurariorum regum Scotorum. Accounts of the Lord High Treasurer of Scotland, 1473-1566. Edited by Thomas Dickson and Sir James Balfour Paul. 11 vols. 1877-1916.

Lyndsay. Works of Sir D. Lyndsay. Edited D. Laing. 3 vols. 1879. Works of Lyndsay, Part IV., E.E.T.S., 1869. The Bannatyne Manuscript. Vol. III., Hunterian Club, 1896.

Mait. Club. Maitland Club publications. Glasgow, 1828-59.

Nichols, J. The Progresses of Queen Elizabeth. 3 vols. 1823. The Progresses of King James the First. 4 vols. 1828.

N.E.D. New English Dictionary.

New Spald. Club. New Spalding Club publications. Aberdeen, 1886, etc.

Petit de Julleville, L. Les Mystères. 2 vols. 1880.
La Comédie et les Mœurs en France au Moyen Âge. 1886.
Les Comédiens en France au Moyen Âge. 1889.
Répertoire du Théâtre comique en France au Moyen Âge. 1886.

Pitcairn. Ancient Criminal Trials in Scotland compiled from the Original Records and MSS., etc., by Robert Pitcairn, Esq. Bannatyne Club. 3 vols. 1833.

Pitscottie. The Historie and Cronicles of Scotland. Robert Lindesay of Pitscottie. Scottish Text Society. 3 vols. 1899-1911.

The Register of the Privy Council of Scotland, 1545-1625. Edited by John Hill Burton and David Masson. 14 vols. 1877-98.

Reg. Sec. Sig. Registrum secreti sigilli regum Scotorum. The Register of the Privy Seal of Scotland. Vol. I., 1488-1529. Edited by M. Livingstone, 1908. Vol. II, 1529-42. Edited by D. Hay Fleming, 1921.

Robertson, J. Inventaires de la Royne Descosse Douairiere de France. Catalogues of the Jewels, Dresses, Furniture, Books, and Paintings of Mary, Queen of Scots. Bannatyne Club. 1863. Statuta Ecclesiæ Scoticanæ. Concilia Scotiæ ecclesiæ Scoticanæ statuta tam provincialia quam synodalia quæ supersunt. MCCXXV-MDLIX. 2 vols. 1866. Translated in Statutes of the Scottish Church, 1225-1559. Scottish History Society. 1907.

S.B.R.S. Scottish Burgh Records Society publications. Edinburgh, 1868-1908.

S.H.S. Scottish History Society publications. Edinburgh, 1886, etc.

S.T.S. Scottish Text Society publications. Edinburgh, 1882, etc.

Spald. Club. Spalding Club publications. Aberdeen, 1839-1870.

Thorpe. Calendar of State Papers relating to Scotland preserved in the State Paper Department of Her Majesty's Public Record Office. Edited by Markham John Thorpe. 2 vols. 1858.

Ward. A History of English Dramatic Literature to the Death of Queen Anne. A. W. Ward. 3 vols. 1899.

Withington, Robert. English Pageantry. 2 vols. 1918.

Wod. Soc. Wodrow Society publications. Edinburgh, 1841-50.

MEDIÆVAL PLAYS IN SCOTLAND.

I.

FOLK PLAYS.[1]

IF we exclude the May game, the evidence as to folk plays in documents of the sixteenth century, and earlier, is, as we might expect, slight and ill-defined. A few prohibitions of the mediæval Church have survived the general wreckage of pre-Reformation ecclesiastical records. A thirteenth-century statute of the Diocese of Aberdeen decrees that neither ' choree ' nor ' turpes et inhonesti ludi ' should be permitted in church or churchyard.[2] Elsewhere wrestlings are strictly prohibited in sacred places, under penalty of excommunication, and sports in which there is a struggle to gain a prize.[3] The fourteenth-century synodal statutes of St Andrews have similar provisions. In order to prevent sacrilege, it is forbidden ' choreas ducere seu lucturam facere vel alios quoscunque [ludos] inhonestos ' in the

[1] I deal only with early records of folk plays and not with modern survivals. My main authority for interpretation of the data is Chambers, *Mediæval Stage*, I, Book II.

[2] Robertson, *Statuta Ecclesiæ Scoticanæ* (*Bann. Club*), II, 38. ' Prohibemus etiam ne choree vel turpes et inhonesti ludi qui ad lasciuiam invitant in ecclesijs vel cimiterijs fiant. . . .' Cf. *Statutes of the Scottish Church*, 1225-1559, *S.H.S.*, p. 40.

[3] Robertson, *Statuta*, II, 40. ' Quod lucte et ludi non fiant in ecclesijs nec in cimiterijs. Huic etiam prohibitioni duximus ad[d]endum vt in aliquibus festiuitatibus infra ecclesias vel cimiteria lucte vel ludi de cetero fieri non permittantur,' 52. ' . . . quod ludi in quibus [decertatur ad bravium assequendum prohibeantur.'] Cf. *Statutes of the Scottish Church*, pp. 42, 56.

A

church or its precincts on festal days.[1] Even from these
scanty survivals we see that in Scotland, as elsewhere,
the ancient rites had been diverted from the pagan temple
to the Christian Church and its environment ; and that
the ' ludi ' associated with the sacrificial ceremony of the
pre-Christian era lingered on.

But it is only when we come to the fuller records of the
Reformed Church that we realise how firmly entrenched
in the life of the people were these semi-Christianised
remnants of heathen ritual. Repeated summonses were
issued by the kirk sessions and presbyteries against those
guilty of pilgrimages to sacred wells.[2] That old homeo-
pathic sun charm, the midsummer bonfire, was the subject
of numerous ecclesiastical edicts ; [3] and the harvest and
seed-time pastimes engaged the attention of various con-
ventions of the Kirk authorities.[4] Yule carols [5] and the
ringing of vessels at Uphaly Day [6] were suppressed with a
heavy hand. The folk custom of playing football in the
churchyard or through the town at Shrovetide survived
in certain districts when the original pagan significance
must have been obliterated.[7]

[1] Robertson, *Statuta*, II, 73. *Statutes of the Scottish Church*,
p. 77.
[2] *B.U.K.*, II, 462 ; III, 874. *Records of Elgin (New Spald.
Club)*, I, 165 ; II, 30, 31. Stirling MS. Presbytery Records,
12th Sept. 1581, 7th May and 11th June 1583, etc. Also *A.P.S.*,
1581, c. 6, III, 212.
[3] *Records of Elgin*, I, 165 ; II, 17, 74. *Aberdeen Kirk Session
Records (Spald. Club)*, 3rd July 1608. Stirling MS. Presbytery
Records, 9th July 1583, 21st Oct. 1589 (Hallowe'en bonfires).
Edinburgh MS. Presbytery Records, 25th June 1588, 2nd and
16th July 1588, etc. Also *A.P.S.*, 1581, c. 6, III, 212.
[4] *B.U.K.*, III, 874. App. I, s.v. *Errol*, 1594, 1596. *Ibid.*,
s.v. *Elgin*, 1596.
[5] App. I, s.v. *Errol*, 1593, 1594-5. *Ibid.*, s.v. *Elgin*, 1600,
1604, 1618. *Ibid.*, s.v. *Aberdeen*—Kirk Session Records, 1574, etc.
[6] *Records of Elgin*, I, 165 ; II, 46, 119, etc.
[7] App. I, s.v. *Errol*, 1594-5. *Records of Elgin*, II, 68, 76, 131
(here it occurs among the prohibited Yule pastimes), etc. ' Sax
futballis ' regularly appear in the Glasgow burgh accounts from

Of more definitely dramatic nature, however, are the
sword dance, morris dance, and mummers' play, which
likewise sprang from the ritual of the seasonal festivals
and symbolised the resurrection of the year in the spring.
Early records of the sword dance in Scotland are rare.
The unique literary Papa Stour dance does not come
within the limits of this survey.[1] The Perth skinners'
dance is interesting as the product of a special craft.[2] As the
earliest records of the Incorporation of Glovers do not
commence until 1593, there is no means of determining the
age of the dance ; but the assurance with which the town
called on the skinners ' to prouyde for ane ſsword dance '
in honour of the King's visit in 1617 gives one the impression of tried skill on the part of the performers. From
the 1633 account we learn that there were thirteen dancers
all clad alike ' with greine cappis silwer strings rid ribbens
whyte shoes and bellis about pair leggis scheiring raperis
in thair handis and all wther abulȝement.' From a
later description the tunic appears to have been fawn-

1574 to 1579 for use at Shrovetide ; and on 31st Jan. 1589-90
John Neill, cordiner, was made burgess without fee ' for fur-
neissing yeirlie during his lyftyme vpoune Fastreinis-ewin of
sex guid and sufficient fut ballis, or ellis tuentie schillingis as the
price thairof '—*Extracts from the Records of the Burgh of Glasgow*,
Vol. I. The conditions for admission to the Perth Tailors' craft
included the presentation of a football for Fastern's E'en—MS.
Records of the Incorporation, 27th April 1546, 11th Feb. 1548-9,
10th May 1550. The MS. Cordiner Book of Perth, 23rd Feb.
1601, has a minute ordaining that whatever freeman of the craft
is married shall make a payment ' for pair futeball at fasterings
evin.' The tournaments which took place at this season at the
Scottish court were perhaps of similar origin. App. III.—Excerpts
from *L.H.T.A.*

[1] Printed in Chambers, *Mediæval Stage*, App. J.

[2] There are some German examples of craft sword dances—
Müllenhoff, *Ueber den Schwerttanz*, in *Festgaben für Gustav Homeyer*,
1871, pp. 119-121, cites dances of the Nürnberg butchers and
cutlers and the Breslau skinners. Other instances are cited by
F. A. Mayer in *Zeitschrift für Völkerpsychologie*, 1889, pp. 238-
40. Cf. also *Creizenach*, I, 409.

coloured.[1] The dance itself was of an intricate nature, five of the dancers being on the ground and five on their shoulders, with the other three dancing through their feet and round about ; [2] but there is no hint either of the ' grotesque ' or the other supernumeraries, who are so conspicuous in the English examples,[3] or of speeches preceding the ' figure '.[4]

The plentiful use of bells lends support to the theory that the sword dance was really identical with the morris dance.[5] Bells for the dancers in the sword dance arranged in honour of Anne of Denmark figure in the Edinburgh burgh accounts for the year 1590.[6] Nor was the morris dance unknown by name in Scotland. Dunbar testifies to its popularity at Court in the early sixteenth century.[7] It is specifically mentioned more than once in the official court records ; [8] and it is probable that those dances for which equipment was provided in December 1506 and May 1508 belonged to the same category. These carefully organ-

---

[1] Müllenhoff, op. cit., 126, cites Winkelmann's theory of a connection between the ' nudi iuvenes ' of Tacitus and the white smocks which he regards as de rigueur in the sword dance. But cf. Chambers, Mediæval Stage, I, 200, who implies that this point has been overstressed, and Mayer, op. cit., 236-8, who recognises this common characteristic, but quotes several records of the dance in which the white smock is not in evidence. Is it possible that the ' fawn ' of the Perth dress is white which has become discoloured ?

[2] Is this a meaningless extension of the ' Erhebung des Königs ' ? It does not seem to correspond to any of the figures cited by Mayer or Müllenhoff.

[3] Chambers, Mediæval Stage, I, 192.

[4] App. I, s.v. Perth—Excerpts from Council Register.

[5] Chambers, Mediæval Stage, I, 195. One of the Perth dresses is still in existence, and is known as a morris dancer's dress. See App. I, s.v. Perth, 271 n.

[6] App. I, s.v. Edinburgh—Municipal Plays. It is difficult to disentangle the sword dance from the ' hieland dansß ' prepared for the same occasion ; but apparently there were twelve dancers who wore white shoes, and, more interesting, ' xij hattis of flouris.'

[7]   ' Sum singis ; sum dancis ; sum tellis storeis ;
     Sum lait at evin bringis in the moreis.'
                   (Dunbar, Poems, II, 206).

[8] App. III, Excerpts from L.H.T.A., 1503-4, 1512.

ised dances would doubtless shed much of their genuine folk character ; but the ' woman ' is prominent, bells are in evidence, and a fool is apparently included in at least one case (1508).[1] The ' buffons ' mentioned among the ' lycht dances ' in the ' Complaynt of Scotland '[2] was probably a morris or sword dance ; and there is a reference to a popular morris in ' Christes Kirk of the Grene.'[3] But, naturally, the less sophisticated versions remain un-chronicled until the kirk sessions bestir themselves to stamp out such ' superstitious ' practices. In December 1605, five men were summoned at Aberdeen for going through the town ' maskit and dansing with bellis ' at Yule.[4] At Elgin, in January 1623, certain ' gwysseris ' were censured by the Session for having ' past in ane sword dance in Paul Dunbar his closs and in the kirkyeard.'[5] The fact that they wore ' maskis and wissoris ' is interesting, as is the gravitation to the kirkyard. A more exhaustive search in early seventeenth-century Kirk records would probably bring to light many other examples of degenerate ' renouveau ' folk dances.

The most fully developed form of folk representation of mock death and resurrection, symbolising the victory of summer over winter, is to be found in the Mummers' Play ; which, in accordance with the tendency of folk customs to follow the Christian calendar, has shifted to Christmas or the New Year. Fragments of the play of Galatians or

[1] At the ' triumph ' prepared by the town of Edinburgh in 1558, thirty-one dozen bells were provided for the six dancers, and there was a fool clad in a coat of ' syndrie hewis.' *Infra*, 84, and App. I, s.v. *Edinburgh*—Municipal Plays.
[2] *The Complaynt of Scotland*, E.E.T.S., 1872, p. 66. Also xcv, where Cotgrave is cited as glossing ' Dancer les Buffons : to daunce a morris.'
[3] *Ibid.*, xcv.
[4] App. I, s.v. *Aberdeen*—Kirk Session Records. Also Jan. 1606.
[5] *Ibid.*, s.v. *Elgin*—Kirk Session Records.

14   MEDIÆVAL PLAYS IN SCOTLAND.

Goloshans,[1] which corresponds to the English play of St George, are still recited in various parts of Scotland, and I have myself collected several new versions from oral sources. But nowhere in the records with which I have been dealing have I come across any definite reference to this play—although the guisard is a familiar personage in sixteenth-century Scotland. Whether ' guisard ' was applied exclusively to these folk mummers or was a general

[1] Chambers, *Mediæval Stage*, I, 210 n., suggests that Galatians is a corruption of Galgacus, who appears in the Falkirk fragment printed by Hone, *Every-Day Book*, 1838, pp. 18, 19. The characters are Galgacus, otherwise Galacheus or St Lawrence, who slays Jack, the Doctor, and Judas, who arrives for the quête. Other versions, more or less corrupt and incomplete, are printed by : Andrew Cheviot, *Proverbs, etc., of Scotland*, 1896, pp. 170-72, Border version—Sir Alexander (presentation), Farmer's son, Wallace, who slays Golaschin, Doctor Brown, Old Beelzebub (quête) ; *Stirling Antiquary*, Vol. I, 1893, pp. 67-9, Stirling version—Sir Alexander (presentation), Farmer's son, Admiral, who slays Galatians, Doctor, Little Diddlie Dots (quête) ; M'Taggart, *Scottish Gallovidian Encyclopædia*, 1824, s.v. Yule boys—Beelzebub and two knights ; Robert Chambers, *Popular Rhymes of Scotland*, pp. 169-177, Peebles version—Talking Man (presentation), Black Knight, who slays Galatian, Young Man, Dr Brown, Judas (quête), a ' Bessy ' who acts as a squire to the vocal guisards ; fragment of Falkirk version—King of Macedon, Prince George of Ville, Slasher ; J. F. Leishman, *A Son of Knox*, pp. 109-116, Forfarshire version—Bol Bendo the Abbot of Fools, who slays Golishan, Sir Alexander (presentation), the Kings of France and Spain (who probably belong to another version), Doctor Beelzebub. Cf. Scott's notes to Canto VI of *Marmion*— ' In Scotland (*me ipso teste*), we were wont, during my boyhood, to take the characters of the apostles, at least of Peter, Paul, and Judas Iscariot ; the first had the keys, the second carried a sword, and the last the bag in which the dole of our neighbours' plumb-cake was deposited. One played a Champion, and recited some traditional rhymes ; another was Alexander, King of Macedon. . . . There was also, occasionally, I believe, a St George.' Cf., too, the Introduction to Canto VI. In Captain Hall's Journal, Abbotsford, 1st Jan. 1825, there is a reference to a Hogmanay guisards' play in which ' the hero was one Golishin.' (Lockhart's *Life of Scott*, 1902, VII, 274.) Notices of English versions are collected by Chambers, *Mediæval Stage*, I, 205-6. See, too, *Folk Lore*, II, 326 ; IV, 162 ; and R. J. E. Tiddy, *The Mummers' Play*, 1923.

term synonymous with ' player ' is not clear. The ' thre gysaris that playit the play ' at the Scottish court in August 1503 may have been none other than John English and his companions, who, according to a contemporary account, acted a ' Moralite ' at the time of the royal marriage.[1] On the whole, however, the term does seem to have been reserved for those groups of local revellers who claimed the right of entry at the festive season [2]—a right handed down from their pagan ancestors, who, carrying branches of sacred trees or wearing parts of the sacrificial beast, sought to bring the whole community into touch with the fertilising spirit. The guisard was in evidence on other festive occasions throughout the year,[3] but the main period of his activities had drifted to the Yule season. He appeared at Court on St John's Day, New Year's Day, 2nd January, Uphaly Day, and even in the beginning of February.[4] The whole energy of the Reformed Church was directed against the keeping of Yule—nowhere more persistent than in Elgin,[5] where, at least until far on in the seventeenth century, the suppression of guising in the ' superstitious days ' occupied the attention of the Kirk Session.

Details as to the performances are rarely given. We may take it that dancing formed at least part of the entertainment.[6] We hear, too, of the ' gysaris that playit to the King '[7]—though the word ' play ' must here, as

[1] App. III, Excerpts from *L.H.T.A.*
[2] *Ibid.*, 1491 (Linlithgow), 1496 (Melrose), 1502-3 (Arbroath); and there are several references to the ' gysaris of the toun of Edinburgh.'
[3] *Ibid.*, Aug. 1488 at Lanark; June 1501 and May 1505 at Edinburgh.
[4] *Ibid.*
[5] App. I, s.v. *Elgin*—Kirk Session Records.
[6] App. III, Excerpts from *L.H.T.A.*, 1491, 1501, 1503-4, 1505. Also App. I, *Elgin*—Kirk Session Records, 1598, 1615.
[7] *Ibid.*, Excerpts from *L.H.T.A.*, 1501-2.

always, be interpreted with caution. Some distinction may be implied between the ' dansaris ' and ' gysaris ' who amused the King at Lanark in 1488.[1] Guising was still in the hands of adults, even if in the post-Reformation period it was limited to a rowdy and lawless section of the population. Characteristic features of the folk play emerge, such as the music of bones and bells,[2] the ' blaikit ' or masked faces,[3] the exchange of garments between the sexes.[4] The carrying of the coat stuffed with straw on a stick suggests the anthropomorphic representation of the deity of fertilisation.[5] The tendency to drift towards the kirkyard, noted already in connection with the sword dance, is also of interest.

But of all the forms of folk play derived from festival rites, none was more popular than that which centred round the election of a mock king, originally the mediator in the sacrificial ceremony. The ' ludus de rege et regina ' crops up at both the winter and summer feasts. The King of the Bean was regularly appointed at Uphaly Day at the Scottish court from at least the.end of the fifteenth century.[6] Occasionally his place was taken by a Queen of the Bean.[7]

[1] App. III, Excerpts from *L.H.T.A.*
[2] App. I, s.v. *Elgin*—Kirk Session Records, 1598.
[3] *Ibid.* Also App. I, s.v. *Dundee*, 1594, 1595, 1597.
[4] *Ibid.*, s.v. *Elgin*, 1615 ; *Aberdeen*, 1575-6, 1606 ; *Perth*, 1609—Kirk Session Records.
[5] Cf. Frazer, *Golden Bough*, Chap. xxviii.—' The Killing of the Tree-Spirit.'
[6] App. III, Excerpts from *L.H.T.A.*, 1489-90, 1491-2, 1496, 1497-8, 1501-2, 1502-3.
[7] *Ibid.*, 1531. See also *Wigtown Papers, Mait. Club Miscellany*, II, 390-2. Thomas Randolphe to Lord Robert Dudley, 15th Jan. 1563-4 : Randolphe had ' allmost forgotten my chiefest matter,' so enthusiastic is his description of the ' great solemnity and royall estate of the Queen of the Beene.' ' Two such sights in one state, in soe good accord, I beleeve was never seen, as to behold two worthie Queens posess, without envie, one kingdom both upon a day.' Cf. Bain and Boyd, *Calendar*, II, 34. Randolph to Cecil, 15th Jan. 1563-4. ' Your honour knows the " solennities " in divers countries on the 12th day of Christmas—it was

Although one may assume that similar elections took place
throughout the land in humbler spheres at the Epiphany,
the only other trace of the custom in early times which I
have found is at the University of St Andrews, where a
minute, dated 1432, regulates the garments to be worn by
the ' Rex ffabe ' and his attendants at the Feast of Kings.[1]

The underlying idea of inversion of status is to be found
likewise in the various ecclesiastical modifications of folk
festivals which were celebrated during the Christmas season.
The incorporation in the statutes of the Scottish Church of
Grosseteste's provision regarding the ' Festum Stultorum ' [2]
shows that the Feast of Fools was not unknown in Scotland. Lyndsay makes use of the *sermon joyeux* on the
theme, ' The number of fuillis ar infinite.' [3] But the special
choir-boys' festival, which centred round St Nicholas Day
or Holy Innocents' Day, is more in evidence. There is
ample testimony to the popularity of the schoolboys' feast
in the enactments made by the ' reformed ' councils and
kirk sessions against the ' taking of the schuill ' and the
play-days at Yule.[4] It is rather surprising, however, that,

no less here, and as much was done as could be for the honour
of the day. . . .' On this occasion Mary Fleming was Queen.
In *Epigrammatum* lib. iii, Valentiniana 6-9, *Ad Mariam Betonam
pridie Regalium Reginam sorte ductam*, Buchanan celebrates Mary
Beton as Twelfth Night Queen. (Cited in Robertson's *Inventories*,
xlviii.)

[1] App. I, s.v. *St Andrews*—Liber Conclusionum Vniversitatis
Sanctiandree. This antedates by half a century the earliest
notice of the Merton ' Rex Fabarum.' Cf. F. S. Boas, *University
Drama in the Tudor Age*, 1914, pp. 4, 5, 6.

[2] Robertson, *Statuta Ecclesiæ Scoticanæ*, II, 52. ' Quod Festum
Stultorum penitus tollatur.' Cf. *Statutes of the Scottish Church*,
p. 56.

[3] Lyndsay, *Works*, 1879, II, 215-21. According to Petit de
Julleville, *La Comédie et les Mœurs en France*, 73, the *sermon
joyeux* is undoubtedly derived from the Feast of Fools. Cf.
infra, 87, the extract from *Reg. Eccles. Colleg. Sancte Trinitatis de
Edinburgh*.

[4] App. I, s.v. *Aberdeen*—Folk Plays (*b*) ; *Elgin*, 22nd Dec.
1596, and footnote.

with the almost universal adoption of the Use of Sarum by
the Roman Catholic Church in Scotland, so few notices of
the Boy Bishop have survived in local records.

In the year 1303-4, Edward I. was entertained at the
royal chapel at Dunfermline by a Boy Bishop, to whom
he gave a present of 40 s.[1] In November 1414 it was
decided that the feast of the St Andrews 'grammatici'
held on St Nicholas Day should be transferred to the day
of the translation of that Saint in summer (9th May);
and that the collection of money from house to house, as
the procession of the Boy Bishop passed from the Castle
to the Monastery, was to be prohibited. For that year,
however, the feast was to be held on the usual date, but
'absque omni exactione et receptione pecuniæ.'[2] A mid-
fifteenth century inventory of vestments belonging to St
Salvator's College, St Andrews, mentions 'a Mytyr for St
Innocentis bishop.'[3] In 1540 there is a payment of 27s.
from the Chamberlain of St Andrews to the St Nicholas
Bishop and his attendants ('ministris') at the feast of St
Nicholas.[4] St Nicholas Bishops from the Abbey and 'the
hie toun' of Edinburgh received grants from the royal purse
from at least 1473 until 1511; and their attendant imps
('deblatis' and 'ruffyis' or 'ruffenis') were rewarded with
proportionately smaller sums.[5] Local 'bishops' in Leith,[6]
Linlithgow,[7] Stirling,[8] and Cupar[9] obtained generous
gratuities from the King. The period of jurisdiction of this

---

[1] App. I, s.v. *Dunfermline.*
[2] *Ibid.*, s.v. *St Andrews*—Liber Conclusionum Vniversitatis
Sanctiandree.
[3] *Mait. Club Miscellany*, III, 199.
[4] *Rentale Sancti Andreæ*, *S.H.S.*, 2nd series, 109.
[5] App. III, Excerpts from *L.H.T.A.*, 1473, 1491, 1497, 1501,
1503, 1507, 1511.
[6] *Ibid.*, 1511.
[7] *Ibid.*, 1496, 1503, 1506, 1507.
[8] *Ibid.*, 1503.
[9] *Ibid.*, 1501.

juvenile bishop apparently commenced with St Nicholas Eve
and extended over the following week ; but in Edinburgh,
at any rate, there seems to have been a second celebration
on Holy Innocents' Day with a ' Sant Innocentis beschop '
(or bishops).[1]

In the copious pre-Reformation records of Aberdeen,
with St Nicholas as the patron saint of the city, one would
expect to find traces of a boy bishop. But it is only by
accident that he comes into the records at all. In 1542
the Council decreed that the master of the Grammar School
was to have 4s. Scots from the soberest person who received
him and the bishop on St Nicholas Day. Other men were
to give him at their pleasure, and whoever refused entry
was to be fined—' and ɣat becauß . . . he hes na vder fee
to leif oñ lyk as his predecessouris hed afor him & vderis
maisteris of vder scuilis.' The yearly pension of ten marks
granted in 1546 had to be eked out with the proceeds of
the St Nicholas ' gaderyng.' Honest citizens were once
more called on to receive the schoolmaster on his rounds
with the bishop and to make contributions ' of ɣe auld
maner efferand to ɣair estatis as ɣa think expedient.' [2]

Of all the types of temporary kings, the Summer King
has made the deepest impression on the extant records of
Scotland. The earliest definite reference to the May game
which I have found is in the minutes of the Faculty of Arts
at St Andrews, 1432.[3] The old practice of the ' magistri '
and ' scolares ' bringing in May or summer (' *importando
mayum seu estatem* ') in disguise on horseback, bearing the
insignia of kings and emperors, is condemned as useless
and dangerous. Two points call for special notice.

In the first place, the St Andrews May game was of a

---

[1] App. III, Excerpts from *L.H.T.A.*, 1506, 1507, 1511.
[2] App. I, s.v. *Aberdeen*—Folk Plays (*b*).
[3] *Ibid.*, s.v. *St Andrews*—Liber Conclusionum Vniversitatis
Sanctiandree.

processional character—that is, consciously or unconsciously, it included the pagan ceremony of spreading the influence of the fertilisation spirit through the community. Whether this surviving piece of ritual was common to May plays in all parts of the country in the fifteenth and sixteenth centuries is uncertain. In Aberdeen there are references to ridings on the Sundays in May ; and in 1562 the burgh bellman was accused of summoning ' þe haill communite or sa mony þairof as wald convene to paſs to þe wood to bring in symmer vpoun þe first sonday of maij.' [1] From the records of the Hammermen [2] we learn that the inhabitants of Edinburgh celebrated the advent of summer in like fashion. In 1496 there are payments for standard-bearers ' passand to newbottill ' and for a mounted minstrel ' þat day at we brocht haym̄ summyr with þe tovne.' In subsequent years there are references to ' þe proclamyne of þe summyr bringin haym̄ ' (1500, 1506) ; horses for the standard-bearers (1501, 1506, 1509) ; ' birkis till our craft at met ws apoñ þe burrowmure ' (1501). At Errol, as late as 1592, the Kirk Session prohibited the ' bringing in off Mayes ' [3] ; while six men were summoned before the Lanark Presbytery in 1625 for ' fetching hame a maypole, and dancing about the same upone pasche sonday.' [4] The minutes relating to the procession to the Dragon Hole at Perth may lend themselves to various interpretations, but some processional May rite is attacked. [5] Finally, there is a suggestion of a processional ceremony in the clause of the 1555 Act of Parliament which prohibits ' ony wemen or vthers about simmer treis singand ' who make perturba-

---

[1] App. I, s.v. *Aberdeen*—Folk Plays (*a*). The winter lustration took place on St Nicholas Day.
[2] *Ibid.*, s.v. *Edinburgh*—Excerpts from the Hammermen's Records.
[3] *Ibid.*, s.v. *Errol.*
[4] *Ibid.*, s.v. *Lanark*—Presbytery Records.
[5] *Ibid.*, s.v. *Perth*—Kirk Session Records, 1580, 1581.

tion to the Queen's lieges 'in the passage throw Burrowis and vthers landwart townis.' [1]

Secondly, it is significant that in our earliest specific notice of the May play there is mention of the mock king. In the Scottish records it is with the election of this king, whether the Abbot of Unreason or Robin Hood, or, more generally, King of the May, that most of the entries deal. The Abbot of Unreason appears under various titles in different parts of the country. In Aberdeen he and his colleague are known generally in the earlier records as the 'Abbot and Prior of Bonacord.' or simply as the 'Abbot and Prior of this burgh,' in the later records as the 'Lords of Bonacord' or 'Domini bonecordie (bonaconcordie).' They also occur as the 'Abbat and prior of Concord' (1507) and 'Abbatis out of ressoun' (1528).[2] In Edinburgh we have the 'Abbot of Narent' or 'Abbat de na Rent'[3] and Lord of Inobedience; in Peebles, the 'Abbot of Unrest'; in Arbroath, 'My Lord of Rason'; in Inverness, the 'Abbot of Unreason' or the 'Lord Abbot'; in Elgin, 'My Lord Abbot'; in Alloway, Arbuthnot, Fintray, and Haddington, the 'Abbot of Unreason.'[4] In the Court records he appears as the 'Abbot de Narentia' or the 'Abbot of Unreason,' according as the entry is in Latin or the vernacular.[5]

---

[1] *Infra*, 30, where the Act is quoted. Cf. also App. I, Glasgow University Records.

[2] App. I, s.v. *Aberdeen*—Folk Plays (a).

[3] I suppose this is to be taken literally as the Abbot of no rent or benefice, 'Narent' or 'Narentia' being the latinised form.

[4] App. I, under the respective headings except the Fintray and Arbuthnot cases, which are cited by Pitcairn, *Criminal Trials*, Vol. I, Pt. II, pp. 81, 15.

[5] App. III, Excerpts from *E.R.*, and from *L.H.T.A.* Cf. Chambers, *Mediæval Stage*, I, 173, who cites from *Flores Historiarum* (R.S.), III, 130, the jest of Robert Bruce's wife after his coronation at Scone, 1306 : ' aestimo quod rex aestivalis sis ; forsitan hyemalis non eris.'

Whether the Abbot is a pure folk creation or a secularised descendant of the Feast of Fools transferred to the May festival need not concern us here. The fact that we find a few stray payments to the Abbot of Unreason at Court in the early months of the year cannot be adduced necessarily in favour of an unmixed ecclesiastical pedigree—though the actual title may have been borrowed from the Feast of Fools,—for the pagan winter festivals also had their *dominus festi*.

In the dearth of burgh records before the sixteenth century, it is impossible to say when or how Robin Hood came to be associated with the folk game. The theory that he was in the May play, either as Woden or as the wood sprite Hode, is apparently discredited.[1] In the absence of any evidence as to interaction between minstrelsy and the folk play, Sir Edmund Chambers has suggested that the Robin Hood of the May game was really the Robin of the French *pastourelles*. Along with Maid Marian, he was introduced from France into England through the 'fête du mai' at a fairly late date, and was subsequently confused with the outlaw of Sherwood Forest. Are we then to assume a similar origin for the Robin Hood of the May game in Scotland ? Whether his exploits were celebrated in the *cantilenæ* of the maidens who sang to the invader, Edward I., as in the days of Alexander, King of Scots,[2] or in the *chansons* of the dancing maidens, who, at a later date, relieved the tedium of royal progresses,[3] and whether the dance of 'Robene hude' in the 'Complaynt of Scotland '[4] is a genuine *carole*, and supplies the missing link between folk play and ballad minstrelsy, are questions which cannot be answered. But to whatever source he

[1] Chambers, *Mediæval Stage*, I, 175 ; Child, *Popular Ballads*, 1882-98, III, 47-8.
[2] Bain, *Calendar*, IV, 475.
[3] App. III, Excerpts from *L.H.T.A.*, Nov. 1501, and footnote.
[4] *E.E.T.S.*, 1872, p. 66.

owed his origin, to minstrelsy, mythology, or history, the
name of Robin Hood was well known in Scotland by the
early years of the fifteenth century.[1] It seems therefore
perfectly natural that this hero, whose deeds were on the
lips not only of the professional minstrel but of the folk,
should be adopted as the lord of the May feast. At any
rate, it is noteworthy that the Scottish records have so far
revealed no trace of Maid Marian, who, says Sir Edmund
Chambers, is inseparable from Robin Hood in the English
May game.[2] This may, of course, be accidental. Though
not elected by. the Town Council, she might well have
been one of Robin Hood's followers. But no woman
appears among the delinquents at Cranston, Haddington, and Linton ;[3] and at Aberdeen, so far as the
official notices are concerned, the celebrants are confined to the male sex.[4] We do find a few references
to the Queen of the May,[5] but there is no need to
postulate a French prototype in these cases. Women

---

[1] Wyntoun's *Orygynale Cronykil of Scotland* (completed c. 1426),
ed. Laing, 1872, II, 263, 467. *Joannis Forduni Scotichronicon*,
1759 edn., II, 104 : ' Hoc in tempore de exheredatis et bannitis
surrexit et caput erexit ille famosissimus sicarius Robertus Hode
et Litill-Johanne cum eorum complicibus, de quibus stolidum
vulgus hianter in comoediis et in tragoediis prurienter festum
faciunt, et, prae ceteris romanciis, mimos et bardanos cantitare
delectantur. De quo etiam quaedam commendabilia recitantur,
sicut patuit in hoc. . . .' John Major, *History of Greater Britain*,
S.H.S., Bk. IV, Chap. 2, p. 156, says that ' the feats of this Robert
are told in song all over Britain.' The *Aberdeen MS. Council
Register* in 1438 has a case in which a ship called ' Robyne hude '
or ' ly Robert hude ' figures (Vol. IV, pp. 133, 134). Later, in
March 1564-5, Randolph writes to Cecil that ' one of the Queen's
chappel, a singing man, said, that he believed as well a tale of
Robin Hood as any word is written in the Old Testament or
New.' (Cited in *Knox*, II, 472.)
[2] *Mediæval Stage*, I, 175.
[3] App. I, s.vv. *Dalkeith, Haddington, Kelso*—Presbytery Records.
[4] *Ibid.*, s.v. *Aberdeen*—Folk Plays (a).
[5] App. III, Excerpts from *L.H.T.A.*, 1506, at Edinburgh and
Ayr. See, too, the 1555 Act of Parliament, *infra*, 30 n[1].

were traditionally associated with the May festival in other lands.[1]

Traces of Robin Hood in the May game are to be found in Edinburgh, Dundee, Aberdeen, Perth, St Andrews, Ayr, Dumfries, Dumbarton, Haddington, Peebles, Arbuthnot, Lasswade, Cranston, and Linton.[2] His relation to the Abbot of Unreason is not quite clear. Even if Dr Maitland Thomson was correct when he implied that Robin Hood was introduced into the Scottish May game from England, the matter cannot be dismissed with his statement that there was a change over from the one to the other after the royal marriage in 1503.[3] It is true that whereas in Aberdeen, from 1440 onwards, there are many references to the Abbot of Bonaccord, and from 1457 to the Prior of Bonaccord, it is not until May 1508 that we hear for the first time of Robin Hood and Little John. In an entry dated November of that year the names recur with the tag ' quhilk was callit in ȝeris bipast Abbot and priour of Bonacord.' [4]   From the volume of excerpts made in the sixteenth century from the original Edinburgh Council Records, we gather that, whereas in 1493 the dignitary in question was known as the Abbot of Narent, by 1518 he went under the name of ' Robin Huid and Little Jhone.' [5] On the other hand, from at least 1492 onwards the Edin-

[1] Chambers, *Mediæval Stage*, I, 170 ; Frazer, *Golden Bough,* 129, 131, 157, 320.
[2] Most of these cases will be found in App. I, under the respective headings. For Lasswade and Cranston, see under *Dalkeith ;* and for Linton, under *Kelso.* For Arbuthnot, cf. Pitcairn, *Criminal Trials,* Vol. I, Pt. II, p. 15 : 31st Oct. 1570. ' Treason—Convocation of the Lieges, etc. (17 men are) Delatit of the Making of ane ragment and ryme in name of Johnne the Commoune-wele and divulgatioune thairof, with conuocatioune, etc. ; and chesing of Robert Hude and Abbot of Unreasoune, within the parochin of Arbuthnot and vtheris pairtis respectiue, in the bounds of Mernis. . . .'
[3] *The Public Records of Scotland,* 1922, p. 154.
[4] App. I, s.v. *Aberdeen*—Folk Plays (*a*).
[5] *Ibid.,* s.v. *Edinburgh*—Folk Plays (*b*).

burgh Guildry gave financial support to 'Robertus Hud,' who by 1500, if not earlier, was joined by his associate, Little John. Further, in the year 1498-9 there seems to have been both a Robin Hood and an 'Abbat de na Rent' functioning under the patronage of the Edinburgh Guildry.[1] To these incontrovertible facts may be added another which would have little weight by itself—namely, that in June 1503, nearly two months before the royal wedding, a payment was made by command of the King to Robin Hood of Perth.[2]

There is little doubt, however, that as the century wore on, the popularity of Robin Hood increased at the expense of the Abbot of Unreason. While the latter apparently drops out of the Lord High Treasurers' Accounts from about 1505, in 1531 we hear of the King's Robin Hood.[2] Further, whereas in Peebles in 1472 burgess silver was paid to the Abbot of Unrest, in 1555 My Lord Robin Hood was the recipient.[3] Yet in many places the Abbot continued to flourish. As late as 1600 a disturbance arose in Elgin in connection with 'ane Abbot play.'[4] In Haddington the Abbot of Unreason held his own until 1552, when he was formally abolished by the Council.[5] But the acts of Presbytery of 1583, prohibiting May plays, Robin Hood, Little John, and Abbots of Unreason, and of 1589, directed against 'pasche playis abbot of onresone robene houd & sic vper prophane playis,' show that he was not forgotten even where Robin Hood and Little John had crept in.[6]

While other folk plays remain unrecorded, the comparative wealth of testimony as to the Abbot of Unreason

[1] App. I, s.v. *Edinburgh*—Folk Plays (*a*).
[2] App. III, Excerpts from *L.H.T.A.*
[3] App. I, s.v. *Peebles*.
[4] *Ibid.*, s.v. *Elgin*.
[5] *Ibid.*, s.v. *Haddington*—Council Records.
[6] *Ibid.*, Presbytery Records.

and Robin Hood—I take the two together as lords of the
May game—is due to the fact that many burghs extended
their patronage to the office, if they did not actually control
the appointment.[1] Thus, in Aberdeen, not only did the
fees come out of the Burgh exchequer, but the election of
two men 'coniunctlie abbatis & priour of bonacord' was
made annually by the Council. The duties must be carried
out to the satisfaction of the authorities, and refusal to
accept such an 'office of honour' was regarded as a contra-
vention of the King's letters and punishable by loss of
freedom.[2] Similarly, in Haddington the election of the
Abbot of Unreason and the payment of his fee was a regular part of the serious business of the Council. In April
1518, Master Frances Bothwell, who had been chosen as
Little John, appeared before the Edinburgh Town Council
and produced a letter of dispensation signed by the Earl of
Arran. The only other actual evidence as to the appointment being in the hands of the burgh authorities is in the
Dumfries records. But there is ample testimony as to the
rewarding of the office (or offices) by conceding the right to
present burgesses and claim their fees or by granting fixed
sums of money (Edinburgh, Dundee, Aberdeen, Perth,
Arbroath, Haddington, Dumfries, Ayr, Peebles, and Elgin) ;
by remission of taxes (Aberdeen) ; by admission to the
freedom of the burgh (Ayr) ; and by miscellaneous awards
(Aberdeen).[3]

The appointment was usually made in April or May
(Aberdeen, Haddington, Dumfries). The duration of sov-
ereignty is less certain. In Aberdeen, in 1531, the Lords of
Bonacord were appointed 'to do plesour and blythnes to

---

[1] See 1555 Act of Parliament, *infra*, 30 n[1].
[2] App. I, s.v. *Aberdeen*—Folk Plays (a), 1531, 1550, 1553.
[3] App. I, under the respective headings. The awards at Aberdeen included a barrel of wheat (1525) ; the fines of the breakers
of the St Nicholas statute (1516) ; 'aucht salmound fysche'
(1571).

þe toune in þis sessoun of Symmir incuming.' But in 1485, 1492, 1495, 1497, 1500, 1538, the offices were held and the fees paid 'for this (instant) year'; and, in 1492, the Council refused payment to the Abbot of Bonacord 'quhil he hede ſseruit it furtht þe ȝere.'

The duty of these officials is generally unspecified. At Aberdeen they seem to have acted as *tribuni voluptatum*, superintending the religious plays (1440, 1445), devising dancing and pleasure for the town's good (1538), assisting in its 'decoratioun and plasour' (1542), organising shows for royalty (1492, 1552), as well as acting as Masters of Artillery (1523) and conducting ridings on the Sundays in May, on St Nicholas Day, and on other holy days. In 1519, six marks was voted to the Lords of Bonacord 'to help to þare abellement.' In 1553, the Council called attention to the superfluous banqueting 'induring þe tyme of þair regnne and specialie in may,'[1] and complained that they had lost sight of the 'cauſ principall' of their election— namely, the 'halding of þe guid touñ in glaidnes and blythnes with dansſ farsſ playis & gamis in tymes convenient.'[2] Banquets were to be strictly limited to three special days, and there were to be 'to generall plais or ane at þe lest with dansſ & gammes vsit and wont.' The Abbot of Narent of the Edinburgh Hammermen[3] conducted ridings and was responsible, at least in 1496, for furnishing Herod and his knights for the Corpus Christi procession. He also had the manipulation of so many pounds of gunpowder. The object of Little John's appoint-

---

[1] Cf. the entries from the Council Register (App. I) under 9th July 1507, 21st April 1539, 21st April 1553, 26th Jan. 1553-4, 15th March 1554-5.

[2] Cf. entry under 21st April 1553.

[3] It seems from the Hammermen's records (App. I, s.v. *Edinburgh*) as if the Hammermen had an Abbot of their own responsible to the Masters of the Craft rather than to the Town Council. We hear of the Abbot of Unreason of the 'pynours' of Leith. (App. III, Excerpts from *L.H.T.A.*, 1504.)

ment by the Edinburgh Council was 'to mak sportis and jocositeis in the toun ' (1518). Play coats were provided by the Haddington Council for the Abbot and his company (1532, 1539). Minstrels were generally in attendance.[1] But, whatever the specified duties, a good deal of horse-play and general rowdiness would arise as a natural consequence of the assumption of authority by the burlesque potentates and of the implicit obedience demanded by them on the part of their subjects.[2] As early as 1445 the office

[1] App. I, s.vv. *Edinburgh*—Hammermen's Records, 1495; *Haddington*—Folk Plays, 1530; *Elgin*, 1549. App. III, Excerpts from *L.H.T.A.*, 1503, 1547.

[2] At Aberdeen 'all maner of Iurisdictiouñ and liberaliteis' granted (1522); power given to correct and punish disobeyers at their own hand (1523); and to summon and poynd non-riders (1508, 1517, 1528, 1539); 'mispersoning' and 'strublance' of the Abbot is forbidden (1508, 1509, 1538, 1542). Cf. *Knox*, I, 40. 'Ane uther day, the same Frear maid ane uther sermoun of the Abbote (of) Unreassone, unto whome and whose lawis he compared the prelattis of that age; for thei war subdewid to no lawis, no moir then was the Abbote of Unreassoun.' Cf. also Scott, *Provincial Antiquities* (Borthwick Castle): 'Eodem die . . . Willielmus Langlandis baculus literarum cititarum Domini Officialis emanatarum super Johannem Dominum Borthwik ad instantiam Magistri Georgii Hay de Mynzeane et literarum excommunicandum pro nonnullis testibus contumacibus juravitque quod Idem Willielmus baculus presentavit literas hujusmodi Curato dicte ecclesie pro earundum executione facienda die dominico decimo quinto die mensis instantis Maij ante initium summe misse. Qui Curatus easdem ante summam missam deponenti redeliberavit, et dixit, se velle easdem exequi post summam missam. Et supervenit quidem vulgariter nuncupatus ye Abbot of Unressone of Borthwick, cum suis complicibus, and causit him passe wy[t] yam quhill he come to ye mylne-dam, at ye south syde of ye castell, and compellit him to lope in ye wattir, and quhan he had loppin in ye wattir, ye said Abbot of Unressone, said ye deponent was not weite aneuche nor deip aneuche, and wy[t] yat keist him doune in ye watter be ye shulderis. And yerefter ye deponent past agane to ye kirk, and deliverit yaim to ye curate for executione of ye samyn. And you ye said Abbot of Unressone, came, and tuke ye letters furt of ye Curate's hand, and gaif ye deponent ane glasse full of wyne, and raif ye letters, and mulit ye samyn amangis ye wyne, and causit ye deponent drynk ye wyne ande eit ye letters, and saide, gif ony maa lettres

was temporarily suppressed at Aberdeen on account of the enormities committed.

In Ayr successive town treasurers played the parts of Robin Hood and Little John. The Aberdeen statute of 1445 appears to have been directed against non-official abbots. The alderman and a bailie were to 'supple that faute' for the year in question. While these honours may not have been reserved permanently for members of the corporation, an examination of the entries will reveal many instances of bailies or councillors holding these posts. In 1531, Saunders Knollis accepted appointment under protest. In 1539, Walter Hay and Thomas Scherar agreed to carry out the duties 'albeit we ar nocht conwenient pairfor.' In 1550, Gilbert Brabaner was warned to accept office by Friday next or to suffer the penalty of the statute. On the whole, however, these elections at Aberdeen passed off smoothly. In Haddington, on the other hand, almost from the commencement of the extant records, there is evidence of unwillingness to assume the burden of office. In 1536, three persons were fined for refusing to play the Abbot of Unreason ; and, in subsequent years, a regular revenue accrued to the burgh coffers from the fines of defaulting abbots. By 1540, so great was the prejudice against assuming the 'abbotschyp' that a short leet of eight names was prepared, the office to be given to the first of those who would accept. It may have been the difficulty of finding suitable nominees which led the bailies in 1539 to deliberate with an assize of twenty-five persons whether it was 'expedient' to have an Abbot of Unreason for that

came yair, salang as he war lord, yai sulde gang ye said gait : propterea judex decrevit Curatum citandum ad deponendum super nomine et cognomine dicti Abbatis de Unressone et suorum Complicium et literas in futurum exequendas in vicinioribus ecclesiis. Et dictus Abbas et complices excommunicandus quam primo constare poterit de eorundem nominibus.' (Extract from the Consistory Register of St Andrews, 16th May 1547.)

year. With eight dissentients the motion in favour of the appointment was carried, and a list of four nominees compiled. In December 1552, there is a curt minute to the effect that the Council ' hes dischargit all abbottis of vnressoun in tymis cumyng.'

The minute of the Haddington Town Council prohibiting abbots was followed by the famous Act of Parliament of 1555.[1] Two forces were at work in the sixteenth century undermining the old folk plays, the one civil, the other ecclesiastical ; and of these the civil movement is at first, perhaps, more in evidence. Revels and disguisings served as a cloak for abuses of all kinds.[2] In the troublous early days of the Reformation assemblies of the people might easily assume a sinister significance. When, in 1561, the Edinburgh bailies as ' cairfull fadderis our their commontie '

---

[1] *A.P.S.*, 1555, c. 40, II, 500 : ' ITEM It is statute and ordanit that in all tymes cumming na maner of persoun be chosin Robert Hude nor Lytill Johne Abbot of vnressoun Quenis of Maij nor vtherwyse nouther in Burgh nor to landwart in ony tyme tocum And gif ony Prouest Baillies counsall and communitie chesis sic ane Personage as Robert Hude Lytill Johne Abbottis of vnressoun or Quenis of Maij within Burgh the chesaris of sic sall tyne thair fredome for the space of fyue ȝeiris and vtherwyse salbe punist at the Quenis grace will and the acceptar of siclyke office salbe banist furth of the Realme And gif ony sic persounis sic as Robert Hude Lytill Johne Abbottis of vnressoun Quenis of Maij beis chosin outwith Burgh and vthers landwart townis the chesaris sall pay to our Souerane Lady x pundis and thair persounis put in waird thair to remane during the Quenis grace plesoure And gif ony wemen or vthers about simmer treis singand makis perturbatioun to the Quenis liegis in the passage throw Burrowis and vthers landwart townis the wemen perturbatouris for skafrie of money or vtherwyse salbe takin handellit and put vpone the Cukstulis of euerie Burgh or towne.'

[2] Pitcairn, *Criminal Trials*, Vol. I, Pt. I, *50, 15th Feb. 1507-8 : ' Eduard Symsoune convicted of art and part of the Stouthreif, by way of ' mummyn,' under silence of night, of certain sums of money . . . from Sir Donald Moffet, Chaplain, furth of his chamber, near the Kirk of Craggy—Hanged.' Similarly Adam Mure, p. *51. Cf. Transcript of the records of the Court of Justiciary (Adv. Lib. MSS.), pp. 5, 12, ' de arte et parte furtive surrepcionis modo le mummyn (velato facie).'

prohibited the May game, they did so on the two specific
grounds of religion and law ; and one can trace a distinct
note of fear of disorders arising from ' convocatioun and
assemblie efter the auld wikit maner of Robene Hude.'
From the details of the prosecutions which follow, one
receives the impression that the gathering had shed most
of the elements of folk play, and consisted of armed processions of hooligans ready and eager for a scrap. The fact
that practically the whole equipment is described in terms
of weapons ' invasive ' need not weigh with us unduly :
this may be due to the biassed pen of Authority. But it
is incredible that the magistrates would have proceeded
to a death sentence unless there was some truth in the charge
that such gatherings savoured of sedition.[1] In the following year another proclamation was issued by injunction
of the Queen, who had heard rumours that the Act of
Parliament was to be defied by certain persons ' quha
vnder colour of Robene Hudis play purpoissis to rais
seditione and tumult within our said burgh.' Yet the play
continued to flourish,[2] and, as late as 1579 and 1580, the
Edinburgh Town Council found it necessary to issue further
proclamations.

Whether all the burgh councils were as active in this
respect as that of Edinburgh is doubtful. The local corporation at Arbroath is found defying the central authority
as late as 1565, when burgess fees were handed over to
' my lord of rasoñ.' In September 1571, Alexander Smith
of Aberdeen was ordered to pay a contribution to the Lords
of Bonaccord. Still more interesting is the fact that in

---

[1] App. I, s.v. *Edinburgh*—Folk Plays, 1561, and notes.
[2] Cf. *D.R.O.*, 263, May 1572 : ' Thair wes in this foirsaid moneth
greit penuritie and scant of vivaris within the burgh of Edinburgh,
sua that all wes at ane exceiding darth. Nochttheles the remaneris
thairin abaid patientlie, and wer of good comfort, and vsit all
plesouris, quhilkis wer wont to be vsit in the said moneth of Maij
in ald tymes, viz., Robin Hude and Litill Johne.'

Dumfries, as late as 1570, not only was financial support
from common good funds forthcoming for the Pasche
Plays, but one of the inhabitants was fined by the burgh
court for having ' incurrit dissobedience at pasche lxx ȝeris
In safar as he vald nocht obbaye And accept on hym ye
office of robert huyd & litill Iohn.' At least acquiescence in
the practice may be deduced from the enforcement by the
Inverness burgh court of the payment of debts incurred in
connection with the revels of the Abbot of Unreason.

Even where the May game was suppressed officially by
the civic authorities, it was in many cases only driven
underground. Vigorous support was lent to the secular
attack by the various ecclesiastical courts ; indeed, the
main burden of administering the Act of Parliament seems
to have devolved on the Kirk. In 1577 the Regent was
petitioned by the General Assembly to ' discharge playes
of Robin Hood, King of May, and sick vthers, on the
Sabboth day.' [1] The following year a supplication was
drawn up for the King and Council asking that they forbid
by open proclamation all kinds of ' insolent ' May plays
' played either be bairnes at the schools or others.' [2] Among
the questions prepared for the General Assembly by the
Synodal Assembly of Lothian in 1579, the following is
not without significance as showing that the custom was
even yet not wholly confined to the younger and rowdier
sections of the population : ' What aught to be done to
sick persons that, after admonition, will passe to May
playis ; and speciallie elders and deacons, and vthers quha
beares office in the Kirk.' [3] The hostility of the Reformed

---

[1] *B.U.K.*, I, 388.

[2] *Ibid.*, II, 407, 410. Probably as a result of this pressure, as
well as on account of the more immediate petition of the Synod
of Lothian, the Privy Council issued a further proclamation against
Robin Hood plays in April 1580. *Reg. Privy Council*, III, 277.

[3] *Ibid.*, II, 440. ' Responsio : They aught not to be admittit
to the sacrament without satisfaction ; in speciall elders and

Church was of a double nature. In the first place, the celebration of the May festival involved Sabbath-breaking : the Sundays in May, and particularly the first Sunday, were sacred to the cult. In the second place, it was a relic of paganism and retained, as we have seen, definite traces of old pagan rites. The General Assembly continued to fulminate against such ' enormities ' as Robin Hood plays.[1] But the old usage died hard, and, at least until far on in the seventeenth century, there were frequent prosecutions of May-time revellers.

The only other point which requires consideration in connection with the summer festival in Scotland is the meaning of the word ' play.' As has already been noted, in more than one town certain duties relating to the regular religious pageants devolved on the May *dominus festi*.[2] But there are many references to Robin Hood plays, May plays, Pasche or Peace plays, King of May plays and Abbot plays, as well as to plays and pastimes generally which took place on the Sundays in May. Is there any dramatic connotation attached to the term ? Or does ' play ' stand generally for the surviving rites of the summer feast, including the election and impromptu frolics of the temporary potentates ? Despite Child and other authorities, Professor Gayley,[3] on account of the reference to ' mimi,' infers acted plays from the ' comedies ' and ' tragedies ' of

deacons.' But cf. *Calderwood*, IV, 366 : ' The king remained at Dirleton twelve dayes. There were in companie with him Arran, Sir Robert Melvill, Secretar Matlane, Phairnihirst, Colonell Stewart, and the Maister of Gray. They passed the time with the play of Robinhood.' (1585).

[1] *B.U.K.*, II, 784 (1591) . ' It is craveit, The acts of Parliament made for suppressing of the enormities following may be put to executioun. First, against Jesuites . . . idolaters, pilgrimagers . . . publick mercatts vpon the Sabboth day ; . . . profaners of the Sabboth day be Robein Hoodes playis ; murderers and blood shedders quhilk overflow the land.'

[2] See *supra*, 27.

[3] *Representative English Comedies*, 1903, I, xl.

Bower.[1] But, as will be shown in Section II., ' mimi ' does
not necessarily carry a dramatic connotation any more
than do the mediæval *comediæ* and *tragediæ*. That plays
of more or less formal nature setting forth the exploits
of the hero of Sherwood Forest were acted north, as well
as south, of the border is not, however, improbable.[2] But,
if we except the interesting Linton Pasche play, where the
' schirreff ' was represented by one of the ' cheiff actoris,' [3]
the individual members of the band, apart from Robin
Hood and Little John, are unchronicled in our records.
This is, of course, not absolutely conclusive. Even if the
principals alone are named in the records, the other members
may have had separate and recognisable identities in the
troupe. At Cranston there appears to have been a third
' principal.' [4] Further, most of the references are post-
Reformation, when, in the face of the determined opposition
of Church and State, the plays were probably shorn of
earlier characteristics. Thus the youths of Haddington
replied to the Presbytery, who had summoned them in

---

[1] Fordun, *Scotichronicon*. See *supra*, 23 n[1].

[2] The only text which has survived is the preliminary ' cry '
for a May game attributed to Dunbar (*Poems*, II, 314-20), entitled in MS. B., ' Ane littill Interlud of the Droichis part of the
(Play),' and in MS. A., ' Heir followis the Maner of the Crying of
Ane Playe.' The influence of a literary genius has not obscured
a close connection with the folk play, which is apparent in the
preliminary patter regarding his pedigree with which the Dwarf
announces himself and in the blessing invoked on the audience
followed by the request for a drink with which the piece ends.
The suggestion of the *S.T.S.* Editor that this ' interlude ' was
represented by John Inglis and his company at the time of the
royal wedding in 1503 seems far-fetched. In stanza 3 ' this amyable
audience Grete of renoune ' is made to consist merely of the
provost, bailies, officers, merchands, and citizens of Edinburgh—
a normal burgh gathering,—and we have the evidence of the
Hammermen's records (as well as the internal evidence of the
piece) for the fact that proclamations were used in connection
with the summer festival. *Supra*, 20, and App. I, s.v. *Edinburgh*.

[3] App. I, s.v. *Kelso*.

[4] *Ibid.*, s.v. *Dalkeith*.

1589, that 'as for thair minstrallis throw the toun . . .
that was callit pasche playis abbot of onresone robene
houd & sic vper prophane playis thay neuer vsit pe effectis
pairof.' At Ayr, where, on the other hand, our notices are
prior to the Reformation and Act of Parliament, details
are meagre. The Frenchmen who received fees in connection with Robin Hood plays in 1546-7 and 1550-51 were
probably minstrels. It would be interesting to know more
of the ' Trik,' the only May play which has survived by
name. Year after year, on the first Sunday of May, this
play was acted in the parish of Samuelston to the delight
of the whole countryside and the embarrassment of the
Laird, who was held responsible by the wrathful Presbytery
of Haddington.[1] Elsewhere we have to be content with
references to communal ridings, dancing, archery contests,
and improvised *ludi*.

[1] App. I, s.v. *Haddington*—Presbytery Records.

II.

MINSTRELSY.

As in England and Western Europe generally, so in Scotland the countryside was overrun with those nomad entertainers, descendants of the Teutonic *scop* or *gleomon* or the Roman ' mime,' who helped to keep alive the dramatic spirit during the Middle Ages.[1] The laws attributed to Macbeth by Hector Boece may be repudiated by the critical historian ; but they must either rest on some traditional basis or else express an ideal code of social legislation as conceived by the later mediæval mind. It is interesting, therefore, to find a special clause directed against ' Histriones, ludiones, mimi et reliquum ociosorum nebulonum genus,' who, unless they enjoy the special favour of the king, are to be compelled to adopt some useful craft ; failing which, if able-bodied, they are to be yoked to the plough.[2]

We are on safer ground historically when we come to the 1449 Act of Parliament against masterful beggars. Inquiries are to be made at every court ' gif þar be ony þat makis þaim fulis þat ar nocht bardis or sic lik vþeris rynnaris aboute.' These are to be warded if and for so long as they have goods to live on : when they are destitute,

---

[1] Chambers, *Mediæval Stage*, I, Bk. I ; Ward, *History of English Dramatic Literature*, I, 13-28 ; Petit de Julleville, *Les Comédiens en France au moyen âge*, 2, 3, 4, 7, 15-28.

[2] See App. II, where I have collected laws relating to minstrels.

their ears are to be nailed to a tree and they are to be banished.[1] Again, in 1457, the justice ayres are to ' ger tak Inquisicione of sornaris bardis maisterfull beggaris or fenȝeit fulys and oȝer bannyſ ȝame ȝe cuntre or sende ȝame to ȝe Kingis presone.' [1]

Although neither Act is explicit on the point, it is evident that the provisions applied, not to the licensed officials of the court or municipalities, but to the unattached minstrels of the road. As early as 1278 we hear of the King of Scotland's ministrels.[2] In the same year the rolls of Durham Priory record a payment ' Menestrallo Regis Scociæ '; and later, in 1335-6, ' histrionibus d'ni Regis Scociæ.' [3] There are ' ministralli ' at the courts of Robert the Bruce and David the Second.[4] From 1377, Thomas Acarsone figures in the Exchequer Rolls as the King's ministrel.[4] During the years from 1442-50, a group of three royal *histriones* or *mimi*, Robert M'Gye, Ade Rede and Marcus Trumpat, receive ' pro suis feodis ' an annual sum of about £20—an additional fee of 28s. being granted to Robert M'Gye ' tempore sue infirmitatis.' [4] We have an occasional glimpse of the enlivenment of the Audit by the presence of minstrels. In the decade commencing 1397, Fulhope and Bergus, minstrels, receive payments varying from 6s. 8d. to 13s. 4d. in the time of the Exchequer ' ex gracia auditorum.' [4] From 1508 onwards, ' histriones ' are definitely attached to the Exchequer and form a regular charge on the expenses.[4]

Not only were there definite appointments at Court,

[1] App. II.
[2] Bain, *Calendar*, II, 28, 29th Oct. 1278, 131. ' Westminster : To Master Elyas, the King of Scotland's harper, 60s. ; to 2 of the King of Scotland's trumpeters, 40s. ; also to 4 minstrels of Scotland, 53s. 4d. ; and to 2 minstrels of the King of Scotland, 26s. 8d ; all by the K.'s gift.' (Wardrobe Accounts, Tower, 6 Edw. I, fol. 39.)
[3] Chambers, *Mediœval Stage*, II, 240, App. E.
[4] App. III, Excerpts from *E.R.*

but about 1430 no fewer than seven ' mimi ' with complete outfit were hired abroad and sent under the leadership of one Martin Vanartyne to the service of the King of the Scots.[1] In the early years of the sixteenth century, French minstrels were much in evidence at the Scottish Court ; [2] troupes of Italians came from Bologna ; [3] and the Norwegian royal household was represented by three ' tubicines et musici.' [4] From time to time, too, royal grants were made to native minstrels to enable them to visit one of the continental ' scholæ ministrallorum ' to perfect their art and increase their repertoire. In 1473, John Brown, luter, was sent ' oure sey to lere his craft.' Later, clothes were sent to ' the Kingis litill lutare ' at Bruges. In 1512, 56s. was sent to ' foure scolaris, menstralez,' to buy instruments and help the expense of their ' fraucht ' ; and a second 56s. was conceded because they ' plenȝeit thai gat our litill expens and fraucht.' [5]

It is not always easy to decide which of the many minstrels who crowd the pages of the Court records [6] were definitely attached to the royal household. At festive seasons wandering performers and strolling companies of all kinds would hasten to the king's palace to participate in the lavish Yule or Pasche rewards. In January 1506-7, no fewer than sixty-nine ' menstrales ' received gratuities. Even the common minstrels of Edinburgh and the Canon-

---

[1] App. III, Excerpts from *E.R.*
[2] *Ibid.*, Excerpts from *L.H.T.A.*
[3] *Reg. Sec. Sig.*, I, Nos. 1456, 1600, 1808.
[4] *Ibid.*, No. 1927.
[5] App. III, Excerpts from *L.H.T.A.* There is no trace of a minstrel hierarchy in Scotland. The ' Rex Robertus ' who receives a reward from the English king for ' menestralciam suam ' at Dunfermline (Bain, *Calendar*, IV, 473), is probably ' Le Roy Robert,' who appears in the English Royal Household Books for 1306 (Chambers. *Mediæval Stage*, II, 234, App. C.).
[6] *Ibid.*, Excerpts from *L.H.T.A.*, *passim.*

gate figure in these periodical lists of awards.[1] Money was distributed, too, with generous hand to various local performers—to jesters, tumblers, dancing maidens, bard 'fallos' and bard 'wives' or 'hussies,' who helped to relieve the tedium of the king's progresses. In addition to the various luters, harpers, and trumpeters, there was, however, at the Court of James the Fourth an official household 'spelar.'[2] The Italian 'spelar boy,' Francis de Luca, and his master, Peter de Luca, enjoyed quarterly pensions of £12, 10s. and 'vestimenta.' Fools, too, are regularly found on the strength of the royal establishment. King Robert the Bruce in his retirement at Cardross diverted himself with Patrick the Fool.[3] 'Gentil Johne the Inglis fule' may have been a temporary resident, but Curry, Nornee, John Bute, and James Geddie, to mention only a few favourites of a later date, were permanent servants of the king. Serat, whose parti-coloured garments are detailed in the household accounts, was the female fool of Mary of Guise ; while Nichola la Jardiniere and Janet Mouche enlivened the court of Mary Queen of Scots.[4]

That minstrels and fools were attached to other establishments we learn from incidental references to the 'Thayn of Caldoris harper,' the 'Lard of Balnagounis harpare,' 'Lord Setounis menstrale,' and Sir William Murray's fool, 'Swaggar.'[4] From an early date common minstrels can

[1] In 1503 there is a grant by the Aberdeen Council to the common minstrels (*lusvribus communibus*) to pass to the King's marriage. App. I, s.v. *Aberdeen*—C.
[2] The Editor *L.H.T.A.* glosses as 'a climber, rope-dancer.' See the entries App. III, Excerpts from *L.H.T.A.*, 1501-2 and 1503 (Aug.). *N.E.D.*, which cites instances only from *L.H.T.A.*, connects with L.G. 'speler' (G. 'spieler'), player, actor, rather than with the verb 'speel' to climb, and glosses as 'a performer, acrobat.'
[3] App. III, Excerpts from *E.R.*
[4] *Ibid.*, Excerpts from *L.H.T.A.*

be traced in the more important burghs. The 'histriones nostri ' of the Aberdeen minute of 1462-63 [1] may not have belonged to this class : the 1393-94 ' menestralli de Perth ' [2] almost certainly did not. But I note references to the Aberdeen common minstrels from 1481 onwards ; [3] at the end of a list of Ayr Burgh officials for 1432-33 there occurs ' Jame faro pipar ' ; [4] and many other cases might be cited from later burgh records. The various craft incorporations, too, made frequent calls on the common pool of minstrels in connection with their ridings and processions. The Edinburgh Hammermen's records [5] show payments for many different minstrels as well as for the common minstrels of the town and for Giljame, tabernar, and Ainslie, who figure so prominently in the accounts of the Lord High Treasurer.

From the above instances it is clear that the harsh provisions of these early laws did not apply to the regular minstrels who came under the patronage of the court and burgh authorities. On the contrary, special provision was made for this privileged section of the profession by the statute of 1471, which granted exemption from the sumptuary laws to knights, heralds, and minstrels.[6] Members of the class were generously pensioned for life or held liferents in certain lands,[7] and were admitted to the freedom of ancient Royal Burghs.[8]

The less fortunate members of the calling, who dis-

---

[1] App. I, s.v. Aberdeen—C.
[2] Bain, Calendar, IV, 475.
[3] App. I, s.v. Aberdeen—C.
[4] Ayr MS. Burgh Court Book (1428-78).
[5] App. I, s.v. Edinburgh.
[6] A.P.S., 1471, c. 7, II, 100.
[7] Reg. Sec. Sig., I, Nos. 194, 237, 238, 465, 1185, 1558 ; II, 2620, 2621, 2622, 2623, 3324.
[8] Dumfries MS. Burgh Court Book, 17th June 1570, has a list of good and geir formerly belonging to ' eduerd moffett mynstrale burges of Drumfres.'

regarded or failed to win influential patronage, continued to lead a precarious vagrant existence in defiance of burghal and parliamentary statutes. About 1548, in order to preserve peace in the community, the town authorities of Dumfries forbade the engagement of minstrels, other than those elected by the Council, at feasts, banquets, or 'conventionis' in the burgh.[1] In 1574, during time of pest, the Glasgow magistrates sought to effect a wholesale clearance from the town of 'pyparis, fidleris, menstrales, or ony wther vagabundis.'[2] The 1574 Act of Parliament against 'strang and ydle beggaris,' confirmed in 1579, was aimed at 'all menstrallis sangstaris and taill tellaris not avowit in speciall seruice be sum of the lordis of parliament or greit barronis or be the heid burrowis and citeis for þair commoun menstrallis.'[3] Victims of the law, these despised outcasts sank lower and lower in the moral scale, and no doubt merited the wrath of the Kirk Fathers who cited among the 'commoun corruptiouns' of all Estates within this realm 'ane great number of idle persons without lawfull calling, as pypers, fidlers, sangsters, sorners, pleasants, strang beggars.'[4]

So far I have used the general term 'minstrel' in the sense of the early mediæval *joculator* to cover a heterogeneous body of professional or semi-professional entertainers ranging from the literary *scop* through wandering scholars, strolling companies of players, jesters, bearleaders, to the lowest of tumblers and buffoons.[5]

[1] App. II, where I have collected various acts against unlicensed minstrels.

[2] *Ibid.*, Acts against unlicensed minstrels (*k*).

[3] *Ibid.* (*e*).

[4] *B.U.K.*, III, 873, 1596. Cf. *A.P.S.*, 1579, c. 12, III, 139 : 'Þe saidis beggaris . . . procuris þe wraith and displesour of god for þe wiked & vngodlie forme of leving vsit amangis þame without mariage or baptizing of a greit nowmer of þair bairnis.'

[5] For examples of various types see App. III, Excerpts from *E.R.* and *L.H.T.A.*, and App. II. I have not come across any

Sir Edmund Chambers's theory as to the ' complete four-
fold equivalence of *ioculator, ministrallus, mimus,* and
histrio, [1] is supported, as indeed he briefly indicates, by
the evidence of the Public Records of Scotland. In 1447-48
there is a note of expenses for musical instruments for
' mimi.' In 1441-42 we meet for the first time Robert
M'Gye and his colleagues, the King's ' histriones.' In
1446-47 a grant is made to this trio under the designation
' mimis et histrionibus.' In the same year a payment is
made in aid of the expenses during illness of Robert M'Gye,
' mimi regis et servitoris.' In 1460-62, Ade Rede is entered
simply as a ' mimus.' Finally, in 1448-49, they are classed
as ' histriones sive joculatores regis.' [2]

It is not always easy to keep clear the identity of the
various Italian performers who frequent the Scottish court
during the early years of the sixteenth century. From a
careful examination of the many entries, however, it seems
as if there were one special group of five or six which
remained more or less identical for many years, enjoying
the patronage of Albany during his visits to this country,
but remaining behind after his departure. This group was
composed of Julian Drummond (Dromont), Julian Richard
(Richet, Rokket), Vincent Pais, who appeared as early as
1505,[3] Sebastian Drummond (Dormon), who came from
Bologna in January 1508-9,[4] another Italian (at one time
' Anthone '), and George Forest, the Scotsman. The
nucleus of this company may perhaps be traced in the four
Italian minstrels who are so familiar from about 1503
onwards.[5] The individual members are definitely specified

example of a minstrel puppet show, although ' pippennis ' or
' poupines ' are found among the inventories of the wardrobe of
Mary Queen of Scots, App. III, pp. 338-39.

[1] Chambers, *Mediæval Stage,* II, App. B.
[2] App. III, Excerpts from *E.R.*
[3] *Reg. Sec. Sig.,* I, No. 1189.
[4] *Ibid.,* No. 1808.
[5] App. III, Excerpts from *L.H.T.A.,* and *L.H.T.A., passim.*

for the first time in combination in 1515, when a payment
of £78, 15s. for fees and expenses is made to ' the v Italian
menstrallis—viz., Vincent, auld Julian, ȝoungar Julian,
Anthone and Bestian Drummonth, and George Forest
scottisman with thame,' and Yule liveries are granted.[1]
At the same time a special payment is made to Bestian
Drummond who passes to ' vesy his frendis in Italie,' but
returns in haste.[2] By 1517-18, Anthone appears to have
dropped out, and the entries refer frequently to a group of
five.[3] In 1524 the place of the late Julian Richart is
assigned to Henry Rudman ;[4] who, in turn, is displaced
by Ninian Brown.[5] Otherwise, the group remains intact
at least until 1529, when the Comptroller decrees that
payments from the fermes of Kintore and Garviauch,
hitherto enjoyed by these minstrels, shall not be made
without the express command of the king.[6]

Taking this small company, then, we see that the members
are referred to indiscriminately as ' minstrels,'[7] ' schawmeris,'[8] ' histriones,' and ' tubicines.'[9] Further, Julian

---

[1] *L.H.T.A.*, V, 53.
[2] *Ibid.*, V, 54.
[3] *E.R.*, XIV, 300.
[4] *Reg. Sec. Sig.*, I, No. 3282 ; *E.R.*, XV, 220.
[5] *L.H.T.A.*, V, 432.
[6] *E.R.*, XV, 220, 495, 682.
[7] 1507 : ' The foure Italien menstrales ' and ' Johne (*sic*)
Forest with thaim ' (*L.H.T.A.*, IV, 56). Also 1508 (*L.H.T.A.*,
IV, 66, 70). 1515 : ' the v Italian menstrallis ' (names) and
' George Forest scottisman with thame ' (*L.H.T.A.*, V, 53). Similarly 1516. Also ' the forsaidis sex menstralis ' (*L.H.T.A.*, V,
87). 1529 : ' the Italiane ministralis ' (*E.R.*, XV, 682).
[8] 1511 : ' The foure Italiane schawmeris and George Forest
with thame ' (*L.H.T.A.*, IV, 270). Also 1511-12 (*L.H.T.A.*,
IV, 324).
[9] 1507 : George Forest ' tubicinis ' (*Reg. Sec. Sig.*, I, No.
1558). 1508-9 : Sebastian Drummond ' tubicine ' (*Reg. Sec.
Sig.*, I, No. 1808). 1517-18 : J. D., V. P., S. D., J. R., G. F.,
' tubicinis et histrionibus Italicis et Scotis ' (*E.R.*, XIV, 300).
1524 : Henry Rudman has assigned to him the place of ' quondam
Juliani Richert, Itali tubicinis ' in company with ' reliquis his-

Drummond appears as a 'musicus'; [1] and Julian Richart, Julian Drummond, Vincent Pais, and George Forest are granted pensions for their services 'in arte musicali.' [2] There is, then, no rigid distinction between those several categories in the Scottish records of the late fifteenth and early sixteenth centuries. Statements, therefore, to the effect that professional stage-players or companies were in the regular pay of the Scottish court from an early date [3] must be accepted with reserve. Owing to the modification, during the mediæval period, in the classical use of the terms *histrio* and *mimus*, a purely dramatic connotation cannot be assumed in any given case without independent corroborative evidence. The versatility demanded on the part of the professional entertainer would naturally tend to prevent such terms retaining or adopting any very specialised significance. But if, on the one hand, the mime and *histrio* had widened the sphere of their activities so that definitely non-dramatic functions entered into, and, it may be, monopolised, their repertoire, on the other hand, the ministrel had not commenced his later specialised career. Even the fidlers, tabroners, and luters had not yet restricted their rôle to the mere provision of instrumental music. French minstrels arrange and participate in a dance in the Abbey ; [4] 'tua fithelaris' sing 'Graysteil' to the King ; [5] Wedderspoon is a 'fithelar and tellar of tales,' [6] and Curry, the court fool, has a 'fithelar' ; [7]

---

trionibus et tubicinis' in the King's service (*Reg. Sec. Sig.*, I, No. 3282). 1522-26 : 'sex tubicinis Italicis et Scotis,' J. D., G. F., V. P., B. D., H. R. (*E.R.*, XV, 220—five names only).

[1] *Reg. Sec. Sig.*, I, 3382.
[2] *Ibid.*, I, Nos. 1189, 1558.
[3] The Editor of the *Exchequer Rolls* glosses 'histrioni' and 'mimi' as 'stage-players.'
[4] App. III, Excerpts from *L.H.T.A.*, 1507-8.
[5] *Ibid.*, 1497.
[6] *Ibid.*, p. 315, n.[5].
[7] *Ibid.*, 1502.

'tawbronars' accompany acrobatic displays;[1] the 'More taubronar' arranges the dance for Fastringis Eve;[2] Guilliam 'taubronar' makes a dance to celebrate the birth of a prince,[3] and, still more interesting, receives £4, 4s. 'for ane fars play to the King and Quenis Gracis in the Abbay.'[4] Were it not that the word 'farce' as used in sixteenth-century Scotland requires further consideration,[5] this last item might be cited as illustrating the derivation of farces from the *jeux* of the minstrels, which was characteristic of France, if not of England.[6] A potential line of dramatic development may, however, be noted in the assumption of special characters by the performers. 'Wantonness' and her companions are rewarded for singing in the King's chamber.[7]

[1] App. III., Excerpts from *L.H.T.A.*, 1496-7, 1497.
[2] *Ibid.*, 1504-5.
[3] *Ibid.*, 1506-7.
[4] *Ibid.*, 1511-12.
[5] *Infra*, 76-8.
[6] *C.H.L.*, V, 4.
[7] *L.H.T.A.*, 1506-7.

III.

COURT REVELS.

THE Court was not altogether dependent on the *amuseur de métier*. From an early date, Yule and other festive seasons were celebrated with amateur disguisings in which king and courtiers took part.[1] The custumars of Edinburgh were called on to make provision for 'le mumre regis erga Natale' in the year 1465-66; and in 1466-67 'ad le mumre grathe in yeme elapsa.'[2] In January 1506-7, two 'mummyng gouns' were made for King James the Fourth. In 1533-34 red and yellow taffeta was provided for a 'play coit' for the King's son; and in December of the following year about £20 Scots was expended on 'certane play gounis to the Kingis grace to pas in maskrie.'[3] Of the nature of these mummings there is no indication. But the fact that at Christmas 1465 the sum of £25, 5s. 10d. was spent on buckram, gold, 'et aliis picturis' handed over to John Rate, painter (who was again in charge in 1466-67), suggests some sort of scenic equipment.[4] Later,

---

[1] Buchanan speaks of masked dances in the time of James the First. *Rerum Scoticarum Historia*, 1762, Bk. X, p. 284. 'Hinc sumptuosa convivia, & nocturnae diurnaeque compotationes, & personatae saltationes, & peregrinarum vestium delitiae. . . .'

[2] App. III, Excerpts from *E.R.*

[3] *Ibid.*, Excerpts from *L.H.T.A.*

[4] *Ibid.*, Excerpts from *E.R.*

at the marriage of Mary Livingstone,[1] a painter was paid
£12 for his services.

There are many references to masks in the years immediately following the return of Mary Queen of Scots
from France. The skill of George Buchanan was enlisted
in the Queen's service, and the Latin verses for several
' pompæ ' are preserved among his works.[2] In October
1561 there was a mask at Holyrood at the farewell banquet
to Mary's uncle, the Grand Prior of the Knights of St
John of Jerusalem, in which parts were taken by Michelet
and Mernat, valets of the Queen's chamber, and by a son
of the Duke of Montmorency ; [3] and it may have been for
this occasion that Buchanan wrote his *Apollo et Musæ
exules.* Knox fulminates against the ' vanitie ' of the
banquet at the marriage of Lord James Stuart early in
1562. ' Thair,' he says, ' began the masking, which from
year to year hath continewed since.' [4] The gaiety of the
Scottish Court in the early months of 1563 is borne out by
Randolph in a letter to Cecil :—

> ' Before M. la Croc's coming, I had nothing to
> write, for we had so little to think on, that we passed
> our time in feasts, banqueting, masking, and running
> at the ring, and such like.' [5]

Six shepherds and two lute players were amongst the
performers in a pastoral mask at the marriage of the
Commendator of St Colme's Inch to the sister of the Earl
of Argyll ; and in December of the same year ' trois grands
bonnetz a la Souisse ' were required for masking pur-

---

[1] App. III, Excerpts from *L.H.T.A.* (1564-65).

[2] Georgii Buchanani, *Opera,* 1725, II, 399-405.

[3] App. III, Excerpts from *Inventories.*

[4] *Knox,* II, 314. *D.R.O.,* 70, speaks only of ' greit and diverse
baling, and casting of fyre ballis, fyre speris and rynning with
horsis.'

[5] Bain and Boyd, *Calendar,* II, 8, No. 7, 15th May 1563.

poses.[1] The mask at Mary Livingstone's marriage has already been noted.[2] A few months later the marriage of Mary and Darnley was celebrated by Buchanan's *Pompa Deorum* and *Pompæ Equestres*. In January 1565-66 the banquets in honour of the French ambassador were followed by masks, in one of which Mary and her ladies-in-waiting, clad in men's apparel, presented daggers to the stranger guests ;[3] and in another of which the Queen, Darnley, Riccio, and seven others took part.[4]

It is clear that frequently mimetic entertainments formed an integral part of the great State banquets. It is interesting to remember that the earliest example of a primitive court mask in these Islands has been traced to Scotland. In 1285, at the marriage banquet of Alexander III. in Jedburgh Abbey, the spectre of Death glided in among the dancers, interrupting the 'choream militarem' and hushing the strains of music.[5] A dance and 'play' was introduced into the banquet which took place in

[1] App. III, Excerpts from *Inventories*.
[2] *Supra*, 47.
[3] App. III, Excerpts from *Inventories* and note.
[4] Randolph to Leicester, Fitch's MSS. Ipswich, cited in Strickland's *Queens of Scotland*, IV, 248.
[5] Joannes de Fordun, *Scotichronicon*, 1759, II, 128 : ' Ubi in nuptiis regalibus dum omnia ritè fierent, factum est tale ludi simulacrum per modum processionis inter catervas discumbentium, praecedentibus in arte illa doctis, cum multimodis organis musicis et tragoedicis instrumentis organicis, aliisque post eos vicissim et interpolatim choream militarem pompaticè agentibus, insecutus est unus, de quo penè dubitari potuit utrum homo esset, an phantasma : qui, ut umbra, magis labi videbatur quam pedetentim transire. Quo quasi, oculis omnium evanescente, quievit tota illa processio phainatica, melos tepuit, musicum dissolutum est, et chorealis phalanx diriguit citiùs insperato. Risus dolore miscetur, et extrema gaudii luctus occupat, et post tantam gloriam regnum ingloriè ululabat, dum postmodum in brevi seipsum perdidit, et consequenter regem.' [The same year the king was killed at Kinghorn, etc.] Withington, *English Pageantry*, I. 103, suggests a connection with the mediæval dance of death. Cf. P. Hume Brown, *History of Scotland*, I, 103.

connection with the great tournament of 1508.[1] An
outdoor mask may be denoted by the ' grate triumph '
which was made in the park of Holyrood house, under
Arthur's Seat, at the wedding banquet of Lord Fleming
in May 1562.[2] The Shrovetide banquet of 1563-64 ' continued with joy and mirth, marvellous sights and shows,
singular devices ; nothing left undone either to fill our
bellies, feed our eyes, or content our minds.'[3] The first
course was ushered in by Cupid to the accompaniment of
Italian verses commencing, ' Queste colui chel mondo
chiama amore ' ; the second and third courses by a fair
young maid impersonating Chastity and a child representing
Time, to the strain of Latin verses written by Buchanan.[4]

The pageant car was probably imported into these
entertainments long before there is any trace in the records.
The ' belle nef laquelle avoit hunne, chasteau, masts, et
les cordes qui estoient d'argent ' at the marriage banquet
of James the Second, in 1449, must, I fear, be taken as an
elaborate dish which was carried in by an attendant.[5]

[1] App. III, Excerpts from *L.H.T.A.*
[2] G. Marioreybanks, *Annals of Scotland,* 14. Cited in Robertson, *Inventories,* xliv.
[3] Bain and Boyd, *Calendar,* II, 47, No. 60, 21st Feb. 1563-64,
Randolph to Cecil.
[4] *Ibid.* ' The last was served by gentlemen apparelled all in
white and black, divers amongst them sang the verses, which
herewith I send your honour.' Cf. *Keith,* II, 220 ; Robertson,
Inventories, lxxxiij.
[5] *Chroniques de Mathieu de Coussy,* p. 156, in Buchon, Collection
des chroniques nationales francaises. ' Eux donc estant assis,
le premier mets qu'on porta et qui leur fut présenté ce fut la
figure d'une hure de sanglier peinte et pleine d'estoupes, dans un
grand plat, autour duquel il y avoit bien trente-deux bannières,
tant des armes du roy, commes des autres seigneurs du pays.
Alors on mit le feu dans lesdites estoupes ; si fut faite grande joie
là dessus dans toute la salle, par tous ceux qui y estoient. Après,
on apporta une belle nef, laquelle avoit hunne, chasteau, masts,
et les cordes qui estoient d'argent, le tout bien ouvré. Ensuite
de quoy vint et marcha le comte d'Orquenay, avec quatre cheva-
liers, précédant.' Cf. Pinkerton, *History of Scotland,* I, 432.

For the principal banquet at the baptism of Prince James
in 1566 at Stirling, however, Buchanan composed his
Pompæ Deorum Rusticorum in co-operation with Bastien
Pagez who devised for bringing the ' meit ' to the great
hall ' ane trym engyn, marching as apperit it alain, with
musiciens clothed lyk maidins, playing vpon all sortis of
instrumentis and singing of musick.' [1] Even more elaborate
' ingegni ' were constructed for the baptismal feast of
Prince Henry at Stirling in 1594. After the first service
there came in a triumphal chariot twelve feet long and seven
feet broad, the ' motion ' of which was ' so artificial within
itselfe, that it appeared to be drawne in onely by the
strength of a Moore.' It had been intended that a lion
should draw the chariot ; but caution prevailed, and the
Black Moor with the assistance of a ' secret convoy '
did the honours of the occasion. About a sumptuously
covered table were placed six gallant dames, Ceres, Fecun-
dity, Faith, Concord, Liberality, and Perseverance, who,
after representing a ' silent comedie,' delivered the dessert
to the sewers. Next came in a ' most sumptuous, artificiall, and well-proportioned ship,' eighteen feet long,
eight feet broad, and forty feet high. The sea, which was
' lively counterfeit with all colours,' was twenty-four feet
long. The ' motion ' of the ship was ' so artificially devised
within herself, that none could perceive what brought her
in.' She carried Neptune, Thetis, Triton, all bearing
symbolic devices, and ' all the marine people,' who repeated
a Latin verse to the strains of the fourteen musicians and
Arion with his harp, and ' made sayle till shee came to the
table, discharging the ordnance in her sterne by the way.' [2]

[1] App. III, Excerpts from MS. Accounts of the Lord High
Treasurer, and note.
[2] Cf. *A True Reportarie of the Most Trivmphant and Royal
Accomplishment of the Baptisme of the most Excellent, right High
and Mightie Prince, Frederik Henry ; By the Grace of God, Prince
of Scotland. Solemnized the 30 day of August* 1594. Printed by

From the meagre data on which the foregoing summary depends, it is difficult to judge how far the characteristics of the genuine mask, where the masked dancers with torchbearers and musicians enter the hall with gifts and after some preliminaries invite the spectators to dance, were reproduced at the Scottish court. No one instance clearly shows all the features. But ' vj maskis ' figure in a list of clothes in 1565 ; [1] Queen Mary plays at dice for a jewel with Lennox [2]—a common feature of the early mask ; daggers are presented by maskers to the spectators, probably as a preliminary to taking them out to dance ; [3]

R. Waldegraue. Cf. Thorpe, *State Papers*, II, 659, No. 23. The summary above is taken from the reprint in Nichols, *Progresses of Queen Elizabeth*, Vol. III. A shorter account is given in *Calderwood*, V, 345 : ' They being refreshed, a certane space, came in a blacke More drawing a chariot, wherin was the desert, presented by ladies Ceres, Facundia, Faith, Concord, Liberalitie and Perseverance. The chariot returning, entered an artificiall and weill proportionned shippe, the lenth of her keell eighteene foote, and her breadth eight foote, from the bottom to the high flag foure foote ; the sea made counterfooted. On her fore sterne was Neptunus, then Thetis and Triton ; about the shippe, mariners and steirsmen. The mast was reid, her taikling and cords of silke, with threttie-five peece of brazen ordinance ; all the sailes of double white taffetie. The pylot in cloth of gold moved the shippe, wherin were musicians, and Arion with his harpe ; and in this maner she sailled, whill she came to the table, discharging her ordinance in the sterne by the way. Out of this shippe was losed and delivered a chrystall glasse, curiouslie painted with gold and azure (as the meases of the chariot were) ; all sorts of fishes made of sugar, as shell fishes, and others. This done, the shippe returned, and shott her ordinance. The bankett ended, thankes being givin to God, there was sung the 128th Psalme, with diverse voices and toones, and musicall instruments playing. The strangers mervelled greatlie at the shippe.' The account in Johnston's *MS. History of Scotland* (Adv. Lib. Hist. MSS., 35, 4, 2), II, f. 622b, is almost identical with the Anglicised version of Calderwood.

[1] App. III, Excerpts from *L.H.T.A.*

[2] Bain and Boyd, *Calendar*, II, 88, Randolph to Cecil, 24th Oct. 1564. ' That night she danced long and in a maske playinge at dyce, loste unto my lord of Lenox a prettie juell of crystall well sette in golde.'

[3] *Supra*, 48.

and masking and dancing are associated in contemporary accounts ; so that there seems no reason to doubt that the 'skippings,' so scornfully condemned by Knox, were orthodox masks 'after the maner of Italie.'[1]

Whether the term 'mask' may legitimately be used to describe those *entremets* instanced above is more doubtful. They may perhaps be regarded as truncated masks adapted to meet the needs of a banquet. In some of the earlier meagre references dancing is mentioned, but 'commoning' with the spectators, the central *motif* of the sixteenth century mask,[2] would be ruled out. The magnificent display at Stirling in 1594 had several points in common with the regular Elizabethan spectacular mask : the use of torches, the pageant car, and Renaissance machinery, borrowings from the moralities or allegorical literature and classical mythology, symbolism run riot, the accompaniment of bands of musicians and the bearing of gifts. Visors are not mentioned, but this may be accidental. The only 'commoning' between the maskers and the guests at the banquet was in the delivery of the dessert and sugar confections. The 'enterlude' culminated, if we may trust the contemporary reports, not in a masked ball, but in the singing of the 128th psalm in seven parts ![3]

By at least the beginning of the sixteenth century, disguisings were an important feature of jousts and tourna-

---

[1] *Knox*, II, 294. The only dance which Knox describes is one called 'the Purpose' in which 'man and woman talkis secreatlie.' In this dance 'the Quene chosed Chattelett, and Chattelett took the Quene.' *Knox*, II, 368.

[2] Cf. Chambers, *Elizabethan Stage*, I, 153.

[3] Nichols, *loc. cit.* : 'And when in this time all the banket was done, after thanks being given, there was sung with most delicate dulce voices, and sweet harmonie, in seven partes, the 128th Psalm, with fourteen voyces ; and that being done, at the sound of Triton's wilke-trumpet, and the pilote's whistle, she wayed anchor, made saile, and with noise of honboys and trumpets retyred, and then discharged the rest of her ordnance, to the great admiration of the beholders.'

ments. The 'torney' which took place outside Edinburgh in 1503, to greet Margaret on her progress north, had all the features of a miniature drama drawn from chivalric romance.[1] If dialogue was introduced into other tournaments of the period, the fact is unrecorded. But the gorgeous spectacular effects, the assumption of special rôles by the participants, the use of allegorical symbolism, the importation of folk characters, reveal a close affinity to mask and pageantry. The 1507 tournament of the Wild Knight and the Black Lady attracted attention far beyond the bounds of Scotland, and, in response to the illuminated 'articules' sent to France, combatants came to Edinburgh from overseas to prove their valour in the Garden of Patience, where grew the Tree of Esperance bearing leaves of Pleasure, the flower of Nobleness and the fruit of Honour. The accounts of the Lord High Treasurer preserve full details regarding the purchase and preparation of dresses, armour, banners, pavilions, the triumphal chair for the Black Lady, harts' horns and goat skins for the wild men, strange winged beasts equipped with reins and saddles, as well as eighteen dozen leaves, six dozen flowers, and thirty-seven pears for the Tree of Esperance.[2] This tournament was repeated, evidently with little change, in May of the following year.[2] There are many other notices of 'hastiludia,' tourneys, running at the ring; but little is said as to disguises. In December 1561 the French Ambassador, Monsieur de Foys, Lord Robert, Lord John, and others ran at the ring 'dysguised and appareled thone half lyke women, and thother lyke strayngers, in straynge maskinge garmentes.'[3] In 1594 the 'rare shewes and singular inventions' of the indoor revels at Stirling were

---

[1] App. III, Excerpts from *L.H.T.A.*, *infra*, 320, n.[2].

[2] *Ibid.*, Excerpts from *L.H.T.A.*

[3] Bain and Boyd, *Calendar*, I, 576, No. 1049, Randolphe to Cecill, 7th Dec.

accompanied by 'martiall and heroicall exploits' in the field. A 'maske' was arranged in which the 'actors' were three Turks, three Christian knights of Malta, and three Amazons, together with nine pages and nine lackies.[1] There should also have been three Moors, but owing to the 'uncertaine presence' of these gentlemen, they were left out. The first law of the pastime was 'that all the persons . . . compeare masked.' The second day's pastime, which had to be abandoned owing to the preoccupation of the artisans with other matters, was to have been 'commendable and wonderfull' with 'such beastes as lyon, elephant, hart, unicorne, and the griphon, together with the camel, hydre, crocadile, and dragon (carrying their riders).' [2]

Were it not that two detailed discharges have escaped destruction, one might dismiss the references to fireworks at court revels as of no value in this connection. For more than a month beforehand, preparations went on at high pressure for the 'triomphe of firework,' costing £190, 17s. 5½d. Scots, which followed the unfortunate episode of the mask of the satyrs at the baptism of Prince James in December 1566.[3] Wrights were employed on the construction of a fort which was illuminated by night with wreaths of fire. Artillery and munitions for besieging the fort were prepared at Edinburgh, conveyed by boat from Leith to Stirling, and carried stealthily by night through the sleeping town 'for feir of knawlege pairof.' 'Play clothes' were provided for the 'men of warre' who made the assault on the fort, goat skins for the 'four hieland wyld mens cleithingis,' buckram of different colours

---

[1] Nichols, *loc. cit.*

[2] *Ibid.* Cf. *Calderwood*, V, 346 : 'The Abbot of Halyrudhous, in woman's apparell tooke up the ring sindrie tymes. The Lord Hume, in Turkish rayment, the king himself, in his masking geir, with a white overthwart croce, the badge of the Knights of the Holie Spirit, which was muche mislyked by good men.'

[3] *Supra,* 50 and note.

for the bands of lance-knights, Moors, and horsemen, and the three ' contrefait ' devils, and lamb skins for false hair for the Moors. Yet it is impossible to reconstruct the allegory ; for the practical John Chisholme was more concerned in recording the various ingredients of the fire- works than the name of the fortress or the object of the attack.[1] Some fifty years later, when King James came back to visit his native country, in 1617, a similar enter- tainment, costing £1014, 14s. 6d. Scots, was provided in Edinburgh. On this occasion St George and the dragon played a prominent part, and ' hielandmen ' again partici- pated. A hobby horse was brought from Berwick, perhaps for the morris dance, and operations were apparently directed by or against the Captain of Envy.[2] No details unfortunately are preserved of the assault on the Pope's ' pallas ' at the marriage of the Earl of Murray's daughter in January 1580-81.[3] As spectacular offshoots from mediæval drama, these displays cannot be ignored. But that they have branched out far from the parent tree is

[1] App. III, Fireworks. Cf. D.R.O., 105, 19th Dec. 1566 : ' thair wes masry and playing in all sortis, befoir supper ; than ane fort haldin in Striueling besyid the kirk-yaird, quhairin wes artailzerie, schote fyre ballis, fyre speris, and all vtheris thingis plesand for the sicht of man.'

[2] Ibid., Fireworks.

[3] Bain and Boyd, Calendar, V, 611. ' On Thursday the King dined at Leith, and after dinner he ran at the ring and beheld such other pastimes as were to be seen, as the assault given to a castle, builded on boats on the river St Angele, named " the Pope's pallas which was wonne and sett one fyre to the Pope's and Papistes great disgrace." Divers ran on the water with boats " justing " one against the other. Some ran their horses on the sands. Three gentlemen fell and were sore hurt, which bred an end to their pastimes.' The original MS. (Harleian MSS. 6999, f. 32) reads : ' and efter dynner he ran at the ring, and beheld such other pastymes as wer to be seen ; As the assault given to a castell builded on boates one the ryver named St Angele, the Popes pallas wch was wonne and sett on fyre to the Popes and papistes great disgrace.'

clear—and particularly so in the 1566 account where the players are regular gunners from Edinburgh and Dunbar, and the Master of Revels is John Chisholme, 'Comptrollar of the artailȝerye.'

To return to the legitimate drama, I cannot find in the Scottish records any real parallel to the influence exerted in England on stage-plays through the activities of the Chapel Royal.[1] Pitscottie states that, at the reorganisation of the Chapel Royal of Stirling, James the Third duplicated the offices—

> 'To that effect that they sould ewer be redy, the ane half to pase witht him quhair ever he pleissit that they might sing and play to him and hald him merrie and the wther half sould remaine at hame in the said chapell for to sing and pray for him and his successouris.'[2]

On the analogy of the testimony furnished by the Northumberland Household Book, the suggestion has been made that the Clerks of the Chapel acted a Nativity play at Christmas and a Passion or Resurrection play at Easter.[3] Very probably they did; but, beyond the fact that they figure in the lists of Yule and Pasche rewards, and that there was a sepulchre in the Chapel Royal at Stirling,[4] no support is given to this conjecture by the official records. Sir Thomas Galbraith, John Goldsmith, and Crafurd, Clerks to the Chapel, sing a New Year 'ballat' to the King in 1491-92; John Goldsmith is elected King of the Bean at Epiphany 1495-96, and again in 1501-2; Sir Thomas Galbraith works along with Piers, the Dutch painter, in the preparation of equipment for the 1507

---

[1] Cf. C. W. Wallace, *The Evolution of the English Drama up to Shakespeare (Schriften der Deutschen Shakespeare Gesellschaft)*.

[2] Pitscottie's *Cronicles*, I, 200.

[3] *L.H.T.A.*, I, ccxl, ccxlv.

[4] *Infra*, 60.

pageant and tournament; the six 'childir' or 'bairnis' of the Chapel appear merely as the recipients of regular gratuities.[1] This seems to exhaust the record.

The suggestion that Patrick Johnson, who was paid £6 'pro suis ludis' at Christmas 1475 and Shrovetide 1476, 'pro certis joccis et ludis' sometime during 1477, and 'pro certis ludis et interludiis' at Christmas 1477,[2] and who appeared in company with the 'playaris of Lythgow' in August 1488 and 1489,[3] was one of the Clerks of the Chapel[4] rests on insufficient evidence, but is more probable than that he was a professional player.[5] If it could be proved that the ceremony of offering the incense at the Epiphany was performed regularly, or, at least, when the King was in Linlithgow, by the Clerks of the Chapel Royal, our difficulties would be simplified; for in 1489-90 a payment was made to Patrick Johnson 'to the censs,' and again in 1490-91 'for the censs.'[6] There are numerous references

---

[1] App. III, Excerpts from *L.H.T.A.* Among the MS. Royal Household Papers (James IV.) at Register House, there is a Bill of Household made 5th Jan. 1507-8 which contains a list of 'The king*is* chapell Riall'—24 men and 'sax child*er*.'

[2] *Ibid.*, Excerpts from *E.R.*

[3] *Ibid,*, Excerpts from *L.H.T.A.*

[4] Dunbar, *Poems*, I, ccxxxvij. The suggestion is based on Johnson's 'association with other persons who received payments at the same time.' On analysis, this amounts to the fact that, according to *L.H.T.A.*, on 15th Jan. 1489-90, Patrick Johnson received a payment for incense and that three days later the Clerks of the Chapel received their usual Yule reward; that, on 2nd Jan. 1490-1, the Clerks of the Chapel were paid for 'thare service at ȝwle,' and on 6th Jan. P. J. was paid 'for the censs' in company with the keepers of the wine cellar, ale cellar and pantry; and that, in August 1489, P. J. is known to have played before the Spanish ambassadors, at which time there was also a payment to the Clerks of the Chapel 'that wes in Lythqow quhen the Imbassatouris wes thare.'

[5] *L.H.T.A.*, I, ccxxxix.

[6] Cf. *L.H.T.A.*, I, ccxliv : 'To furnish this (the incense) seems to have been a perquisite of the clerks of the chapel.' But no authority is stated. Payments for this ceremony were made to the priests of Linlithgow (*L.H.T.A.*, IV, 95), the Parish Clerk

D

to Patrick Johnson in the Exchequer Rolls, but never a
hint as to his profession. The fact seems to have been
generally overlooked that from 1466 to 1468 he acted as
one of the 'ballivi ad extra' for Linlithgowshire. It may
have been in recognition of these services that, in 1467,
the King granted under the Privy Seal the life-rents of
Kingisfielde 'dilecto familiari servitori nostro Patricio
Johneson, pro suo fideli servicio nobis impenso et impendendo,' and to his wife Janet if she should survive him.
His association with the 'playaris of Lythgow,' the fact
that he is not known to have played outside Linlithgow,
and that the Chamberlain of Linlithgowshire is debited
with the expense of the earlier group of these plays, his
official position as receiver of fermes for the shire—all
this points to a strong local interest.[1] If his services at
the Epiphany involve of necessity an ecclesiastical connection, may he not have held some minor post at the
Parish Church of Linlithgow ? The omission of the courtesy
title of 'Sir' and the recognition of his marriage by royal
charter (for celibacy was not enforced in the lower ranks)
might thus be explained. In any case, there seems no
reason to doubt that the plays provided by Patrick Johnson
were genuine dramatic productions. 'Ludi' and 'jocci'
are indeterminate as usual; but the use of the term 'in-
terludia,' and the fact that Patrick Johnson is one of
Dunbar's 'makaris,'[2] are details not without significance.
Were we not dealing with the barren dramatic history of
Scotland, the theory of a local 'puy' would be tempting.

> 'Quho can say more than Schir James Inglis sayis,
> In ballattis, farses, and in plesand playis ? '

---

of Edinburgh (IV, 181), the priests of St Giles (IV, 402), and the
priests of Glasgow (IX, 272), as well as to various unspecified
singers and 'men that brocht the sensouris.'
    [1] App. III, Excerpts from *E.R.*, *infra*, 311 and notes.
    [2] Dunbar, *Poems*, II, 50.

asks Lyndsay.[1] But, prior to the date of his appointment
to the Abbacy of Culross which ' hes his pen maid impo-
tent,' there are only two notices in the Lord High Treasurer's
accounts which reveal Inglis in the rôle of actor, if not
playwright.[2] Similarly, so far as the official records are
concerned, the dramatic activities of Sir David Lyndsay
at the Scottish Court begin and end in October 1511, when
he was provided with a blue-and-yellow taffeta play coat
costing £3, 4s. for ' the play playt in the King and Quenis
presence in the Abbay.'[3] The entries relating to the play
coats made by the tailor ' agane uphalyday ' 1539-40 occur
in a section devoted to ' Expensis debursit upoun the
King and Quenis personis ' ; and therefore, presumably,
were not intended for the players of the *Satyre of the Thrie
Estaitis*, which we know to have been acted on this day
in Linlithgow.[4] The services of George Buchanan in connection with the mask have already been noted.[5] A
payment to William Lauder for a ' play ' at Lady Barbara
Hamilton's wedding [6] concludes the recorded services of
the ' makaris ' in regard to Court drama.

[1] *Works*, 1879, I, 62.
[2] App. III, Excerpts from *L.H.T.A.*, 1511-12, 1526.
[3] *Ibid.*, Excerpts from *L.H.T.A.*
[4] Gairdner, *Letters and Papers of the Reign of Henry VIII*,
XV, 36 ; Pinkerton, *History of Scotland*, II, 494 ; Ellis, *Original
Letters*, 3rd series, Vol. III, 279.
[5] *Supra*, 47 ff.
[6] App. III, Excerpts from *L.H.T.A.*, 1548-49.

IV.

MUNICIPAL PLAYS.

(Where authorities are not cited, see App. I.)

PRE-REFORMATION church service books in Scotland are very rare, and the liturgical drama has left few traces. The directions in the *Holyrood Ordinale* for the services on Good Friday and Easter Sunday reveal a magnificent Passion play in embryo.[1] The Arbuthnot Missal, which follows the Sarum model, gives directions for laying the Cross ' pariter cum corpore Dominico in sepulchro,' and for the censing and closing the sepulchre until the Resurrection.[2] A payment for the mending of the sepulchre at the Chapel Royal at Stirling [3] leads one to suppose that at least a *Quem quœritis* was played by the Clerks of the

[1] *The Holyrood Ordinale*, Old Edinburgh Club, 1916, pp. 109-112, 124-5. p. 110 (In die parasceue): ' In passione cum diaconus dixerit · *partiti sunt vestimenta mea* · sint iuxta altare illi duo qui vltimum tractum cantauerunt · vnus ex una parte et alius ex alia parte trahentes ad se linthea que ante officium ad hoc ibi fuerat posita.' The ceremony of the veneration of the Cross is described in detail. There is no definite reference to a sepulchre. ' Hijs peractis · prelatus ac ministri · stolis et manipulis resumptis · solo prelato calciato · et casula induto · cum thuriferario et ceroferarijs · pergant ad locum vbi pridie corpus domini posuerunt.'

[2] *Liber Ecclesie Beati Terrenani de Arbuthnott*, missale secundum usum Ecclesiæ Sancti Andreæ in Scotia. Burntisland, 1864.

[3] *L.H.T.A.*, I, 228, 1494-5, ' Item, for the mending of the sepulture, the chapell dure, and Judas crois, iijs.'

Chapel at Easter. A passage in Buchanan purports to give the origin of a liturgical Passion play in the reign of James the First :—

> 'Certoque psalmorum penso, quod in singulos dies imperabatur, emurmurando colluderunt, et nunc alternis versibus contendentes, nunc choros inter actus adhibentes tragoediae speciem exhibebant, quae Christi morte imaginaria claudebatur.' [1]

But there are no clear instances of either a fully fledged liturgical drama or miracle plays and religious pageants prior to the stage at which these came under the control and patronage of the burgh authorities.

The earliest definite reference to a religious play in Scotland is in 1440, when a Corpus Christi Passion play at Aberdeen seems to be indicated. On 13th May of that year, a fortnight before the Corpus Christi festival, the right of presenting a burgess and claiming the fee was granted to the Abbot of Bonaccord in consideration of his expenses 'factis et faciendis in quodam ludo de ly haliblude ludendo apud ly Wyndmylhill.' Whether the play was performed annually is uncertain. It is mentioned again in 1445. In 1449 the notary public, Walter Balcancole, received 5s. either for copying out or rearranging the old Haliblude play, or for writing out a new play for Corpus Christi Day ; from which we may assume that we are dealing with articulate drama and not mere dumbshow.

Up to this point there is no suggestion that these plays were of the cyclical type usually associated with Corpus Christi Day. From the brief entries, one would almost be inclined to infer detached 'standing' plays. Of organised craft participation there is not a hint ; and indeed the

[1] George Buchanan, *Rerum Scoticarum Historia*, 1762, Bk. X, p. 283.

fact that, in 1479, the expenses for the 'arayment & vɣiris necessaris of ɣe play to be plait in ɣe fest of corpus xp̄i nixt tocum' were to be defrayed from common good funds points rather to the contrary.

The only other early play in Aberdeen of which the name has survived has hitherto completely escaped notice. In July 1471 there is a reference in the Council Register to expenses incurred in connection with a 'ludum de bellyale.' From the date of the entry, this may have been another Corpus Christi miracle play ; but there is no reason for ruling out a morality play of the type of the *Castle of Perseverance*.

The loss of the pre-Reformation craft records in Aberdeen is to be deplored.[1] The earliest evidence in the burgh records as to the association of the crafts with the Corpus Christi celebrations occurs in the statute of January 1512-13, ordaining the provision of torches for the Corpus Christi and other processions. It is not, however, until 1530 that pageants are definitely mentioned in connection with the Corpus Christi procession. On 17th June of that year the Council decreed that the craftsmen should 'keip ɣair pagganis in ɣe processiouñ oñ sonday nyxt cumis,' [2] under penalty of 40s. for each craft which failed. I am able further to confirm the fact (which could only be conjectured from the printed records by Sir Edmund Chambers [3]) that the 1531 list of 'panȝeanys' referred to the Corpus Christi procession. The heading 'Ordour of corpus xpi processioun' and the addition to the marginal note 'and of corpus cristi,' omitted in the Spalding Club transcript, were almost certainly added at the same time as the list of pageants scribbled in at the end of the original

[1] Cf. E. Bain, *Merchants and Craft Gilds*, 1887. I have not made any independent investigation of the Aberdeen craft records.
[2] This is the only case where the procession is mentioned as taking place on a day other than Corpus Christi Day.
[3] *Mediæval Stage*, II, 333.

entry—all three additions being made, if not by another hand, at least in ink different from that in which the rest of the entry was written.

It is doubtful whether the later Aberdeen evidence can be construed to signify a professional cycle of the Chester type. The nature of the pageants themselves would seem to preclude any such theory. The old Haliblude play may perhaps be traced in the Crucifixion and Resurrection pageants, to which might be added the St John pageant and the Litsters' pageant of the Coronation of Our Lady. But there is no parallel for incorporating a series of martyrdoms of the saints in a connected Passion cycle.[1] Further, from various regulations we know the stereotyped order in which the crafts passed in procession before the sacrament, which order corresponds with the 1531 list of pageants. But these pageants could not be played in succession to form an evolutionary history of the Passion. The absence, too, of any regulation as to ' stations ' is significant, if not conclusive.

It may be that the Corpus Christi pageants at Aberdeen were mere dumb-show accompaniments of the religious procession,[2] or that they incorporated the characters and scenes of a play which would take place at the playfield either before or after the procession.[3] As we have seen, the scanty evidence is against rather than in favour of associating the crafts with the earlier plays at the Windmill Hill. The absence of reference to any such ' standing ' play in the later records is, however, no absolute proof of its non-existence. It would be interesting to know

[1] But see infra, 69.
[2] Cf. K. L. Bates, The English Religious Drama, 1893, p. 21, who points out that in France the Corpus Christi pageants never yielded to the spoken drama, but that this one feast was devoted to procession and dumb-show.
[3] This may have been the arrangement at Newcastle. Cf. Chambers, Mediæval Stage, II, 134. But see The Non-Cycle Mystery Plays, E.E.T.S., 1909, p. xli.

not only the exact uses for which the new playfield made
in 1559 was designed, but also the nature of the ' playis '
for which the Abbot of Bonaccord was held responsible.[1]
Were these ' to generall plais ' the May revels and St
Nicholas riding ? Or did the Abbot of Bonaccord, as in
the days of the Haliblude play, still superintend genuine
religious dramatic performances ? It is, of course, possible
that the reference may be to the Corpus Christi and Candlemas pageants—though there is no evidence for associating
the Lords of Bonaccord, as distinct from the ordinary
bailies, with these functions.[2]

The enactments of the Council regarding the Corpus
Christi pageants show that they were regulated in much
the same way as south of the Border. The ordering of the
procession was in the hands of the bailies ; and the jealousy
with which their respective positions or ' roumes ' were
guarded by the crafts is illustrated frequently in the
records. The deacons or masters of the crafts were responsible to the town for furnishing the pageants (1530,
1534, 1538, 1551), and a defaulting craft was held liable
for a considerable fine. In 1532 the Baxters were summoned
for ' wanting of pair pagane.' The following year the
Litsters and Barbers appeared in court for failure to provide
' pangeaniß ' ; and again, in 1539, the Litsters were summoned and fined for ' non-ganging ' in the procession.
The costs of the pageants were borne by the respective
crafts. Each of the craftsmen was to contribute ' eftir
pair faculty ' (1538—baxters), and powers were given to

[1] App. IV, *Playfields* ; App. I, s.v. *Aberdeen*—Folk Plays,
14th April 1553.
[2] For the statement of C. Davidson, *Studies in the English
Mystery Plays*, 1892, p. 95, that on Corpus Christi Day the procession was under the direction of the Abbot of Bon-Accord,
later under that of Robin Hood, and that a fusion of May Day
and Corpus Christi Day seems probable, there is no support apart
from the ambiguous 1553 entry regarding the duties of the Lords
of Bonaccord. But see duties of Edinburgh Abbot, *supra*, 27.

the deacons to 'stent' the members of their own crafts 'and gif nead beis to pund and distrenȝe ȝame ȝairfor' (1551).

As has been pointed out by authorities on the subject, the Passion and Nativity cycles were never merged at Aberdeen.[1] From 1442 there are traces of a Candlemas play centring round the Presentation in the Temple, but including apparently a *Prophetæ*, Annunciation, and a *Magi* or *Stella*. It is evident that here, too, there was a processional pageant, in which the honest squires and the woodmen and minstrels figured. But, despite the 1505-6 regulation providing for the attendance of two craftsmen, 'to paß with the pageant ȝat ȝai furnys to keip thare geire,' the instructions as to the order of the crafts are again too specific to render plausible any suggestion that there was a processional play composed of independent scenes in the hands of the various incorporations. A Candlemas play would scarcely conclude with the Magi— the pageant of the Smiths and Hammermen, who brought up the rear of the civic procession next the sacrament,— but would culminate in the Presentation in the Temple, with Simeon as one of the characters. Nor does the early date of the first entry in 1442, taken in conjunction with the fact that more than sixty years later the pageants were substantially the same, suggest that a process of decadence had set in which would account for the confused nature of the scheme.

Sir Edmund Chambers queries Professor Davidson's contention that there was never more than a 'mystère mimé' at Aberdeen at Candlemas, and cites the references to the 'play' in 1506, 1507, and 1510.[2] But, even with

[1] Chambers, *Mediæval Stage*, II, 128, 333; *The Non-Cycle Mystery Plays*, p. xi.
[2] *Mediæval Stage*, II, 333; *Studies in the English Mystery Plays*, 96.

the additional entries which I have transcribed from the original manuscript, I find it difficult to determine the exact signification of the word 'play' in this connection. The word occurs in the entries of (1) and (2) 29th January 1503-4 ('thare—*i.e.*, the Skinners' and Walkers'—part of candilmeß play'; 'thar part of ye said play'); (3) and (4) 3rd February 1503-4 ('ye processione of (in) candilmeß play'); (5) 5th February 1503-4 ('ye situacione[1] of candilmes play'); (6) 30th January 1505-6 ('in ordire to ye Offering in ye play'); (7) 31st May 1507 ('in ale processionis baitht in candilmeß play & vyeris processionis'); (8) 29th January 1507-8 ('yar part of candilmes play'); (9) 1510-11 ('in ordour to the offering in ye play').

From (5), almost certainly, and (7), if we read 'in candilmeß play' as in apposition to 'in ale processionis,' it is arguable that 'play' is really synonymous with 'procession.' On the other hand (3), (4), (6), (9), and (7), if we read 'in candilmeß play' as a phrase qualifying 'procession,' do not lend themselves to this argument. The balance of probability seems to lie in favour of interpreting the word 'play' in the widest sense to cover both the processional pageantry and the 'offerand.'

Apart from this, however, it seems fairly certain that the procession was not an end in itself. The phrases 'ye inordinate passing one candilmes day to ye offerand' (1492-93), and 'yai sale in ordire to ye Offering in ye play' (1505-6 and 1510-11), suggest that the procession was preliminary to the main part of the proceedings—namely, the 'offerand.' I may be laying too much stress on the actual wording of the entry when from the 1442 statute, with its exhortation to the crafts to 'fynd ȝerely in ye offerand of oure lady at candilmes yire persones vnderwrittin' (taken along with the list of 'persones' and the order in which they occur), I infer that the original idea,

[1] See note on this entry in App. I, s.v. *Aberdeen*.

at least when first recorded, was the furnishing of so many characters for one common ' play,' rather than the representation of independent scenes in a processional cyclical play by the several crafts.

Where the ' offerand ' was performed cannot be ascertained. An elaborate *al fresco* performance in the playfield seems unlikely at this time of year. In the absence of any more plausible interpretation, I suggest that the Candlemas celebrations at Aberdeen may have been similar in nature to, if more elaborate in detail than, those of the Beverley Guild of St Mary [1]—that is, a preliminary riding or procession with a dramatic ceremony in the church. Whether a simple drama or a ' mystère mimé ' would be enacted at the high altar must, of course, remain uncertain.

Otherwise, the Candlemas regulations resembled closely those relating to the Corpus Christi festival. The obligation of furnishing the ' persones ' or pageants rested on the crafts who bore the expense. In January 1503-4 the Skinners and Walkers were ordered to uphold their part of the play, and to ' extent ' reasonably all unfree persons

---

[1] Toulmin Smith, *English Gilds*, 149 : ' Every year, on the feast of the Purification of the Blessed Mary, all the bretheren and sisteren shall meet together in a fit and appointed place, away from the church ; and there, one of the gild shall be clad in comely fashion as a queen, like to the glorious Virgin Mary, having what may seem a son in her arms ; and two others shall be clad like to Joseph and Simeon ; and two shall go as angels, carrying a candle-bearer, on which shall be twenty-four thick wax lights. With these and other great lights borne before them, and with much music and gladness, the pageant Virgin with her son, and Joseph and Simeon, shall go in procession to the church. And all the sisteren of the gild shall follow the Virgin ; and afterwards all the bretheren ; and each of them shall carry a wax light weighing half a pound. And they shall go two and two, slowly pacing to the church ; and when they have got there, the pageant Virgin shall offer her son to Simeon at the high altar ; and all the sisteren and bretheren shall offer their wax lights, together with a penny each.'

of their crafts ' eftir ᵹe faculte of thare gudis,' and, if need be, to distrain.   In January 1507-8 the deacon of the Walkers was summoned at the instance of John Reid 'for ᵹe wranguiſs withhaldin fra him of ij đ to ᵹe furnising of ᵹar part of candilmes play.'   In 1515-16 the deacons of all the crafts were to furnish ' ᵹar partis and badgeandis ' of the procession.   Absentees were to be punished.   There were convictions for ' non-ganging ' in 1483-84, 1492-93, 1503-4, 1510-11, and 1523-24.   The order was regulated by the statutes of 1505-6, 1507, 1507-8, 1510-11, and 1531. The Candlemas procession, though not specified, was surely included in the enactment of 1512-13 concerning torches ; details as to the payments for which by the individual skinners are given in a subsequent entry.   The acts of 1484-85 and 1523-24 testify to the wearing of their special tokens by the craftsmen.   In all probability the Candlemas play would survive until the Reformation, but it is mentioned for the last time in the Council Register in 1531.

The loss of the early records of Perth has almost certainly deprived us of valuable information relating to mediæval drama.   The few available sources indicate not only a long-established dramatic tradition, but an extraordinary tenacity on the part of the inhabitants in preserving their old plays in the face of ecclesiastical persecution.[1]

In 1485 a payment of 20s. was made through the Dean of Guild at the command of the Council to a priest named Robert Douthle ' pro suis laboribus et expenſsis factis in processione et ludo corporis x͠pi.'   The payment was repeated in the following year ; and again in 1487-88, when, however, the ' ludus ' alone is mentioned.   Any doubt as to whether the term ' ludus ' has here a claim to dramatic connotation must, I think, be resolved by the fortunate

---

[1] For the latter point see Section V, also App. I, s.v. *Perth*— Kirk Session Records.

preservation of one of the pre-Reformation craft books, that of the Hammermen. In 1518 there is a list of payments to the ' playaris on Corpus Christie Day.' The interpretation of this list is not clear. Adam and Eve, the Devil and his ' Man,' the Devil's Chapman,[1] the Angel and 'Marmadin ' indicate the Creation and Fall. St Eloy, as patron saint of the Hammermen, might be fitted into the cast. But there was apparently a second play on the subject of St Erasmus, the gruesome story of whose martyrdom must have been portrayed with astonishing realism by the aid of the Cord-drawer and the three Tormentors.[2] By 1553, if we trust the official minutes, the play of Erasmus had disappeared, leaving us with only the Old Testament drama, in which George Allan plays the part of the Trinity, Robert Colbert impersonates the Serpent, while the parts of Adam and Eve, St Eloy, the Mermaid, and the various angels and devils are taken by members of the craft under penalty of half a stone of wax. There are the usual payments for banner-bearers, minstrels, and for food and drink to the players.

The only other evidence which I have found regarding the pre-Reformation Corpus Christi play in Perth is contained in a manuscript volume belonging to the Wrights' Incorporation. It is not easy to disentangle the special

[1] This character may, however, belong to the play of St Erasmus.

[2] Cf. Bollandus, *Acta Sanctorum*, s.v. Junius ii, 208 : ' Certe in hujus Actis antiquis nusquam legitur quod intestina ei fuerint extracta de ventre, in quo tamen tormenti genere, Romanis Tyrannis ignoto, sed Barbaris non insolito, constitutus Erasmus, in Belgio et Germania passim exprimitur . . . Ita in Antuerpiensis suburbii Borgerhautana aedicula, conspicitur tabella, nudum cum insignibus Episcopalibus Martyrem repraesentans humi stratum, sub tornatili cylindro (alii veru pingunt) cui circum volvuntur lente extracta e ventre intestina.' In 1520, iijd was paid by the Perth Hammermen for ' Sanct Erasimus cord.' Petit de Julleville, *Les Mystères*, II, 630, has a play of ' Saint Erasme,' performed at Metz in 1438, in his list of ' mystères perdus.'

Corpus Christi items from the rest of the account, but at least payments are recorded for repairing the play-gear and for 'menden of ye castell.' The expenses, too, of the minstrel and banner-bearers and of the bread and ale supplied to the players, are noted.

Little information as to the Wrights' play itself can be gleaned from these scanty entries, which are of importance rather as proving—what could be surmised—that the Hammermen's play was not an isolated play but the commencement of a cosmic cycle. Whether this craft cycle was of a processional character is not, however, quite clear. The entries in the Guildry manuscript and the Hammermen's book suggest a close connection between the 'ludus' and 'processio.' But exactly how does the rather ambiguous Hammermen's minute (1520) regarding the money gathered about the town 'to furneis the play afoir the procession' affect the question ?

At Lanark, where a few mutilated fragments of accounts belonging to the late fifteenth and early sixteenth centuries have escaped destruction, we again find traces of the Corpus Christi festival. There was certainly a 'procession of Corpus Christi,' the costs of which were borne by the town. The 'chapell' was carried round ; and St George in armour, complete with the dragon,[1] figured in the procession. But reference is made also to a 'Corpus Christi play,' the subject of which was apparently 'Cristis pascione.' Expenses in connection with Christ's coat and gloves, the making and repairing of the Cross, the 'ladis crownis' and certain 'hattis' are noted in the accounts. Another interesting item is the sum of money voted for a quire of paper to 'bill the pla.' If we may assume that the 'Kingis of Cullane' were attached to the Corpus Christi play,[2]

---

[1] The dragon was apparently a stock character in the communal ridings, and was borne round also at Martinmas.

[2] But see note on this entry, App. I, s.v. *Lanark*, 1507.

then at Lanark the Crucifixion was preceded by the *Stella*—that is, the Passion was extended to cover the Nativity. There is no suggestion in the records that any of the crafts of Lanark took part in their corporate capacity. The relation of the ' play ' to the ' procession ' is uncertain.

At Haddington in 1534, 1537, and 1541 there are traces of a cycle of craft pageants. Unfortunately no details have been entered in the Council books, and the old craft books are lost. The absence of any reference to pageants in connection with the 1532 regulation of the crafts in the Corpus Christi procession, though significant, must not be over-emphasised. More important perhaps is the minute of Council of 1537, ordering the crafts to play their pageants that year on Midsummer Day instead of Corpus Christi Day ; from which the inference may be drawn that, at any rate by this date, there was no inseparable connection with the ecclesiastical procession of Corpus Christi Day.

A mid-fifteenth century inventory of the 'grayth of ꝑe prossession of corpus xp̄i,' miraculously preserved in the Book of the Kirk, induces speculation as to the nature of the celebration of this feast at Dundee. Without further corroborative evidence we are not justified in assuming anything more definitely dramatic than an elaborate processional pageant with the Host, incorporating *tableaux* from the Old Testament stories, the Nativity, Passion and Resurrection, and legends of the saints. Yet there was an old-established playfield in Dundee, in which the Wedderburn plays are known to have been acted at a later date.[1]

The fact that it is not until 1553 that we come across the first references in the Edinburgh town records to municipal plays (apart from folk plays under the patronage of the Council) need not, in itself, prejudice the possibility of genuine miracle plays having been acted in this city,

[1] App. IV, *Playfields.*

for the pre-Reformation burgh records are far from complete.[1] In 1503 the Accounts of the Lord High Treasurer register the provision of equipment 'agane the Kingis passing to the Corpus Christi play,' presumably in Edinburgh. In 1504 there is a payment for grass to the royal 'chamires' on 'Corpus Christi day, at the play.'[2] In connection with the Corpus Christi celebrations in 1494 (the date of the commencement of their records), 1496, 1498, 1504, 1505, 1507, and 1516, the Hammermen's book chronicles payments for the furnishing of Herod and his knights, who are accompanied on several occasions by two doctors and, in 1507 only, by four 'wiffis.' After 1516 this Herod group falls out of the records, and, so far as can be judged from the official entries, the Hammermen confined their energies to providing minstrels, bannerbearers, and the 'twa knapis' or 'werlotis.' Until the Reformation the procession of Corpus Christi and the Octaves held an important place in the economy of the Hammermen and the associated crafts.[3]

Again the lack of parallel records renders doubtful the interpretation of the data. The Herod group furnished by the Hammermen is practically identical with the cast of the Towneley play of Herod the Great. If, however, the Hammermen of Edinburgh, even prior to 1532,[4] held the place of honour in the Corpus Christi procession in immediate proximity to the sacrament, then the idea of an evolutionary processional pageant must be dismissed. A drama representing Herod's rage at the departure of the Magi and the slaughter of the Innocents would scarcely form a fitting climax to a Corpus Christi craft cycle. Nor in the very full records of the Hammermen is there any

[1] I deal with the question of the Edinburgh town records at length in my concluding section, pp. 97-8.
[2] App. III, Excerpts from *L.H.T.A.*
[3] App. I, s.v. *Edinburgh*—Excerpts from Hammermen's Records.
[4] *Ibid.*, s.v. *Haddington*—Corpus Christi Procession.

mention of movable pageants.[1] Herod and his companions certainly took part in the Corpus Christi procession (1498), and apparently rode on horseback (1504). There seems, indeed, to be little to distinguish them from the numerous torch-bearers and standard-bearers and minstrels ; and there may have been nothing more dramatic than a spectacular religious riding with Biblical characters. ' Procession ' is the word used regularly in the accounts.[2] In 1494 a payment was made to a minstrel ' on sownday quhen ᵹe processioun was playd for ᵹe king,' [3] and the ' play ' to which allusion is made in the Accounts of the Lord High Treasurer for 1503 and 1504 may amount only to processional pageantry. On the other hand, the furnishing of bread and ale ' throw ᵹe gait,' as well as both before and after the procession, suggests a prolonged function with stoppages. It may be that the procession included a play on a fixed stage at one or more of the ' stations ' hallowed by tradition for pageants at royal entries. But there is no means of deciding whether the clerk play for which a scaffold was made in 1553 was a Corpus Christi play ; and there is no indication as to the type of performance which Mary of Guise witnessed from her carefully prepared ' luging ' on Corpus Christi Day, 1554.

If the burghs organised religious plays in connection with other church festivals, the records preserve an almost unbroken silence on the matter. At the feast of St Giles, the patron saint of Edinburgh, which fell on 1st September, the crafts went in procession with relics of the

[1] There is certainly a ' cart to ᵹe danß ' mentioned in 1506, but this may have been for the summer folk festival.

[2] I take it that the ' play ' for which money was gathered through the town by the Hammermen in 1500 was the folk play which was made this year at the bringing in of summer.

[3] But this detachment from Corpus Christi Day and the suggestion of a command performance for royalty imply a definitely dramatic conception.

E

saint,[1] but there is no hint of 'disguisings.' In 1580 the inhabitants of Elgin were forbidden to ride in 'disagysit maner'
on St Nicholas Day or eve. At Aberdeen the statutes
governing the winter lustration on St Nicholas Day vary
the decree concerning 'best array' only by a prosaic
reference to 'watter clokis' (1522). The Perth Baxters
held an annual riding in honour of their patron saint on
10th December, when the devil figured among the
celebrants ; and at Lanark there seems to have been a
Martinmas procession. But all these instances savour of
surviving pagan folk rites rather than organised Christian
ceremonies. The notice of the play of Good Friday and
Whitsunday, produced by a priest at Dumfries under the
patronage of the Town Council, is unique ; for I take it
that the 'histriones' who were rewarded at Easter 1462-63
at Aberdeen were the common minstrels.

Sir Edmund Chambers defines 'clerks play' as a variant
of miracle play.[2] In the few Scottish instances where it
is possible to check the meaning, it is probable that plays
on religious subjects are under consideration. The 'vane
Clerk play' at Haddington, against which Wishart directed
his scorn in 1546,[3] was in all likelihood the Corpus Christi
craft cycle. The subject of the clerk play in which the
scholars of the grammar school at St Andrews took part

---

[1] Cf. *Knox*, I, 259. In the Edinburgh Dean of Guild Accounts
(*City of Edinburgh Old Accounts*, Vol. II) there are entries concerning the painting of St Giles (1554-55, 1555-56), the mending
and polishing of his arm (1555-56), the mending of 'Sanct Gelis
capis' (1555-56), etc. See, too, App. I, s.v. *Edinburgh*—Excerpts
from Hammermen's Records, 1495, 2nd quarter, and note.

[2] *Mediæval Stage*, II, 104.

[3] *Knox*, I, 138 : 'O Lord, how long shall it be, that thy holy
woord shalbe despysed, and men shall not regard thare awin
salvatioun. I have heard of thee, Hadingtoun, that in thee
wold have bein at ane vane Clerk play two or three thowsand
people ; and now to hear the messinger of the Eternall God, of
all thy toune nor parishe can not be nombred a hundreth
personis.'

in 1574 was ' the comede mentionat in Sanct Lucas Euuangel
of the forlorn sone.' As the outcome of the ensuing controversy between the General Assembly and the St Andrews
Kirk Session, it was decided that ' no Clerk playes, comedies,
or tragedies be made of the Canonicall Scripture alsweill
new as old.' [1] The subject of the thesis set by the Stirling
Presbytery to John Brown, schoolmaster, ' Is it lesum to
play clark playis oñ ye sabboth day or nocht And qwethir
gif it be lesum or nocht to mak clark playis oñ ony part of
ye scriptur,' would seem to imply that the plays acted
by his pupils at Strageath were drawn from the Scriptures.
In the absence of any evidence to the contrary, then, the
assumption is justified that the clerk plays subsidised by
the town of Ayr in 1534-35 and 1541 were based on Biblical
or hagiological themes ; and that miracle plays [2] were
represented on the scaffolds erected in Edinburgh in June
1553, and at Uphaly Day, 1554-55.

The term ' interlude ' occurs but seldom in the Scottish
records. Its early use in England, embracing alike religious and secular plays, is too general to be of much
value for the purposes of interpretation.[3] Patrick Johnson
was rewarded for his ' ludis et interludiis ' at Court. The
provisions laid down in 1462 for the annual celebration of
the feast of the Translation of St Nicholas at Glasgow
University contemplated an ' interludium ' : but we know
only that the players were to be ' magistri aliqui vel studentes ' ; that it was to take place at some convenient spot,
presumably out-of-doors ; that it was to be of a popular
character, ' quod iocundare potest populum ' ; that it was
to be approved by the authorities ; and that special
privileges were to be enjoyed by those who took part.

[1] *Infra*, 93 n[2].
[2] I know no instance of the use of the term ' miracle ' play
or ' mystery ' play in Scotland.
[3] *C.H.L.*, V, 55 note.

While the early printed edition of the *Satyre of the Thrie Estaitis* employs 'interlude' in the frequently accepted sense of a representation made in the interval of something else, and while Bannatyne uses the word to denote the separate short sections of this play, Eure in his famous letter to Cromwell describes the whole piece as 'ane Enterluyde.' But at all events Lyndsay's play was not the only interlude known to the citizens of Edinburgh. In 1552, at least two years before the *Satyre of the Thrie Estaitis* was acted at the Greenside, James Henderson petitioned the Town Council of Edinburgh to concede to him a certain plot of ground for a playfield because 'thair is no wther place left to play interludis in to draw pepill till the toune nor pastyme ground for the induellaris.' [1]

As the word 'farce' is all but unknown in contemporary England,[2] it is interesting to find it employed fairly freely in Scotland. In view of the intimate relations between Scotland and France, one would expect to find the term used in the French sense of a short racy comedy.[3] It is, however, obvious that with Scottish scribes and historians of the sixteenth century the application was wider, if not entirely different.[4] A contrast between religious and secular plays may be implied by the terms in which the claim of John Walcar to the freedom of the burgh of Perth in 1546 is stated—' pe surfat and gret expenß mayd be Johne walcar . . . apoñ gemmys ferchis and clerk playis making.' To Pitscottie a 'farce' meant something in the nature of a 'triumph,' a spectacular effect produced with the assistance of machines or *ingegni*. Thus he describes the 'trieumphant frais' made by Sir David

---

[1] App. IV, *Playfields*.
[2] Chambers, *Mediæval Stage*, II, 202 ; *N.E.D.*, s.v. *farce*.
[3] *Petit de Julleville, La Comédie en France*, 51-54.
[4] I find that this point has been dealt with in some detail by J. A. Lester, *Some Franco-Scottish Influences on the Scottish Drama, Haverford Essays*, 1909.

Lyndsay at St Andrews in honour of Mary of Guise when
a great cloud came out of the heavens and opened, dis-
closing an angel who delivered the keys of Scotland.[1]
Again he relates how at the banquet held at the time of
the great Tournament of 1508 there was between every
service—

> ' ane phairs or ane play sum be speikin sum be
> craft of Igramancie quhilk causit men to sie thingis
> aper quhilk was nocht. And so at the hennest bancat
> pheirs and play . . . thair come ane clwdd out of
> the rwffe of the hall as appeirit to men and opnit
> and cleikkit vp the blak lady.' [2]

Nor is this use of the word peculiar to Pitscottie. In
1561 the Edinburgh Town Council dealt with equipment
for the ' triumphis and fairssis ' at the Over Tron, Tolbooth,
Cross, Salt Tron, and Nether Bow ; and Knox castigates
the masking and ' ferses ' prepared at this time. Yet
none of the contemporary accounts of the entry of Mary
Queen of Scots hint at anything remotely resembling a
farce in the modern English or the later mediæval French
sense of the word ; and there is no record of representations
of that nature in connection with any of the later royal
entries at Edinburgh.[3] Nor, to judge from his extant
works, would the ' litill farsche and play ' made by William
Lauder belong to the rollicking tribe of the immortal
Maître Pathelin. It is noteworthy, too, that Bannatyne
never uses ' farce ' to denote any of the ' mirry and sportsum

---

[1] App. I, s.v. *St Andrews.*
[2] App. III, Excerpts from *L.H.T.A.*, May 1508, notes. *Pitscottie* seems to distinguish here between ' farces ' and ' playes,'
He speaks elsewhere of ' great treumph and blythnes of phrassis
and playis ' (I, 379), ' playing and phrassis efter denner ' (*ibid.*),
' sic bankattin feirceis and playes ' (I, 240), ' phraissis and playis
that sould haue bene maid to hir ' (I, 369).
[3] But see reference to ' antikis,' App. I, s.v. *Aberdeen*—Miscellaneous entries, 13th May 1580.

interludis ' in the *Satyre of the Thrie Estaitis ;* [1] and when
Henry Charteris speaks of Lyndsay as the author of ' Fairsis
and publict Playis,' [2] he may have had in mind his services
in connection with the reception of Mary of Guise at St
Andrews and Edinburgh and other similar functions.

On the other hand, the farces played on the floor by
Sir David Lyndsay to amuse the young prince [3] suggest
performances of a much less formal nature.   In the Scots
version of Bishop Lesley's *Historie,* Albany was received in
1515 by the citizens of Edinburgh with ' sindre ferses and
gude playis ' ; in the Latin original he was greeted with
' comœdiis facetissimis, spectaculis exquisitis, ac rebus id
genus ludicris.' [4]   The farces required from the Abbot of
Bonaccord of Aberdeen (1553) may not have amounted to
more than boisterous gambols with a crude extempore
plot.   There is no mention of apparatus for the ' gyse
and farce ' played by the gentlemen of the country at St
Andrews in 1580, the stage apparently consisting of a
' place read with a fear circuit ' in front of the Abbey.

In addition to subsidising and controlling religious
pageants, clerk plays, interludes, and farces—not to
mention their interest in folk plays,[5]—the municipal
corporations were responsible for the entertainments in
honour of royal guests.   There are many references to
entries at Dundee, Perth, Aberdeen, Stirling, and other
towns,[6] but, with the exception of solitary cases at Aberdeen (1511) and St Andrews (1538), no details have been

---

[1] Cf. *Bannatyne Manuscript,* Vol. III, Hunterian Club.

[2] Preface to 1582 edition of Lyndsay's Works.

[3] Lyndsay, *Works,* 1879, I, 1, ' *The Dreme—Epistil to the
Kingis Grace.*'

[4] *Historie of Scotland,* Bann. Club, 102 ; *De Origine Moribus
et Rebus Gestis Scotorum,* 1578, p. 375.

[5] See Section I.

[6] There are references in the burgh records themselves ; and
cf. *Pitscottie,* I, 240, 369 ; Lesley, *Historie of Scotland, S.T.S.,*
247 ; *D.R.O.,* 69, 73.

preserved outside of Edinburgh. Even as regards Edinburgh, the loss of the early original records has probably deprived us of much information on the subject ; [1] and it is to an English chronicler that we must look for the earliest account of a royal entry in 1503.[2]

There was not much variation in the entertainment on these occasions. At Edinburgh scaffolds of one or more tiers were erected at certain points along the route hallowed by ancient custom. The West Port or Over Bow was selected for that favourite device of Renaissance pageantry, in which by means of some mechanical contrivance a cloud or globe descended and opened out, revealing an angel, who with appropriate verses handed over the keys.[3] The actual setting for this *ingegno* with the accompanying choir of celestial spirits owed something, no doubt, to the more elaborate ' nuvole ' and ' paradiso ' of Brunelleschi.[4] In 1503 there was the ' yatt of Wood painted, with Two Towrells, and a Windowe in the Midds,' with angels at the windows of the ' Towrells ' singing joyously, and with another angel at the middle window presenting the keys. At St Andrews in 1538 Sir David Lyndsay—

' Caussit ane great clude come out of the heavins done abone the zeit . . . and oppin in two halffis instantlie '

---

[1] *Infra*, 97-8.

[2] App. I, s.v. *Edinburgh*—Municipal Plays ; App. III, Excerpts from *L.H.T.A.*, Aug. 1503, note.

[3] The origin is perhaps to be traced in the religious drama. Cf. D'Ancona, *Origini del teatro italiano*, I, 29 : ' Dalle finestre, cioè, della volta scendeva per funes un Angelo ' (Feast of the Annunciation at Parma). *Ibid.*, I, 240 : ' Essendo in questo luogo giunto il Pontefice, ecco a un tratto, come volasse dal cielo, calare per una fune un vaghissimo fanciullo, alato come angelo, che con volto serafico e voce divina e col cenno salutò il presule, e cantando un inno annunziò subito la futura resurrezione del Salvatore.' (Viterbo, Corpus Christi celebrations.)

[4] Cf. L. B. Campbell, *Scenes and Machines on the English Stage during the Renaissance*, 1923, pp. 59, 60 ; J. A. Symonds, *Italian Literature (The Renaissance in Italy)*, II, 318.

to reveal an angel with the keys of Scotland.   In 1561 at the Edinburgh Butter Tron there was a—

> ' Port made of tymber . . . cullorit with fyne
> cullouris . . . vpon the quhilk port wes singand
> certane barneis in the maist hevinlie wyis ; vnder the
> quhilk port thair wes ane cloud opynnand with four
> levis, in the quhilk was put ane bony barne.' [1]

The ' Arches ' which figured so conspicuously in 1633 followed, therefore, on traditional lines. Details as to the decoration of the earlier pageants are lacking. Payments for the painting of the stages and stage properties occur in the burgh accounts for 1588-90. No fewer than five artists or craftsmen painters, including George Jamesone, were employed with their assistants during the seven months from December 1628 to September 1629, either continuously or on special pieces of work connected with the stage decorations for the expected entry of Charles the First. In 1633, for the first time, we hear of gorgeously executed ' landskips ' ; [2] of a ' Citie situated on a rock, which with pointed Clifts, Shrubs, Trees, Herbs, and Verdure did appeare in perspectiue upon the battlements ' ; of a curtain or ' vale ' falling to ' discover ' the theatre ; of a mountain which moved at the approach of the King.

The influence of the miracle plays, if not so unmistakable in the later Biblical scenes, the ' Korah, Dathan and Abiram ' of 1561, and the ' Wisdom of Solomon ' of 1579, can surely be detected in the ' Salutation of the Virgin,' the ' Kings of Cologne,' and the ' Expulsion from Paradise ' of 1511 at Aberdeen. Whether at Aberdeen the representation of those pageants was directly in the

---

[1] The same device recurs in the later entries. See analysis opposite.

[2] L. B. Campbell, *op. cit.*, 167, discusses the use of the term ' landscape ' in stage descriptions.

hands of the craft gilds is uncertain. While the Nativity scenes may have derived from the Candlemas play, there is no trace of a Creation pageant in the Corpus Christi cycle as we know it. In Edinburgh, so far as one can judge from the town records, the various incorporations were not responsible for the separate pageants. The only direct charges for royal entries which I have noted in the accounts of the Hammermen are for drink to the four men on the tolbooth head, and for ' graithing ' of their ' harnes ' in 1538, and for halbert men in 1590.[1]

The influence of allegorical literature, if not of the morality plays, is apparent in the stock characters of the Virtues who, from at least 1503 onwards, appeared on successive occasions, frequently in conjunction with the corresponding Vice. Even as late as 1633 the conflict between good and evil was represented in the trampling of Superstition by Religion and of Oppression by Justice. Incidents from Greek mythology were utilised as early as 1503, when the Judgment of Paris was enacted on one of the scaffolds. Professor Withington claims this as the earliest instance in Great Britain of the introduction of the classical element into pageantry, and suggests a French influence which, through Scotland, reacted on pageants in England.[2]

The royal genealogy was expounded in various ways, by means of pageants introducing illustrious ancestors, or by portraits of the kings of Scotland. In honour of Charles the First's entry, George Jamesone was commissioned to paint his hundred and seven royal ancestors. The conjunction of the heavenly bodies at the birth of the sovereign was represented by concrete embodiments of the planets. With the possible exception of the Giant

[1] *Calderwood*, III, 458, describing the 1579 entry, says the crafts' standards and ' pinsells ' were set at the Tolbooth.
[2] *English Pageantry*, I, 81, 169.

Bruce at Aberdeen in 1511, the folk element was confined
to the Moors, who acted as whifflers, clearing the way for
the royal guests. Other essential features were the wine-
swilling at the Cross, the spreading of the streets with
flowers, the tapestry decorations, and, of course, the
propine.[1]

The question arises as to how far the pageants represented
on these scaffolds were dramatic in character. A royal
entry, by its very nature, would tend to discourage any
marked development on such lines. Certainly the familiar
' oraisons ' of the groups of Virtues who ' spak ilkane in
pair awin degrie ' can claim but distant kinship with
genuine drama. And indeed these allegorical pageants
seemed to approximate more and more to *tableaux vivants*,
expressing their message by means of symbols and even
scrolls bearing moral epigrams. But this does not hold
necessarily regarding the other types of pageants. In his
Deploratioun of the Deith of Quene Magdalene (1537),
Lyndsay speaks of—

> ' Disagysit folkis, lyke creaturis divyne
> On ilk scaffold to play ane syndrie storie.' [2]

Although the directions issued by the Edinburgh magistrates in 1538 to various persons to ' ansuer ' for the Nether
Bow, Tron, Cross, Tolbooth, Over Bow, West Port, ' and
awaitt vpoun the grathing of thair rowmes in skaffetting
personages and ordour thairof ' rather imply that the
action was of minor importance, it is well to remember
that here, as at St Andrews, the master of ceremonies was,
in all likelihood, Sir David Lyndsay.

In this particular connection little stress need be laid

---

[1] See analysis of Edinburgh pageants at Royal Entries, opp.
p. 80.
[2] Lyndsay, *Works*, 1879, I, 121. Other details of the preparations by the town of Edinburgh are given in lines 99-175.

on the ' comœdiis facetissimis ' with which Duke Albany
is said to have been welcomed to Edinburgh in 1515 ; [1]
for there are no records to support this late generalisation
by Bishop Lesley. Randolph's letter, however, referring
to the spectacles, plays, and interludes with which Queen
Mary was received into Aberdeen in 1562, if lacking in
detail, has at least the value of a contemporary document
written by an eyewitness.[2] Further, if the brief contemporary description of the Edinburgh royal entry in 1503
can be relied on, the ' Judgment of Paris ' was a simple
play where the action was not interrupted, as in the later
London representation in 1533, to make an application
fitting to the occasion or to indulge in a gratulatory speech.[3]
Professor Withington cites this pageant as an instance of
the rare débat in pageantry.[4] Other instances of ' intensive
drama ' may fairly be inferred from the 1579 representations
of the ' Wisdom of Solomon ' and the ' brieff fabill for
abolisching of the paip & of the meß,' if not from the 1511
scriptural pageants at Aberdeen. The only extant text [5]
relating to such a function—that of 1633—exemplifies the
characteristic trend of pageantry elsewhere with its devotion
to ' spectacle ' rather than to dramatic action. The
' actioune ' of the horoscopal pageant of the seven planets
resolves itself into a string of loyal addresses in the usual
stilted style.

None of the contemporary diarists have noted the
' Triumphe and Play ' made at Edinburgh in 1558 on the
occasion of the marriage of Mary to the Dauphin. At
the Trons, Cross, Butt, and Nether Bow, stages were
erected, which were covered with turf for deadening the

---

[1] *Supra*, 78.

[2] Cited in App. I, s.v. *Aberdeen*—Miscellaneous entries.

[3] App. I, s.v. *Edinburgh*—Municipal Plays.

[4] *Op. cit.*, I, 111.

[5] See notes on 1633 ' entry,' App. I, s.v. *Edinburgh*—Municipal
Plays.

' din ' of the players' feet.   There was the traditional wine-
swilling at the Cross.   Canvas for hose and coats, taffeta
of various colours, red skin buskins and a golden crown
were provided for the seven planets, who might be trusted
to make the usual astrological exposition.   The presence
of Cupid needs no explanation in an age which revelled
in topical symbolism.[1]   So far, then, the main features of a
royal entry appear to have been reproduced.   But perhaps
on this occasion it was possible to allow more scope for the
dramatic as opposed to the spectacular side of the entertainment.   The vernacular could be employed : there was
no obligation to prepare stiff orations in some foreign
tongue to greet a stranger guest.[2]   And it looks as if the
scaffold at the Tron had been reserved for a genuine play,
composed by either William Lauder or William Adamson,
in which a Grey Friar and a Black Friar took prominent
parts.   Here the scenic decoration was not confined to the
' symmer treis ' which relieved the bareness of the other
scaffolds.   The stage was carefully covered with clay and
woodbine, into which yellow flowers were stuck erect,
and the *pièce de résistance* was a tree decorated with two
dozen gilded tennis balls and a hundred cherries.[3]   Thirty-
one dozen bells were required for some kind of morris
dance which may or may not have formed part of the
Tron play.   There were six dancers, three in red taffeta,
three in white, and a fool who wore a buckram coat of
' syndrie hewis.'   A wooden ' convoy cart ' drawn by horses
brought the players to the various scaffolds ;   and the

[1] In 1590 the Nether Bow was ' beautified with a marriage of
a King and his Queene,' App. I, s.v. *Edinburgh*—Municipal Plays.
[2] In 1538 a French oration was prepared to welcome Mary of
Guise ; and, in 1590, the speeches of the seven planets, at least,
were in Latin ' becaus the queane wnderstood na Scotis.'   App. I,
s.v. *Edinburgh*—Municipal Plays.
[3] Cf. G. F. Reynolds, *Trees on the Stage of Shakespeare, Modern
Philology*, V, 159, 160.

extensive order for ' staffs to convey the playaris ' implies
the regular troupe of Moors to ward off the crowds.   The
yellow and red garments of the minstrels and the gaily
coloured banners added to the riot of colour.   The shooting
of ordnance, with a firework display, brought the official
rejoicings to a close.

V.

INFLUENCE OF THE REFORMATION.

As has been noted in the section on Folk Plays, the Catholic Church from time to time promulgated statutes prohibiting ' ludi.' [1] In the absence of any qualifying epithet, there is no reason to suppose that these ' ludi ' were regular miracle plays—and, indeed, the context points rather to folk plays of pagan origin. Archibishop Hamilton's Catechism condemns ' carreling and wanton synging in the kirk, and all uther vice quhilk commonly hes bein maist usit on the sunday.' [2] There are stray enactments, too, forbidding priests to look on at minstrels (' histriones ') performing,[3] and prohibiting monks from frequenting ' spectacula.' [4] In 1527, Michael Disard, sacrist of the Holy Trinity Church, Edinburgh, was accused of consorting with the laity in public places and using the divine office

---

[1] *Supra,* 9.

[2] Ed. T. G. Law, 1884, p. 68.

[3] Robertson, *Statuta*, II, 52 : ' Quod non intendant histrionibus.' (Ecclesiastical Statutes of the 13th century.) Cf. *Statutes of the Scottish Church, S.H.S.*, p. 55.

[4] *Antiquities of the Shires of Aberdeen and Banff* (Spald. Club), IV, 9 : ' Nullus sub eadem pena presumat ire ad nupcias aut ad prandia festorum aut spectacula vel tabernas frequentare sed seruentur capitula regule *De fratribus in via directis* et *De fratribus qui non satis longe proficiscuntur*. (Copy of the constitutions for the better rule of the Cistercian monasteries in Scotland, 1531, sent to the convent of Deir.)

disguised in the garments ' histrionum et fatuorum.' He
was forbidden to do so in future unless for the King's
entertainment or among his brethren, and then only
' moderate et discrete.' [1] This attitude of hostility towards
folk plays and itinerant minstrels and of disapproval of
clerical participation in lay revels was characteristic of the
mediæval Church in Western Europe. But there is no
reason to suppose that in Scotland the Church evinced
any antagonism towards the civic religious plays and
pageants. In Perth a priest was rewarded by the Guildry
for his services in connection with the Corpus Christi play
and procession ; [2] and at Dumfries Sir Harry Merser
received a burgess fee for the play of Good Friday and
Whitsunday.[3]

As regards folk plays and the *spectacula* of the minstrels,
the Reformed Kirk of Scotland merely reinforced the

---

[1] *Registrum Ecclesie Collegiate Sancte Trinitatis de Edinburgh,*
Bann. Club, 1861, pp. 208-10, 5th Aug. 1527. ' . . . Quemquidem
dominum Michaelem (Disard) tunc presentem dictus prepositus
de consensu auisiamento et consilio capituli et prebendariorum
subscriptorum calumpniauit et accusauit prout sequitur In primis
quod citra mandata canonum ac contra statuta et fundacionem
predicte ecclesie necnon contra honestatem clericalem in pernicio-
sum exemplum ecclesiasticorum et in detrimentum ac dampnum
non modicum officii sacristie eidem Michaeli commissi noctiuagus
goliator existit multociensque vestibus dissimulatiuis histrionum
et fatuorum tabernis viis publicis ac diuersis aliis locis inhonestis
et societate laicorum minime honesta sed vilium personarum
vtitur exercicium sui officii predicti et diuinorum dicte collegiate
ecclesie obmittens ostia ipsius ecclesie ac capituli eiusdem et
custodiam iocalium ac vestimentorum prefate ecclesie verum
eciam pulsacionem campanarum temporibus statutis . . . Qua-
propter dicti prepositus et capitulum suam determinacionem
ordinacionem et decretum pronunciarunt in hunc qui sequitur
modum . . . pronunciamus decernimus et declaramus atque tibi
in his scriptis mandamus quatenus in futurum non sis noctiuagus
neque goliator nec tabernis neque societate vilium personarum
nec locis inhonestis neque vestimentis dissimulatiuis histrionum
et fatuorum nisi tantummodo pro domini regis solacio aut inter
tuos confratres et hoc moderate et discrete vtaris. . . .'
[2] App. I, s.v. *Perth*—Excerpts from MS. Guild Book.
[3] *Ibid.*, s.v. *Dumfries.*

declared official policy, if not the consistent practice, of the Roman Catholic Church. Its work in suppressing May games, which had already been condemned as illegal by Act of Parliament, and in stamping out other folk *ludi* associated with the pagan winter and summer festivals, has already been discussed.[1] The traditional dislike of the professional *histrio* may be traced in the ban placed on the performances of the English travelling companies.[2]

During the period of the Reformation, however, there is no evidence of a frontal assault on plays as plays.[3] On the contrary, the drama was employed by the early Scottish Reformers as a valuable means of propaganda. The scanty notice of Friar Kyllour's Passion play, which was represented in Stirling about 1535 and ' enflammed the hartes of all that bare the beastis mark,' points to Reformation teaching in the frame of the conventional miracle play.[4] A few years later, in his *Beheading of Johne the Baptist* and *Historie of Dyonisius the Tyrane,* acted at Dundee, James Wedderburn exposed the abuses of the Papists.[5] Lyndsay's *Satyre of the Thrie Estaitis* in its unrestrained attack on the corruption of the clergy claims kinship with the contemporary French moralities, and its value to the cause of the Reformers has never been questioned. Knox himself was present at a play embodying his doctrines which was made at St Andrews by John

[1] Section I.
[2] App. I, s.v. *St Andrews*—Kirk Session Records, 1598 ; App. II, Travelling English Companies, 1599.
[3] I have not been able to trace Christie, *Account of Parish Clerks,* cited by Chambers, *Mediæval Stage,* II, 202, as his authority for the statement that in 1558 the Scottish General Assembly forbade ' farseis and clerke playis.' But *prima facie* the statement is incorrect : the first General Assembly did not meet until December 1560. I suppose it is on the same authority that Chambers, *Elizabethan Stage,* II, 265, refers to the General Assembly in 1574 as utterly forbidding, *not for the first time,* clerk plays, etc.
[4] App. I, s.v. *Stirling.*
[5] *Ibid.,* s.v. *Dundee.*

Davidson, one of the foremost champions of the Protestant cause.[1] Mention has already been made of the mask
or firework display representing an assault on the Pope's
palace, which took place at the wedding festivities when
the Earl of Murray's daughter was married in January
1580-1.[2]

Pageants at royal entries presented invaluable oppor-
tunities for inculcating the new faith. Psalms were sung
and a Bible presented ' and the praise thereof declared '
in 1561 ; and some children made a speech concerning the
' putting away of the mess.' A more daring stroke of
propaganda was withheld only at the instance of the Earl
of Huntly ; for preparations were in hand for a pageant
representing a priest burned at the altar at the elevation
of the host. A compromise was reached on Korah, Dathan
and Abiram ; from which each side was able to extract a
suitable moral.[3] A service at St Giles formed the central
feature of the 1579 entry,[4] Dame Religion having invited
King James to pass into the church. And, lest the inter-
vening secular pageants should blot out the effect of the
sermon from the mind of the youthful monarch, the pro-

---

[1] App. I, s.v. *St Andrews*. For the attitude of the continental
Reformers to the drama cf. *Letters of John Calvin*, Dr Jules
Bonnet, trans. David Constable, 1855-7, II, 47-8, No. clxviii ;
The Life and Letters of Martin Luther, Preserved Smith, 1911,
p. 350 ; Chambers, *Elizabethan Stage*, I, 245-9. Knox's attitude
to dancing in particular is well defined in the following passage :
' And of dansing, Madam, I said, that albeit in Scripturis I fand
no praise of it, and in prophane wryttaris, that it is termed the
jesture rather of those that ar mad and in phrenesye then of
sober men ; yitt do I not utterlie dampne it, provyding that
two vices be avoided : the formare, That the principall vocatioun of those that use that exercise be not neglected for the
pleasur of dansing ; Secoundly, That they daunse not, as the
Philisteanis thair fatheris, for the pleasur that thai tack in the
displeasur of Goddis people. . . .' (*Knox*, II, 333.)
[2] *Supra*, 55.
[3] App. I, s.v. *Edinburgh*—Municipal Plays.
[4] Similarly in 1590.

F

ceedings terminated with the ' brieff fabill ' for abolishing
the Pope, enacted at the Canongate Cross.[1] No details
have survived regarding the reception of Anne of Denmark
at Perth in 1591 ; but one doubts if the Kirk Session
would have suspended its sitting on 28th June had not a
strong dose of Protestant doctrine been administered with
the pageantry.[2]

School plays, too, were regarded by the opposing parties
as useful vehicles for religious instruction. A Haddington
schoolmaster made a play ' to exercise his scholars against
the ministers.' [3] The short minute regarding the Edinburgh
High School ' tragedies ' prepared in honour of the King
in 1579, gives no information either as to their subject
or as to whether they were to be incorporated in the civic
pageantry.[4] There can be no doubt, however, as to the
central *motif* of the ' comedie ' of 1598, in which the rôles
of the pope, two cardinals and five friars were undertaken
by the master and scholars of the High School.   This
representation, at any rate, was not confined to the school
precincts. A second scaffold was erected at the Tolbooth,
where a more popular form of the play may have been
given for the benefit of the citizens of Edinburgh.[5] Beyond
the fact that they were subsidised from the burgh funds,
no details are available concerning the Dundee High

---

[1] App. I, s.v. *Edinburgh*—Municipal Plays.

[2] *Ibid.*, s.v. *Perth*—Kirk Session Records.

[3] *Keith*, II, 269 : ' (There were) two notable blasphemies against
God, yet not worthily punished, though somewhat with difficulty
enough to have the doers committed to prison. A schoolmaster
at Haddingtoun made a play to exercise his scholars against the
ministers, and baptised a cat in the name of the Father, the
Son, etc.' (Randolph to Cecil, 20th March 1564-5.)

[4] App. I, s.v. *Edinburgh*—Municipal Plays.

[5] *Ibid.* Cf. Herford, *The Literary Relations of England and
Germany in the Sixteenth Century*, 72, where, speaking of the
school drama in Germany, he says that a Latin performance at
the school might be followed by one in the vernacular at the
Rathaus.   The Magdeburg school statutes prescribed such a
double performance.

School play of 1595-6, or the later Perth school plays.[1] In all probability there were many other propagandist school plays during the period ; but, if these were self-supporting, the expenses would not be engrossed in the ordinary town records.

If, however, apart from the folk plays and the performances of the professional stage-players or *scenici*, no general denunciation of dramatic performances as such is on record,[2] yet, in the years following the triumph of Protestantism and particularly in the last quarter of the century, a series of special acts came into force which gradually caused the production of plays to be hedged about with irksome and almost impossible conditions.

In theory, at least, the Scottish Reformed Church led the way in the suppression of feast days. In 1566, in reply to a letter from the Churches of Geneva, Berne, and other Reformed Churches, the Scottish Superintendents stated that they were in complete agreement with the continental policy, ' albeit in the keeping of some Festivall days, our Church assented not ; for only the Sabbath-day was kept in Scotland.' [3] Some slackness, however, must have crept in in practice. In 1575 the General Assembly drew up an article to be presented to the Regent for the abolition of all holy days but the Sabbath, and the punishment of all those who kept Yule and other festivals by ceremonies, banqueting, playing, fasting, ' and sick vther vanities.' [4] In 1581 the matter was taken up by Parliament and an act was passed prohibiting, *inter alia*, the observing of the festival days of the saints.[5] The feast of Corpus Christi,

---

[1] App. I, s.vv. *Dundee, Perth.*

[2] Even in the late 1599 controversy (App. II), the ministers, in their interview with the King, do not appear to have made a direct attack on the drama after the fashion of the English Puritan pamphleteers.

[3] *Knox*, II, 534.

[4] *B.U.K.*, I, 339.

[5] *A.P.S.*, 1581, c. 6, III, 212.

which was so intimately associated with the Roman Catholic doctrine of transubstantiation, must have been peculiarly obnoxious to the Protestant mind. The only place where the Corpus Christi pageants are known definitely to have survived the Reformation, and that in an unofficial form, is at Perth.[1] In July 1577 the Kirk Session met to deal with those who, in defiance of magisterial statutes and pulpit edicts, participated in ' Corpus Christeis play.'[2] Various Corpus Christi players were summoned before subsequent meetings of the Session and pledged themselves to renounce this idolatrous superstition ; while baptism was refused in the case of certain infants unless their fathers promised ' neuir to mell with sik thingis again.' As the July minute is incomplete in the manuscript register as now extant, the penalties for breach of the ordinance are not on record. But, to judge from the fact that on 16th December of that year a batch of Corpus Christi players appeared before the Session for the last time, they must have been very effective. It took longer to stamp out the baxters' ' sancttobertis play,' which was apparently a saint's day riding ; and it was only in 1588, after the deacons and craft had made common cause with the Kirk Session, that it was finally eradicated.[3]

At first, it would appear, powers to allow or disallow

[1] But, excepting at St Andrews and Aberdeen, few traces of the earliest Kirk Session enactments remain. See note on Local Records at commencement of App. I. It is not clear whether the act of the Privy Council against ' playis ' on festival days at Aberdeen (App. I, s.v. *Aberdeen*—Miscellaneous entries, 1576-7 n., and Kirk Session Records, 1574) was directed against the old religious pageants or against folk plays. See, too, App. I, s.v. *Glasgow*, 1599, and n.

[2] Unfortunately, the previous volume of minutes has disappeared, so that it is impossible to say whether drastic action had been taken prior to this date. It is curious to find the civil authorities enforcing fulfilment of an obligation contracted in connection with this same Corpus Christi play. (App. I, s.v. *Perth*—Excerpt from MS. Register of Decreets.)

[3] App. I, s.v. *Perth*—Kirk Session Records.

Sunday plays were vested in the local authorities. Thus, in 1574, the St Andrews Kirk Session gave permission to Mr Patrick Authinleck to play the Comedy of the Forlorn Son on Sunday, 1st August, provided that it did not interfere with the attendance at forenoon or afternoon preaching.[1] This decision was challenged by the General Assembly, which promulgated the Act of March 1574-5, unconditionally vetoing Sunday plays of any kind.[2] In July 1574 the Dunfermline burgh records chronicle an incident which took place ' vpone the sabbothe day being also the playday and maist confluence of peple convenit pairto.'[3] In 1576, however, the General Assembly flatly refused to allow the town of Dunfermline to perform on a Sunday afternoon a play which otherwise, to all appearance, was in conformity with the official regulations.'[3] Two years later, in April 1578, the Assembly drafted an article stipulating that the Sabbath day should be universally observed and that ' mercats, playes, and all other impediments, which may hinder the people to conveen to hear the word, be discharged.'[4] In 1583 the schoolmasters of Muthil and Strageath were summoned by the Presbytery for allowing their scholars to act clerk plays on Sunday.[5]

[1] App. I, s.v. St Andrews—Kirk Session Records.
[2] B.U.K., I, 322 : ' (Forsamikle as it is considered, that the playing of Clerk playes, comedies or tragedies upon the Canonical parts of the Scripture, induceth and bringeth with it a contempt and profanation of the same ; therefore C.) It is thoght meit and concludit, That no Clerk playes, comedies or tragedies be made of the Canonicall Scripture, alsweill new as old, neither on the Sabboth day nor worke day, in tyme comeing ; the contraveiners heirof (if they be Ministers) to be secludit fra thair functioun, and, if they be vthers, to be punischit be the discipline of the Kirk : and ordaines ane article to be given in to sick as sitts vpon the policie, that, for vther playes, comedies, tragedies, and vthers profane playes as are not made vpon authentick partes of the Scripture, may be considderit befor they be proponit publicklie, and that they be not playit vpon the Sabboth dayes.'
[3] App. I, s.v. Dunfermline.
[4] B.U.K., II, 405.
[5] App. I, s.v. Stirling—Presbytery Records.

In 1590, out of deference to the objections raised by the Edinburgh ministers, the pageants arranged for the entry of Queen Anne were postponed from Sunday to a week-day.[1]

It is interesting to find a reference to the Comedy of the Forlorn Son played by the pupils of the Grammar School of St Andrews.[2] This play, which as *Der verlorne Sohn* had a great vogue in Germany, and was known in France (*L'enfant prodigue*) and Italy (*Il figliuol prodigo*), as well as in the vernacular literatures of Spain and the Netherlands and in the Latin versions of Macropedius (*Asotus*) and Gnaphæus (*Acolastus*), embodied the vital characteristics of a ' Christian Terence,' and as such was warmly espoused by the humanist Reformers on the Continent.[3] But, in spite of the fact that its theme could readily be adapted to inculcate the tenets of Calvinism in a youthful audience in Scotland, as based on 'Sanct Lucas Euuangel,' it came under, if indeed it did not actually precipitate, the 1574-5 interdict of the General Assembly on plays made on canonical parts of the Scripture.[4]

Mr Patrick Authinleck's play was to be submitted to a body of censors to be ' revisit ' before production.[5] It is uncertain if, prior to the Act of March 1574-5, this was obligatory in all cases. Certainly thereafter all plays not ruled out under one or other of the above conditions were to be submitted for consideration of the Kirk authorities. In 1582 the Dalkeith Presbytery dealt with an offender who produced a play without license of the elders.[6] In June 1589 permission to act a certain play at Perth was given on condition that it was free from swearing and scurrility ; and, lest a bowdlerised draft of the actual

---

[1] App. I, s.v. *Edinburgh*—Municipal Plays.

[2] *Ibid.*, s.v. *St Andrews*—Kirk Session Records. Also *supra*, 74.

[3] Herford, *Literary Relations*, 152 ; H. Holstein, *Das Drama vom verlornen Sohn*, Halle, 1880, pp. 10, 50, 51 ; D'Ancona, *Origini del teatro italiano*, I, 269.

[4] *Supra*, 93 n².

[5] App. I, s.v. *St Andrews*—Kirk Session Records.

[6] *Ibid.*, s.v. *Dalkeith*.

version should be presented for the official investigation, it was decreed that none of the players should make additions to what appeared in the ' register.' [1] The register of John Brown's clerk play was found by a committee of the brethren to contain ' mekill baning & swering sum badrie and filthie baning.' [2] In 1595-6 the master of the St Andrews ' sang scole ' craved forgiveness of the Session for producing a play at St Leonard's College without their ' advys.' [3] The Elgin schoolmaster, having been responsible for the acting of a play by Terence in May 1600, was forbidden to ' practeis any comedie ' in future without special licence of the Session. [4]

Finally, while Calvin was not so rigid and uncompromising in his view of the stage as some of his followers, he pronounced judgment in no uncertain tones on the exchange of garments between the sexes. [5] While this attitude is reflected in the Scottish Kirk records only in connection with folk guising, [6] one may feel sure that it would colour the whole outlook of the Scottish Calvinist, and act as a restrictive factor in the composition and production of plays.

The suppression of feast days traditionally associated with dramatic performances, the absolute prohibition of Sunday plays, limitations as to subject-matter, and a slavish acceptance of the Deuteronomic law regarding disguisings, a rigid censorship—all these restraints were bound to militate against the preservation and stimulation of the drama. An Act of Parliament or even an edict of the Assembly might have been disregarded : it was less easy to defy the ' visitations ' of the presbyteries and the inquisitorial methods of the local kirk sessions.

---

[1] App. I, s.v. *Perth*—Kirk Session Records.
[2] *Ibid.*, s.v. *Stirling*.
[3] *Ibid.*, s.v. *St Andrews*—Kirk Session Records.
[4] *Ibid.*, s.v. *Elgin*.
[5] Chambers, *Elizabethan Stage*, I, 248.
[6] App. I, s.v. *Aberdeen*—Kirk Session Records, 1605. See also *supra*, 16.

VI.

CONCLUSION.

No attempt to estimate the growth of the early Scottish drama can ignore the nature and extent of the existing records. Any detailed comparision of the extant pre-Reformation records of Scotland with those of England leaves us hopelessly outclassed. The only burgh records which date back to the fourteenth century are those of Aberdeen ; while even the fifteenth century is very sparingly represented.[1] Further, there is nothing in Scotland to set beside the English Churchwardens' Accounts, from which so much information regarding mediæval drama in England has been derived.

When dealing with the early religious municipal plays, for instance, two types of local records are specially valuable —the common good accounts and the detailed discharges of the various craft gilds. Both of these types are extremely rare. There are fragments of pre-Reformation accounts at Aberdeen and Lanark ; the regular series of Edinburgh Treasurers' and Guildry accounts commences in 1552 ; Haddington has preserved a few odd compts from 1554 onwards ; Perth, Dundee, and Dumfries can produce nothing within the period. In short, the only burgh associated with religious plays—and, indeed, the only

---

[1] See Note on Local Records, *infra*, 114.

Scottish burgh at all—which can produce a continuous record of pre-Reformation municipal expenditure over any length of time is Ayr, where the common good accounts date from 1535. It is more difficult to trace the records of the trade incorporations, which, outside of the more important burghs, have been extinct since the passing of the Municipal Reform Act. It is probable that there are still important craft manuscripts in private hands. According to the historian of the Incorporated Trades of Aberdeen, the earliest records have all perished. Dundee is in scarcely better plight ; and inquiries in Haddington, Lanark, Ayr, and Dumfries have failed to bring any useful material to light. The only burghs, then, which are known to have supported religious plays and which have preserved at least one set of detailed craft records are Edinburgh and Perth ; and just there, unfortunately, not only the early burgh accounts but the pre-Reformation Council registers have disappeared. Thus, even the positive evidence can rarely be complete.

Sir Edmund Chambers notes the Edinburgh municipal plays of 1554, but is not satisfied that they were miracle plays proper or of long standing ; and he implies that this apparent outburst of dramatic activity was forced on the half-hearted bailies by the new regent, Mary of Lorraine.[1] It is necessary, however, to recall the important fact that the original Council minutes date only from 1551, that the regular town accounts commence in 1552 (and expenditure on a clerk play is registered in the 1552-3 treasurer's discharge), and that material for the printed

---

[1] *Mediæval Stage*, II, 366-7. Cf. C. Davidson, *Studies in the English Mystery Plays*, 99 : ' The Records of Edinburgh are remarkable for their silence concerning plays. In 1503 an ordinance in restraint of plays was passed, from which one infers that *English innovations* [italics mine] were not viewed wholly with approval.' Unfortunately Davidson does not give his authority, and I am not aware of any such ordinance.

volumes of records prior to that date has been collected
from protocol books, odd documents, and from late sixteenth - century excerpts from the early registers.[1] My
theory, supported by the general nature of these excerpts,
that the compiler was a keen Reformer was partially
confirmed when I referred to the manuscript for details of
the 1538 royal entry. The scribe has placidly copied all
the other acts made ' for ꝑe honorabill entrie of the quene,'
but, when he comes to the minute arranging for the
pageants, his impatience finds vent in a caustic marginal
comment—' this act Inproffitabill.' [2] Still less ' proffit-
abill ' in his eyes would be the old miracle plays which
savoured so strongly of papistry ; and it is at least a
plausible contention that any references to such plays in
the original registers would be omitted from his compila-
tion. It may be, however, that apart from the Corpus
Christi pageant and the clerk plays already noted,[3] Edinburgh, even in pre-Reformation days, followed London in
conserving her energies and resources for the frequently
recurring pageants at royal entries.

Similarly, it is rarely possible to deduce a satisfactory
negative result. The majority of the old royal burghs
of Scotland are entirely unrepresented as regards continuous records, such as accounts, burgh court books,
council registers, or burgess rolls, in the period prior to
the Reformation,[4] while in others the records are so meagre

[1] These excerpts are contained in a ' Brevis et Compendiosa
Collectio veterum et maxime vtilium statutorum ' (in the burgh
archives) and a volume of excerpts from the original records
(in the Advocates' Library), both compiled about 1580. Cf.
E.B.R. (S.B.R.S.), I, xxxii.

[2] Adv. Lib. Hist. MSS., 31. 4. 9., f. 190 : ' This act [nihil ad
rem (deleted)] Inproffitabill.'

[3] Supra, 71 ff.

[4] This is true as regards Annan, Auchtermuchty, Bervie,
Brechin, Cullen, Culross, Dingwall, Dornoch, Dumbarton, Dunbar,
Falkland, Forres, Fortrose, Glasgow, Inverkeithing, Inverurie,
Irvine, Jedburgh, Kinghorn, Kirkcaldy, Kirkcudbright, Lauder,

and incomplete that no reliable inference can be made.[1] Where the burgh records are full and complete over a series of years, it is reasonable to conclude that at least nothing existed in the shape of a municipally directed drama. Linlithgow is one of the few places which fulfils these conditions to some extent—and there only for a short period. In a burgh court book which is notable for the wide range of interest of the entries, there are detailed accounts of expenditure for the years 1529-37. But here again the craft records fail.

When early burgh court books or council registers survive (unsupported by accounts or craft records), a negative deduction must be made with caution. From 1442 to 1483-4, a period of over forty years, there is no reference in the Aberdeen Council Register to the Candlemas play, which presumably was an annual event. The pageants of the Aberdeen Corpus Christi procession did not, one may feel reasonably sure, spring into existence in 1530, when they are mentioned for the first time. So long as innovations were eschewed and the crafts continued to furnish their pageants in satisfactory manner, there was no need to write elaborate minutes on the subject. Use and wont, rather than acts of Council, regulated these annual functions. Occasionally some irregularity was committed—the Litsters failed to produce a pageant, members of the craft were not in their places,[2] someone borrowed a trumpet [3] or a garment [4] and failed to return it,—whereupon

Lochmaben, Nairn, North Berwick, Renfrew, Rothesay, Rutherglen, St Andrews, Tain, and Whithorn, many of which were flourishing royal burghs by this time.

[1] Arbroath, Banff, Crail, Cupar, Elgin, Inverness, Montrose, Newburgh, Wigtown, and even Stirling, may be included in this category.

[2] App. I, s.v. *Aberdeen*—Religious Pageants.

[3] *Ibid.*, s.v. *Dundee*, 1553 ; but the nature of the play is not stated.

[4] *Ibid.*, s.v. *Perth*—Excerpt from MS. Register of Decreets.

the authorities intervened and the clerk wrote up the case.

Further, entries may be inscribed in such a form as to disguise their full import. Reasons for admission to burgess-ship may be suppressed, and the objects on which the burgess fees are expended may be omitted. This happens when the manuscript is not contemporary with the events chronicled. Thus one must be careful not to base a negative conclusion on the fact that the Dundee Burgess Roll dates from 1513. The earlier entries were copied into the present Lokkit Book in 1582, and there was no need to record the disposal of the funds.

As with the religious pageants and miracle plays, so, in the more important towns at least, the pageantry for royal entries was prepared as a matter of course ; and, where the extraordinary discharges of the town treasurer have disappeared, few vestiges of these functions remain. Thus in 1511 it was decided to receive Queen Margaret at Aberdeen 'als honorablie as ony burgh of scotland except edinburgh allanerlie,' and to expend as much money thereon as the Council allow. The specific minutes in the Council Register deal with the decoration of the town with tapestry hangings and evergreens, with the cleansing of the streets and removal of swine, and with the means of defraying the costs. There is not a word about pageants, and, were it not for Dunbar's glowing description, we should be left in total ignorance as to the fare devised 'for ȝe honour of ȝe towne and plesour of hir gud grace.' Such trite and indefinite phrases as ' ȝe decoryng & preparing of ȝis gud toune ' or the ' preporatioun and decoratioun of ȝe toun ' cover the entries of Mary of Guise and Mary Queen of Scots in 1541 and 1562 respectively. It is left to the contemporary historian or the foreign ambassador to furnish testimony as to the triumphs and interludes arranged for these occasions. In 1580, in connection with the prospective visit of James the Sixth, the Provost of Aberdeen reminded the Council of the lovable custom of the burghs of Scotland 'obſeruit perpetuallie in all tyme bigane' (and not neglected by that town) whereby kings and princes at their first entry were received 'with fasceis, playis, historeis, antikis, and sic vther decoratiouñ as was thocht expedient for ȝe tym.' Regarding these, so far as the Aberdeen Council Register is concerned, not a single concrete detail remains. Once and once only, in 1526, does the Register go so far as to define in terms of 'pageantis & sportis and plesand pastymes·' the entertainment to be provided for a royal guest.[1] There is no need to labour this point, which could be amply illustrated also from the records of Edinburgh, when the treasurers' accounts are awanting.

There is, of course, no suggestion that the miracle plays and religious ridings in Scotland ever approached the magnificence of the great English craft cycles, or that the pageantry prepared by the citizens of Edinburgh in honour of royal guests could compete with that of London. Less favourable climatic conditions, the relative poverty of the country, the scanty population,[2] and the comparatively late development of civic institutions, would all act as deterrent factors. But the difference was one of degree rather than of kind. Too much stress has been laid on the dramatic isolation of the *Satyre of the Thrie Estaitis*. As was inevitable from the fact that it is the only complete text of a mediæval play which has survived in Scotland, Lyndsay's morality has come to be regarded as a kind of literary sport. Professor Gregory Smith holds that the composition of the *Satyre of the Thrie Estaitis*

---

[1] App. I, s.v. *Aberdeen*—Miscellaneous Entries.
[2] Hume Brown, *C.H.L.*, III, 139, estimates the population of Scotland in the sixteenth century as about 500,000, only half of whom used a Teutonic form of speech.

and the *Droichis part of the Play* proves rather the extraordinary versatility of Lyndsay and Dunbar than a
popular love of the drama.[1] The latter piece has survived
only by accident and without signature, and there is no
absolute proof that Dunbar was the author. But there
were very good reasons why the *Satyre of the Thrie Estaitis*
should have been preserved when other texts perished.
The position of the poet at the Scottish Court, the circum-
stances under which a command performance of the play
was given at Linlithgow, and the manner in which it was
used by the King to expose the ' noughtines ' in religion,
the effect on the Catholic clergy and their desire for revenge
on the author, the subsequent canonisation of the works
of Lyndsay in the eyes of the Protestant leaders, would all
contribute to save the text from the normal fate of such
manuscripts. It was not as a dramatic masterpiece that it
received notice at the hands of Eure,[2] Charteris,[3] and
Row.[4] Had it not been for the ' grave matter,' it is question-
able whether any ' mirry interludis ' would have survived
for George Bannatyne to copy.

The farcical episodes, commencing with the *cry* of the
Auld Man and his Wife, and ranging through the interlude
of the ' Puir Man and the Pardoner ' to the concluding
' Sermon of Folly,' as well as many individual touches
throughout the play, suggest that Lyndsay was writing
for a popular audience accustomed to food of this kind.

[1] Gregory Smith, *The Transition Period*, 293. He admits,
however, that there are indications in both pieces that the poets
were only stimulating a prevalent taste. Rogers, *Social Life in
Scotland*, 1884, p. 325, states categorically that the ' first performance of the articulate drama ' took place in January 1539-40—
i.e., the *Satyre of the Thrie Estaitis*. On the other hand, T. F.
Henderson, *C.H.L.*, III, 122, is of the opinion that ' lack of
information does not imply a lack of plays.'

[2] *Supra*, 59 n[4].

[3] App. I, s.v. *Edinburgh*—Municipal Plays, 1554, notes.

[4] John Row, *Historie of the Kirk of Scotland*, Mait. Club, 1842,
I, 3 ; II, 312.

The fact that no other farces have survived [1] must not be pressed too far. The fifteenth and sixteenth century farce was by its very nature doomed to a speedy death, and, in many cases, was probably never committed to writing.[2] And although, as has been pointed out, the actual epithet 'farce' was frequently applied to representations of a very different character, that does not mean that the type did not exist in Scotland. The 'scurrillitates et infamationes,' which characterised the plays and proclamations of the St Andrews students in the early sixteenth century, make one suspect a close kinship with the farces of the Paris 'écoliers.' [3] Indeed the broad homely humour of the typical farce is related to one of the most characteristic strains in Scottish literature.

The wholesale loss and destruction of manuscripts in a country which lay for centuries in the grip of a merciless puritanism is at least an easier hypothesis than that the *Satyre of the Thrie Estaitis* was, from the dramatic standpoint, unusual, still less unique ; for of all forms of art, the drama is least likely to develop in a hostile or alien environment. The fact that Lyndsay, Kyllour, Wedderburn, and later, Davidson, used the drama as a vehicle for propaganda [4] speaks volumes in itself.

In short, while Lyndsay's *Satyre* may represent the culminating point of mediæval drama in Scotland, it was written against what, especially in view of the imperfect state of the early records, must be regarded as a promising

[1] See note on *Inglis, infra,* 329 n[2].
[2] Cf. Petit de Julleville, *La Comédie en France,* 57-8 ; *Théâtre comique en France,* 322.
[3] App. I, s.v. *St Andrews.* Cf. Petit de Julleville, *Les Comédiens en France,* Chap. ix. See, too, W. J. Lawrence, *Early French Players in England, Anglia,* 1909, for a suggestion that the Frenchmen who played before the King in Dundee in 1490 (App. III, Excerpts from *L.H.T.A.*) may have had some connection with the Paris 'Clercs' or 'Enfants.'
[4] *Supra,* 88-9.

background. All over civilised Scotland, as we have seen, the town authorities either personally or vicariously through the Abbot of Unreason catered in one form or another for their play-loving ' neighbours.' They arranged for the pageants at royal entries, regulated the craft representations at religious festivals, subsidised clerk plays and interludes,[1] controlled the organised folk games and ridings,[2] budgeted for the preparation and upkeep of the playfields.[3] Troupes of professional minstrels, in defiance of civil and ecclesiastical interdict, roamed the countryside, playing their *spectacula* to delighted townsfolk,[4] tempting students from their classes [5] and monks from their cells.[6] The members of the two older Universities of St Andrews and Glasgow not only organised ridings [7] in disguise,[8] but celebrated the feast of St John with scurrilous farces and popular interludes. Household minstrels, court ' makaris,' members of the royal retinue, wandering bards and jugglers, Clerks to the Chapel, bands of folk players from the town, professional jesters, all combined in the late fifteenth and early sixteenth centuries to make the Scottish Court a favourable nursing ground for dramatic activities.[9] The idea that the masks of Mary Queen of Scots were delicate exotic products introduced from France in 1561 is untenable.

The May play was proscribed by a definite Act of Parliament,[10] and thenceforth, with some notable excep-

---

[1] Section IV.

[2] Section I.

[3] App. IV, *Playfields.*

[4] Section II ; App. II.

[5] App. I, s.v. *St Andrews*—Excerpts from Liber Conclusionum, 1460.

[6] *Supra,* 92 n[4].

[7] App. I, s.vv. *Glasgow*—Munimenta ; *St Andrews*—Liber Conclusionum.

[8] At St Andrews, at least.

[9] Sections II, III ; App. III, Excerpts from *E.R.* and *L.H.T.A.*

[10] *Supra,* 30 n[1].

tions,[1] sank from its position as a municipally controlled and subsidised folk play to that of a surreptitious game practised by prentice lads and farm labourers.[2] The municipal clerk play and interlude were smothered by the cumulative force of a series of inhibitions,[3] coupled with a remarkable transformation in the outlook of the nation.[4] The effect of the Reformation on the dramatic development of Scotland has already been discussed in detail. With the prohibition of the observance of the ' superstitious ' days of the Catholic Church and the subsequent legislation against Sunday plays, the popular communal drama was doomed. In Scotland the Reformation was a middle-class movement ; and, generally speaking, these acts were imposed not from above by a tyrannical minority, but with the sanction of the main body of the nation. The concession of a Monday holiday in 1598 came too late to save the situation ; [5] and where, as in Elgin, ' guysing ' was one

---

[1] *Supra*, 31-3.

[2] Cf. *Poems of Alexander Scott* (1525-84 ?), *S.T.S.*, 1896, p. 23.

> ' In May quhē men ȝeid everich one,
> Wᵗ Robene Hoid and Littill Johne,
>   To bring in bowis and birkin bobbynis ;
>   Now all sic game is fastlingis gone
>   Bot gif it be amangis clovin Robbynis.'

[3] *Supra*, 91-5.

[4] Cf. *Maitland Quarto Manuscript, S.T.S.*, 1920, f. 8. ' Quhair is the blyithnes that hes beine.'

[5] *Register of the Privy Council*, V, 462 : ' Monday appointed to be a weekly pastime and exercising day over the realm from the first Monday of August next. No courts to sit on Monday thereafter ; no household labour to be required from servants on that day ; masters of colleges and schools to give liberty to their students and scholars to exercise themselves in their pastimes after 12 o'clock ; cottars, tenants and fermorers, astricted to shear their masters' corns, to be exempted from the said service that day. The Act is passed to avoid profanation of the " Saboth day, quhilk suld be allanerlie bestowit and imployit in Godis service and na utherwyis," whereas " the samyn has bene abuisit be the haill leigis of this realme be hanting and using of gaimis and pastymis upoun the said day, pretending ane lauchfull excuis

of the pastimes, the Kirk Session saw to it that an effective supervision was maintained.[1]

Even in the post-Reformation period the burgh records are far from complete. There is a gap in the Ayr accounts from 1561-2 to 1574-5. When they recommence one looks in vain for notices of burgh plays. It is not until the last quarter of the century that Dundee and Glasgow can produce a regular series of accounts, while records of the expenditure of other burghs have either disappeared entirely or are represented by a few disconnected compts.[2]

The Edinburgh records, however, are almost continuous from now onwards, and may be taken as reflecting faithfully the organised dramatic life of the capital. The Edinburgh bailies appear to have concentrated their efforts almost entirely on the shows at royal entries ; which, if stereotyped in form, were carried out with a high degree of technical skill. There is an occasional grant in aid of a Grammar School play or an official inspection prior to the performance.[3] Otherwise, a single reference to a subsidised play by Robert Semple [4] and a jealous regard for the bounds of the playfield, represent the positive activities of the Town Council in connection with the drama.

The only playfield shows at Dundee which are detailed in the treasurers' accounts, commencing in 1586, are witchburnings and executions. But the 1635 reference to

for thame in the said mater that na day in the oulk wes grantit to thame for thair releif fra thair lawbour except the said Sabboth." ' (Printed in full in *A.P.S.*, IV, 160.)

[1] App. I, s.v. *Elgin*—Kirk Session Records, 1599.

[2] This is true even of Aberdeen. And see note on early Kirk Session records, *supra*, 92 n[1].

[3] App. I, s.v. *Edinburgh*—Municipal Plays.

[4] *Ibid.*, 20th Feb. 1567-8, and note. If this Robert Semple can be identified with the fiery Reformation poet, his play was probably produced in the interests not of the drama but of Protestant propaganda,

the Aberdeen playfield, ' whair comedies were wont to be
actit of auld,' suggests that all dramatic performances
did not cease with the Protestant régime ; for this particular
playfield was acquired only on the eve of the Reformation.[1]
The all too short minute decreeing the compulsory attendance of the inhabitants of Glasgow at the play and pastime
on Corpus Christi Day 1599 [2] must, I think, be taken as
evidence of the persistent survival of the mediæval communal play in some form, rather than as proof of fresh
enterprise in municipal drama at that particular period.
Perth is one of the few towns where signs of dramatic
vitality can be detected.   Proclamations were broad-
casted throughout the land enjoining the observance of
the 5th of August, the day of the King's deliverance from
the Gowrie conspiracy, with attendance at the preaching
and ' all civill and lauchfull glaidnes.' [3] We hear of bonfires,[4] drinking of wine and breaking of glasses at the
market cross,[5] minstrels,[6] sermons and psalmsingings.[7]
But, with the possible exception of Dunfermline,[8] in
Perth alone, if the records are to be trusted, the day was
celebrated with dramatic entertainments.[9]

[1] App. IV, *Playfields.*
[2] App. I, s.v. *Glasgow.*
[3] *Register of the Privy Council,* VI, 257 ; *A.P.S.,* 1600, IV, 213.
[4] Dunfermline MS. Burgh Court Book (Treasurers' accounts for
1605-6 ? 1606-7).
[5] Aberdeen MS. Council Register, XL, 104 ; St Andrews MS.
Treasurers' Accounts, 1611-12.   Cf., too, the accounts of the
Aberdeen Dean of Guild and Burgh Treasurer (Spalding Club
Miscellany, Vol. V) for annual expenses of wine, confections, and
glasses.
[6] St Andrews and Dunfermline MS. Treasurers' Accounts.
[7] Aberdeen Council Register, *loc. cit.*
[8] The 1606 entry cited in App. I, s.v. *Dunfermline,* is followed
in the MS. by an entry of expenses for ' tua tar barrellis and
thrie laidis coallis and wagis to the minstrallis at the Tounis
congratulatioun for his Maiesties delyverance fra his enemies.'
This may, however, be for Gunpowder Plot celebrations.
[9] App. I, s.v. *Perth*—Excerpts from Council Register.

In England, where the gild plays and parish plays were suppressed or died a natural death, other forces were operating to save the drama and infuse it with new life. Scotland was relatively unaffected by the Renaissance. The Universities were hampered by inadequate resources, and there were no richly endowed schools. During the period when London was evolving a rich and varied civic life, Edinburgh was the main battleground of the opposing forces of the French and English parties. For months at a stretch the Castle was under siege, and the inmates suffered all the rigours of an intermittent blockade. Above all, the Court was no longer the centre of the national life. The long minority of James the Sixth, synchronising with a period of bitter internal strife, resulted in a succession of short regencies of precarious tenure. From 1579 the ascendancy of Lennox, the emissary of the Guises, and the secret intrigues of the young King for the overthrow of the religious settlement served to accentuate the gulf between the Court and the now articulate middle-classes led by the ministers.

The faithful reports of the English envoys and the fulminations of Knox against the levity of the Queen, supplemented by detailed inventories of the royal wardrobe, have preserved for us a vivid picture of the revels at Holyrood during the brief personal reign of Mary Queen of Scots. If we were dependent on the Accounts of the Lord High Treasurer, our information would be limited to three brief entries.[1] Even the mask of the rural gods at Stirling in 1566 passes unnoticed, save for a record of the delivery of taffeta to Bastien Pagez 'to be sovm preparatenis for ꝑe baptisme.' [2] It is doubtful, then, if the later Treasurers' accounts, covering the period after

[1] App. III, Excerpts from *L.H.T.A.*
[2] *Ibid.*, Excerpts from MS. Lord High Treasurers' Accounts. Cf. *supra*, 50.

James assumed the reins of power, represent any more accurately the Court life of that date. In January 1580-1 there are details of ' masking claithis ' for the Earl of Murray's marriage, in preparation for which the royal ' balladine ' taught the young King to dance. The following year £66, 13s. 4d. was expended on apparel and ' wappinnis ' for a mask dance.[1] The spectacular ' enterlude ' which graced the baptism of Prince Henry in 1594 is, however, unremarked in the official records save for a reference to the ' transporting of the lyoun fra haliruid houß to striuel-ing.' [2] It is possible that the expenses for the masks both in 1594 and in 1566 may have been included in the records of the Master of Works for Stirling Castle ; but the records for these particular dates have not been preserved among the manuscript Master of Work Accounts now at Register House. Intermittent grants to troupes of comedians from 1594 to 1603 [3] represent the sum total of dramatic activity at the Scottish Court during this late period, as recorded by the Lord High Treasurer. Yet it is difficult to believe that Anne of Denmark spent thirteen years in the northern capital without indulging her taste for masks in the ' dansing chalmer ' at Holyrood.[4] Whether the ' greit abuß ' in the King's house at Yule, against which the Edinburgh Presbytery so strenuously protested,[5] consisted in masking

[1] App. III, Excerpts from MS. Lord High Treasurer's Accounts.
[2] *Ibid.*
[3] *Ibid.* ; App. II, Travelling English Companies.
[4] App. III, Excerpts from MS. Lord High Treasurers' Accounts, 1581-2. In September 1589 a mask for six maskers and six torchbearers was sent to Scotland for the King's marriage by command of Queen Elizabeth. Cf. J. P. Collier, *Annals of the Stage*, I, 263 ; A. Feuillerat, *Documents relating to the Office of the Revels*, 1908, p. 392.
[5] Edinburgh MS. Presbytery Records, 26*th December* 1598 : ' The presbyterie being informit of ye greit abuß that hes bene in ye king*is* maiesties houß, in the town of ed*inburgh* and vther part*is* about ye keiping of ȝule hes ordanit that(t) his maiesteis minister*is* speik his maiestie that ordour may be takin with his

and plays, such as enlivened the Christmas season at the Elizabethan Court, must be a matter for conjecture.

One of the last struggles in which James the Sixth was engaged with the Kirk, prior to his accession to the English throne, centred round the establishment of a 'pastyme hous' in Blackfriars Wynd, Edinburgh, in the autumn of 1599. The King was victorious in the first round of the contest. The ministers were forced to acquiesce in the annulling of their act against the English comedians.[1] The first public theatre in Edinburgh has left no further mark on the contemporary records.[2] But, in all probability, for the next three years [3] the acting of comedies proceeded apace ; and when the English players travelled north to Dundee and Aberdeen, they were fêted and rewarded by the civic corporations.[4]

It is idle to speculate on what might have happened if the Court had not removed to London in 1603. Signs are not lacking that, on occasion, the town authorities were unable to see eye to eye with the more puritanical section of the ministers. The enforced postponement of the Sunday pageants arranged in honour of Queen Anne in 1590 was not to their liking ; indeed, according to Calderwood, they 'reviled despitefullie' the ministers.[5] In July 1598 the citizens of Edinburgh were entertained by the exploits of a daring funambulist, and the Presbytery

houſ And ꝰat ꝰe ministeris of edinburgh and ꝰat ꝰe rest of ꝰe ministeris about tak ordour with thair flockis be ressoun godis word, the actis of ꝰe kirk & lawis of the realme hes damnit ꝰe samin.' 18th December 1599 : ' Ordanis [two ministers] to ga to ꝰe kingis maiestie and to crawe that ʒoolkeiping may be stayit.'

[1] App. II, English Travelling Companies.

[2] Infra, 300 n[2].

[3] It is probable that the Blackfriars company did not survive the departure of the King from Edinburgh. Certainly Fletcher appears in England in 1603 as a member of the King's company (J. Tucker Murray, English Dramatic Companies, I, 104).

[4] App. II, Travelling English Companies.

[5] App. I, s.v. Edinburgh—Municipal Plays.

met to censure the magistrates ' for suffering sic spectacles
in pair citie.' Notwithstanding this rebuke, the very next
day £6, 13s. 4d. was paid from the burgh exchequer to the
said ' maister of activitie.' [1] If the Council records are a
faithful guide, an attitude of neutrality was preserved
regarding the 1599 controversy between the King and the
Kirk. The Provost, it is true, intervened ; [2] but as the
affair is ignored in the municipal Register, this may have
been in an unofficial capacity. On the whole, however,
the Town Council appears to have seconded the ministers
loyally in their regard for the reputation of their ' reformed '
city.[3]

Whether, then, with the continued patronage of the
Court, this exotic English drama, imposed against the main
current of the nation's thought in a period which was
singularly barren of literary activity in any form, could

---

[1] App. II. The popular love of *spectacula* died hard in spite of
the opposition of the Kirk. The King showed his appreciation
of this point when, in 1600, he arranged for a French funambulist
to give a display at Falkland ' to mitigat the Quein and peiple
for Gowrie's slauchter ' (*ibid.*).

[2] *Infra*, 304.

[3] Cf. Sir Anthony Weldon's Description of Scotland, 20th June
1617, cited in Nichols, *Progresses of James I*, III, 340 ff. : ' Ffor
his Majestie's entertainment, I must needes ingenuously confesse
he was received into the parish of Edenborough (for a City I
cannot call yt) with great showts of joy, but no shewes of charge ;
for Pageants, they holde them idolatrous things, and not fit to
be used in so reformed a place. . . . They holde their noses yf
youe talke of beare-bayting ; and they stop their eares yf you
talke of a playe. . . . To conclude, I am persuaded that yf God
and his angells at the last day should come downe in their whitest
garments, they would run away and cry, " The Children of the
Chappell are come againe to torment us ; let us fly from the
abomination of these boyes, and hide ourselves in the mount-
aynes ! " ' Weldon's satirical strictures are probably justified,
though the Edinburgh bailies may have considered that the
official entry of James the First had already been celebrated in
1579, and that of his consort in 1590. At any rate, this ' parish '
spared no expense on the pageants for the entry of Charles the
First in 1633.

ever really have flourished and extended is doubtful. So far as one can judge from the meagre notices, the dramatic history of Scotland in the period following the Reformation is that of the gradual extinction of the once flourishing but now effete mediæval drama in its several forms. There was no fresh stimulus and no new growth. The sole surviving texts of *Philotus*, drawn indirectly at least from the Italian *novella*,[1] and the *Monarchicke Tragedies*,[2] based on Senecan models, serve mainly to accentuate the poverty of the post-Reformation drama as compared with that of contemporary England. Here and there schoolmasters encouraged a carefully supervised ' Christian Terence,' and the University of St Andrews continued to celebrate its ' Bachelar Act ' with plays of some kind. The drama as a popular institution and a force in the national life was now dead.

[1] Printed in 1603 by Robert Charteris. In the testament of Margaret Wallace (spouse to Mr Robert Charteris, printer), who died 1st Feb. 1603, there occurs, ' Item, fyve hundreth Philotus buikis, at ijs. the pece, summa Lł.' (*Collections of the Wills of Printers and Booksellers in Edinburgh*, Bann. Club, *Miscellany*, Vol. II). The plot is borrowed from Barnaby Rich—' *Riche, his Farewell to Militarie Profession* '—who apparently claims it as original. (*Philotus*, Bann. Club, 1835, p. viij.) The editor of Barnaby Rich's work for the Shakespeare Society, 1846, however, considers that the play was the earlier, and suggests derivation from a common source. This latter suggestion is favoured by Professor Moore Smith in *Riche's Story ' Of Phylotus and Emilia*,' Mod. Lang. Rev., 1910. In any case, the influence of the Italian ' novella ' is apparent.

[2] *Poetical Works of Sir William Alexander, Earl of Stirling*, Vol. I, *S.T.S.*, 1921.

APPENDIX I.

EXCERPTS FROM LOCAL RECORDS.

Other excerpts from local records will be found in
Appendix II. and Appendix IV.

NOTE ON LOCAL RECORDS.

A certain amount of information regarding early burgh records is to be found in the *Report of the Committee on Local Records*, 1902. By means of personal inquiry and investigation all over Scotland, I have been able to supplement, and occasionally to correct, this information. The results have been published in *An Inventory of the Manuscript Records of the Older Royal Burghs of Scotland* (St Andrews University Publications, XVII.), 1923. Details as to the extant kirk session, presbytery, and synod records are to be found in the various reports of the Church of Scotland Committee on Church Records, and have been published in collected form by Dr Thomas Burns in his *Church Property*, 1905.

ABERDEEN.

[Extracts from the Council Register, 1398-1625, have been published in two volumes by the Spalding Club (*A.C.R.*, Spald. Club); but, as roughly forty volumes of the Council and Burgh Court Register prior to 1600 have been preserved in the burgh archives, this represents only a small proportion of the manuscript records. As the transcript of these printed volumes is generally slovenly and the dates are often inaccurate, it seemed better to transcribe from the original manuscripts not only the additional material which I have discovered but the relevant portions of the Register in detail. In order to economise space below, I cite the marginal notes only when these are of interest. Some earlier extracts from the Register, dating from 1317, have been printed in the Spalding Club *Miscellany*, Vol. V., 1852; while excerpts from later volumes, 1625-42, were published by the Burgh Records Society. A few early town accounts which have survived have been printed in the Spalding Club *Miscellany*, Vol. V. A register of burgesses is printed in the New Spalding Club *Miscellany*. Other publications include : *Selections from the Records of the Kirk Session, Presbytery, and Synod of Aberdeen*, Spalding Club, 1846 ; *Merchants and Craft Guilds*, Ebenezer Bain, 1887 ; *Records of the University and King's College, Aberdeen* ; *Fasti Aberdonenses*, Spalding Club, 1854 ; *Registrum Episcopatus Aberdonensis*, Spalding Club, 1845.]

EXCERPTS FROM MANUSCRIPT BURGH RECORDS.

A. Religious Pageants.

13th *May* 1440   IV, 203

Item eod*em* die p*er* comm*une* consili*um* concess*um* fuit Ric*ardo* kintor tu*nc* abbati de boneacord vnus burgens*is* futur*us* faciend*us* ad libitu*m* suu*m* qua*n*docu*n*que ips*um* prese*n*tauerit p*ro* expensis suis fact*is* et faciend*is* in quoda*m* ludo de ly haliblude ludend*o* apud ly Wyndmylhill

V (2), 661 1442 [1]

Þire craftez vnderwrittin sal fynd ʒerely in þe offerand [2]
of oure lady at candilmes þire persones vnderwrittin þat is
to say

   þe littistarez sal fynd

þe emprioure and twa doctourez / and alsmony
   honeste squiarez as þai may

  þe smythez and hammirmen sal fynd

þe three kingis of Culane and alsmony honeste
   squiarez as þai may

   þe talʒourez sal fynd

oure lady / Sancte bride [3] Sancte helene Iosepħ
   & alsmony squiarez as þai may

   þe Skynnarez sal fynd

twa bischopes / foure angelez / and alsmony honeste
   squiarez as þai may

  þe webstarez and walkarez sal fynd

Symion [4] and his discipłez / and alsmony honeste
   squiarez & etc

   þe Cordonarez sal fynd

þe messyngeare and moyses / and alsmony honeste
   squiarez & etc

  þe fleschowarez (sal) fynd

twa or foure wodmen / and alsmony honeste squiarez
   & etc

  þe brethire of þe gilde sall fynd

þe knyghtez iñ harnace / and squiarez honestely
   araiit & etc

   The baxstaris sal fynd

the menstralis and alsmony honest squyaris as
   thai may & etc

708 1445

Thomas lawsoñ ad instanciam Ricardi kintor receptus fuit
ex eo quod fuit eidem per commune consilium concessum
nuper quando fuit abbas de boneacord / pro expensis suis
factis in quodam ludo de ly haliblude luso apud ly wyndmylhill / et prestitit solitum Iuramentum plegio pro eo
eodem Ricardo kintor

  [1] Possibly 2nd Jan. 1442 3.
  [2] 'p' is deleted in MS. before 'offerand.' The scribe may at first have
intended to write 'play.'
  [3] The first of February, Candlemas Eve, was the festival day of St Bride
(Bridget), heathen goddess of fertility. Cf. Frazer, *Golden Bough*, 134-5.
  [4] *A.C.R.* (*Spald. Club*) has 'Symon.'

1449

Nicholai*us* benyng recept*us* fuit in libero*s* burgensem et confr*atrem* gilde *ratione* pater*ne* libertat*is* p*ro* v s̄ quos p*repositus* dedit walt*ero* balcancole [1] p*ro* sc*ri*ptura ludi iñ festo corp*oris* x̄p̄i

30*th July* 1471

thomas Watsoñ receptus fuit in liber*um* burgen*sem* et confr*atrem* gilde hui*us* burgi ex fauore *con*silii concessa [2] phillippo de drumbrek *se*riando p*ro* suis expen*sis* fact*is* *circa* ludu*m* de bellyale qui p*re*stitit solitu*m* Iurame*n*tum

14*th May* 1479

þe samy*n* dai þe *con*sale & breþ*er* of þe gilde beand p*re*sent for þe ty*m* has *con*sentit & ordanit þe ald*ir*ma*n* to mak þe expenſ & cost*is* of þe *common* gude apon þe arayme*n*t & vþir*is* necessar*is* of þe play to be plait i*n* þe fest of corp*us* x̄p̄i nixt tocu*m* & *etc*

9*th Feb.* 1483/4

Iohñ of lam*m*yntoñ & a*n*dro lam*m*yntoñ *con*vict be ane assise a*r* adiugit ilkane of þaim i*n* am*er*ciame*n*t for þe wrangwiſ absenti*n*g of þaim fra þe offerand on ca*n*dilmesday

4*th Feb.* 1484/5 [3]

The ferd dai of februar*e* þe ȝer*e* of god *etc* lxxxiiij It is ordanit & decretit be þe ald*ir*man & counsale þat þe talȝour*is* & al vþir*is* craftti*s*men wi*th*in þe toune sal i*n* tyme tocu*m* beyr þare takyn*n*is of þare craft apon þare breist*is* i*n* þare best aray on Candilmes day at þe offerand And quha þat *con*tempnis [4] & dois nocht sal tyne þare fredu*m* for a ȝer*e*

9*th Feb.* 1484/5

Iames kenn*er*ty *con*vict be ane assise was adiugit i*n* am*er*cia*me*nt for breki*n*g of *common* ordina*n*ce at þe offerand on candilmes day & *etc*

---

[1] Notary Public. See *Reg. Epis. Aberd.* I., 255, 258, 259.
[2] Apparently ' cuius compositio ' is understood.
[3] *A.C.R.* (*Spald. Club*) has 1st Feb. 1484.
[4] *Ibid.*, ' contervinis.'

VII, 399 *4th Feb.* 1492/3

The saide day the assiſs ordanit Ionhne of lammyntone to bringe v ℔ waxe to ꝑe haly blude licht Ande Williame lammyntone to bringe v ℔ waxe to ꝑe saide licht for the brekin of commoñ ordinance in ꝑe inordinate passing one candilmes day to ꝑe offerand as vꝑeris thar nichtbouris passit Ande atour gif euere ꝑe saidez Ionhne or Williame brekis commone ordinance in tyme to cum And beis conuikit ꝑairof Ilkane of tham beinge conuikit sal pay xl ſ to Sanct nicholes Werk vnforgevin gif ꝑai occupy the craft

403 *8th Feb.* 1492/3

[Andrew Lamyngtone accused ' for ꝑe Inordinat passinge to ꝑe offerand one candilmes day '].

VIII, 186 *3rd Feb.* 1502/3 [1]

The saide day Iohne rede wobster Iohne william-
for Candilmeſ sone Alexander mernothe Andro hill thome
day wobsteris wobster gilbert mernothe williame wobster
& talȝouris Archibalde wobster & Ihone paule Ilkan of
tham was conuict be ane suorne assiſs Alexander Rede forspeker [2] becauſs thai dide nocht It that accordit thame to do one candilmeſs day in the processione [3] eftir the auld honorable & lovabill consuetude of the burghe etc for ꝑe quhilkis thai were in ane amerciament of ꝑe court & to amende as law will & forbere in tyme to cum becauſs thai pretendit thame to precede and paſs in the place of the processione quhare the talȝouris had vyſs to paſs tymes bigane

The saide day Iames crukschank was conuict be the saide assiſs Alexander Rede forspeker for ꝑe breking of commone ordinance in ꝑe situacioun & ordoure of the processiouñ one candilmeſs day etc Ande for trubulance of Williame of mar dekin of the Skynneris in ꝑe executioun of his office & to amende as law wil & forbere in tyme to cum

---

[1] A.C.R. (*Spald. Club*), 1502.
[2] MS. repeats ' forspeker.'
[3] A.C.R. (*Spald. Club*), ' Passioun.'

29th Jan. 1503/4 316

Skinnaris
walcaris

The saide day the ald*irman* & bal3eis ordanit
þe skin*naris* & walcar*is* tile vphalde & sustene
thar*e* p*art* of candilmeß play aucht & wount
etc [1] Ande þai lefit & gif thame charge tile extent resonabtie
ale vnfre p*er*sonis of þ*air* craft*is* eft*ir* þe faculte of thar*e*
gud*is* & to raiß þe samy*n* & gif neid be to *com*pel & dis-
tren3e þ*air*for to þe vphaldin of thar p*art* of þe said play

3rd Feb. 1503/4

The said day It was deliu*er*it be ane suorñ assiß patry
red forspekar þat Alex*ander* coup*er* was in ane am*er*ciame*nt*
of þe court for brekin of *com*mouñ ordinance of þe tovne /
becaus he kepit no*ch*t þe processione of candilmeß play
siclik as vþir craft*is*meñ did

William belty william blinseile & And*r*o mortim*er* be þar
avin tounge grant was Ilkañ in am*er*ciame*nt* of þe court
for þe brekin of *com*moñ ordinance becaus þai kepit no*ch*t
þe processione in candilmeß play

5th Feb. 1503/4 317

The saide day It was deliu*er*it & ordanit be ane suorne
assiß gilb*er*t men3eis forspek*er* þat gif eu*er*e dauy litst*er*
*com*mitt*is* ony offence tile ony of h*is* craft in tyme to cu*m*
& beis *con*uict þair*of* sal pay xl ß to sanct nicholes Werk
vnforgevin becauß of þe offence done to gilbert litst*er* at
þe sit*u*acione [2] of candilmes play

30th Jan. 1505/6 [3] 543

situacio
artificum
in processione
in die
purificacionis

The said day It was fundin be þe ald lovabile
consuetud & Rite of þe burghe þat in þe honor
of god & þe blissit v*ir*gin mary þe craft*is*meñ
of þe samy*n* in thar best aray kepit & decorit
þe processiouñ one candilmeß day 3erlie quhilk*is*
alde & louabile consuetude ye pr*o*uest ballies & counsale
riplie auisit Ratifeit ande appro*u*it þe said Rit Ande ato*ur*

---

[1] The MS. read originally ' . . . . . . of candilmeß play þat is þe empr*i*our*e*
etc.,' but was altered as above.
[2] ? Arranging of crafts in order. Cf. entries of 3rd Feb. 1502-3 and 30th
Jan. 1505-6.
[3] *A.C.R.* (*Spald. Club*) has 1505.

statut & ordanit ꝑat the saide craftismeñ & thare successoris
sale ꝑerpetualie In tyme to cum to obſserue & keipe the
saide processiouñ alſs honorabily as ꝑai cane Ande ꝑai
sale in ordire to ꝑe Offering in ꝑe play paſs tua & ij to
gidder socialie In ꝑe first ꝑe flesſseris barbouris baxturis
cordinaris skinneris couparis wrichtis hatmakaris & bonat-
makaris togidder walcaris litstaris wobstaris tailȝouris
goldsmithis blak smithtis & hammiremeñ And ꝑair craftismen sale furnyſs ꝑair pageantis / ꝑe cordonaris ꝑe messinger [1]
wobstaris & walcaris symeoñ ꝑe smythis & goldsmithtis
iij kingis of cullane ꝑe litstaris ꝑe Empriour / ꝑe masounis
ꝑe thre knichtis ꝑe talȝouris our lady Sanct brid & Sanct
elene Ande ꝑe Skynneris ꝑe tua bischopis Ande tua of ilke
craft to paſs with ꝑe pageant ꝑat ꝑai furnys to keip thare geire
And gif ony ꝑersone or ꝑersonis happinnis to failȝe & breik
ony pont befor writin & beis conuict ꝑairof sale pay xl s̃
to Sanct nicholes werk & ꝑe balȝeis vnlaw vnforgevin Ande
to ꝑe obſseruing & keping of ꝑe Samyn ale ꝑe said craftismeñ
was oblist be ꝑar handis vphalding.

699 **31st** *May* 1507

The said day ꝑe prouest and bailȝes statut and ordanit
ꝑat ale skynnaris sale gang befor ꝑe cordinaris in ale
processionis baitht in candilmeſs play & vꝑeris processionis
ꝑat accordis ꝑame to gang in

797 **29th** *Jan.* 1507/8

The saide day ꝑe borgñ fundin be Iohnne reid one william
walcar dekin of ꝑe walcaris for ꝑe wranguiſs withhaldin
fra him of ij đ to ꝑe furnising of ꝑar ꝑart of candilmes play
was fundin awaile for ꝑe quhilkis ꝑe said william was in
ane amerciament of ꝑe court etc be ane suorñ aſsiſs thomas
lesly forspeker

799 **31st** *Jan.* 1507/8

cordonaris
skynnaris
The said day it was deliuerit & fundin be ꝑir
personis eftirwritin eldast maist famouſs ande
dekynnis of ꝑar craftis ꝑat is to say dauid
themañ gilbert litster cristy prat alexander tailȝour Iohnne
wi(l)ȝeamsone wobister Iohne lorirmar Iohnne red &
wilȝeam walcar suorñ ꝑe gret aitht at command of ꝑe

---

[1] *A.C.R. (Spald. Club)* 'messing.'

aldirman & bailȝes ȝat ȝe skynneris of ȝis burgh̃ sale paſſ
& gang befor ȝe cordonaris in ȝe processiouñ of candilmes
day & ale vȝer processionis ȝat ȝai viſſ to paſſ intile within
ȝe said burgh̃

3rd Feb. 1510/11 [1]

1153

craftismen
absent fra ȝe
processioñ
one candilmes
day

The said day thomas meldrum william paton-
sone Andro lousone ȝonger Iok allane & Richerd
wricht was Ilkan of thame in Amerciament of
ȝe court be ȝar avne toung graunt becauſſ ȝai
passit nocht in ȝe processioñ of candilmes day
to decore ȝe samyn etc & tile amend as law wile & forber
in tym̃ to cum

ȝe cit(uation)
of ȝe pro-
cess(ioun) one
candilmeſ
day of ȝe
craftis men
of ȝe tovne

. . . . . . and fyve . . . . and ten ȝeris 1212
the copy of ȝe act . . . . . . the offering
. . . candilmeſſ day eftir follouys on . . . . . .
. . . .
wes fundin be the auld lovabłe consuetud &
Rite of ȝe . . . . . . in ȝe honour of [etc. etc.] [2]

14th Jan. 1512/13 [3]

IX, 177

Ratificacio
acti pres-
entis facti
pro cero-
ferariis le
torscheis

The said day ȝe prouoist bailȝeis and counsaile
present for ȝe tyme Ratefeit and apprevit the
actis maid obefoir ȝat euery craft within ȝis
townne sall haue a pair of Torcheiſſ honestlie
maid of foure pund of wax to decoir and worschip
ȝe sacrament one corpus xp̄i day and at ȝe
fest of pasche at ȝe resurrexiouñ at ȝoule and at all vthir
tymes quhene neid is to ȝe honour of ȝe townn And ordanit
all fre & vnfre to loit and scot and pay ȝar part ȝairto as
ȝai ar extentit to be ȝe deknys of ȝar craftis

28th Jan. 1512/13

186

Statutum
pelliparorum

The said day It was statut & ordanit be ȝe
prouost & balȝeis with aviſſ of the consale ȝir
personis eftir writin sale pay ȝir somes of money
to furneſſ ȝar torchis to decoire ȝe towne ȝat is to say

---

[1] A.C.R. (Spald. Club), 1510.
[2] The rest of the entry is practically identical with the corresponding
portion of the January 1505-6 statute. At the commencement the MS. is
defective ; but, from the minute of 4th July 1525, we may take it that the
date is 12th Jan. 1510-11.
[3] A.C.R. (Spald. Club), 25th Jan. 1512.

William skynner iiij s̃ Andro burat iiij s̃ henry brovne xij
đ Ionhne kempy ij s̃ Ionhne patersone xviij đ Charlis skynner
xvj đ Robert blak xvj đ Andro skynner vj đ & Ionhne
horne vj đ

553 31st Jan. 1515/16

Statutum pro
processione
in die purific-
acionis

The said day It was statut and ordanit be ꝑe
gudmen of ꝑe townñ & thoucht expedient ꝑat
ꝑe auld laudibile consuetud amang ꝑe craftismen anent ꝑe processiouñ one candilmes day
be vphaldin as it has bene obefor in all thingis And ordanit
ꝑe officiaris to pas to ꝑe deknys of all ꝑe craftis and warne
thame to furnys ꝑar partis and badgeandis of ꝑe samyn
vnder ꝑe panis of ane vnlaw of euery craft to ꝑe bail3eis
vnforgevin & vꝑer panis contenit in ꝑe statutis maid obefor

XI, 399 5th Feb. 1523/4 [1]

Statut of
candilmes
processiouñ

The said day ꝑe provest with ꝑe awiſs of ꝑe
haill counsell present for ꝑe tym fand & deliuerit
ꝑat ꝑe craftismen of ꝑe said Ꝫurgñ had fail3eit
in ꝑe obſſeruing & keping of ꝑe lovable auld
statut maid be ꝑair predecessouris with ꝑe consent of ꝑe
haill craftismen in ꝑe decoring & honoring of ꝑe processiouñ
oñ candilmeſs day becauſs ꝑai wer absent for ꝑe maist
part & ꝑat ꝑai ꝑat wer present buyr nocht ꝑe taikins of
ꝑair craft eftir ꝑe forme of ꝑe said statut And ordanit ꝑe
bail3eis to wptak ꝑair vnlawis of ꝑe absente & ꝑai ꝑat
fail3eit in ꝑe bering of ꝑair taikins to amend in tym cumin
vnder al payne contenit in ꝑe auld statut to be wptakin
but ramissioñ.

statut pill
amerciament

The said day Iohne pill tail3our wes conuikit
be his awin tong grant maid in Iugment for
ꝑe dissobeing of dauid andersoñ bail3e becas he
rafusit to paſs in ꝑe candilmeſs processiouñ with his taikin
& sing of his craft in ꝑe place lemit to his craft And in
likwiſs for ꝑe mispersoning of ꝑe said dauid And [2] ꝑe
merchandis of ꝑe said guid touñ in calling of ꝑaim coffeis [3]
& bidding of ꝑaim tak ꝑe salt pork & herboiſs in ꝑair
handis ffor ꝑe quhilk ꝑe provest & hail [4] chargit ꝑe said

---

[1] A.C.R. (Spald. Club), 1523. Order of entries inverted.
[2] Ibid., 'Anderson' inserted and 'And' omitted.
[3] Merchants.   [4] 'Counsell' omitted in MS.

Iohne he beand obleist in Iugment be his hand wphaldin to fulfill [1] ꝑair deliuerance to cum oñ sonday ꝑat nixt cumis in ꝑe tyme of hiemes barfut and bairheid with ane candil of ane pund of wax & offir ꝑe samyn to ꝑair patrouñ sanct nicholace And sit douñ humilie oñ his kneis besekand ꝑe provest & guydtouñ to ramyt him his forsaid falt and inobedience doyne to ꝑe bailȝe & guydtouñ And to bring oñ his breist ꝑe wsit taikin of his craft ꝑat is to say ane pair of pantit [2] scheris And gif euer ꝑe said Iohne committis ony siclik falt in tym cuming to pay to sanct nicholace wark x merkis but ramissioñ

12th or 13th June 1525   589

vobsteris in
amerciament

The said day Iohnne wilȝeamsoñ vobster sande moir & thome murra wes in amerciament of ꝑe curt be ꝑe deliuerance of ane suorne assiſs Iohnne collisoñ forspekar for ꝑe strublance of ꝑe bailȝeis oñ corpus xpi day in tyme of processiouñ & for inobediens done to ꝑe touñ And ꝑe amendis ꝑairof continewit quhill mononday to ꝑe provest & counsell & ꝑe said persons to compeir ꝑe said day afore ꝑe samyn

4th July 1525   594

ratificatioun
of ꝑe statut
of craftismen

The said day the bailȝeis ratifeit & apprevit ꝑe lowable statut maid be ꝑar noble progenitour prouest & conseill of ꝑis burght ꝑe xij day of Januar anno xvᶜxº tueiching ꝑe ordoure of ꝑar craftismen in all ꝑar processiouñ [3] and ordanit ꝑe samyñ ordour to be keipit vnder ꝑe pannis contenit in ꝑe samyñ etc

9th Feb. 1525/6   671

hammirmen
massonis

The baillies assignit william lorimour in nayme of ꝑe hammyrmen to preif ꝑe auld wſs gif ꝑe massonis & sclataris ȝeid with ꝑaim in processiouñ oñ candilmes day & pait ꝑair dewite with ꝑaim ꝑairfor

---

[1] A.C.R. (Spald. Club) omits.
[2] Ibid., ' patent.'
[3] Sic in MS.

XII(2), 833 *17th June* 1530

The provost bailȝeis and counsaill commandit
ȝe craftismen   ȝair officiaris to pas and charg all ȝe craftismeñ
processiouñ   of ȝis burght to keip ȝair pagganis in ȝe pro-
keiping   cessiouñ oñ sonday nyxt cumis commandit ȝañ
be ȝe haill tovnn wnder ȝe pane of xl s̄ ilk craft ȝat falis
to be pait vnfo(r)gewiñ *etc*

XIII, 160 *22nd May* 1531

Ordour of corpus x*pi* processioun

ordour of can- The said day It was statut and ordanit be ȝe
dilmeſ pro-   prouest bailȝeis and counsaile present for ȝe
cessiouñ and   tyme conforme to ȝe auld lovabill consuetudis
of corpus   and ryte of ȝis burgħ and of ȝe nobill burgħ of
cristi
Edinburgħ of ȝe quhilk rite and consuetude ȝe
forsaid prouest has gottiñ copy in write That is to say ȝat
in ȝe honour of god and ȝe blissit virgyne Marye The
craftiſsmen of ȝis burgh in ȝair best array keipe and decore
ȝe processiouñ oñ corpus cristi dais and candilmes day als
honorabillye as ȝai can Euery craft with ȝair awiñ baner
with ȝe Armez of ȝair craft ȝairin And thay sall pas Ilk
craft be ȝame self tua and tua in ȝis ordour That is to say
in ȝe first ȝe flescharis and nixt ȝame ȝe barbouris nixt
ȝame skynnaris and furrowris togidder nixt ȝame ȝe
cordonaris nixt ȝame ȝe tailȝouris eftir ȝame ȝe vobstaris
and valcaris togidder nixt ȝame ȝe baxtaris And last of all
nerrest ȝe sacrament pasſ all hemmirmen That is to say
Smythtis wrichtis masonis cuparis sclateris goldsmythis
& armouraris And euery ane of ȝe said craftis in ȝe candilmes
processiouñ Sall furniſ ȝair pageane conforme to ȝe auld
Statut maid in ȝe ȝeir of god Im v^c and x ȝeris quhilk Statut
was maid with ȝe awiſ of ȝe haile counsaile And approvit
be ȝe craftis men of ȝe toune for ȝe tyme for ȝame And
ȝair successouris And oblist ȝame to ȝe keping of ȝe Samyn
vnder ȝe pane of xls̄ and ȝe bailȝeis vnlaw vnforgeviñ to
be vptakiñ of ȝame ȝat beis absent but ane resonabill
cauſ fra ȝe said processiouñ or ȝat makkis trubill or per-
turbatiouñ ȝairiñ To ȝe quhilkis ȝai var oblist be ȝair
handis vphaldiñ in iugement And the prouest bailȝeis and
consaile present for ȝe tyme ratifeis and apprevis ȝis
present statut and ȝe panez contenit ȝairin to be kepit
Inviolablye In all maner in tyme cuming

etc   *etc*   *etc*

The craft*is* ar chargit to furneiſ ɲair panȝeanys
vnderwrittin

ɲe fleschar*is* sanct
bestien̄ and his trum-
matour*is*
ɲe barbaur*is* sanct
lowrence & his trum-
mentour*is*
skynnar*is* sanct
stewin' torment*ouris*

ɲe cordonar*is* sanct
martyne
ɲe tailȝeour*is* ɲe
coronatioun̄ of
our lady
litstar*is* sanct
nicholeſ
wobstar*is* walcar*is*
and bonetmakar*is*
sant Ion

baxstar*is* sanct
georg
writt*is* messounſ
slater*is* & cupar*is*
ɲe resurextioun̄
ɲe smyth*is* and
hem*ir*men to
furneſ ɲe barmen̄[1]
of ɲe croce[2]

31*st* *May* 1532   453

baxsteris conuik

The said day all ɲe baxst*eris* of ɲe guid tovn̄n̄ put ɲame in provost and bailȝeis will for ɲe wanting of ɲair pagane in corpus xp̄i proces-sioun̄ ɲa vsit afore And siclik for ɲe vanting of ane dekin to ɲair craft quh*il*k ɲa au*c*ht to cheiſ ȝeirlie quharfor ilk ane of ɲame is in ane am*er*ciam*ent* of ɲe court to forber in tyme to cum and mend as law vill and ɲat is gevin for dovme And ɲe said baxst*eris* chargit to cheiſ ɲame ane dekin betuex ɲis & mou*n*onday nixt cu*mis* and pr*es*ent afore ɲe said provost and bailȝeis in iugiment

13*th* *June* 1533   XIV, 204

litsteris barbour*is* amerciament

The said day It is fundin and deliu*er*it be ane sorne assise thomas menȝeis forspeikar ɲat ɲe litst*eris* and barbour*is* hes failȝeit ɲat ɲa decorit no*c*ht ɲe processioun̄ on̄ coppus xpi day w*ith* ɲair pangeaniſ as ɲa suld haue done quharfor ɲa and ilk ane of ɲame is in am*er*ciam*ent* of[3] ɲe court to forber in tym to cum and mend as law will and ɲat is gevin for dovme and ɲe mendis ɲa*ir*of *con*tinevit to be modifeit be ɲe provost and consale[4]

[1] *A.C.R.* (*Spald. Club*), ' bearman.'

[2] The heading ' ordour of corpus xpi processioun,' the phrase ' and of corpus cristi ' in the margin, and the list of pageants scribbled in at the bottom of the page in the MS., all seem to have been added later in different ink.

[3] MS. repeats ' of.'

[4] Under this date in *A.C.R.* (*Spald. Club*) is quoted a statute ' from a MS. now in the possession of a Member of the Club,' which is practically identical with that of 22nd May 1531, as far as ' nixt ɲame ɲe baxtaris.' Then follows : ' Nixt thame the wrichtis, masonis, sclaters, and coupers togidder, and last, and nixt the sacrament, passis all the smithis and hammyrmen. And euery craft in the said processionis sall furneiss thair pegane and banar honestlie as effers, conforme to the auld statut maid in the yeir of God jaj vᶜ and tene yers . . .' No list of pageants is given.

tailȝouris
amerciament

The said day It is fundin and deliuerite be ane sorne assise thom menȝeis forspeikar ɯat ɯe tailȝeouris of ɯis guid tovnñ hes failȝeit to smythis and halmirmeñ and [1] siclik to ɯe valcaris and vobsteris in ɯe keiping of ɯair placeis of ɯe processiouñ oñ corpus xpi day quharfor ilk ane of ɯame is in ane amerciament of ɯe court to forbeir in tym to cum and mend as law vill and ɯat is gevin for dovme and ɯe mendis ɯairof continevit to be modifeit be ɯe counsale

387 1st *June* 1534

The prouost chargit Iohne mor maister messvne to caufs and compele ɯe laif of his craft to furneifs ɯair onest pagane to ɯe towns honour as he wil ansuer to ɯame ɯar apone and ɯai suld caufs his craft & ɯair nychtbouris sic as writtis cuparis & sclattaris to obey ɯame

388 5th *June* 1534

The bailȝeis assignit mounday nixt to cum to Iohne Iamesone skynner to produce his ressonifs quhy he suld gang afor ɯe writtis and tailȝeouris in processiouñ

574 31st *May* 1535

litsteris
amerciament

The Said day It is fundin and deliuerit be ane sorne assise gilbat menȝeis forespeikar that ɯe litsteris of ɯis burgh hes vranguslie brokin ɯe staitut maid be ɯe tovnñ for corpus xpi processiouñ quharfore ɯa ar in ane amerciament of ɯe court and ordinit to pay ɯe panis contenit in ɯe said statut and ɯe bailȝeis vnlaw vnforgeviñ *etc*

XV, 637 27th *May* 1538

command to
baxteris

The balȝes chargit duncan gall george crawy Iohn vysman & ɯe remanent of ɯe baxteris to intend & obey to ɯar deykynnis of craft for ɯe furnessing of ɯair peggane agane corpus xɯi day Ilkan to pay eftir ɯair faculty & ɯe sayd dekynnis to mak compt to ɯaim quhat ɯai rasaif

[1] MS. repeats 'and.'

21st *June* 1538 659

protestatio
hay

The sayd day walter hay goldsmyth dekyne of
ɥe craft of hemmirmen compeirit In Iugment
and complenit to ɥe balȝes allegiand wrang doñ
to ɥame be ɥe marenaris [1] in vsurping of ɥair place in ɥe
processiouñ oñ corpus xp̄i his day and ganging behind
ɥame aganis ɥe commound ordinance & statutis of ɥis
nobill burght & all vder borrowis within ɥis realm requyrand
ɥaim for remeyd of law protesting gyf ɥai refusit ɥat It be
lesum to call ɥe said marenaris befor vder Iugis sperituall
or temporall & for remeid of law

6th *June* 1539 XVI, 266

tinctores
amerciament

The said day alexander freſſour Iohne litstar
Iohne crystesone And Iohne reaucht litsteris
and ɥe laif of ɥair craft wes conwict for diss-
obeyng in ɥe nonganging In corpus criste processiouñ and
braking of ɥe commound ordinans & statutis of ɥis toun
maid ɥairupouñ quhairfor ɥai var put in amerciament of
court to forbeir in tym cumyng and amend as law will
And ɥat wes gewin for dome

23rd *June* 1539 291

ɥe litsteris
vnlaw
remittit

The consall prowest and balȝes remittis ɥe
litsteris of ɥe townis wnlawis quhilk ves conwict
obefor for ɥe braking of ɥe commoun ordinans
& statutis of ɥis toun for ɥe nonpassing in ɥe
processiouñ oñ corpus christe day as ɥai ɥat aucht to hef
done ɥe same bot ɥai ordane ɥaim to pay ɥe balȝes wnlaw
oñ remettit with fauouris oñ ɥair gud bering bot gyf euer
ɥai commit ɥe said falt In tyme cumyng ɥai ordane ɥame
to pay bayth ɥe townis wnlawis bygane & tocum oñ for-
gyffin bot to be dewly takin oup *etc.*

25th *June* 1546 XIX, 143

ɥe chesyn
of litsteris
decane

The said day ɥe haill Litsteris of ɥis burght
chesit alexander freſſour litster ɥair dekyne of
ɥair said craft for ɥis instant ȝeir quhilk accepit
ɥe said office oñ him and is sorne ɥe grit ayth
to exerce ɥe same lelile and treuly during ɥe said ȝeir And

---

[1] *A.C.R. (Spald. Club)* has 'ameraris,' which may be correct, though the
word 'marenaris' recurs in this entry.

þe bailȝeis inter̃ponit þair auctorite þairto and ordinit þame to haue þair banar and pagane as wþer craftis of þe said burght hes ilk ȝeir oñ corpus xp̄i day and candilmeſs dayis processionis vnder þe panis contenit in þe statut maid þairupouñ

xx, 567 25th May 1551

The said day þe bailȝeis ordinit william barclay

þe craftis-
mennis
charge

officiar to pas and charge all þe craftismeñ of þis guid tovnñ to obſerue keip and decoir þe processiouñ one corpus xp̄i day nixt cumis with þair banaris and baganis ilk craft in þair avin place conforme to þe auld statut maid þairupouñ ilk persouñ vnder þe pane of ane vnlaw vnforgevin

dekynnis
craftismeñ

The said day þe bailȝeis committit and gaif povar to þe dekynnis of euery craft of þe said burght to stent þe nychtbouris of þair avin craftis for þair partis of þe furnesing of þair paganis and bannaris of þe processiouñ oñ corpus xp̄i day nixt cumis And gif nead beis to pund and distrenȝe þame þairfor as efferis þat vill nocht pay þair part þairof

xxi, 423 5th June 1553 [1]

The said day þe dekyn and haill craft of þe

Smythtis
convickit

smythis wer convickit be ane suorne assiſs for þe disobeying of þe baillies in refusing contempnandlie [2] to gang in ordour in þe processioun oñ corpus xp̄is day last bipast befor þe sacrament as þai ȝeid in ordour þe ȝeir Immediatlie bypast And þe baillies wer maid quit be þe said assiſs of all strublens of þe said craft And þat wes gevin for dome

protestatio
artificum

The said day alexander kempt dekyne of þe baxter craft protestit in name of þe said haill craft þat quhat þe baillies did oñ corpus xp̄is day þat last wes or ȝit hes done sensyne anent þe rewling and ordouring of þe passage of craftismen in þe processioun þe said day be nocht preiudiciall to þair prevelege obserwit obefor bot þat þai ma haf þe samin ordour keipit þat vtheris principall burrowis of þis realme observis conform to þe ald statutis & actis maid þairupoun vpoune þe quhilk

---

[1] A.C.R. (Spald. Club) has 4th June.   [2] Ibid., ' contempurindlie.'

he desyrit act of court & instrument And Ierom blak
dekyne of ꝑe covperis Iames hunter in name of ꝑe haill
smythis protestit inlykmaner as Is aboun vrittin

9th June 1553

425

Smythis
convickit

The said day ꝑe baillies & consell ordanit ꝑe
panes contenit in ꝑe statitut maid obefor anent
ꝑe ordour of craftismen to gang in ꝑe processioun oñ corpus xp̄is day viz ꝑe soum of xl s̃ Togidder
with ꝑe baillies vnlaw To be tane vp of ꝑe smythis ffor ꝑe
dissobeying of ꝑe baillies vpoun corpus xp̄is day ꝑat last
wes ffor ꝑe quhilkis ꝑai wer convickit be ane Suorne assifs

21st May 1554

666

protestationis
of craftismen
anent ꝑe
ordour of ꝑe
procession
oñ corpus
xp̄i day

The said day androw bissett dekin of ꝑe
wrychtis william Iamesoune dekyne of ꝑe
masonis and Ierome blak dekin of ꝑe cowperis
compeirit in iudgement and exponit to ꝑe ballies
quhow ꝑat Iohnne Ienour ꝑair officiar at ꝑair
command had chargit ꝑame and ꝑair haill
craftis to pafs in ordour vpouñ corpus xp̄i day now approcheand in ꝑe processiouñ by ꝑe ald maner and ordour
That is to say to pafs be ꝑame selffis and with ꝑe sklateris
all togidder hawand ane honest baner and pegane of ꝑair
awin Immediatlie befoir ꝑe smythis and vtheris hammyrmen
quhair ꝑai had wont to gang with ꝑe said smythis as ꝑai
allegit all Togidder vnder ane baner and pegane And
producit ane staititut maid ꝑairupoune of ꝑe dait ꝑe xxii
day of may ꝑe ȝeir of god mvᶜ xxxj ȝeir And williame
robertsone dekin of ꝑe smythis compeirit in iudgement And
allegit ꝑat ꝑai wer in vse of gangging be ꝑame selffis in ꝑe
said processione vnder ꝑair awin baner hanmaist and nixt
ꝑe sacrament And ꝑe saidis wrychtis masonis cowperis
and sklaitteris to proceid Togidder befoir ꝑame vnder ane
baner and pegane siperat fra ꝑe saidis smythtis And producit ane statitut maid ꝑairupouñ of ꝑe dayt ꝑe xiij day of
Iunii ꝑe ȝeir of god mvᶜ xxxiij ȝeiris And ꝑe ballies decernit
and ordanit ꝑe last statitut to be obseruyt and keipit vnder
ꝑe panes contenit in ꝑe same Becaus ꝑai all wer present
and consentit ꝑairto and oblist ꝑame to obserf ꝑe same as
ꝑe said statitut proportis at lynth And ꝑe saidis wrychtis
masonis cowperis & sklayteris protestit ꝑat quhat ꝑe ballies

I

dois or decernis ꝃis day Anent [1] ꝃe ordour forsaid mak na
dirogatioune to ꝃe forsaid statitut first maid producit be
ꝃame in iudgement bot ꝃat ꝃai may haf ꝃair ald prewelege
obseruyt And for remeid of law quhen tyme and place
requiris   And allexander kempt dekyne of ꝃe baxsteris
allegit inlykwyiſ ꝃat ꝃai ar put by ꝃair rowme and ordour
vsit obefor And protestit siclyk ꝃat quhat be done ꝃis
ȝeir be ꝃe ballies Anent ꝃe said ordour hurt ꝃame nocht in
tyme cuming

671 *28th May* 1554

Litstaris
accusit for
ꝃe braking
of ꝃe
commound
ordinance

The said day Iohnne litster symone burnet
androw murdow alexander litster walter waldy
Iohne rowcht androw chalmer and alexander
andersoune litsteris wer accusit in iudgement
for ꝃe braking of ꝃe commone ordinance and
publict statitut of ꝃis guid toune And dissobeying of ꝃe charge gewin to ꝃaim be ꝃe officiaris at
command of ꝃe prouest and baillies, Nocht gangand in
ordour vnder ane banere in ꝃe processioun vpoun corpus
xp̄i day And ꝃe saidis personis allegit ꝃat It is nocht ꝃe
vse and consuetud of edinburght nor na vther borrowstoune
of scotland ꝃat litsteris ganggis in ꝃe said processioun be
ꝃame selffis bot amang ꝃe burges and breithir of gild And
allegit ꝃat ꝃai all ar burgesſ and breider of gild And
ꝃairfor ꝃat ꝃai aucht nocht to be compellit to keip ꝃe said
statitut And ꝃe ballies assignis to ꝃame ꝃe auchten day of
Iunii nixt to cum to preif ꝃair said allegiance dewly as
efferis

XXII, 77 *14th June* 1555

The said day alexander kempt elder dekin of ꝃe baxteris
allegit ꝃat ꝃe baillies vpoune corpus xp̄i day lastbipast
hes put ꝃame fra ꝃair rovme and place of ꝃe processioune
be way of deid by ꝃe ald ordour and statut maid ꝃairupone
And protestit ꝃat ꝃe said compulsioune preiuge nocht
ꝃaim and ꝃair ordour & place in ꝃe said processioune in
tym cuming Bot ꝃat It be lesum to ꝃame to Ioiſ and
brovk ꝃair ald plaice and priuilege conforme to ꝃe vse of
edinburght and ꝃe remanent burrowis of ꝃis realme
The said day Ierome Blak dekyn of ꝃe cowperis allegit
in Iudgement ꝃat ꝃe baillies vpoune corpus xp̄is day

---

[1] MS. repeats ' anent.'

lastbypast hes put þaim fra þair rovme and place of þe
processione by þe ald ordour and statut maid þairupoune
And protestit þat quhat þe baillies dois & hes done þe
said day mak na dirogatione to þair awin ald statutis
maid þairupone obefor Bot þat It ma be lesum to þaim to
brovk & Ioiß þair ald place & priuielege conform to þe vse
of edinburgh & vþer burrowis of þis realm

29th May 1556   325

Statut of þe   The said day þe counsell ordanit þat þe ald
processione   statut be obßeruit & keipit Anent þe ordour
one corpus   of þe processioune of þe craftmen one corpus
xp̄is day   xp̄is day nixt cumis wnder þe panis contenit
In þe said statut

          B. *Folk Plays.*   (a) *Lords of Bonaccord, etc.*
                   (b) *Boy Bishop, etc.*
                                                          (a)
13th May 1440   IV, 203
     (See under A.)

28th July 1440   207

Quo die Robertus Johannes et angusius Iohannes [1] Recepti
fuerunt in liberos burgenses et confratres gilde prestito ab
eis solito Iuramento ob fauorem Ricardj de kyntor abbatis
de boneacord pro feodo suo anni instantis

30th April 1445   V(2), 701

It was concludit statute and ordanit be the commoune
counsaile and mony othir of the gilde / for lettyng and
stancheyng of diuerß enormyteis done in tyme bigane be
the abbotis of this burgh callit of bone acorde / that in
tyme to cum thai will give na feis to na sic abbotis
Item it is sene speidful to thaim that for this instant yhere
thai will haue na sic abbot / bot thai will that the Aldirman
for the tyme and a balyhe quhom that he will tak til him /
supple that faute

1445   708

     (See under A.)

  [1] According to the previous minute, only one burgess-ship has been conceded.

734 *13th Dec.* 1448

Item penes foedum abbatis de bone acorde / consilium ordinauit quod prepositus in cuius tempore electus fuit satisfaciet sibi foedum suum secundum consideracionem consilij

[1453   The compt of Richard Kintor, Dean of Guild of Aberdeen, has :— Item to ꝑe abbot ande ꝑe priour viij ꝉib vjš viij đ.]

793 1456

Iohannes knokynblew ex gracia consilii et Abbatis de bonacorde et prioris receptus fuit in liberum burgensem et confratrem gilde pro v š in alba bursa prestito iuramento solito

797 1457

Michael blaklug ex gracia consilii receptus fuit pro xl š donatis abbati et priori de bonecord

VI, 480 *14th April* 1477

pro edific-
acione chori   [The same day the Council] has grantit to ꝑe biging of ꝑe queyr / al feis of alderman balȝeis dene of gilde Abbot & prioure of ꝑis burgh with ꝑe common gude & al vꝑeris proffitis ꝑat may be gottin for sevyn ȝeris tocum [etc.]

940 *28th Nov.* 1485

ꝑe samyn day ꝑe Aldirman & consale has deliuerit & decretit ꝑat gif Alexander of chavmer aldirman of ꝑe ȝere bipast be extra expendit in his compt sa ꝑat his son Alexander of chavmer Abbot of boneacord may nocht get payment of his fee concerning his office / than ꝑe said Aldirman & consel has grantit & tayn vppon ꝑame to pay & content him his fee of ꝑis instant ȝere / ꝑe said Abbot doand his dewiteis ꝑarfor as acht & wount was

966 *7th Aug.* 1486

The aldirman ballies counsale & cominte of abirden has gevin & grantit til Iohne of culane [1] in contentacion of his fee ꝑe tyme ꝑat he was Abbot of boneacord al ꝑe profite

----

[1] Member of Council, 1484-5 and 1485-6.

& avail þat he may get of ony twa sufficent men quhilkis
likis him erast to present to be resavit in þe fraternite of
burgesſ & gild of þe said burgħ / becauſ he had acquit-
ance of William blindsel ane of þe ballies for þe tyme of
þe some of ten merkis for his said fee þe quhilk some was
optenit apon þe said Iohñ of culan be þe said aldirman / And
þai sal resaue þe said twa personis to þe samen fraternite
& fredom of þe said burgħ quhen & quhat tym conuenient it
beis likand to þe said Iohñ or his factouris & etc

9th Aug. 1492   VII, 340

þe saide day Alexander chamer ȝonger offrit him redy to
preyf þat he pait his watter maile þe first ȝere þat he enterit
in þe office of Abbat of bonacorde

17th Aug. 1492 [1]   341

þe said day comperit Andro culane ȝonger abbat of bonacorde & askit at þe aldirman & ballieis ande diuerſ of
þe consal present for the tyme pament of his fee promittit
to him as vþeris hed abefor quhilkis ansuerd þai coud
fynde nay way to pay him quhil he hede ſeruit it furtht þe
ȝere & he protestit for remede of law

16th Nov. 1492   364

þe samyn day the aldirman & consal present for þe tyme
assignit to Androw Culane & Iames colison x markis of
thar watter malys for þe office of Abbat of bonacord to be
excersit this ȝere alſ honorabily as þai cane for þe wourschip
of þe tovne agen þe cumin of our Souerane lorde & the
lordis of consale

9th Dec. 1493   479

þe said day Androw barkare be his avne tonge grant was
In amerciament of þe court becauſ he raid nocht with
þe Abbat of bonay corde
þe saide day Androw lister was conuikit be his avne grant 480
becauſ he raid nocht with þe Abbat of bonacord

11th Sept. 1495   655

þe saide day the balȝeis & mast part of þe consale present
for þe tyme grantit & consensit to pay be þe haile tone to

---

[1] A.C.R. (Spald. Club), 1491.

Alexander chamer ʒonger [1] tene markis Scottis money for
ꝑe ſſeruing of ꝑe office of Abbat of bonacord for ꝑis Instant
ʒere & ꝑe ʒeris bigane

800 *8th May* 1497 [2]

Abbat of
bonacord

The viij day of may the ʒer forsaid ꝑe aldirman
balʒeis & consale present for ꝑe tyme at ꝑe
Womanhill for vphaldin of ꝑe ald louabile
consuetud honor consalaciovn & plesour of ꝑis burghe lik
as has bene vsit in tymez of ꝑare wourthie & honorable
progenitoris chesit thomas leslie [3] & Robert of cullane [3]
coniunctlie abbatis & priour of bonacord tile vyſſ & excerce
ꝑe saide office ꝑis Instant ʒer & grantit to pay ꝑame v
merkis of ꝑe common gudis this tyme tuelf monetht

1003 *9th Dec.* 1499

ꝑe saide day thomas narne & Wat of gareauche accusit
for ꝑe non Riding one Sanct nicholes day with ꝑe abbat
& priore of bonacord for ꝑe vphaldin of ꝑe honor of ꝑe
tone put ꝑame in ꝑe aldirmannis will Ande richerdredhed
in likuyss accusit referrit him to ꝑe Aldirman etc

1050 *1st May* 1500

electio
abbatis et
prioris de
bonacard

One may day ꝑe ʒere forsaid Ionhne of mar [4] &
dauid mar Was chosin be ꝑe aldirman ballieis
consale & comminte in ꝑe office of Abbat &
priore of bonacord for ꝑis ʒere tile excerce &
vyſſ the saide office eftir ꝑe lovabile consuetud & vyſſ
of ꝑe burghe for ꝑe quhilk ꝑai promittit to content &
pay to ꝑe saide Abbat & priore of bonacord tene markis
vsuale money of Scotland

1088 *10th May* 1501

Assignacio
Abbatj et
priorj de
bonacord

The said day ꝑe balʒeis consale & comminte of
ꝑe tone assignit to Ionhne of mar & dauid mar
abbat & priour of bonacord Sax merkis of ꝑe
malys of ꝑe gardin & foure merkis of ꝑe malis
of schothoysley to be rasit at ꝑare avine handis at ꝑe
termes vsuale within ꝑe saide burghe for thare gude &
solaciouſſ ſſeruice to be done Anent ꝑe saide office of bonacord for ꝑis Instan ʒere eftir ꝑe ald louabill consuetud of

[1] Member of Council at this time.
[2] A.C.R. (Spald. Club), 1496.
[3] Elected bailie, Oct. 1496 ; VII., 755.
[4] Bailie, 1499-1500 ; VII, 987.

ɥe said burghe quhilk*is* x m*erkis* was gra*n*tit & assignit
to ɥa*m* one may day last biga*n* at ɥe woma*n*hill quhe*n* ɥai
wa*re* new chosin in office last

29*th Nov.* 1504   VIII, 397

The said day it was statut and ordanit be ɥe
bail3eis and counsaile riplie auisit for ɥe vphaldin
and p*er*seuerans of ɥe auld louabile honor consuetud and rit of ɥe said burgħ vsit and sustenit
in tymes bigane in ɥe honor of thar glorius
patrouñ Sanct nicholes that ale personis burges
nichtbour*is* burges and burges sonnys habille to rid to
decoir and honor ɥe touñ in thar array co*n*ue*n*ient
ɥarto sale Rid wi*th* ɥe abbot and prior of bonacord
one eu*ery* Sanct nicholes day thro*w* ɥe toune as viſſ
and wont has bein quhen ɥai ar warnit be ɥe sad
abbot and prior obefor And gif ony man hawand tak of
wat*er*is and fisching of ɥe tone habill to rid be warnit be
ɥe said abbot & prior of bonacord and wile no*ch*t rid sale
tyñ ɥar tak*is* quhilk*is* ɥai haue of ɥe toune at ɥe nixt
assedaciouñ bot gif ɥai haue ane ressonabɬe cauſſ & Impedme*n*t ɥat ɥai may no*ch*t rid quhilk*is* thai sale schaw and
be considerit be ɥe aldermañ bail3eis and counsaile obefor
and vɥir personis beand warnit habile to Rid and fail3eis
ɥai*ri*n wi*th*out ane ressonabɬe cauſſ schawin to ɥe ald*ir*man
bail3eis and counsaile for ɥe tyme sale pay to Sanct nicholes
werk xx^ti ſ vneforgevin And viij ſ to ɥe bail3es for ɥar vnlaw

Statut pro
equitantibus
cum domino
abbate et
priore de
bonacord

16*th Dec.* 1504   402

The saide day Syme ellouñ was in ane am*erciamen*t of ɥe
co*ur*t be h*is* avne tong graunt for ɥe brekin of *comm*oñ
ordinance ɥat he Raid no*ch*t at Sanct nicholes day *etc*
The saide day Iohne patirsone was *con*uict be ane Suorne 403
assiſſ mathou*w* branche forspek*er* for brekin of *com*mone
ordinance ɥat he raid no*ch*t one Sanct nicholes day wi*th*
ɥe abbat & p*ri*or of bonaycord to decoire ɥe [1] for ɥe quhilk*is*
he was in ane am*erciamen*t of ɥe co*ur*t & to amende as law
wil & forber*e* in tyṁ to cu*m*

31*st Jan.* 1504/5   418

The saide day Alex*ande*r hay was *con*uict be ane suorne
assiſſ du*n*cane colisone forspekar for breking of ɥe statut

---

[1] ' toun ' omitted.

& ordinance of ȝe tovne ȝat he Raid nocht with ȝe Abbat
& prior of bonacorde one sanct nicholes day to decoire
the towne eftir ȝe auld lovabite consuetud of ȝe samyñ

528 *12th Dec.* 1505

abbas de
bonacord et
non equitantes
The said day ȝe aldermañ and bailȝes assignit
ȝe law day eftir ȝouyll nixt heireftir to ȝe personis ȝat ȝe abbot of bonacord was plantuiß
one quhilkis Raid nocht at sanct Nicholeß meß
to decoire ȝe toune to ansuer ȝaranent And ordanit williañ
scrimgeour Officiar to warñ ȝe said personis to ȝe said day

642 *27th Nov.* 1506

Renouacio
statuti pro
equitantibus
in festo Sancti
Nicholaij [1]

695 *17th May* 1507 [2]

ȝe abbat &
prior of
bonacord
The saide day It was statut & ordanit be the
prouest balȝeis & counsale for the vphaldin of
ȝe alde louabile consuetude honor & Rite of
ȝe tone ȝat ale manere of ȝonkheris [3] burges &
burges sonis conuenient [4] salbe redy euere haly day to paß
with the abbat & prior of bonacord in thare array conuenient
ȝairto vnder the pane of xxᵗⁱ͡s Ilkane persone ȝat falȝeis
& beis [5] conuict [5] ȝairof for thar vnlavis vnforgevin quhilkis
vnlavis salbe departit betuix Sanct nicholes werk & ȝe said
abbat & prior equalie Ande in likuiß ȝai ordanit ȝe iiijᵒʳ [6]
officiaris to be redy & paß with ȝe said abbatis & prior
continualie for ȝe honor of the tone etc

709 *9th July* 1507

The said day thomas chamer [7] & dauid Stevart [7] grauntit
to pay to gilbert menȝeis [8] ȝe Rest of the wyne tane be
thame ande ȝar ßeruandis Sene thar entreyß in ȝe office
of Abbat & prior of Concord of ȝis burghe ȝis day or to
morne

[1] Minute blank in MS.   [2] A.C.R. (Spald. Club), 16th May.
[3] Ibid., 'youthis.'   [4] Ibid., 'conuenient' omitted.
[5] Ibid., a blank.   [6] Ibid., 'tounes.'
[7] Member of Council, Oct. 1506.   [8] Common Clerk, 1506.

8th May 1508   828

Bonacord   The said day It was statut and ordanit be ꝑe
Alderma*n* baillies & counsale ꝑ*at* ale personis
ꝑ*at* ar abill wi*th*in ꝑis burgꝣ salbe reddy wi*th* ꝑar array-
me*nt* maid in grene and ȝalow bowis Arrowis brasſ And
all vꝑ*er conu*enient thing*is* according ꝑarto to paſ w*ith*
Robyne hvyd & litile Iohnne all tymes *con*venient ꝑarto
quhen ꝑai be Requirit be ꝑe saidez Robyne & litile Iohne
eft*ir* ꝑe tenou*r* of ꝑe statut*is* & ꝑroclamatiouñ maide be
ꝑe ꝑrouoist*is* baillies & counsaill obefor And gif ony of the
said personis happi*n*nis to failȝe in ony poynt befor w*ri*tyne
sal pay fourty schilling*is* vnforgevin And sall no*ch*t breuk
nor Ioiſ tak fischeing nor land of ꝑe said burgꝣ

17th Nov. 1508   899

         The said day the Prouoist bailȝeis counsaill &
approbacio
acti *presentis*   *com*minte of ꝑe said burgꝣ representand the
confecti pro   haill body of the samyne warnit be the hand
equita*ntibus*   bell & [1] circualie [1] Inquerit [1] ale in ane voice con-
in die *sancti*
nicholaij *etc*   cordand [2] Riplie auisit for ꝑe auld Rit and
         lovabiƚe consuetud of ꝑe said burgꝣ vsit and
perseuerit all tymes bigane past memor of mañ in ꝑe
honou*r* of ꝑar glorious patrouñ sanct nicholace statut and
ordanit ꝑat all personis burges nichbour*is* and Inhabitar*is*
burges sonnys habill to Rid to decor and honou*r* ꝑe towne
in ꝑar array *con*veniant ꝑarto sall Rid w*ith* Robert huyd
and litile Iohne quhilk was callit in ȝer*is* bipast Abbot and
priou*r* of Bonacord one eu*er*y Sanct Nicholas day throw
the towne as wse and wont has bene quheñ ꝑai war warnit
be ꝑe said Robert huyd or litile Iohnne or ony ane of thame
And gif ony man haffand tak*is* of watt*er*is fischeing*is* landis
or ony pensiouñ or proffit of ꝑe towne habile to Rid beand
warnit be ꝑe saidez Robert huyd or litile Iohnne forsaid and
will nocht Ryd and beis *con*uikit ꝑair*in*till be ane suorne
assiſ of ꝑe said burgꝣ sall tyne ꝑar tak*is* pensionis and
proffit*is* ꝑat ꝑai haue of ꝑe said burgꝣ & salbe secludit removit & vtirlie expellit fra ale tak*is* pe*n*sionis proffit*is* quhat-
su*meue*r ꝑai haue of ꝑe said burgꝣ in tyme tocum wi*th*out
ressonabƚe cauſ schawin & ꝑroponit to ꝑe ꝑrouoist bailȝeis
counsaill Robene and litile Iohne obefor and be consid*er*it
be thame to be lauchful Impedme*nt* and excuſ quharthrow
ꝑai my*ch*t no*ch*t Rid And the personis havand na tak*is*

---

[1] *A.C.R. (Spald. Club)* omits.   [2] *Ibid.*, 'considerand.'

of ꝑe said burght beand warnit be the said robert hyud
or litile Iohnne & will no*ch*t rid sall pay xx^ti schilling*is*
to Sanct nicholace werk & viij đ to ꝑe bail3eis vnlaw vnforgevin

908 *15th Dec.* 1508

The said day dauid Colp was *con*uikit be ane suorne assiſß
ſß*ir* Iohnne Rutherfurd forspekar for ꝑe stroublance of
mathou branche Abbot of bonacord in the executiouñ of
his office and till amend as ꝑai will & forbeir in tyme
tocum and ꝑat was giffin for dome And ꝑe said mathou was
maid quyt be ꝑe said assiſß of all strublance of ꝑe said
dauid

962 *22nd May* 1509

d*o*mini de
bonacord &
hay

The saide day Alex*ande*r hay saide he was
nocht complanteouſß one ꝑe Abbot ande priour
of bonacorde and haid nay thing to say to
ꝑame bot gud Ande referrit ande put him in ꝑe
prouestis wile and ꝑe counsel of ꝑe toun in ꝑe thingis ꝑat ꝑai
war complanteouſß on him

1132 *25th Oct.* 1510

Ratificac*io*
act . . .
. . . . . .
pro equi-
tan*tibus* in
die S*an*cti
nicholaij

The saide day the *pr*ouost bal3eis & counsale
ale in ane *con*sent ratifeit affirmit & app*r*ouit
ꝑe Act & louabile statut maide obefor Anent
ꝑe *per*sonis deuisit & ordanit to Rid one Sanct
nicholes day w*ith* ꝑe abbat & p*r*ior of bonacorde
throw ꝑe toune as vyſß & wount has bene tymes
biga*n* & ale pont*is* *co*ntenit in ꝑe samy*n*

1137 *10th Dec.* 1510

The *per*sonis
ꝑat raid no*ch*t
one sanct
nicholas day

The said day patry chernsid and*r*o meldrum
dauid fynne and Iohnne archo*u*r war accusit
for ꝑe breking of ꝑe statut and Act maid obefor
& newlie Ratefeit ꝑat ꝑai raid nocht one Sanct
nicholes day w*ith* ꝑe Abbot and p*r*ior of bonacord To
decor ꝑe towne eftir ꝑe auld laudabile consuetud and Rit
of ꝑe said burgh to ꝑe pleso*u*r of ꝑar glorious patrone Sanct
Nicholas and ꝑe towne *etc* Quhilk*is* *per*sonis put ꝑame in
wil of ꝑe *pr*ouost & bail3eis ffor ꝑe quhilkis ilkane of thame
was i*n* am*er*ciame*nt* of ꝑe court be ꝑar avin toung grant

And til amend as law wil and forber in tyme tocum And
þat was gevin for dome

The saide day Ionhne Andersone alias loche-
hillis dauid lame & Ionhne quhitcorne be þar
avne toung grant for þe brekiñ of the Act &
statutis maid obefor to rid one Sanct nicholes
day with þe abbat & prior of bonacorde to
decoire þe toune etc was in Amerciamentis of
þe court & tile amend as law wile & forber in tyme to cum

þe personis þat Raid nocht one Sanct nicholes day to decoire þe toune

21st Nov. 1511

IX, 59

Pro equitantibus in die sancti nicholaij [1]

The said day It was statut and ordanit be
prouost bailзeis counsaile & comminte present
for þe tyme representand þe body of þe tovne
circualie Inquerit be gilbert prestone officiar for
þe auld rit & louabile consuetud of þe said burgħ
vsit & perseuerit all tymes bigane past memour of man
In þe honour of our glorious patrouñ sanct nicholes þat ale
personis burges nychbouris burges sonis and Induellaris
withìn þe said burgħ abill to Rid to decoir & honour þe
tovne in þar best array conuenient þairto sal rid euery
sanct nicholes day al tymes tocum quheñ þai ar warnit be
þe prouost and bailзeis And gif ony burges or burges sonis
havand takis of wateris fischeingis landis or ony pensiouñ
or proffit of þe tovne abill to Rid beand warnit be þe prouost
and bailзeis and wil nocht Rid and be conuict þairintile
be ane suorne assifs sal tyne þar takkis pensionis and pro-
ffittis þat þai haue of þe said burgħ & salbe secludit removit
& vterlie expellit þairfra in tyme tocum without ressonable
caus schavin and exponit to þe said prouost and bailзeis
& to be considerit be þame gif it be lauchfule Impediment
& excufs quharthrou þa may nocht rid And als þat all
personis burges merchand men & craftismen havand na
takis habill to rid beand warnit be þe prouost & bailзeis
as said is & wil nocht rid sall pay xxtis to sanct nicholace
werk vnforgevin & aucht schillingis to þe bailзeis vnlawe
without lauchfule Impediment as said is conformand to þe
vthir actis maid þairapone obefoir

Statutum pro equitantibus in die sancti nicholaij

---

[1] *A.C.R. (Spald. Club)* omits this heading.

520 *19th Nov.* 1515

The said day It was statut and ordanit be þe provest bailȝeis and counsaill *present* for þe tyme þat þe auld lovabill consuetud and rit þat has bene vsit withtin þis burgħ all tymes bigane past memor*e* of man in þe hono*u*r of our glorious̄ patroun̄ sanct nicholace & vphalding of þe auld consuetud þat all burges sonnys / marchand men̄ and craftismen̄ habill þarto thoucht expedient be þe pr*o*vost bailȝeis & þe gud me*n* of þe town̄ and to be billit [1] be thame / address̄ þame in þar best array to rid at þis instant fest of our said patroun̄ sanct nicholace siclik as has bene vsit obefor tymes for hono*u*r to þe towine & loving to o*u*r patroun̄ And quha þat failȝeis and riddis no*c*ht he being warnit þarto be ane bailȝe þat salbe lymyt þ*air*to to be punyst eftir þe forme of þe act and statut maid þ*air*apone in þe monetht of nouem̃ber anno qui*n*gentesimo vndecimo with̃out ony fauou*ris*

Statutum pro
equitan*tibus*
in die sancti
nicholaij

---

641 *24th Nov.* 1516

The said day the pr*o*vost and counsaile gaif grantit and assignit to þe Alexan*d*er ruþerfurd [2] & Alexan*d*er menȝes [2] bailȝeis þe vnlawis of þe p*er*sonis þat ar warnit to Rid at sanct nicholesmes̄ and Ridis no*c*ht

---

703 *15th May* 1517

The said day þe bailȝeis Robert huyd & litiłe Iohnne chosin be þe town̄ continewit þe inobedientis & ȝoung [3] þat wald no*c*ht pass̄ with̃ thame to sanct devi*n*nis eftir þe teno*u*r of þe pr*o*clamacioun̄ & statut maid be þe town̄ apoun̄ þar gud bering And warnit þaim oppi*n*lie i*n* iugment of new to obß*er*ue & keip þe said pr*o*clamacioun̄ and pas with̃ þe saidez Robert & Ioh*n* all þe sondais of may & vther tymes quhen̄ þai be warnit for hono*u*r of þe town̄ And quhar contempnis & wil no*c*ht pas þai being i*n* þe town̄ with̃out resonabile caus or licence askit to pay ane vnlaw of viij ß vnforgevin & to be accusit for breking of com̃mon̄ ordinance

ȝong me*n*
Robin &
litile Iohn̄

---

[1] *A.C.R. (Spald. Club),* ' villit.'
[2] These names are inserted later in a different hand.
[3] ' men ' omitted.

2nd May 1519   X, 72

Lordis of
bonacord

The said day the prouest bailჳeis and conseill gaf grantit and assignit to alex*ande*r rud*e*rfurd [1] and willeam turing lordis of bonacord sex m*e*rkis to be pait of the rediest of ჳar*e* com*m*ont gudis to help to ჳar*e* abellem*e*nt for hono*ur* of the gud tovne

18th Nov. 1519   138

The said day ჳe prouest bailჳeis and consaill pr*es*ent for ჳe tyme granttit and consentit to ჳe allowance of ჳe sex m*e*rk*is* deliu*e*rit be the gudma*n* androv culleñ to alex*ande*r rud*e*rfurd [1] lord of bonacord quhilk ჳai assignit to him *with* the consent of ჳe consaill as ჳe act*is* maid abefor proportts and ordanit ჳe samyñ to be allowit in the said androv valt*ir* maill of ჳis ჳeir*e* instant *etc*

5th May 1522   XI, 83

electio
dominoru*m*
bone cordie

The said day ჳe pr*o*vest baitties & counsell grantit in iugm*e*nt ჳat ჳai *with* ჳe awiჴ of ჳe com*m*inte beand pr*es*ent for ჳe tyme had chosyne maist*e*r a*n*dro tulidef and robert wod lord*is* of bonacord for ჳis instan*t* ჳeir gevand and gra*n*tand to ჳame all maner of Iurisdictiouñ / and liberaliteis according to ჳe said office wsit & wont Requirand & chargand all maner of abill p*e*rsonis till obey to ჳe said*is* lord*is* of bonacord *with* intimatiouñ to ჳame ჳat quhasa dois in ჳe contrar*e* in tyme to cu*m* sall no*ch*t be abill till Ioiჴ nor bruyk na maner of tak p*er*tening to ჳe fredome of ჳis said burgñ or office of hono*ur* farthinfurtht / and ჳis Act & statut maid be ჳe haill touñ & ordand to be kepit / in-violabte in all maner of tyme to cu*m*

17th Nov. 1522   207

statut for
ჳe ridar*is*
oñ sanct
nicholace day

The said day ჳe baillies chargit ჳ*air* officar*is* to paჴ & warne all ჳe ჳong abte meñ *within* ჳis towñ duelling quhilk*is* salbe gevin ჳaim in bill to addreჴ ჳame in ჳ*air* best abilჳem*e*nt honestlie horsit *with* ჳ*air* watt*er* clok*is* to ryd oñ sanct nicholace day eftir noyne eft*ir* ჳe auld wჴ & *con*suetud of ჳe samy*n*

----

[1] Elected bailie, Oct. 1519 ; X, 119. See also under 24th Nov. 1516, above. Oct. 1518 ; X, 6, elected Dean of Guild.

272 *13th April* 1523

ꝑe chesing
of ꝑe lord*is*
of bonacord

The said day ꝑe hail touñ all in ane voce maid constitut and ordanit hon*o*rable men thomas men3es of petfoddells & pat*r*ik lesly [1] burgeſſ of abirdeñ lord*is* of bonacord for ꝑis instant 3eir & ordanit al man*er* of 3ong abłe men wit*h*in ꝑis touñ duelland to riſſ & obey to ꝑame quheñ ꝑai ar requirit eftir ꝑe auld rit & wſſ of ꝑe said burgħ gevand ꝑame power to correk & puneiſſ ꝑair dissobear*is* at ꝑair awin hand and chesit ꝑa*im* inlikwiſſ to be maiste*r*is of ꝑair artail3ery for ꝑis *instant* 3eir

650 *17th Nov.* 1525

The said day Iohne chamo*ur* grantit In Iugme*nt* ꝑat he deliu*er*it a berrell of q*uh*e*i*t to ꝑe lord*is* of bonacord at *com*mand of the prouest mast*er* andro*w* tulidef Iohne malesone & Iohne hay q*uh*i*l*k*is* war p*er*tinar*is* of the said q*uh*e*i*t

XII, 149 *29th April* 1527 [2]

The said day ꝑe prouest bail3eis Consall and comi*nt*e ordinat ꝑat ꝑe lord of bonnacord and his fallow be ansuerit of x me*r*kis of ꝑe fyrst freme*n* ꝑat hapy*n*nis to be frathinfurt*h* becauſſ it is ꝑe ald wſſ and hes bene vsit a lang tyme of before wit*h*in ꝑis guid tovnne

388 *3rd Aug.* 1528

assignac*io*
ratray
malisone

The said day ꝑe prouest bail3eis and Counsaill gaif grantit & assignit to ꝑair lovit*is* Ihone ratray [3] and gilbert malisouñ ꝑair Abbat*is* out of ressouñ of ꝑis instant 3eir ffor ꝑair feis ꝑe nyxt tua freme*n* ꝑat hapnis to be maid and desirit be ꝑame

XII (2), 463 *11th Dec.* 1528

The said day Androw losouñ w*illia*m a*n*nand androw durty w*illia*m kemp Ihone Iamesone skynnar & georg bissait ꝑa and ilk ane of ꝑa*m* put ꝑa*m* in ꝑe prowost and bail3eis willis for ꝑair non riding One ꝑair patrownñ day *con*forme to ꝑe statut*is* maid be ꝑair predecessour*is* and

---

[1] Member of Council, Oct. 1522 ; XI, 183.
[2] *A.C.R.* (*Spald. Club*), 30th April.
[3] Member of Council and Dean of Guild, 1527 and 1528 ; XII, 240, 433.

approwit be ꝑam Quharfore ꝑa and ilk ane of ꝑame was
in amerciament of ꝑe court to forber in tyme to cum and
mend as law will and ꝑat was gewin for dowme

The said day Saundris bissat was in ane amerciament of
ꝑe Court in falt of presens of his persone as he ꝑat was
lauchtfullie warnit to ꝑis to ꝑe instance of ꝑe prowest
bailʒeis and lordis of bonacord for his non-riding one sanct
nicolas his patrouñ day to forber in tym̃ to cum and mend
as law will and ꝑat was gewin for dowme

17th April 1531 [1]   XIII, 127

The Said day Sandris gray exponit [2] in [2] iuge-
protestacio   ment [2] to ꝑe prouest and bailʒeis how he and
gray   Sandris knollis was chosiñ be ꝑame lordis of
bonacord to do plesour and blythnes to ꝑe toune in ꝑis
sessoun of Symmir incuming offerand him alwayis reddy
to ꝑe Samyn effect for his part to do all plefsour to ꝑe toune
eftir his gudlye powar thay findand ane marrow sufficient
furthfilland his part in ꝑe samyn effect protestand alwais
gif ꝑai did nocht ꝑat he wald nocht except ꝑe said office
on him nor na part ꝑairof for ꝑis instant ʒeir oñ ꝑe quhilk
he tuke note & instrument

The prouest exponit to ꝑe communite present
expositio   for ꝑe tyme how he had ꝑe kingis grace lettrez
prepositi   vnder his signet impetrat be ꝑair awiſs Charge-
and ꝑe nichtbouris of ꝑis burgñ ꝑat nane of ꝑame Suld
refuſs quhatsumeuir office of honour ꝑai happin to be chosin
to be ꝑe Said communite vndir ye panes of tinsall of all and
sindry thair takkis & rovmes ꝑai had of ꝑe samyn And
inlikuiſs how ꝑe prouest and counsall had chosin alexander
gray and alexander knollis to be lordis of bonacord for
ꝑis instant ʒeir quhilk has bene ane office of honour ꝑis
tymez bygane and inquirit at ꝑe commonite gif ꝑai thocht
expedient ꝑat gif ony of ꝑe saidis parteis refusit ꝑe said
office ꝑat our souerane lordis lettrez suld be execut on ꝑame
in ꝑe charpest maner quhilk ꝑe haile counsall and commonite thocht expedient to be done

The said day sandris knollis exponit to ꝑe
protestatio   bailʒeis and commonite present for ꝑe tyme how
knollis   ꝑat he was chosin be ꝑe prouest counsall and
part of ꝑe commonite as ꝑai allegit to be ane of ꝑe lordis

[1] A.C.R. (Spald. Club), 16th April.   [2] Ibid., ' opponit iugement.'

of bonacord for þis instant ȝeir to þe quhilk office he was
nocht abill as he allegit for diuerſs cauſs ane becauſs he
was nocht present at þe said electiouñ ane vþer becauſs
þair [1] waſs mony vþeris mair abill for sic officis in þe toune
and had gretar proffite þairof Thridlye becauſs he had þe
kingis lettrez dischargeand him of all Sic thingis nonþeles
he was ȝeit reddy to except þe said office gif þe toune wald
gif him þe auld fee quhilk þai had wont to pay for þe
Samyn and vþerwais nocht protestand quhat beis done
be þe toune heirintill turne him to na pregiteis.

XIV, 283 *11th Oct.* 1533

þe lordis
bonnacordis
feis

The said day þe prouest and counsale consentit to gif þair lordis of bonacord of þe ȝeir
bigane tene merkis for þair feis of þe first mone
þe tovnñ gettis in and ma guidlie forbere how
sovne it ma be gottin

555 *30th April* 1535

Statut oñ
þe grene
cottis

The said day It is thocht expedient & ordinit
be þe consale þat all þe ȝovnng abłe meñ within
þis guid [2] haue þair grene cottis and agit meñ
honest cottis efferand to þame and obey and
decor þair lordis of ƀonacord conforme to þe auld lovable
vse of þis guid toun vnder þe panis of braking of commond [3] and statutis of þe guid tovnñ þat beis conuikit
þairof and to be punnest conforñ þairto

XV, 609 *29th April* 1538

The sayd day þe prowest balȝeſs & consell present for þe
tyme consentit all in ane voce þat gilbert fraſsour and henrik
collisouñ lordis of bonacord for þis instant ȝeir suld haf þe
compositiouñ of ane burges to supple þame of þair expensſs

626 *21st May* 1538

The sayd day robert arthur and Iohnn arthur sonis to
Iohnn arthur war accusit for þe strublens of my Lordis
of bonacordis & of þis gud toun in Iugment . . . . . .
[The assise decided that] þe saydis robert & Iohn hed

---

[1] MS. repeats ' þair.'   [2] ' toun ',omitted.
[3] ? ' ordinance ' omitted.   A.C.R. (*Spald. Club*) reads ' command.'

strublit ꝩe lordis of bonacord & ꝩis gud toun in stoping
of dansing & plesour dewisit to ꝩe plesour of ꝩe same
quharfor ꝩai & Ilkane of ꝩaim ves in amerciament of curt
to forbeir in tym cuming & ꝩe amendis ꝩairof continevit
to be maid be ꝩe awyſſ of ꝩe prowest & consell . . .

25th May 1538   634

The sayd day ꝩe prowest balȝeſſ and consell present for
ꝩe tym ordanit and chargyt robert arthur & Iohnn arthur
ȝongar sonis to Iohn arthur to cum ꝩe morne within ꝩe
queyr of sanct nicolace kyrk in tyme of ꝩe hemes barheyd
Ilkane of ꝩame with ane candill of vax of ane pound in
ꝩair hand & syt downe on ꝩair kneis & beseyk ꝩe prowest
in ꝩe townis name to forgyf ꝩame for ꝩe strublens doñ
ꝩairto be ꝩame in tyɱ of ꝩair solace & play & Inlykwyſſ to
beseyk ꝩe sayd prowest & gudmen of ꝩe touñ to mak
request to ꝩe lordis of bonacord to forgyf ꝩame ꝩe falt &
strublens done to ꝩaim And gyf ꝩai or ony of ꝩame committis ony siclik falt to pay v merkis to sanct nicolace
wark ꝩe committar ꝩairof on forgewin

14th Feb. 1538/9   XVI, 5

Eodem die willelmus gariocht receptus fuit in liberum
burgensem et fratrem gilde burgi de abirdene de communi
omnium burgensum consensu quia composuit cum dominis
de bonacord viz gilberto freſſour et henrico collisone de
mandato prepositi balliuorum et consilij Necnon solutis
preposito quinque solidis in alba bursa et prestito solito
Iuramento [1]

23rd June 1539   6

Eodem die Iohannes michelsone receptus fuit in liberum
burgensem et fratrem gilde de commine omnium burgensum
consensu quia composuit cum dominis bonaconcordie de
mandato prepositj balliuorum consilii et decani gildy per
eosdem ipsis assignatos Necnon solutis preposito quinque
solidis in alba bursa et prestito per eum solito Iurimento

[1] And see under p. 152 of the MS. cited below.

K

152 *14th Feb.* 1538/9

The balȝes chargit Iames litstar of his awin grant maid in Iugment to pay gilbert freſſour & henry collisone lordis of bonacord vjs scottis within terme of law

213 *14th April* 1539 [1]

Heir followis þe lordis of bonacordis desyr

petitio dominorum boneconcordie — My lord prowest balȝeis and consall of þis gud towne oñ to ȝour /m/ humely menis & schawis we waltir hay and thomas scherar lordis of bonacord That quhar ȝour /m/ put ws in þe said office þis Instant ȝeir albeit we ar nocht conwenient þairfor Nochtþeleſſ we sall god willand do þe best we may to ȝour /m/ honour and þe gud townes Quharfor we exhort ȝour /m/ þat we hef þe auld lowable vse lang vsit and keipit within þis gud towne now in our tyme lyk as It hes bene in our predecessouris tymes That is to say all þe ȝong able meñ within þis gud towne to conwoy ws euery sunday & haly day and wþer neidfull tymez aboulȝeit as ȝour /m/ hes deuisit & agit meñ to meit ws at þe crabstane or kirk-ȝard And þai þat compeiris nocht þat we may poynd þame conforme to þe auld vse or ellis mony of þame will nocht obey *etc* And als at ȝour /m/ pleyſſ rattefy & afferme þe saying ȝe promyst ws þe tym of our chesing in office That is to say ane of þe first fremeñ þat be gud at our chesing þat we heff securite in ȝour bukis þairof And ȝour /m/ ansur heirapouñ maist humely we beseik *etc* The quhilk petitiouñ forsaid þe prowest balȝes consall and communite present for þe tym ratefeit aprewit & affermit & ordanis þe same to be keipit & obſeruit in all poyntis þairof wnder þe panis contenit in þe same to be ouptakin & poyndit be þe forsaid lordis at þair plesur

224 *21st April* 1539

protestatio of þe lordis of bonacord — The said day waltir hay and thomas scherar lordis of bonacord exponit in Iugment þat how þai drank in thomas brechynis hous certane beir extending to (*blank*). s quhow þai had offerit hym payment þairfor and he had refusit to ressaue þe same And als þai offerit hym in Iugment payment ȝairfor quhilk he refusit to ressaue And þai protestit þat þe payment þairof turne þaim to preiudice [2] *etc*

---

[1] *A.C.R.* (*Spald. Club*), 4th April.   [2] 'na' omitted before 'preiudice.'

23rd June 1539   290

The balȝes & *pro*vest assignis to ȝe lord*is*
ane frema*nis* of bonacorde of ȝis Instant ȝeir viz thomas
*compositio*un scheres & valt*ir* hay Iohne michelsonis *com*-
to ȝe lord*is*
of bonacord positioune of frema*n*schip to be taky*n* oup be
ȝai*m* *con*forme to ȝe act maid be ȝe haill
*con*sall of befor

14th July 1539   312

The said day valt*ir* hay & thomas scheres lord*is* of bonacord quietclamit & dischargit Iohne michelsone in Iugme*n*t
for *com*positiouñ of his frema*n*is schip of vj m*er*k*is* q*uhi*lk*is* vas
assignit ȝai*m* be ȝe touñ obefor oñ ȝe q*uhi*lk he tuk nott *etc*

19th July 1540   567

The said day walt*ir* hay & thomas scheres
protestatio req*ui*rit Io*n*n brabn*er* to inquyt & bowrrow
hay et
scheres In his chargeour q*uhi*lk ȝai haf in ved of viij š
for his vnlav of absens in may quhe*n* ȝai var
lord*is* of bonacord *pro*testing gif he vald no*ch*t wyt*h*in
aucht dayſß ȝat gyf It hapnis to be put away ȝat ȝai be
no*ch*t indettit to anſßer eft*ir*wart for ȝe same

17th Jan. 1540/1   693

The *con*sell ordanis ȝe *com*po*sitio*une of ane
*compositio*un freman & burges to be maid to be gewine
of ane frema*n*
*con*signit to ȝe & *con*signit to maist*er* Io*h*n gordoune [1] &
lord*is* of
bonacord maist*er* Io*h*n freſßour [2] lord*is* of bonacord of
ȝis i*n*sta*n*t ȝeir becaus ȝe same*n* ves promittit
to ȝai*m* obefor

17th April 1542 [3]   XVII, 153

The said day ȝe prowest balȝes and *con*sall
*compositio*un *con*signis & gyff*is* to al*ex*ande*r* gray [4] & dauid
of a frema*n*
*con*signit to ȝe kyntoir ȝair lord*is* of bonacord chosin ȝis instant
lord*is* of
bonacord ȝeir ȝe *com*po*sitio*un of ane frema*n* & burg*is*
of gyld to help to ȝe decora*ti*oun & plasour to
be done be ȝai*m* to ȝis gud toune and ordanis ȝe officiar*is*
to pound ȝa*ir*for gif neid be

[1] Bailie, Oct. 1540 ; XVI, 592. Also Oct. 1541 ; XVII, 3,
[2] Member of Council, Oct. 1540 ; XVI, 595.
[3] *A.C.R.* (*Spald. Club*) gives this entry also under 1541.
[4] Member of Council, Oct. 1541 ; XVII, 10.

162 *24th April* 1542

The sayd day alexander kayn wes accusit in Iugment for his vyff becauſs he oblegit hym to anſser for hir [1] deidis for ꝑe hawy strublens & vyill myspersoning of alexander gray & dauid kyntoir lordis of bonacord & ꝑair company present with ꝑame for ꝑe tyme sayand commound beggaris & skaffaris ꝑair meltyd wes bot small for all ꝑair cuttit out hoyſs with mony vder Iniurious vordis unlefull to be expremytt quhilk ꝑe said alexander denyit and ꝑaireftir It wes fundin be ꝑe haill consell present for ꝑe tym ꝑat ꝑe said alexander vyf hed havely strublyt & myspersonit ꝑe saidis alexander & dauid & ꝑe remanent off ꝑair cumpany for ꝑe tym in maner abown wrytin quharfore he wes convict & put In amerciament of courtt to forbeire In tym cumyng & amend as law wyll & ꝑat weſs gewin for dome & ꝑe amendis ꝑairof continewit to be modifyt eftirwartt be ꝑe consell

XVIII, 512 *24th July* 1545

ꝑe lordis
of bonacord
fremañ

The said day ꝑe prouest bailӡeis and counsale present for ꝑe tyme assignis dauid mar [2] and maister Iames torre ꝑair lordis of bonacord ꝑe first fremannis compositioun siluer ꝑat hapnis to be maid within ꝑis guid tovnñ frathinfurth within ꝑis burgh at ꝑar desire and gettis and producis ꝑe mañ ꝑam self to be fremañ

XX, 14 *20th April* 1548

ꝑe granting
of xij merkis
to ꝑe lordis
of bonacord

The said day ꝑe counsale assignit and gaif ꝑe xij merkis scottis promittit for andro huntaris fremanschip to maister patre Ruderfurd [3] and Iohn losouñ ꝑair lordis of bonacord of ꝑis instant ӡeir and ordinit thame to be thankfully obeit of ꝑe same to help to mak ꝑair expenſs in ꝑe said office

69 *9th July* 1548

denis of
gild lordis
of bonacord

The said day ꝑe prouest bailӡeis and counsale present for ꝑe tyme ordinit dauid mar and gilbert malysouñ ꝑair denis of gild for ꝑe tyme to deliuer and pay to maister patre Ruderfurd [3] and Iohn losouñ ꝑe tovnis lordis of bonacord for ꝑis instant

---

[1] MS. has 'his.'   [2] Member of Council, Oct. 1545 ; XVIII, 535.
[3] Member of Council, Oct. 1547 ; XIX, 402.

ʒeir ꝑe **xij** merkis ꝑa haue ressauit fra Andro huntar for his fremanschip within xlviij houris and ordinit ꝑe same to be alovit to ꝑame in ꝑair nixt comptis ꝑairof

14th April 1550   398

ratificatioun of ꝑe statut vpouñ offices within ꝑe burght

The said day ꝑe haill tovnñ beyng conuenit as said is in ꝑair heid court ratifeit affermit and approuit ꝑe statut maid one ꝑe burgessis of ꝑis guid tovnñ ꝑat acceppis nocht and exercis nocht ꝑe offices ꝑat ꝑa ar chosin to be ꝑe tovnñ within ꝑis burght and ordinis ꝑe same to be keipit and obſſeruit in tymes cuming conforme to ꝑe same And forder ordinit gilbert brabaner [1] quhilk was chosin be ꝑe tovnñ ane of ꝑe lordis of bonacord ꝑis instant ʒeir to be varnit to friday nixt cumis to accept ꝑe said office or to refuiſſ ꝑe same ꝑat ꝑe tovnñ ma do ꝑairintill ꝑaireftir eftir ꝑe tennour of ꝑe said statut

27th May 1552   XXI, 161

compositionis assignit to ꝑe lordis of bonacord

The said day ꝑe prowest ballies & consall present for the tyme ordanit ꝑe sax pound of Iohnne robertsonis compositiouñ for his fremanschip and ꝑe nixt compositioune of ony burges of gild ꝑat hapnis to be maid of grit or small degre, to be gewin to patre menʒes and thomas nicholsoune [2] lordis of bonacord of ꝑis instant ʒeir to help to mak ꝑair [3] expensſſ Be ressoune ꝑat ꝑai ar put to grytar coist ꝑis ʒeire nor vtheris ꝑat bur office befor ꝑaim hes bene put to And ꝑat be ressoun of cumyng of ꝑe quenis grace, my lord governour & ꝑe maist part of ꝑe lordis & gritmen of ꝑis realme presently to ꝑis toune

3rd Feb. 1552/3   320

command to ꝑe den of gild

The consall ordanis ꝑe den of gild to pay to thomas nicholsoun [2] tene merkis in compositioune of tene pound quhilk ves grantit to hym obefor for his part / to his support of ꝑe expensſſ deburſit be hym in may as ane of ꝑe lordis of bonacord as ꝑe act mayd ꝑairupoun obefore bairis / vithin viij dais

[1] Member of Council, Oct. 1549 ; XX, 296.
[2] Member of Council, Oct. 1551 ; XXI, 57.
[3] A.C.R. (Spald. Club), 'mair.'

And siclik ordanis ꝑe den of gild to pay villiam rannaldsvn
x ß & Iohnn howe iiij ß for scorcheattis tane vp fra ꝑaim /
within ꝑe said terme

387 14th April 1553 [1]

staititut
for electioun
of lordis
of bonacord The said day ꝑe counsell all in ane voce havand
reispect and considderacioune ꝑat ꝑe lordis of
bonacord in tymes bigan hes maid our mony
grit sumpteous & superfleous banketing induring
ꝑe tyme of ꝑair regnne and specialie in may quhilkis wes
thocht nother profitabill nor godlie and did hurt to sindry
ʒoung men ꝑat wer elekit in ꝑe said office becaus ꝑe last
elekit did ay pretend to surmont in ꝑair predecessouris
in ryetoußs & sumpteous banketing And ꝑe cauß principall
and gud institutioun ꝑairof quhilk wes In halding of ꝑe
guid touñ in glaidnes and blythnes with dansß farsß playis
& gamis in tymes convenient neclekit and abusit Thairfor
ordanis ꝑat in tyme cuming all sic sumpteous bankating
be laid doun aluterlie Except thre sobir and honest viz
vpouñ ꝑe senʒe day ꝑe first sonday of may and ane Iunion [2]
vpouñ tuisday eftir pasche day And na honest man to paß
to ony of ꝑair bankettis Except on ꝑe said thre dais allanerlie And in place of ꝑe forsaid superflouß banketing to be
had and maid ʒeirly to generall plais or ane at ꝑe lest with
dansß & gammes vsit and wont And quhasoeuer refuisis to
accept ꝑe said office in tym cuming beand elekit ꝑairto be
ꝑe toun to tyne his fredome priuelege takis and profitt
he hes or ma haf of ꝑe toun and neuer to be admittit frathinfurth to office honour nor dingnete

388 The counsell ordanis ꝑe denis of gild to pay to patrik
menʒes [3] and thomas nicholsoun [3] lordis of bonacord of ꝑis
last ʒeir bigane ꝑe sowme of tuenty merkis betuix ꝑis and
vitsonday nixt cumis In satisfactioun of ꝑe compositioun
of ane freman quhilk wes grantit to ꝑam for ꝑair suport

390 21st April 1553

lordis of
bonacord The said day ꝑe prowest & ballies decernyt &
ordanit alexander Scot ane of ꝑe lordis of bon-
acord of ꝑis instant ʒeir to deburß satify & pay
to patre lesly his nychtbour & colleg of ꝑe said office, ꝑe

[1] 1552 in MS. and A.C.R. (Spald. Club).
[2] A.C.R. (Spald. Club) omits and leaves a blank.
[3] Members of Council, Oct. 1552 ; XXI, 225.

Iust & equall half of all expensſß necessar ꝑat he debursis
for ꝑe honeste & plesour of ꝑis gud toune *conforme* to ꝑe
last act & statut mayd ꝑairupoune in making of bankatis
playis farsis da*n*sis & games *con*forme to ꝑe ald & ancient
ryt vsit obefor

1*st Sept.* 1553 496

The baillies chargit patre men3es in Iugeme*n*t to releif
*willia*m barclay at ꝑe handis of Io*h*n chalm*e*ris wif of ꝑe
half of saxtene š viij đ scottis money ffor tua gallonis of
wyne resauit be ꝑe said *willia*m fra hir in ꝑe said patrik*is*
name and *thoma*s nicholsonis as lordis of bonacord in
a*nn*o fyfty tua 3er*is* qu*h*ilk ꝑe said *willia*m Is actit for to
ꝑe said Io*h*n chalm*e*ris wif

26*th Jan.* 1553/4 594

The ballies chargit alex*ande*r scott ane of ꝑe Lordis off
bonacord for ꝑis instant 3eir to pay Iohnne andersonis
wif sewin š iij đ wit*h*in xxiiij houris of ꝑe rest of ane ba*n*ket
maid be hir in hir awi*n* howſß in may lastbypast at *com*mand
of ꝑe said alex*ande*r scott And patrik lesly his marrow quhilk
wes sufficiently prowine in Iugement And ꝑat in compleit
payme*n*t of ꝑe said alex*an*dris ꝑart of ꝑe said bankett

15*th March* 1554/5 XXII, 3

peticio
men3es
My Lord prouest and baillies of ꝑis guid toune
of abirden vnto 3o*ur* m/ humily menis and
*com*plenis I patrik men3es burgis of ꝑe said
bur*gh*t vpoune Thomas nicolsoune combur*gis* of ꝑe sami*n*
That q*uh*ai*r* in ꝑe 3eir of god mvᶜ fyfty tua 3eiris in ꝑe
monet*h* of may or ꝑairby we bea*n*d lordis of bonacord
wit*h*in ꝑe said bur*gh*t for ꝑe tym we botht Togidder ane
last of beir fra ane duyche ma*n* for ꝑe sowme of xvj ħ xvj š
of ꝑe q*uh*ilk I pait for my ꝑart viij ħ viij š scottis money
q*uh*ilk haill last of beir wes input in ꝑe said Thomas sallar &
disponit be hi*m* as he thocht guid & sua I want compt &
rakni*n*g of my half ꝑairof forsaid And siclyk ꝑat Ilk tyme
I coft sax barrell of beir fra dauid king and patrik mal-
eaoune q*uh*ilk cost vj ħ viij š ꝑat wes ru*n*in in my howſß
at ꝑe said thomas *com*mand and my*n* of ꝑe q*uh*ilk his ꝑart
ꝑairof extend*is* to iij ħ iiij š And as 3it hes gottin na payment ꝑairof And als he is awa*n*d me ten š for ane crovne
ꝑat he tuik fra alex*ande*r men3es q*uh*ilk ves Liand in plege

ꝑairof of ꝑe quhilkis premisſ ꝑe said Thomas vrangovslie
& aganis ꝑe lawe postponis and deferris to mak ane pament
of ꝑe same To my hewy dampnage & skaith without he be
compellit ꝑairto be iustice Beseikand heirfor ȝour m/
prouest & baillies forsaidis to decerne caus and compell
ꝑe said Thomas be iustice to refound content and pay to
me ꝑe forsaid sowmes of money abouñ vritin reparatioune
for ꝑe causſ forsaid insafar as he will grant or ꝑat I ma
sufficientlie preif According to iustice And gyf neyd be
ꝑis my complent to be reformit of newe And to haf ꝑe
strynth of ane peticioune gyd neid beis

XXIV, 415 *4th May* 1562

The said day Iohnn Kelo belman wes accusit in Iugement
for ꝑe passing throw ꝑe rewis of ꝑe toun with ꝑe hand
bell be oppin voce to convene ꝑe haill communite or sa
mony ꝑairof as wald convene to paſ to ꝑe wood to bring
in symmer vpoun ꝑe first sonday of maij contravinand ꝑe
actis and statutis of ꝑe quenis grace and lordis of consell
eppeirandlie to raiſ tumult and Ingener discord betuix ꝑe
craftismen and ꝑe fre burgesſ of gild and ꝑe saidis craftismen to dissobey and adtempt aganis ꝑe superioris of ꝑe
toun gif it stuid in ꝑair power as ꝑe saidis prowest and
baillies ar informit The said Iohnne hawing na command
of ꝑe saidis prowest and baillies to do ꝑe same And inlykwyiſ
alexander burnatt alias potter wes accusit for passing throw
ꝑe toun with ane swech to ꝑe effect and occasioun aboun
wrytin Quhilkis Iohnne and alexander confessit ꝑe samyñ
alleigand thai did ꝑe samyn of na ewill mynd bot conforme
to ꝑe auld wse and be command of Iohnne grant quha is
ane fre burgeſ and brothir of gild and had done na wrang
ꝑairin as ꝑai alleigit And ꝑe said Iohnne grant inlykmaner
beand accusit for giffing command to ꝑe saidis Iohnne and
alexander as is aboun wrytin and passing throw ꝑe toun
fortifeing and menteining ꝑame as he mocht to ꝑe effect
forsaid, grantit and apprewit ꝑe same and denyit ony
wrang done be him ꝑairintill Quhilk mater wes put to ꝑe
decisioun and knawleg of ꝑe assiſ aboun wrytin chosin
suorne and admittit in Iugement quhilkis accepit ꝑe said
mater on ꝑame and efter detfull consultatioun & con-
sideratioun ryplie awisit enterit in court fand and deliuerit
all in ane voce be ꝑe moutht of gilbert menȝes elder chancellar of ꝑe said assiſ for ꝑe tyme that ꝑe saidis personis

had grytlie wrangit in ꝑe *com*mitting of ꝑe said enormitie
and hey*ch*t atemptat but ꝑe awiſs of ꝑe *pro*west baillies and
superioris of ꝑe toun [Ordered to appear next Sunday in
the Parish Kirk and ask forgiveness] [And] gif ꝑai be *con*-
victit for sic offens in tym *cum*ing to tyn ꝑair fredome
proffit and *pri*velege of ꝑis guid toun and to be seperat
and exulat fra ꝑe societie ꝑair*of* frathinfurtht and quha
of ꝑame dissobeyis ꝑe said ordinance to incur ꝑe samyn
pane but fauo*ur* or request to be hard in ꝑe *con*trar

[On 11th May John Grant is accused for not making amends 423
on Sunday.   Loses his freedom and is expelled.]

11*th May* 1565   XXV, 574

The said day henry m*er*schell Is *con*vickit for being in
*con*ventioun w*ith* his colleggis in making of robin huid &
litill Iohnne aganis ꝑe act of *par*liament & *con*temptioune of
ꝑe prowest baillies & charge gewin be the belman at thair
*com*mand Quhairfor he was *com*mandit to sit doune vpoune
his kneis And ask ꝑe prowest & baillies & *con*sell forgifnes
of ꝑe said offens And gif eu*er* he beis *con*vickit for sic offens
in tym *cum*ing to be baneist of ꝑis toune

14*th May* 1565   577

The said day Iohnne kelo belman maid faytht in Iugement
that he at *com*mand of ꝑe prowest and baillies past oñ
setterday was viij daiſs viz ꝑe v day of maij & oñ setterday
last was viz ꝑe xij day of maij throw all the rewis and
gettis of this toune be oppin voce And maid inhibitioune
to all burges men craftismen & all vtheris inhabitantis &
induellaris of ꝑe said toune That nane of thame tak vpone
hand to mak ony *con*ventioune w*ith* taburne plaing on
pype or fedill or haue anseing3es to *con*vene ꝑe quenis legis
in chesing of robin huid litill Iohnne abbot of ressoune
queyne of maij or siclyk to *con*traveyne ꝑe statutis of *par*-
liament or mak ony tumult scism or *con*ventione
The said day Iames masar lourens masar mathow guild
thomas huntayr & androw wysma*n* war conuickit for ꝑe
*cum*yng throw ꝑe toune vpon sonday last wes eftir none
w*ith* ane me*n*strall playand befor ꝑaim thro*w* ꝑe gallow-
gett In *con*temptioune of ꝑe townis actis & *pro*clama*ti*onis
maid obefor & breaking of ꝑe actis of parliame*nt* & *con*-
travening of ꝑe same*n* q*uhai*rfor ꝑai war put In am*er*cia-

ment of court and war ordanit to remane In ᵹe tolbut*h*
qu*h*ill ᵹai find sou*e*rte for fulfilling and satisfeing of ᵹe
eme*n*d*is* to be modifyt be ᵹe *con*sall

580 18*th May* 1565

[Minute on the ' dischargeing of masaris guild wysma*n* &
huntar*is* fredome.']

588 28*th May* 1565

[The whole town was summoned and the above statute
was explained to them.]
[The provost has been to Edinburgh in connection with
the above " enormiteis " and reads the following letter
from the Queen] :

590   Marie be the grace of god queyne of scottis, To
The quenis   the provest and ballies of ᵹe burgh of abirdene
Lettres vpoun
craftismen   greting fforsamekill as be ᵹe *com*plaint laitlie
           maid to ws in ʒour name we haue vnderstand
quhow certane seditious p*er*sonis craftismen cutlaris baxter*is* saidlers swerdslipparis cordinaris blaksmyt*his* gold-
smyt*his* cowparis barboris and vᵹeris within our said burght
p*ro*wokit to a certane bauld raschnes throw ᵹe publica-
tioune of our l*ett*rez laitlie grantit in fauoris of ᵹe honest
craftismen of our borrowis hes in thair maner schakine
of all debtfull obedience aught to ʒow our maiestratis
And *con*temptuuslie and malignantlie refusis to obey ᵹe
louabill actis and *con*stitutionis maid be ʒow for keiping
of *ou*r said burght in decent ordour and quietnes As alsua
expreslie *con*trar the tennor of *ou*r actis of p*ar*liament hes
arrogantlie atte*m*ptit in this instant monet*h* of maij to
elect amangis thame selffis Robene hude and Litil Iohnne
And to mak oppine *con*vocatioun in weirlyk maner alsweill
oñ the sabbaoth as vᵹeris prophane dayis Tending as
appeiris to na thing vᵹer bot a plane seditioune and wproar
and witht tyme to aspure vnto farther Lice*n*tious libertie
gif thair temerarius attemptatis be no*ch*t quiklie repressit
[Their punishment is approved by the Queen. She com-
mands them also to pass immediately to the Market Cross
and command all craftsmen to obey the laws of town and
parliament under pain of loss of freedom . . . At Stirling,
23rd May 1565.]

9th July 1565   621

[The craftsmen assure the authorities ' ᵽat thai menit no
evill nor ȝit did ony thing in *contem*ption of the maiestratis
of this bur*ght*.' They ' obleist thame selff*is* to abstene fra
sic enormiteis in ty*m* cu*m*ing ' and were restored to freedom.]

28th Sept. 1571   XXVII, 584

Bonacord
Smytht

The Bailȝeis ordanis alex*ande*r smyt*h* to co*n*tent
refound and pay to the Lordis of Bonacord
auc*ht* salmound fysche wit*h*in auc*ht* dayis

(b)

27th Nov. 1542   XVII, 328

ordinans for
resaving
of sanct
nicolas
Byschoip

The sayd day ᵽe haill co*n*sell pr*esen*t for ᵽe
tyme all In ane voce ordanit ᵽat ᵽe maist*er* of
ᵽair gram*m*ar scuyll sall haf iiij š scott*is* of ᵽe
sobirest p*er*soun ᵽat resauis hi*m* & ᵽe byschop at
sanct nicholace day till h*is* vage at ᵽe leyst
and eu*er*e vd*er* honest me*n* to gif hi*m* at ᵽair plasour and
gyf ony honest ma*n* of ony reputat*i*oune od*er* craftisma*n*
or vd*er* hald*is* furt*h* ᵽe bischop & giff*is* hy*m̃* noc*ht* e*n*tres
he sall pay iiij š to ᵽe maist*er* & viiij š to ᵽe ballies oñ
forgewin for ᵽair vnlaw & ordanis ᵽe officiar*is* to pound
& distrenȝe for ᵽe sami*n* and ᵽat becauß It ves co*n*siderit
be ᵽai*m* ᵽat he hes na vd*er* fee to leif oñ lyk as h*is* pre-
decessou*ris* hed afor hi*m* & vd*er*is maist*er*is of vder scuilis

25th March 1546   XIX, 65

ᵽe maist*er*
of ᵽe gramm*er*
skuillis pro-
uisiouñ *etc*

The said day ᵽe counsale pr*esen*t for ᵽe tyme
co*n*sentit all in ane voce ᵽat maist*er* hew monro
maist*er* of ᵽe gram*m*er skuilhill of ᵽe said
burgh haue guid and thankfull pame*n*t of ᵽe
tovnñ of his ȝeirly pentiouñ of tene m*er*k*is* scottis mone
*con*forme to ᵽe act maid ᵽairupouñ abefore Salang as he
remanis co*n*tinevaly and techis in ᵽe said skuilhill as he
auc*ht* and suld do of ressouñ And als ᵽat eu*er*y honest
mañ fremañ wit*h*in ᵽe said burgh bayt*h* m*er*chandis and
craftismeñ ressaue him and ᵽe bischop at sanct nicholace
meß wit*h*in ᵽair houisß co*n*forme to ᵽe auld lovabill vse
of ᵽe said burgh and gif him ᵽair wagis of ᵽe auld man*er*
efferand to ᵽair estatis as ᵽa think expedient And gif ony
honest mañ m*er*chand or craftismañ ᵽat ma guidly gif his
wag*is* ressauis him noc*ht* and ᵽe bischop at ᵽe said tyme

That he sall complane oñ þe dissobeyar*is* to þe bailȝeis þat
hapnis to be in office for tyme and þa to caus him haue
his quyte of þame be þe aviſſ of þe counsale *con*forme
to þe auld vse of þis said burgh *etc*

XXVII, 211 *9th Jan.* 1569/70

[Supplication presented ' be Epistill in Latein ' by the
scholars of the Grammar School concerning the abrogation
of their old privileges and liberties. Protest by the master.
The Council decide that the scholars ' sall haif previlege
and Libertie to remaiñ fra the scuill þai keipand guid ordour
quhair þai pleiſſ fra Sanct thomas evin befoir ȝoull quhill
vpouñ the morne efter þe epiphanie day allanerlie and all
wther preuilege of skaling q*uhi*lk was vsit at ony tyme in
þe ȝeir of befoir to be dischargit and abrogatit in all tyme
*cum*ing *etc.*']

XXX, 293 *21st Dec.* 1580

Ordinance
Anent þe
preuilege
of the
bairns

The said day þe prouost ballies and co*n*sale
reasony*ng* and *con*sulting vpon þe enormiteis
*com*mittit be disordourit barnis & scholaris of
þe gra*m*mer schuill of þis bur*gh*t and vþeris
schuilis wi*th*in þe same in taking of þe schuill
vsurping aganis þe maister & magistratis this tyme of ȝeir
afoir ȝuill callit natiuite of our lord þair by fosterand þe
ald ceremonie & rite of preuilege þat was wont to be gra*n*tit
to þame quhilk þe co*n*sell obefoir throchlie aduysit hes
altogedder abrogatit and dischargit for remeid þair of þat
Na sic attemptatis nor enormiteis be *com*mittit in ony
tyme heireftir The prouest balles and co*n*sale hes statut &
ordanit þat in all tyme *cum*ing all gentilma*n*nis soneis to
landward as burgesſſ soneis wi*th*in þe bur*gh*t þat sall
happy*n* to be *pre*sentit to ony maister of schuill wi*th*in
þis bur*gh*t The scholar & bairne salbe be þe maister to
quhome he is enterit be presentit to þe prouost & ballies
or euir he be receavit wi*th*in ony schuill of þis bur*gh*t and
sall set cautiouñ of burgesſſ induellaris of ab*er*d*een* þat þe
scholar presentit sall obey þe magistrat & maister and sall
nawayis vsurpe aganis þame in halding of þe schuill or
attempting ony vþ*er* thing aganis þe ordinance of þe co*n*-
sell vnd*er* þe pane of ten poundis monie of penaltie to be
pait be þe cautionar for þe barne transgressing and ane
act to be maid þairoñ and þe barne & cautionaris name

registrat in ᵹe townis buikis and this act to be publist
oppinlie in ᵹe pulpit oñ sonday nixt

26th Dec. 1581

The said day ᵹe provest ballies & consale taking ordour
with ᵹe disordourit barnis & scholaris of ᵹe grammer
schuill of ᵹis burght quha presentlie hes takin ᵹe schuill
menyng to have ᵹe ald preuilege quhilk was wont to be
grantit to ᵹame at this tyme of ȝeir about ȝuill quhilk
altogidder ᵹe consale obefoir be dyuerſs actis & statutis
had dischargit remittit & dischargit frelie ᵹe saidis scholaris
of all offenceis bypast And statut & ordanit in presens of
ᵹe maister of ᵹe said grammer schuill and ᵹe maist part
of ᵹe saidis scholaris ᵹat na priuilege salbe grantit to ᵹame
nor na scholaris of ᵹe said grammer schuill nor ȝit na vᵹer
schuill within this burght at ᵹe tyme of ȝuill in na tym
cuming and in place ᵹairof ᵹe provest ballies & consale
ordanit ᵹe saidis scholaris to have in ᵹe begynnyng of ilk
raith or quarter in the ȝeir thre dayis makand in ᵹe haill
tuelf dayis in ᵹe ȝeir

C. Miscellaneous Entries.

11th Jan. 1444/5

Item eadem assisa dixit quod willelmus quhite sutor fouet
in domo sua et receptat lusores malorum ludorum in
dampnum veniencium ad istum burgum quare percipitur
sibi quod decetero de talibus non communicatur / aut inde
iusta querimonia non audiatur sub pena exulacionis ab
isto burgo

4th March 1462/3

Eodem die duncanus de byrsſs receptus fuit in liberum
burgensem et confratrem gilde ad fauorem consilii sibi
concessam pro duabus togis deliberatis histrionibus nostris
ad festum pasche eiusdem anni qui prestitit Iuramentum
solitum

1st March 1481

Item ᵹe assise deliuerit ᵹat ᵹe said dauid gethane had
brokin commoñ ordinance in ᵹe denying of mett & wage

giffing to þe *commoñ* menstralis of þis burgh quharfor he
was adiugit *in* am*er*ciam*ent* and to gif þe said me*n*stralis
þare met & wage in tyme tocu*m*

VII, 386 18*th* **Jan.** 1492/3

The saide day it was statut . . . . . . þat Ionhe & Robert
thar *com*mone me*n*st*r*alis sal haue resonabile diet*is* circualie
throw the nichtbo*ur*is of the towne Ande gif ony p*er*sone
or p*er*so*n*s refuſs to resaue þame to þ*air* diet*is* it salbe lesum
to þame to gif to þe said menstral xij đ one the day bat*h*
for mett d*r*ink*is* & wag*is* for simpile folk*is*

VIII, 241 24*th* **July** 1503 [1]

Assignacio
x ħi ſusvribus
communibus

The saide day þe ald*irman* balȝeis & consale
assignit to thar *com*mone menstrallis tene ħi to
be takin fra þe denys of gilde to furnyſs thame
to þe passage wit*h* þe ald*irman* & vþ*er*is hon-
*orab*le nyc*h*tbo*ur*is to þe fest of our Soue*r*ane lord*is* mariage
at *com*mavnde of his hienes & to þe plesou*r* of h*is* maieste

1182 5*th* **May** 1511 [2]

The quenys
propin

[The Council unanimously] consentit to Ressaue
oure Soue*r*ane lady þe queyne als hon*or*ablie as
ony burgħ of scotland except edinburgħ allanerlie and to mak als larg expenſs þairapone as þe p*r*ouost
and counsail diuiſs for þe honou*r* of þe towne and plesou*r*
of hir gud grace . . . . . .

[Arrangements for raising the money and cleaning the
town.]

1183 10*th* **May** 1511 [3]

for þe star*is*

Item it was statut and ordanit þat all personis
duelland vteucht þe forgait in þe bakstretis [4]
samony as salbe warnit & chargit þairto & billit be þe
prouost & bailȝeis furnys & graitht þe star*is* of þe forgait
wit*h* arreſs werk daily as effer*is* vnd*er* þe pane of ilk p*er*sone
þat beis requirit þairto & furnisſs noc*h*t þe samyñ of (*blank*)

[1] *A.C.R.* (*Spald. Club*), 1501.   [2] *Ibid.*, 4th May.
[3] *Ibid.*, 10th May 1501.   [4] *Ibid.*, ' bak steris.'

s̃ vnforgevin for ỹe Ressaving of our Souerane lady ỹe queyne

[13th May, and subsequently, arrangements for raising money for Queen's entry.] [1]

16th April 1526 XI, 701·4

[Arrangements for an 'honest propyne' to the King—wax, wine, scorcheatis, etc. Methods of raising money, as the good town is 'superexpendit']. . . . Thir ar ỹe personis & sovmes promist be ỹame to ỹe furnessing of ỹe said propyne Togiddyr with all pageantis & sportis & plesand pastymes quhilk salbe diuisit to ỹe plesour of oure said souerane lord hiṣ mast noble lordis of Counsell & yair tryne

3rd Oct. 1541 XVII, 5

[Certain persons chosen, including the provost and bailies,] to dewyſ ane certane sowme of money for ỹe decoryng & preparing of ỹis gud toune agane ỹe quenis cuming and to propyne hir eftir ỹair power as ỹe ald wſ hes bene within ỹe burght at ỹe first cuming of princis And to consult & considder ỹe mayst eisy way quhow ỹe said sowm of money ma be gottin . . . [2]

12th Jan. 1561/2 XXIV, 324

propyne devysit to ỹe quenis grace

The said day thomas menȝes prowest exponit to ỹe consell ỹat he is suirlie informit ỹat ỹe quenis grace is to cum to ỹe north partis to vesy ỹe same betuix ỹis and peace nixt to cum or ỹairby And ỹat it is nocht onknawin to ỹame of hir grace

[1] Dunbar, The Quenis Reception at Aberdeen, S.T.S., II, 251, mentions pageants of the 'salutatioun,' the offering of the 'orient kingis thrie,' and the expulsion from Paradise, the representation of the genealogy of the Stuarts, the playing and singing of 24 maidens, the decoration of the streets with tapestry, &c.

[2] Cf. Leslaeus, De Origine Moribus et rebus gestis Scotorum, 1675, 430 : 'Rex deinde ac plurima nobilitas Reginam ad Aberdonensem Academiam comitabantur : in qua cives ac scholastici, officiis diversis, illi triumphis publicis, hi exercitationibus privatis, animos voluntatesque suas certatim conabantur declarare. Nam nulla effluxerat dies, in qua aut comoediae in theatrum non inducerentur, aut controversiae ex omni artium genere depromptae non agitarentur, aut orationes in Graeca Latinaque lingua, summo artificio instructae, non haberentur, aut aliae id genus exercitationes non instituerentur.' The Scots version of Lesley's History, Bannatyne Club, 1830, 159, has : 'and fra that maid journay to Aberdene, the King being alsua in company, and wes ressavit thair with diverse triumphes and playes maid be the town, and be the university and sculis theirof, and remanit thair the space of fiftein dayes, weill intertenit be the bischop quhair their wes excersise and disputationes in all kind of sciences, in the colledge and sculis, with diverse oratiouns maid in Greke, Latine and uther languages . . ."

honorabill resauing at hir first entre and prencely propynis
giffin to hir grace in edinbur*ght* and du*n*de and v*p*er townis
*p*at hir grace hes veseit and inquirit *p*ame quhat *p*ai tho*ch*t
expedient to be dun *p*ai*r*anent Quha all in ane voce dewisit
and ordanit *p*e sowme of tua thowsand me*r*kis to be vpliftit
for prepora*t*ioun and decora*t*ioun of *p*e toun and to be
propynit to hir grace as viſs hes bene in tymes bypast to
be done to king*is* and princis of *p*is realme at *p*air first
entre *with* co*n*sultat*i*oun to be had quhair *p*e said sovme
may be best easalie collekit and gottyn

498, etc. [26th August 1562 and subsequently, arrangements for
raising money for the Queen's entry. Expenses are to
exceed the sum originally voted.] [1]

XXIX, 98 25*th Jan.* 1576/7

[The deacons of the Hammermen, Baxteris, Cordiners,
Tailors, and Websters were accused] for thame selffis and
*p*e remane*n*t of thair craft for *p*e ma*n*tening of *p*e tuentie
fyft day of december last bipast as 3will day halding *p*e
same halyday and absteni*n*g fra labour for *p*e maist p*art*
with festing and playing co*n*trar *p*e tenno*u*r of *p*e act maid
be my lord regent /g/ and lordis of secreit counsell at his
being in Abirdene vpoun *p*e auchtene day of august *p*e
3eir of god Jmvc threscoir fourtene 3eiris [2] quha anſserit
that thay and *p*e remane*n*t of thair craft that was suspectit
of *p*e said Innormortie war callit and accusit thairfoir befoir
*p*e minister and essemblie of *p*e kirk, and at thair desyir
purgit thame selffis thairof particularlie ilkane for him
selff vpoun his consciens And lykwayis *p*e sadis decanis
prese*n*tlie at *p*e desyir of *p*e counsell purgit thame selffis
on thair consciens that thay ma*n*tenit noth *p*e said superstitious festuall dayis nor knew noth ane of thair craft
that ma*n*tenit *p*e same*n*. And *p*e counsell ordanit thame
to obſserue *p*e said act and ordinance of *p*e dait forsaid
in tymecu*m*ing, And geiff thay come in *p*e co*n*trar ilk
decain to pay fyve markis and ilk craftisman fourtie ſ to

---

[1] See also *Calendar of State Papers (Foreign) Elizabeth*, V, 319: 23rd Sept.
1562. ' On Tuesday last she arrived at Old Aberdeen, preparing herself against
her entry the next day into the new town, where she was honorably received
with spectacles, plays, interludes, and other things as they could best devise.'
[2] *Register of the Privy Council*, II, 390: 18th August 1574. ' Certane in-
junctionis to the Provest and Baillies of Abirdene. (1) That thay suld inhibite
and expreslie punishe the superstitious keping of festuall dayis usit of befoir
in tyme of ignorance and papistrie, and all playis and feisting at thay tymes . . .'

be applyit to ꝑe hospitall and to sett cautioun for ꝑe samin.
And ilkane of ꝑe saidis decanis become cautioun for thame
selff and thair awin craft.[1]

13th *May* 1580

[The Provost informs the Council that the King is shortly
to visit the town] And ꝑat it is nocht onknawin to ꝑame of
ꝑe rait and lowabill consuetud of ꝑis realme obſ̄eruit [2]
perpetuallie [2] in all tyme bigane And ꝑat at quhatsumeuir
tyme his grace progenitouris kyngis of scotland of gud
memorie happynnit to visie and repair to ꝑe maist honorabill burrowis of ꝑis realme ꝑat at ꝑe tym of ꝑair first entre
and presentatiouñ of ꝑame selffis ꝑairto Thay vſ̄ to receaue
ꝑair said souerane lord and kyng with willing and glaid
hartis schawing significatiouñ ꝑairof at ꝑair vtermaist
power to recreat [3] and glaid ꝑe kyngis maiestie with fasceis,
playis, historeis, antikis & sic vther decoratiouñ as was
thocht expedient for ꝑe tym And also To propyne ꝑair
graces with ane honorabill propyne of gold, walx and
spyce and vther prouisiouñ to ꝑe furnesing of his g/ houſ̄
And specialie this burght was euir radie to do sic decoratioun and plesour at ꝑe first entre of ꝑair prince and kyng
at ꝑair vtermaist power according to ꝑair substance and
facultie. And Inquyrit at ꝑe communite being convenit
be lauchtfull warnyng as said is for ꝑe maist part to ꝑe
effect vnder writin gif ꝑai wald do ꝑe lyk now as ꝑair predecessouris burgessis & Inhabitantis of ꝑis burght did obefoir
gif it happynnit our said maister ꝑe kyngis grace to hald
furth his purpoſ̄ and progres in visiting this his /g/ puir
towne Of ꝑe quhilkis ꝑai all in ane voce but contradictioun
war glad content and consentit ꝑairto And for preparatioun
of ꝑe premissis consentit to collect lift and gadder ane
taxatiouñ of ꝑe sowme of thre thousand markis vsuall
monee of ꝑis realme. And for setting of ꝑe said stent and
taxatiouñ Nominat and chesit thir personis vnder wretin
[12 *names*] stentaris and taxtaris quha war sworne ꝑe
gryt aitht to stent ꝑe same vpon ꝑe Nychtbouris and
Inhabitantis of ꝑis burght ilk ane conforme to his substance
and facultie according to ꝑair conscience knawlege and
vnderstanding

---

[1] See below, in Excerpts from Aberdeen Kirk Session Records, under 16th
Feb. 1574.
[2] *A.C.R.* (*Spald. Club*) omits.
[3] *Ibid.*, ' receive.'

EXCERPTS FROM KIRK SESSION RECORDS.

16th Feb. 1573/4

The said day, inhibition made to the decanis of the cor
dinars, vobstars, telyers, and baxteris, to remoif all superstition and occasion thairof, in keeping of ony holy day,
or ony wther festuall dais quhilk wes vsit of auld tyme
befor : bot to keip only the Sabet day, callit the Sounday,
to be keipit in preiching and prayers.

24th April 1574

(Admonition given to the master of the ' sang schole ' to
give no play or privilege to scholars ' in the dayes dedicated
to superstition in Papistrie ')

30th Dec. 1574

(Fourteen women charged ' for plaing, dansin and singin off
fylthe carrolles on Yeull Day, at evin, and on Sonday, at
even, thairefter ')

18th Aug. 1574

Comperit Gilbert Menzies of Cowly, Maister Patrick Rutherfurd, Maister George Middiltoun, and Alexander Chalmer,
baillies of Aberdeen, quhilks wer admonyshit be my Lord
Regentis grace, in presence of the Lords of Secreite Counsal,
in maner and to the effect following :

That thay suld inhibite and expresslie pvnishe the superstitious keping of festuall dayis vsit of befoir in tyme
of ignorance and papistrie, and all playes and festing at
thai tymes. . . . [1]

9th Feb. 1575/6

(A woman fined ' for the abusing of hir selff in claything of
hir with mennes clayes at the like (wake) of George Elmislyes
wife ')

10th Jan. 1575/6

(Several women convicted as ' dansares in mennes claythes
vnder silence of nycht ').

[1] Cf. Excerpts from Burgh Records, p. 160 and n².

4th Aug. 1605

The said day, anent the delatioun geven in to the sessioun
aganis sum young men and young wemen of this citie, for
dansing throcht the towne togidder this last vlk, the tyme
of the brydellis ; the young men being cled in wemennis
apparell, quhilk is accompted abhominatioun be the law
of God that ony man suld put on wemennis rayment,
Deuteronomie 22, vs. 5 ; and the young wemen for dansing
opinlie with thame throw the streittis, with maskis on
thair faces, thairby passing the bounds of modestie and
schamefastnes, quhilk aucht to be in young wemen, namelie,
in a reformed citie : Quhilk mater being referrit to the
provinciall assemblie, haldin at this burt in this vlk immediatlie begane, to be judged be thame quhat punischment
suld be inflicted vpon suche offendaris in tyme cumming,
thay fand . . . that if any man or woman be convict in
the lyk monstruous behaviour in tyme cumming, to vit,
ather men dansing in wemennis apparell, or wemen in
mennis apparell, or yitt gif wemen be fund dansing publictlie throw the streittis maskit and disagysit in sic a
wantoun and vnchast forme, in cumpanie with men, that
the doaris sall pay a pecuniall penaltie to the puir, according
to the modificatioun of the sessioun, as also mak thair
publict repentance on the stuill, for the first fault ; and
for the secund fault, sall mak thair publict repentance in
sack cloth, conforme to the act of the said provinciall
assemblie sett doun thairvpon : quhilk act is ordanit to
be intimat from pulpitt on Sonday nixt, that nane pretend
ignorance thairof in tyme cumming.

29th Dec. 1605

(Five men accusit of being 'fosteraris of superstitioun in
going throch the towne maskit and dansing with bellis on
Yuill day last at night.' Intimation to be made from the
pulpit 'that nane gang throch the towne on Newyeiris
evin singing any songis ')

19th Jan. 1606

(Ordained that 'na man nor woman in this burght about
the superstitious tyme of Yuill or Newyeris day, or ony
vther superstitious tyme, sall presume to mask or disagyse
thame selffis in ony sort, the men in wemennis claythis,
nor the wemen in mennis claythis, nor vtherwayes, be dans-

ing with bellis, ather on the streittis of this burt or in privat houss, in ony tyme cumming . . .' The five men accused above of the said crime are admonished.)

14th May 1609

(William Stewart, fiddler, warned to refrain from ' his wounted superstitioun, in playing & singing the Sondayes of Maij, in the morning.')

ARBROATH.

[Manuscript records in the burgh archives : (1) Burgh Court Book, 1491-1550, 8 fol., fragments ; (2) Burgh Court Book, c. 1528-30, 38 fol. ; (3) Burgh Court Book, 1563-75 ; (4) Regality Minute Book, 1605-47. So far as I could learn, no early craft or guildry records have survived. Detailed treasurers' accounts are inserted in the minute books only from 1605 onwards.]

2.   f. 5. *28th July* 1528

ꝑe ordinans to gyf xiij ſ & four ꝺ to ꝑe play the q*uhi*lk day ꝑe balȝeis *con*sall & *commun*ite hes ordand char*les* bro*un* [1] to gif a*ne* merk of monay to al. ly. & his *com*-panȝonis to by ꝑaim a*ne* barrell of ayll w*ith* to ꝑair play & ꝑe said m*er*k of monye to be allowit to ꝑe said C [2] *in* his compt

3.   f. 12. *11th May* 1565

grant fre

The q*uhi*lk daj thom̃ grant is maid fre ma*n* of ꝑe broith and hes maid ꝑe aith to ꝑe touñ as ws is and sall paj to my lord of rason vj ſ viij ꝺ

neill wallas
Ingreffi
ferrour } fre

The q*uhi*lk daj rob neyll ȝowng*er* andro wallas Iames Ingreffi Ihoñ ferro*ur* soñ to dauid ferro*ur* ar maid fre me*n* and hes maid ꝑe aith to ꝑe towñ as ws is for Ilk ma*n* half ane mark gyffy*n* to my lord of rasoñ

[Similarly, f. 13, 26th May 1565, James Durward and Rob Bardy are made freemen ' and ꝑair fredu*m* sillu*er* giffy*n* to my lord of rasoñ.']

---

[1] MS. ' char/br.'   [2] Charles (Brown).

AYR.

[Manuscript records in the burgh archives : Burgh Court
and Council Books, 1428-78, 1547-53, 1580-9, 1589-96,
1596-1606, 1598-1611 ; Accounts of the Common Good,
1535-1603, with gap, 1561/2-1574/5 ; Court Book of
Alloway, 1492-1535.]

17*th May* 1496
[At the Whitsunday Court of the lands of the Barony of
Alloway, ' ye abbat of wnresson ' appears as pledge for
Jame Lech in his loft.] [1]

1534/5
Item defalkit to hym for ayll & meitt to ye clerk play
viij ş ij đ [2]
Item to georde blayre to bye skynnis with to ye clerk play
xxviij đ [3]

1539/40
Item to Williame nesbit for robert hudis plais v merkis
Item alexander kennedy for ye samyñ plais ye ȝeir
ȝaireftir v markis [4]

1540
Item deliuerit to william nesbit at command of ye provost
& baitties for ye expensſś maid at ye triumphe of my
Lord ye princis birth   xvij tib [5]

1541
Item gevin to robert boymañ for powdir at ye birth of my
lord prince vj ş Item for sewing of ye townis arraſś
workis v đ. Item to maister patrik andersouñ for his
fe ye last witsounday v ti Item plus to ye said maister
patrik for his expensſś in ye clerk playis
xxvj ş viij đ

[1] Court Book of Alloway.
[2] Discharge of John Dalrymple.
[3] Discharge of Thomas Schanks, treasurer.
[4] Dean of Guild's account rendered Jan. 1540-41 for the past two years.
[5] Treasurer's account.

Iteɱ to william nesbit for vyne to ꝑe quenis grace

v ƚi

Item to ꝑe said william for tua quartis of vyne to ꝑe egiptianis quhen yai dansit to ꝑe baillies   iij s̃ iiij đ

Item for breid & vyne to ꝑe first clerk playis at ꝑe baillies
command   xv s̃ ij đ [1]

1542/3

Item to Robert hudis play   iij ƚi vj s̃ viij đ [1]

1544/5

Item ꝑe said androis expensſß quhen he wes robert hude
iij ƚi vj s̃ viij đ [2]

1546/7

Item to george duñ for ꝑe franchemennis lawingis in robert
hvdis playis   xxxv s̃ viij đ [3]

1547/8

Item in nicol gervanis handis x merkis quhilk suld haue
bene gevin to George dun and hew montsode quhen ꝑai
wer robert hude & litle Johnn [4]

18th Nov. 1549

Quo die William Wallace in qhytehouſß refferit to ꝑe Inqueist To enter to ꝑe fredome of burgesrie for his lawbouris
done ꝑe tyme ꝑat he wes robert hwde enterit for ꝑe samyñ
cauſß [5]

Quo Die Willelmus Wallace in le quhytehouſß factus fuit
burgenſß gratis pro suis laboribus et benemeritis per ipsum
factis tempore quo ipse factus fuit robertus capitius viz ;
le Robert hwde et Iuravit fidelitatem supreme domine
nostre Regine et communitati &c [6]

2nd Dec. 1549

Quo die Iohne campbƚe barbour desyrit to enter to ꝑe
fredome of burgesrie gratis for his lawbouris ꝑe tyme ꝑat
he wes litill Johne with williame wallace in quhythouſß ꝑat
wes robert hude for ꝑe tyme enterit be ressoñ forsaid [7]

---

[1] Treasurer's account.   [2] Account of Andrew Dalʒell, treasurer.
[3] Treasurer's account.   [4] Dean of Guild's account.
[5] Council Book, p. 128.   [6] *Ibid.*, p. 131.   [7] *Ibid.*, p. 133.

Quo die Joha*nn*es ca*mp*b*ł*e barbitonsoris factus fuit burgensis gratis pro suis laboribus tempore quo ip*se* fuit le
litiljohne vo*catus* Will*elm*o Wallace in qhytehouß le robert- twa *merkis*
hude pro tempore et Iuravit fidelitate*m* [etc.] [1]

1549/50

Item to Jo*hn*n Jamesone quhen he wes robene hude v
m*erkis* [2]

19*th May* 1550

Quo die Iohnne ada*m̃* cadger referrit to *ꝑ*e inqueist to
Enter to *ꝑ*e fredome of burgesschip for *ꝑ*e payme*n*t /
ent*er*it for *ꝑ*e payme*n*t w*ith* *ꝑ*is restrictio*ñ* *ꝑ*at he be
honestlie cled as ane honest man as effer*is* to ane burges
ma*ñ* to be betuey*ñ* & su*n*day nixt tocu*m* to serf robert hud [3]

1550/1

Item for *ꝑ*e expensß of four frenchmen quhen george dun
wes robene hude in his hous xl *š* . . . Item to charles
campbel quhen he wes robene hude v m*erkis*. Item to
ro*b*ert m*c*millane quhen he wes litle Johne v m*erkis* [4]

1553/4

Item for powder To robene hud*is* playis iiij *š* vj *đ* [5]

1557/8

Item for vyne at *ꝑ*e tryumphe of *ꝑ*e quenis mariage in
fraunce xviij *š* [5]

1560/1

(Payment for ' certane vynes at *ꝑ*e tryumphe of *ꝑ*e quenes
hamecumyng.') [5]

---

[1] Council Book, p. 134.
[2] Treasurer's account.
[3] Council Book, p. 156.
[4] Treasurer's account. Robert Macmillan was treasurer for this year.
[5] Treasurer's account.

CUPAR.

The date of the performance of the ' Satyre of the Thrie
Estaitis ' at Cupar is uncertain.   In the 1806 edition of
Lyndsay's Works, Chalmers argued in favour of 1535
(I. 60-1).   Laing, *Works of Lyndsay*, 1879, I. xxxiii., rejects
this theory ; and, reading the reference to Whitsun Tuesday
falling on the 7th of June in the ' Proclamatioun maid in
Cowpar of Fyffe ' in connection with the preceding heading
' Heir begynnis the Proclamatioun of the Play, made be
Dauid Lynsayis of the Month, Knicht in the Playfeild, in the
Moneth of   , the yeir of God 155   yeiris '
(*Bannatyne Manuscript*, f. 164 a., Hunterian Club, 1896,
Vol. III.), fixes the date as 1552 (Laing, *op. cit.*, I. xxxiv.;
II. 363).   But it is possible that the year ' 155 ' given by
Bannatyne refers, not to the performance on the Castle
Hill, Cupar, but to that in the Greenside playfield at
Edinburgh (*Bannatyne Manuscript*, ff. 177 a, 210 a) ; in
which case the date must be determined by internal evidence.   In any case, if we are to accept the ' Auld Man
and his Wife ' as the ' cry ' for the ' Satyre,' the date 1535
is incorrect.   The only other dates within the period on
which Whitsun Tuesday fell on 7th June were 1530, which
is too early for even Chalmers's arguments, and 1541.   Unfortunately, the burgh records of Cupar are no help.   There
are no treasurers' accounts ; and the only sixteenth century
Council and Court Book, 1549-53, ignores the event if it took
place in 1552.

DALKEITH.

[Manuscript Presbytery Records, Vol. I., 1582 - 1630,
in the custody of the Clerk to the Presbytery.   Only partially examined.]

EXCERPTS FROM MS. PRESBYTERY RECORDS.

f. 17 [1] *24th May* 1582

Ordanis the haill *personis* ꝑat ar defender*is* taker*is* vpoun
thame to raſ vp or play abbott of vnressones play*is* or

---

[1] There is some confusion in the binding of the folios in this volume.

robene hud*is* to be varnit aga*ne* this day aucht dayis & gif
thay dissobay the disciple of the kirk salbe pit in executio*n*

6*th Sept.* 1582.

The q*uhi*lk day compeirit m*aiste*r andro alane being accusit
for the priuie co*n*ferri*ng* wit*h* m*aiste*r ro*b*ert m^c garie being
excom*uncat . . . . . .* And as tuiching his play as playit
in the castell of Dalkeyt*h* wit*h*out Licence of the eld(er)schip
ordanit tua of the bretheren to sycht his . . . . . .[1]

27*th June* 1583

Item the said day It wes complanit be the said m*aiste*r
george *p*at the lard of drydane eldar semit negligent in
no*ch*t causing   [2] tail3o*u*r and   [2] scott
his tenna*n*tes to satisfie the kirk for p*r*ophanatio*n*e of the
sabboth day be the vsing of may playis *p*airon. The said
lard being present a*n*swered as co*n*cerni*ng* the first man he
knew him not bot as to *p*e v*p*er he p*r*omisit to cau*fs* him
satisfie the kirk for his offens as accordis

4*th July* 1583

prophaneris
of the
sabboth (in)
lesswaid
The q*uhi*lk day also the p*er*sonis m*aiste*r george
Ramsay co*m*plenit vpon in the visita*t*io*n*e of
lesswaid we*fs* ordanit to be su*mm*ondit to *p*e
nixt furesday to a*n*f*s*er to the headis of the sam
co*n*cerni*ng* the prophanatio*n*e of the sabboth day wit*h*
Ro*b*ert hude & litill Ihone & may playis

12*th* Sept. 1583

The q*uhi*lk day also Ihone Abell wit*h* the rest of his band
p*r*ophaner*is* of the sabboth be Ro*b*ene huidis play in lesswaid we*fs* callit and *p*air co*m*perit for thame Ihone sincleir
of drydane 3onger q*uh*a excusit thame becaus of sindrie
thing*is* q*uhi*lk*is* occurrit and p*r*omisit in name of the said
Ihone abell his *fs*ervant and the rest of his fa*p*eris *fs*ervantis
& te*n*nantes q*uh*a wor callit and accusit for p*r*ophani*ng* of
the sabboth to caus thame wit*h* all humilitie to submit
thame to the ordina*n*ce of kirk in all poyntis for the offence

---

[1] The last word in the Minute has faded, and is now quite illegible.
[2] Blank in MS.

*com*mitted be thame [The matter was remitted to their own minister in Lasswade.]

Part II. 30*th April* 1590

f. 23 The q*uhi*lk day c*er*tane p*er*sons of cranstone bei*n*g called as ȝej wer su*mund* be m*aiste*r ada*m* Iohnestone & not *com*pera*nd* y*air* cryme bei*n*g ȝe p*ro*phana*ti*one of ȝe sabbath day be maij playſs It was statut ȝ*at* i*n* visita*ti*one of ȝ*at* kirk sik ordor suld be taken w*ith* ȝame aſs might stay vȝ*er*s i*n* tyme cu*m*i*ng*
Ite*m* ȝ*at* day it is statut ȝ*at* ȝe haill brethren giue publick admoni*ti*one ȝe nixt su*n*day i*n* ȝ*air* pulpit*is* ȝ*at* nain of ȝ*air* p*er*oschiner*is* p*re*sume to uſse may playes vpo*n* ȝe su*n*day wnd*er* pain off ȝe censuris of ȝe kirk to stryk vpo*n* thame

f. 25 *b* 28*th May* 1590

Cranstoun

The q*uhi*lk day co*m*p*er*it [13 men] as they wor su*mmon*dit to ȝ*at* day for p*ro*phani*ng* the sabboth w*ith* pasch playis as robene hud*is* abbott*is* vnresson *etc* and being accusit ȝ*air*foir *con*fessit their falt & submittit thame to ȝe kirk. The breȝ*er* vnderstanding the no*m*ber to be gret & the haill to stand to be bot ane mokage as also haifing sure intelligence the first thrie weſs the autho*uris* devyſs*eris* and tha quha bure the office of Robene hud*is etc* tho*ch*t best seing thair enormitie lastit bot ane ho*ur* & weſs stayit in tyme be the *com*missionar m*aiste*r adam Ihonestoun q*uha* inco*n*tine*n*t send & su*mmon*d thame at ȝe hering of the swesch tymelie in the morni*ng* They ordanit the said first thrie to acknawlege ȝ*air* falt oppy*n*lie & mak ȝ*air* repentance ȝ*air*foir & becauſs ȝai wantit ane minister ordanit m*aiste*r Iames be*n*net to ressaif the sam aſs lykwyſs to baptiſs wattie me*n*teythis [1] barn q*uha* weſs tryit (?) to haif beine In ȝ*air* co*m*panie be compulsion & not vȝ*er*wyse

[1] One of the thirteen.

DUMFRIES.[1]

[Manuscript records in the burgh archives : Burgh Court
Books c. 1506-c. 1548, 1561-4, 1569-74, etc. Manuscript
accounts at Register House from 1590, with many gaps.]

EXCERPTS FROM MS. BURGH RECORDS. Vol. I.

31st July 1532   f. 117

Iohne mertin is maid burgeß & suorn ꝑairto & frely gevin
to ßir hary merßer for ꝑe play of gude fryday & vitsonday
payand xl ₫ to sanct mychellis werk borcht Iohn merting

9th Oct. 1534   f. 143

Quo die Iok wilsoun and wille thomsoun ar maid fre
burges and suorn ꝑairto frely gevin till Robin hude & litill
Iohne quhilk was chosin at pasche last was / ather of ꝑaim
payand xl ₫ to sanct (michellis) werk ꝑe spice & wyne . . .

27th April 1536   f. 164

Quo die ꝑe Inquest ordanis & deliueris ꝑe fredom of ij
sufficient men choissin be ꝑe gud toun to be gewin to robert &
litill Iohne swa ꝑat ꝑai be maid in ꝑe tolbuyth afoir ꝑe baillies
ane or ma payand sanct mychellis werk & clerkfe & officeris

14th June 1536   f. 168

Quo die Iohne pawtonson is maid fre burgeß & suorn
ꝑairto gevin to Robin hude & litill Iohne payand xl ₫ . . .

21st April 1537   f. 185

Quo die symeon crokket is maid fre burges & suorn ꝑairto
frelie gevin to Robin hude & litill Iohne . . . . . .

Vol. III.

17th June 1570

The quhilk day ꝑe provest ballies & consale ordanis herbert
ranyng elder to be payit for his taffiteis resauit fra hym at
paische lxx ȝeris of ꝑe first of ꝑe fredomes to be rasit to
ꝑe vse of robert huyd quhilk extendes to   pundis &

[1] I am indebted to Mr G. W. Shirley, Dumfries, not only for valuable information regarding the Dumfries records, but for his kindness in making a
final collation of my transcript with the original manuscripts.

allevin ℔ xj ℥ [1] money of this realm quhilk salbe admytit
to ꝑam in ꝑair compttis be this present

3rd Nov. 1570

The quhilk day ꝑe person of the counsale present fyndis
ꝑat thom trustre incurrit dissobedience at pasche lxx ʒeris
In safar as he vald nocht obbaye And accept on hym ꝑe
office of robert huyd & litill Iohn be resson of ꝑe sam͂ he is
decernit to pay of his expenſẜ lyik as archibald velsche vsit
in ꝑat office & to vnderly ꝑe chargeis for his dissobedience
as efferis & resave ꝑe fredoum of ane condigne burges & etc

dettis awand be ꝑe commond
item to bessie cunyngham for rest to paſẜ playis x ℥
item to Iames vallace at ꝑe pasche playis & for his raleiff

v ℔is x℥

DUNDEE.

[Manuscript records in the Burgh archives : The earliest
volume of the Register of Burgh and Head Courts commences 1520.   There is a gap in the Burgh Court Records
from 1524 to 1550, from which date a regular series of
19 volumes brings the records up to about 1600.   There
are separate Council Minute Books from 1553.   The Lokkit
Book, as now extant, dates from 1582, but the scribe has
copied entries from an earlier book dating from 1513.   The
earliest volume of Treasurers' Accounts runs from 1586 to
1606 ; but at Register House there are various odd compts
of the Common Good for 1574-5, 1575-6, 1576-7, 1580-1,
1581-2, 1582-3, and others from 1601 onwards with gaps.]

EXCERPTS FROM MS. BURGH RECORDS.[2]

ꝑe grayth of ꝑe prossession of corpus xp͂i deliuerit
ſẜir thomas barbour to kepyng

In primis iiixx of crownis vj pair of angel veynis iij myteris
cristis cott of lethyr with ꝑe hosſẜ & glufis cristis hed xxxj

---

[1] Originally, according to Mr Shirley, *two* blanks seem to have been left
for the insertion of the sum with the word 'pundis' between.   When the
sum was filled in, the scribe seems to have entered the wrong amount in the
first blank ; whereupon the whole sum was transferred to the second blank.

[2] Some of this material has already been used by Maxwell in his histories
of Dundee and by other local historians.

suerd*is* thre lang corßis of tre sanc tho*m*as sper a cors til sanc blasis sanc joħnis coit a credil & thre barnis maid of clath xx hed*is* of hayr ye four evangellist*is* [1] sanc kat*er*ins quheil sanc androwis cros a saw a ax a rassour a guly knyff a worm of tre [2] ye haly lam of tre sanc barbilł [3] castel abraamis hat & thre hed*is* of hayr [4]

4th April 1521

Rob huyd

Quo die ye p*ro*uost & balȝeis has gra*n*tit to Roby*n* huyd to ye biggene of ye buttis a burgesschip or v m*er*k*is* of mone ye next y*at* yai sall be *pres*ent to ye thesaurar & maid at h*is* will & ye balȝeis [5]

13th Sept. 1553

The q*uhi*lk day elspet ky*n*monthe is adiugit to delyver to Jhone fothringhame his trumpat q*uhi*lk ye said Jhone fothringhame lent to ye said williaȝ̃ in tyme of ye play at ye vestfeild [6]

21st Feb. 1568/9

Anent dansing and playing

Item it is statut and ordanit for eschewing of tumult seditioune drinking and vyer vncumlie insolans and vantownes and yat na persone pretend to cum furth of his awin lugeing w*ith* menstrallis or ony vyer maner of vay efter nyne houris at nycht to vse ony kynd of dansing drinking playing or sice wane exersyces vnder ye pane of ye breking of ye menstrallis Instrumentis and ya personis to be imp*re*sonit and nocht to depert q*uhi*ll yai pay xx s̃ to ye puer [7]

[1] Is a word omitted here ?

[2] Is this the serpent or a dragon ?

[3] Saint Barbara.

[4] This entry is found on f. 170 *b* of the earliest volume of the Burgh Court Register. Generally known as the 'Book of the Kirk,' this volume was miraculously preserved from destruction. Originally an inventory of the ornaments belonging to the altars of St Mary's Church, &c., the book came into the possession of the town clerk early in the sixteenth century, and the blank pages were used for court records. Many folios have been cut out. The above entry is undated, but probably belongs to the mid-fifteenth century.

[5] Burgh Court Register, I, f. 21.

[6] Burgh Court Register.

[7] Head Court Laws, 1550-1622, p. 56.

6th Oct. 1594

Anent Blasphemer*is* and monie vther vyces

. . . . . . And forder That ye actis maid anent drunkardis royatus bankates danseris nicht walkers maskingis and gysingis perturbar*is* of ye kirk and kirk3eard intym of sermone . . . . . be put in executioun aganis all transgresso*uris* yairof but respect to persoun [1]

6th Oct. 1595

. . . . . . And becaus the sabboth day hes bene maist slaunderouslie prophanit In tymes past be making of surffett & Ryotus banquet*is* yairvpon vsing of maski*ngis* gyissing*is* & vy*er* Insolenceis To ye dishono*ur* of god & slaunder of ye Relligiouñ qu*h*ilk hes procedit cheiflie fra ye solennizatioun of Mariagis vpon ye said sabbot*h* day . . . . . . It is statute w*it*h advyi*ſs* of ye Ministeris & elderis of ye kirk of ye said bur*ght* That Na mariages sall be solemnizit wit*h*in ye kirk of ye said bur*ght* vpon ye sabbot*h* day heirefter And yat na p*er*soun preswme to mak ony banquettis and feistis vpon ye said sabbot*h* day Or to vse ony maski*ngis* gyising*is* or Inordinat behavio*ur* ather in ye nicht seasoun or day efter ye xv day of October Instant In ty*me* cu*ming* at ye lest ay & qu*h*ill ane mair substa*ntious* ordo*ur* be sett douñ yair*anent* be advyi*ſs* of ye kirk vnder ye pane of ane hundret*h* ɫib to be vptane of ye contravenare heirof but respect to p*er*souñ [2]

3rd Oct. 1597

[The Court has under consideration the ' sclanderous behaveo*ur* of c*er*tane personis Inhabitantis of yis bur*ght* quha keipis superstiouslie c*er*tane dayis specialie 3ull day Be absteni*ng* fra yair handiewark & Laubo*ur* yairvpoñ closing of yair buth doris and spending that day In ge*mming* or vy*er*wayis Idlie / to ye offence of god . . . . . . ' Penalties to be attached.] [3]

. . . . . . fforder ye said*is* provest & balleis co*n*saill & commintie Ratiffeis and approvis ye auld actis maid anent ny*ch*twalkeris danseris vseris of masking(is) & gysingis Ryotous banketteris specialie on ye sabbot*h* day [*etc*] [4]

[1] Head Court Laws, 1550-1622, p. 74.   [2] *Ibid.*, p. 78.   [3] *Ibid.*, p. 80
[4] *Ibid.*, p. 82.   Similarly, p. 100, and Council Book, I, 131.

9th Jan. 1595/6

To thomas kinneir for bigging the scafhold the tyme the
    barnis of the school playd   5 ŝ

To *willia*m authinlect for bigging ane scafhvld wpon the
    head of the scafhold   3 ŝ 4 đ

for carying of dealis and puncheonis wit*h* wther furnich-
    ment to the said play   13 ŝ 8 đ [1]

Excerpt from Calderwood's History of the Kirk of Scotland.
Wodrow Society. I. 142.

This James (Wedderburne) had a good gift of poesie, and
made diverse comedeis and tragedeis in the Scotish tongue,
wherein he nipped the abusses and superstitioun of the
time. He composed in forme of tragedie the beheading
of Johne the Baptist, which was acted at the West Port
of Dundie, wherin he carped roughlie the abusses and
corruptiouns of the Papists. He compiled the Historie of
Dyonisius the Tyranne, in forme of a comedie, which was
acted in the playfeild of the said burgh, wherin he likewise
nipped the Papists. He counterfooted also the conjuring
of a ghaist, which was, indeed, practised by Frier Laing,
beside Kingorne, which Frier Laing had beene confessor
to the king. But after this conjuring the king was con-
strained, for shame, to remove him.

DUNFERMLINE.

[Manuscript records in the burgh archives : Burgh Court
Books, 1488-1584 (printed by Erskine Beveridge, 1917),
1572-5, 1606-13.]

Edward I
1303-4.

Dona—Episcopus Puerorum in Nocte Sancti
Michaelis. Johanni filio Johannis le baillyf de
Dunfermelyn episcopo puerorum in capella
regis apud Dunfermelin in nocte Sancti Michaelis anno
presenti de dono ipsius regis per manus proprias apud
Dunfermelyn vj die Decembris xl s [2]

---

[1] Treasurer's Accounts.

[2] Bain, *Calendar of Documents relating to Scotland*, IV, 473. In both cases
' Michaelis ' should read ' Nich*o*lai.' See Brit. Mus. Addit. MSS., 8835, f. 42.

20th July 1574

(A case of ' strublance ' committed by two men ' vpone the sabbothe day being also the playday and maist confluence of peple convenit pairto.') [1]

1576

Anent the supplicatioun given in be the toun of Dumfer-line, for liberty to be granted them to play upon a Sunday afternoon, a certain play which is not made upon the Canonical parts of the Scripture : The Assemblie refuses to give libertie to the Bailzie of Dumfermling to play upon the Sonday afternoone, a certaine play quhilk is not made upon the Canonicall parts of the Scripture, in respect of the Act of the Assemblie past in the contrair ; exhorting the Bailie of Dumfermling, presenter of the bill, to requiest the toun to keep the ordinance of the Assemblie. [2]

27th July 1580

(Edinburgh Town Council) hes consentit and ordanit that Andro Steuinsoun, thesaurer, sall len and deliuer, in name of the guid town, ane of the townis anseingyeis to James Wemys of Pittincreif for owtsetting of the play to be maid at Dunfermeling ; and Hary Smyth merchant is become souerty to rander and deliuer the same agane to the said thesaurer, als haill, guid and sufficient as the same is pre-sentlie at the lenning thairof. [3]

1606 ?

In the first debursit be him to Margaret murray for aill furnischit be hir to the playeris vpoun the play day xxxij s [4]

2nd May 1609

(The Curis Capitalis ratifies former acts concerning night-walkers, drinkers, ' insolent dansaris and playaris throwcht the toun in the nycht.') [5]

[1] MS. Burgh Court Book.
[2] *Booke of the Universall Kirke*, I, 375.
[3] *Edinburgh Burgh Records, S.B.R.S.*, IV, 172.
[4] MS. Burgh Court Records, Treasurer's Account, 1605-6.
[5] MS. Burgh Court Book.

EDINBURGH.

[Four volumes of Burgh records, with index, have been published by the Scottish Burgh Records Society, 1869-92. *E.B.R. (S.B.R.S.)* Two volumes of *City of Edinburgh Old Accounts*, comprising Bailies' and Treasurers' Accounts, 1544-67, and Dean of Guild Accounts, 1552-67, were published by the Town Council in 1899. In addition to the above, which, where necessary, I have compared with the original manuscripts, I have made use of the following manuscripts in the Burgh archives : Guild Register, 1487-1579; Council Registers from 1589 to 1636 ; various volumes of Bailies', Treasurers', and Dean of Guild Accounts from 1568 onwards. Of the manuscript Presbytery records in the custody of the Presbytery Clerk, I have examined the first two volumes, 1586-1601, in detail, and a third volume, 1601-3, less exhaustively. The *Book of the General Kirk* has been printed in part by the Mait. Club, *Miscellany*, Vol. I., 1834, pp. 97-126. Few of the Craft records appear to have been preserved. *Extracts from the Minute Books of the Skinners of Edinburgh*, 1549-1603, were printed in the Old Edinburgh Club Publications, Vol. VI. I obtained permission to examine all the papers belonging to the Incorporation of Wrights, and found that a rough Minute Book, with very sparse entries from 1547-54, and a few loose pages, are all that have survived of the early period. Fortunately an excellent series of accounts of the Hammermen's Incorporation, which date from 1494, are still extant. Copious extracts from these were printed in *The Hammermen of Edinburgh and their Altar*, John Smith, 1906 ; but, as the transcript is inaccurate, and as several important items have been omitted, I have made a fresh transcript of the relevant portions from the original manuscript now in the custody of the city authorities.]

A. *Municipal Plays and Pageants at Royal Entries.—*
Excerpts from Burgh Records, etc.

15th May 1509

Wobsteris
Walkaris

The quhilk day the provest baillies counsale and kirk-maisteris hes consentit and ordanit that in tyme to cum baith the craftis—viz., webstaris, wakeris, and scheraris—in all tymes of pro-

M

cessioun quhair euir thair bannaris beis borne, that thai
pas togedder and be incorporat vnder ane baner in als
formis as thai pleis . . . and the said scheraris and
wakeris to pas vnder the bannar of the wobstaris quhill
thai may gudlie furnis thair awin, and the armys of the
said scheraris and wakeris to be now put in the webstaris
bannaris gif thai may be gudlie formit and gottin thairvntill [1]

7th August 1503

At the Entryng of the said Towne was maid a Yatt of
Wood painted, with Two Towrells, and a Windowe in the
Midds. In the wich Towrells was, at the Windowes, revested
Angells syngyng joyously for the Comynge of so noble a
Lady ; and at the sayd middle Windowe was in lyk wys
an Angell presenting the Kees to the said Qwene.

Within the Towne ny to the said Yatt came in Processyon
the College of the Perysche of Seint Gilles, rychly revested,
with the Arme of that Seint ; the wiche was presented to
the Kynge for to kysse ; wherof he did as before, and
began to synge Te Deum Laudamus.

In the Mydds of the Towne was a Crosse, new painted,
and ny to that same a Fontayne, castynge forth of Wyn,
and ychon drank that wold.

Ny to that Crosse was a Scarfawst maid, wher was represented Paris and the Thre Deessys, with Mercure, that
gaffe hym th Apyll of Gold, for to gyffe to the most fayre
of the Thre, wiche he gave to Venus.

In the Scarfawst was represented also the Salutacion of
Gabriell to the Virgyne, in sayinge Ave gratia, and sens
after, the Sollempnizacion of the varey Maryage betwix
the said Vierge and Joseph.

More fourther was of new maid One other Yatt, apon
the wiche was in Sieges the iiij Vertuz. Theys is to weytt,
Justice, holdynge in hyr right Haunde a Swerde all naked,
and in the t'other a Pair of Ballaunces, and she had under
hyr Feet the Kyng Nero : Force, armed, holdyng in hyr
Haund a Shafte, and under hyr Feete was Holofernes, all
armed : Temperance holdyng in hyr Haund a Bitt of an
Horse, and under hyr Feete was Epicurus : Prudence,
holdynge in hyr Haunde a Syerge, and under hyr Sardena-
palus. With thos war Tabretts that playd merrily, whill
the noble Company past thorough. Under was a Licorne

[1] E.B.R. (S B.R.S.), I, 122.

and a Greyhound, that held a Difference of one Chardon
florysched, and a Red Rose entrelassed . . . The Towne
of Edenbourgh was in many Places haunged with Tappissery
. . . And in the Churches of the sayd Towne Bells range
for Myrthe.[1]

19th May 1531
[The Websters on the one side and the Walkers, Shearers
and Bonnetmakers on the other side appear before the
Council, and submit themselves to its judgment in regard
to various matters in dispute, ' and in speciall anent the
ordering of thame to pas in the processioun on Corpus
Christi day and the octauis tharof, and all vthir generall
processionis and gatheringis in all tymes tocum.' The
Council ordains ' that the saidis dekin and brethir of the
Wobstar craft sall ressaif and suffir the saidis dekin ouerman
and brethir of the saidis Walkaris, Scheraris and Bonet-
makaris to resort and pas with thame all togidder in ane
place on Corpus Christi day and octauis tharof and in all
vther generall processionis and gatheringis in all tymes
tocum, without ony stop or impediment to be maid to
thame tharintill, and als to spley and bere thar baneris
ilkane with vtheris as the maner is in syk tymes, quhilk
place and rovme salbe callit the Wobstaris place and rovme
for euir, and the saidis Walkaris Scheraris and Bonet-
makaris and thar successouris to be with thame in brether-
heid and bruke the said place of licence and tollerance of
the saidis brethir of Wobstaris and thare successouris in
all tymes tocum . . .] [2]

17th July 1538
[Various statutes re the ' craftis araying,' the clothing of
the inhabitants, the cleansing of the town and expulsion of
beggars in honour of the entry of Mary of Guise.] [3]

Item, the provest baillies and counsale ordanis Robert
Hector to compleitt the wark taikin on hand be him vpoun
the croce at the entrie of the Quenis Grace. . . .
Item, it is devysit that thir persouns following, viz, James
Bassenden Alexander Spens, for the Nether Bow ; Robert
Graham, William Tod, for the Trone to ansuer ; Patrik

[1] Leland, *Collectanea*, IV, 289-91.
[2] *E.B.R.* (*S.B.R.S.*), II, 48.
[3] For these and the following statutes, see *E.B.R.* (*S.B.R.S.*), II, 89-91.

Lindsay, Jhone Purves, George Leche, for the Croce to ansuer; Robert Hector, Robert Watsoun, for the Tolbuith to ansuer; Maister Dauid Ireland, William Symsoun, and Jhone Symsoun, for the Over Bow to ansuer; the Archidene of Sanctandrois, William Loch and James Hill, for the West Port to ansuer; Dauid Lindsay and Robert Bischope, and awaitt vpoun the grathing of thair rowmes in skaffetting personages and ordour thairof, ilk ane for thair awin rowme, and quhat expenssis thai mak thairvpoun ordanis Thomas Vddart thesaurer to answer thame at all tymes as he or his chaplane beis requyrit, quhilkis expenssis sall be gevin in to him in writt, and this to be done with avyse of the said Dauid Lindsay anent all ordour and furnesing.[1]

Item, it is devysit that Maister Henry Lawder be the persoun to welcum the Quenis grace in sic abulyement, and with the words in Fransche, as sall be devysit with avyse of Maister Adame Otterburne, Maister James Fowlis and Dauid Lyndsay.

1553

Item, the xxij of Junij, gevin to George Tod for making of ane skaffalt on the hill to the clerk play, the bering of daylis and punschonis thairto, and the aill and the wyne that day thai playit, and furnessing of sax sparris thairto,

xxvj s [2]

1554

Item, payit for beireing of burds and trestis to the Queenis luging on Corporischristeis day,[3] to Mr Abraham Creichoun forehoir and for flouris and raichis and vj menis lauboris that day awating thairon   xx s [4]

Item, the day of the playing of the play at the trone, with the convoy of the moris; payit for graithing of the Quenis luging foiranent the samyn, for flours, beirks, and rocheis, and beiring of furmes and trestis thairto   xvj s [5]

---

[1] This modern punctuation may not be correct. The previous entry indicates that Robert Hector was associated with the preparations at the Cross; and David Lyndsay may have been responsible for the opening pageant at the West Port as well as general supervision of the whole pageant.
[2] *City of Edinburgh Old Accounts,* I, 76. Would this be for a Corpus Christi play, acted on 1st June, or for a midsummer play?
[3] 24th May.
[4] *City of Edinburgh Old Accounts,* I, 108.
[5] *Ibid.,* I, 109. The dates in this account are rather confused. This item occurs between entries dated (1) 16th June and (2) 7th June, and may refer to the play of 10th June in the next entry quoted.

15th June 1554

Precept
anent the
expenssis of
the play

The prouest baillies and counsale ordanis the thesaurar Robert Grahame to pay the werkmen, merchandis, carteris, paynterris, and vtheris that furneist the grayth to the convoy of the moris to the Abbay and of the play maid that samyn day the tent day of Junij instant the sowm of xxxvij li. xvj s. ij d. as the compt producit be Sir William Makdougall maister of werk thairupoun proportit, prouiding alwayis that the said Sir Williame deliuer to the dene of gyld the handscenye and canves specifiit in the said tikkit to be kepit to the behuif of the toun.[1]

18th August 1554

Precept
menstralis

The prouest baillies and counsale ordanis the thesaurer Robert Graham to content and pay the xij menstralis that past afoir the convoy and the plaaris on Sonday last bypast xls.[2]

Item, payit on the day of the play, for the dennar maid to the playars,   iiij li. xviij s. ij d.
Item, payit for the making of the Quenis grace hous on the playfeild, besyde the convoy hous under the samyn, and the playaris hous, the jebbettis and skaffauld about the samyn, and burds on the playfeild, careing of thame fra the toun to the feild, and thairfra agane, the cutting and inlaik of greit and small tymmer, with the nallis and warkmanschip of vj wrychts twa dayis thairto, pynoris feis, cart hyre, and uther necessaris, as Sir William M'Dougall, maister of wark, tikket beiris

xvj li. v s. iiij d.[3]

[1] *E.B.R. (S.B.R.S.)*, II, 193.
[2] *Ibid.*, II, 197.
[3] *City of Edinburgh Old Accounts*, I, 110. These items occur between entries dated 18th August and 18th October, and may, perhaps, be taken in conjunction with the entry in the Council Register dated 18th August (see above), in which case the entry of 12th October may be regarded as a belated payment in connection with the same play. Was this, then, the occasion on which the *Satyre of the Thrie Estaitis* was acted at the Greenside ? The playfield there we know to have been completed by the middle of August 1554. (See App. IV, Playfields and Pageants, p. 351.) The *Bannatyne Manuscript* (Hunterian Club, 1896) definitely refers to this play having been acted ' in the Grenesyd besyd Edinburgh ' (fol. 168) ; and ' in the Playfeild of Edinburcht ' (fol. 177) ; and ' in the Grensyd besyd Edinburcht in anno 155- yeiris ' (fol. 210). Henry Charteris, in his *Works of Sir Dauid Lyndsay*, 1582 (originally published in 1568), says : ' Na les ernist and vehement was he aganis them (*i.e.*, the Clergy) in his Fairsis and publict Playis, quhairin he was verray craftie and exoellent. Sic ane spring he gaue them in the Play, playit beside Edinburgh, in presence of the Quene Regent, and ane greit part of the Nobilitie, with ane exceiding

12th October 1554

The prouest baillies and counsale ordanis the thesaurar Robert Grahame to content and pay to Walter Bynnyng the sowme of v li. for the making of the play graith and paynting of the handsenye and the playaris facis ; providand alwys that the said Walter mak the play geir vnderwrittin furthcumand to the town quhen thai haif ado thairwith, quhilkis he hes now ressauit, viz., viij play hattis, ane kingis crowne, ane myter, ane fulis hude, ane septour, ane pair angell wyngis, twa angell hair, ane chaplet of tryvmphe.[1]

28th Dec. 1554

Anent the
Quenis
propine

The prouest baillies and counsale findis it necessar and expedient that the litill farsche and play maid be William Lauder be playit afoir the Quenis grace, and that scho be propinit to hir nether gift with sum cowpis of siluer.[2]

1554/5

Item, on Uphaly day, the vj day of Januar 1554 for beiring of daillis, greit treis and punschionis to mak ane skaffald

greit nowmer of pepill, lestand fra nyne houris afoir none, till six houris at euin, quhair amangis monie baith graue materis, and merie trikkis, he brocht in ane Bischop, ane Persone, ane Freir, and ane Nun, deckit vp in thair papisticall ornamentis, and maner of rayment. And thairefter brocht in King Correctioun, quha reformand sindrie deformiteis in his Realme, passit to the tryall of his Clergie. And findand them to be altogidder Idiotis, vnworthie of onie Functioun Ecclesiasticall, decernit them to be degradit of thair digniteis, and spulzeit of thair officis : quhilk beand executit, and they denudit of thair vpmaist Garmentis, they war found bot verray fulis, hypocrites, flatteraris, and nouchty persones. Quhairby he signifyit to the pepill, that howsaeuer they war estemit of the warld, they had na thing quhairin they micht iustlie glorie to be Pastouris of Christis Kirk, and feidaris of his flock, bot onlie thair outward ornamentis, and triumphant tytillis. Bot beand inwardlie considerit, they wald be fund bot verray hyrelingis, enemeis to Christ, and deuoraris of his flock. This play did enter with sic greif in thair hartis, that they studyit be all meanis, to be auengit thairof. . . .' From both Bannatyne (f. 177) and Charteris one gets the impression that Lyndsay, who died before April 1555 (*D.N.B.*, s.v. Lyndsay), was himself present on this occasion ; and as, according to Charteris, the play lasted nine hours and was played before Mary of Guise as Regent, this would seem to point to a date during the summer of 1554. Sunday, 18th August 1554, may then have been the date of this notable event. While the articles of play gear handed over to Walter Bynnyng are suggestive of any stock piece (see next excerpt, 12th October), it is not without significance that they can be definitely assigned to individual characters in Lyndsay's play.

[1] *E.B.R.* (*S.B.R.S.*), II, 198.
[2] *Ibid.*, II, 206.

in the Tolbuith to play the Clerk Play on, and away bringing
of it agane. vj s. viij d.[1]

1558 [2]

Item, gevin to ane officiar twa syndrie dayis at the in-
warning of the vij men quha wes the vij planets to gif
agane thair play and clayths [3] xij d.

The expensis maid upone the *Triumphe and Play at the* Play
Marriage of the Quenis Grace, with the Convoy the (blank)
day of *Julij anno* 1558.

Item, in primis, coft fra James Adamsoun iij elnis and ane
half of yallow taffetis of the cord till the ansenze, price
of the ell xxiiij s. : summa is, iiij li. iiij s.

Item, coft fra William Lawsoun iij elnis and ane half quhit
taffeteis of the cord, . . . iiij li. iiij s.

Item, coft fra Marroun Scott iij elnis and ane half of blew
taffettis, . . . iiij li. iiij s.

Item, bocht fra Johnne Johnnestoun iij elnis and ane half
of reid taffeteis of the cord, . . . iij li. x s.

Item, gevin Patrik Durhame for making of the said ansenze
with the freiris clayths iiij li.

Item, gevin for silk ij s. iiij d.

Item, for ane staf to the ansenze ij s.

Item, gevin to William Adamsoun for writting of ane part
of the play, and for the recompance of his part of the
play, quhilk he had in keping, at the presidents command,
iiij li.

Item, gevin to William Lawder for the making of the play
and wrytting thairof x li.

Item, gevin Walter Bynning for paynting of the vij planets
of the kart with the rest of the convoy
xvj li. xiij s. iiijd.

Item, for xxiiij elnis of small canves tilbe the vij planets
coitts and hoiss, with cupid, price of the ell iiij s. ;
summa is, lvj s.

Item deliverit to the vij planets with cupid, xxiiij ells of
forbati [4] taffeteis of syndre sorts of hewis, . . .
xiiij li. viij s.

---

[1] *City of Edinburgh Old Accounts,* I, 133.
[2] The following entries relating to the play in honour of the marriage of
Mary, Queen of Scots, to the Dauphin are excerpted from the *City of Edinburgh
Old Accounts,* I, 241, 269-73.
[3] MS. has ' *pair* play & clay*this.*' ' & ' is clearly deleted.
[4] N.E.D. gives ' ? counterfeit, imitation.'

Item, till William Ury, ij elnis iij quarters of greinn taffeteis of the cord, quha was ane of the said planets, . . .

iij li. vj s.

Item, gevin for vij reid skynnis tilbe thair schort broty-kynnis, . . .   xxj s.

Item, gevin for four golden skynnis bocht fra ane skynnare tilbe ane crown to ane of the planets   vj s.

Item, for xiiij elnis of blak and quhyt grayis to be the freiris weids, . . .   lix s.

Item, gevin for twa ledderone skynnis till be ane pair of breiks to the gray freir, . . .   iij s.

Item, gevin ane tailzeour for making of thame   xij d.

Item, bocht iij dosoun fyrsparis to mak symmer treis with birkis about thame on the Nether Bow & Butt, and Nether Trone, . . .   xxv s. vj d.

Item, for upbringing of thame furth of Leith be vj men,

iij s.

Item, gevin for xij laid of byrks with vj byrk treis to cleyth the But, Trones and Croce, . . .   xxxvj s.

Item, gevin for small skenze threid and small towis to bynd all the birks about on thir partis foirsaid   x s.

Item, gevin for vij skenze of flanderis gyrthis till put round about the convoy horss, . . .   x s. vj d.

Item, gevin for iij^{xx} arrowis, . . .   x s.

Item, gevin for canves, bruntstane, salt peter, lumbard paper, to the fyre balls,   viij s. viij d.

Item, gevin to twa men for furnessing of clay and wodbynd to clay the Trone agane the said play for upstikin of jonet [1] flowers upone the samin   viij s.

Item, gevin iiij^{xx} xiij elnis and $\frac{1}{2}$ round canves, price of the ell ij s. : summa is   ix s. vij d.[2]

Item, mair, vj elnis of canves, . . .   xv s.

Item, gevin for als mekle clayth till be freris hoiss, and making of thame   ij s.

Item, gevin for ane wyne puntioun till put wyne in till be run upone the Croce,   iij s. vj d.

Item, gevin for xx quartis of wyne tilbe run on broche upone the said Croce,   lviij s. iiij d.

Item, gevin to Johnne Weir, puderar, for making of pypis to the out passage of the wyne and awaiting upone the samin, with the recompance of his leid and lawbores done be him in the tyme   xxx s.

---

[1] Jaunette, yellow.   [2] 'ix li. vij s.' in MS.

Item, gevin for xxiiij elnis of quhyt taffeteis and reid taffeteis forbati to be the vj dansors clayths, price of the ell xij s : summa is,   xiiij li. viij s.

Item, gevin for xij elnis lynning clayth to lyne the thre stand of quhyt clayths, . . .   xviij s.

Item, gevin for vij elnis ½ of reid boukrum till lyne the thre stand of reid clayths, . . .   xxij s. vj d.

Item, gevin to Robert Gray, merchand, for xxxj dosoun of bells till the said dansors till be put upone thair bodyis and leggs, price thairof,   xxxviij s.

Item, gevin thame iij quarteris of quhit taffeteis forbati, and iij quarteris reid of the samin sort to be hung upone thair heids, . . .   xviij s.

Item, gevin for iij leddroun skynnis to be thair schone
                                 vj s.

Item, gevin for making of thir vj stand of clayths with thair breiks, and on setting of the said bells all the parts of thair bodyis thyis, . . .   xlviij s.

Item, gevin for meit and drink furneist to thame in Johnne Litillis houss at the on putting of thair clayths afoir the dance and eftir the dance   xj s.

Item, gevin for vij elnis and ½ boukram of syndrie hewis tilbe the fuillis coit, . . .   xxij s. vj d.

Item, for making of it   iij s.

Item, for vj elnis and ½ boukram tilbe twa coitts, ij pair of breiks and to be thair bonets till the twa men that callit the cart, . . .   xix s. vj d.

Item, gevin to ane tailzeour for making of thir twa stands with thair bonetts, price of the stand iiij s : summa is
                                 viij s.

Item, for twa dosoun of cachepull [1] balls cled with gold fuilze till hing upone the tre upone the Trone, price
                                 viij d.

Item, for ane hundreth cheryis till hing upone the said tre,
                                 xij d.

Item, gevin to Jacques and his twa sonis with ane uther man, at the command of the presidents and counsale, vj elnis of yellow staming, . . .   v li. viij d.[2]

Item, for iiij elnis of reid taffeteis forbati to draw thame out with, . . .   xlviij s.

Item, for iiij elnis of quhyt lynning to lyne thair hoiss with, . . .   x s. viij d.

---

[1] Tennis.   [2] 'v li. viij s.' in MS.

Item, four elnis of reid taffeteis forbati to be thame dow-
blaitts, . . .   iiij li. viij s.
Item, for xij elnis of quhyt lynning fustiane to lyne the
dowblaitts, . . .   xxxvj s.
Item, for iiij reid bonnets to thame, . . .   lvj s.
Item, for making of the iiij pair of hoiss, iiij dowblatts,
price of the pece iiij s : summa is,   xxxij s.
Item, for sylk to thair dowblatts,   v s.
Item, for ane barrell of aill till the playars of the skaffetts,
contenand v gallonis and ane half, . . . xiiij s. viij d.
Item, for bering of it be twa men to the said skaffetts,
                                                      iiij d.
Item, for ane barrell of wyne, contenand vj gallonis iiij
pynts, . . .   iij li. ix. s.[1] iiijd.
Item, for bering of it to the skaffetts be twa men, iiij d.
Item, for vj mayn schotts [2]   xij d.
Item, for casting and leding of ij° scheiratts [3] till the
skaffetts for latting of dyn to be maid be the playars
feit, price of the hundreth casting and leding vij s : summa
is,   xiiij s.
Item, gevin to Robert Fynder and his servand iij dayis
wage, and Johnne Stewart, William Stevinsoun, George
Tod, Gilbert Cleuths servand ij dayis wage at the upputting of the skaffetts, . . .   xliij s. iiij d.
Item, gevin to viij werkmen for bering of daills, grit tymmer,
puntionis and byrkyn of the But, Trone, Croce, with
the ovir Trone, and upputting of skaffetts and away
taking thairof be the space of ij dayis and iij nychts,
ilk man in the day and nycht,
                                    ij s. vj d : summa is xl s.
Item, gevin ane man ane dayis wage that keipit the ansenze
quhilk stude upone the Croce,   xviij d.
Item, gevin for grit garroun naills, plancheour naills and
dure naills to the said skaffetts,   xvj s.
Item, gevin to the wrychts for v dosoun viij staffs to convey
the playaris, . . .   iij li. viij s.
Item, gevin to the calsay maker for mending of the calsay
quhair the skaffetts stuid and labors done be him,
                                                    vj s. v d.
Item, gevin four men for inputting of xix pece of artailzerie
within the flesche market efter thai wer schot in the
tyme of nycht   v s.

---

[1] 'x s.' in MS.   [2] Manchets, loaves of fine wheaten bread.
                           [3] Green turfs.

Item, for candill the samin tyme,   vj d.
Item, gevin Andro Williamsone, wrycht, for making of the
    convoy kart with sparris, rauchteris, gyrstingis, naills,
    werkmanschip, and all :   v li. iiij s. ix d.
Item, gevin ane puir man for recompance of his yaird trod
    doun be convoyaris horss,   x s.
Item, ane man ane dayis wage for awaiting upone the kart,
                                                        xviij d.
Item, gevin Maister Johnne Spens, baille, for ane horss
    houss quhilk was tynt on the play day,   vj s.
Item, gevin to Patrik Vernor, for labors done be him
    quha rad [1] the blak freris part of the play,   xx s.
Item, gevin Richard Trohop for furnessing of wyne and
    meit to the playars in his houss in tyme of the said
    convoy,   iij li. xij s.
Item, gevin to Paul at kirk dur and to uther twa men for
    certane bells quha wes stowin of the horss in the convoy
    kert,   xxxviij s. x d.
Item, bocht fra Johnne Hucheoun to be deliverit to James
    Drummond, trumpator, at the command of the president,
    viij elnis of tafteis of the cord, . . .   viij li.
Item, mair, fra the said Johnne viij elnis of tafteis of the
    four threidds, . . .   vij li. iiij s.

1558

The presidenttis ballies and counsale ordanis James Adamsoun thesaurer to delyuer to William Adamsoun for his
travell takin in the play maid at the tryumphe of our
Souerane Ladyis mariage the sown of foure lib ; . . . to
Walter Bynning, painter, for his panting and all his lawbouris takin be him in the tryumphe maid at our Souerane
Ladyis mariage the sown of xxv merkis ; to William
Lauder the sowm of aucht lib., by the fourtie schillingis
quhilkis he hes ellis ressauit for his travell and lawbour
tane vpone him in setting furth of the play maid at our
Souerane Ladyis mariage ; . . . to all the wrychtis quhilkis
wrocht the play grayth in the play maid at the tryumphe
of our Souerane Ladyis mariage for thair tymmer and
workmanschip the sowm of fyve lib. four s. nyne d. . . .
to Patrik Dorane for his travell takin on him for making
of certane claythis agane the tryumphe of our Souerane
Ladyis mariage the sowm of four lib. . . . to Adam Smyth,

_____
[1] 'had' in MS.

takkisman of Andro Mowbrayis ȝarde the sowm of vj s.
viij d. for the dampnage and skayth sustenit be him in
tramping down of his gers of the said yard be the convoy
and remanent playeris the tyme of the trumphe.[1]

26th Aug. 1561

[Preparations for the Queen's entry when a banquet is to
be given and ' a triumphe to be maid of hir graces entre
within this toun.'] [2]

27th Aug. 1561

Ordanis Louke Wilsoun, thesaurer, with all diligence possible, to mak preparatioun for the banquet and triumphe.[3]

28th Aug. 1561

[Clothing for the twelve ' seriandis ' ' agane the tyme of the
triumphe.']
(Also) to furnes and deliuer to Patrik Schang, wrycht, and
Walter Bynning tymmer, canves, and all vther necessaris
convenient for the triumphis and fairssis (at) the over
trone, tolbuth, croce, salt tron, and Nether Bow.
[Regulations re the dress of the various town officials, the
' pale ' bearers, etc.] and euerye man to gang in his dew
and gude ordour ; and the seriandis to ordour the calsay
and to mak rowme for the nobelitie and nychtbouris foresaid ; and siclike that the young men of the toun devise
for thame selffis sum brawf abulyement of taffate or vther
silk and mak the convoy before the cairt triumphant.[4]

3rd Sept. 1561

Extent of
xxviijᶜ li.

The prouest baillies and counsale, efter avise-
ment with the lairge and greit sowmes contenit
in the compttis debursit vpoun the banquet,
triumphe, and propyne to the Quenys grace, quhilk will

---

[1] E.B.R. (S.B.R.S.), III, 26.
Cf. Maitland Quarto MS., S.T.S., 1920, f. 10 b :—
 All borrowis tounis everilk man ȝow prayis
 To mak baine fyris fercis & clerk playis
 and throw ȝour rewis carrous daunce & sing
 and at ȝour croce gar wyne rin sindrie wayis
 as wes the custome in our elderis dayis
 Quhen that ȝai mad Triumphe for ony thing
 And all ȝour stairis with Tapestrie gar hing
 Castellis schut gunnis schippis & galeyis
 Blaw vp ȝour trumpettis and on ȝour drummis ding.
[2] E.B.R. (S.B.R.S.), III, 119. [3] Ibid., III, 121. [4] Ibid.

extend to the sowme of iiij m. merkis or thairby, ordanis, conforme to the ordinance maid of befoir, that ane generall extent be set and lyftit of all the nychtbouris of this burgh, bayth merchant and craftisman, to the quantite of the said sowme of iiij m. merkis, and with all deligence to be collectit and debursit for the releif of the creditouris, furnissaris of the necessaris of the said banquet triumphe and propyne.[1]

> [Although the following description of the entry of
> Mary, Queen of Scots, is well known to Scottish his-
> torians, it has frequently escaped notice in the annals
> of drama and pageantry. Thus, in his comprehensive
> survey of English pageantry, Professor Withington
> confines himself to the notices of the ' banquet and
> tryumphe ' in the Council Records, and comments :
> ' It is hard to say whether there was pageantry in the
> strict sense of the word ; if there were, we do not know
> of what it consisted.'—*English Pageantry*, 1918, I.,
> 203.]

And thairefter, quhen sho was rydand down the castellhill, thair met hir hienes ane convoy of the ȝoung mene of the said burgh, to the nomber of fyftie, or thairby, thair bodeis and theis coverit with ȝeallow taffateis, thair armes and leggs fra the kne doun bair, cullorit with blak, in maner of Moris, vpon thair heiddis blak hattis, and on thair faces blak visouris, in thair mowthis rings, garnesit with intellable precious staneis, about thair neckkis, leggis and armes infynit of chenis of gold ; togidder with saxtene of the maist honest men of the toun, cled in veluot gownis and veluot bonettis, berand and gangand about the paill wnder the quhilk her hienes raid ; quhilk paill wes of fyne purpour veluet lynit with reid taffateis, freinȝiet with gold and silk ; and efter thame wes ane cart with certane bairnes, togidder with ane coffer quhairin wes the copburd and propyne quhilk suld be propynit to hir hienes ; and quhen hir grace come fordwart to the butter trone of the said burgh, the nobilitie and convoy foirsaid precedand, at the quhilk butter trone thair was ane port made of tymber, in maist honourable maner, cullorit with fyne cullouris, hungin with syndrie armes ; vpon the quhilk port wes singand certane barneis in the maist hevinlie wyis ; vnder

---

[1] *E.B.R. (S.B.R.S.)*, III, 122.

the quhilk port thair wes ane cloud opynnand with four
levis, in the quhilk was put ane bony barne. And quhen
the quenes hienes was cumand throw the said port, the
said cloude opynnit, and the barne discendit doun as it
had bene ane angell, and deliuerit to hir hienes the keyis
of the toun,[1] togidder with ane bybill and ane psalme buik,
coverit with fyne purpourit veluot;[2] and efter the said
barne had spoken some small speitches,[3] he deliuerit alsua
to hir hienes thre writtingis, the tennour thairof is vncer-
tane. That being done, the barne ascendit in the cloud,
and the said clud stekit; and thairefter the quenis grace
come doun to the tolbuith, at the quhilk was (blank) vpoun
twa skaffattis, ane abone and ane vnder that; vpone the
vnder was situat ane fair wirgin, callit Fortoune, vnder
the quhilk was thrie fair virgynnis, all cled in maist precious
attyrement, callit (blank) Justice and Policie.[4] And efter
ane litell speitche[5] maid thair, the quenis grace come to
the croce, quhair thair was standand four fair virgynnis,
cled in the maist hevenlie clething,[6] and fra the quhilk
croce the wyne ran out at the spouttis in greit abundance;
thair wes the noyiss of pepill casting the glassis with wyne.[7]
This being done, our souerane ladie come to the salt trone,
quhair thair wes sum spekaris; and efter ane litell speitche,[5]
thaj brunt vpoun the skaffet maid at the said trone, the

---

[1] Cf. *Johnston's MS. History*, II, f. 356, Advocates' Library Hist. MSS.:
'Cled as ane angell.' *Knox*, II, 288 : 'The keyes war delivered unto hir by
a pretty boy, descending as it war from a cloud.' Wright, *Queen Elizabeth
and her Times*, I, 73, Randolph to Cecil : 'A boy of six yeres of age, that
came as yt were, from heaven owte of a rownde globe.' Herries, *Historical
Memoirs :* 'At the head of the Strait-bow there was a pageant richlie adorned,
and upon it a number of boys singing musick, and playeng upon instruments ;
one of which cam doune in a cloud.' (An 'abridgment' only of the original
description is given by the transcriber of this manuscript.)

[2] *Knox :* 'The verses of hir awin praise sche heard and smyled. But when
the Bible was presented, and the praise thairof declared, sche began to frown ;
for schame sche could not refuise it. But she did no better, for immediatelie
sche gave it to the most pestilent Papist within the Realme, to wit, to Arthoure
Erskyn.' *Herries :* The Bible and Book of Psalms ' were signified by a speech
made by the boy to be emblems of her defending the Reformed Religion.'

[3] Cf. Rait's *Mary, Queen of Scots*, 1900, p. 21, where the four stanzas are
quoted. Thorpe, *State Papers*, I, 174, quotes the first stanza.

[4] *Johnston :* 'At the qu*h*ilk was set wpone twa skaffald*is* ane aboue the
wther Wpone the Ouer was cituat ane virgin callit fortoun wnder the qu*h*ilk
was thrie fair virgines callit Luiff Iustice and policie.' *Herries :* 'At the
Parliament hous a double pageant, one above another, was presented with
many devyces and musick.'

[5] 'Space ' in *Johnston*.

[6] *Johnston* omits this detail.

[7] *Johnston* adds : 'Cryand throw all the streit God saiff Marie queane of
Scotis.'

maner of ane sacrifice ; [1] and swa that being done, sho depairtit to the nether bow, quhair thair wes ane vther skaffet maid, havand ane dragoun in the samyn, with some speiches ; and efter that the dragoun was brynt, and the quenis grace hard ane psalme song, hir hienes past to hir abbay of Halyrudhous with the said convoy and nobilities ; and thair the bairneis quhilk was in the cairt with the propyne maid some speitche concernyng the putting away of the mess, and thairefter sang ane psalme ; and this being done, the cart come to Edinburgh, and the said honest men remaynit in hir vtter chalmer, and desyred hir grace to ressaue the said copeburd, quhilk wes double ourgilt ; the price thairof wes ij m. merkis ; quha ressauit the samyne, and thankit thame thairof.[2] (*Diurnal of Remarkable Occurrents*, pp. 67-9, *Bann. Club*.)

20th Feb. 1567/8

Precept   The samyn day ye baillies and counsall ordanis the thesaurar to deliuere to Robert semple ye sowme of x merkis in support of ye expensĩs maid be him at ye play the same to be allouitt in his comptis [3]

[1] There is some discrepancy in the accounts here. *Johnston :* ' Ane sacrifice as it had bene ane preist *pair* sayand meĩ (at the quh*i*lk hir grace was not content).' *Herries :* ' But at the Trone there was a pageant that seemed to many ridiculous, but to the French it seemed contemptible. Upon the top of this pageant, there was a speech made tending to abolishing of the mass, and in token that it was alreddie banished the kingdome, there was the shape of a priest in his ornaments reddie to say mass, made of wode, which was brought forth, in sight of all, and presentlie throwen in a fyre made upon the scaffold and burnt.' This was ' diverslie constructed ' and the Queen not pleased. *Wright :* ' There, for the terrible sygnifications of the vengeance of God upon idolatrie, ther wer burnt Coron, Nathan (*sic*) and Abiron, in the tyme of their sacrifice. Thei were mynded to have had a priest burnt at the altar, at the elevation. The Erle of Huntly stayed that pagient.'
[2] *Johnston :* ' Quh*i*lk with great deficultie scho ressauit And thanked thame of all *pair* proceeding, saveand onlie for burneing the sacrifice quh*i*lk micht (as hir grace said) weill *an*neugh done.' (Later hand has obliterated ' done ' and inserted ' haif bein undon.') *Knox*, commenting on the whole, says : ' Great preparationis war maid for hir enteress in the town. In ferses, in masking, and in other prodigalities, faine wold fooles have counterfooted France. Whatsoever myght sett furth hir glory, that sche heard, and glaidlye beheld.'
[3] MS. Council Register, Vol. IV, f. 213. Cf. *The Diarey of Robert Birrel,* Dalyell's Fragments of Scottish History, 1798 : 17th Jan. 1568. ' The 17 of Januarii a play made by Robert Semple, and played befor the Lord Regent, and divers uthers of the nobilitie.' In the MS. Accounts of the Lord High Treasurer there are several references at this time to a Robert Simple or Semple. In April 1567 he receives a payment of £140 (Vol. 1566-7, f. 34), a signed receipt for which, dated 27th April, is preserved among the Manuscript Household Papers (Miscellaneous Accounts, Precepts, &c., 1544-67) at Register House.

Aug.-Sept. 1579

[20th Aug. Arrangements re propine to the King. 26th Aug.
' Rex, villa, triumphe.' Arrangements for triumph and
propine. 27th Aug. An ' extent ' of £4000 to be raised ' for
making of ane copbirde of syluer or gold to the Kingis
Maiestie and vther trumphis agane his cuming to this
burgh.' 11th, 14th, 18th Sept. Ordinances concerning
apparel of merchants and craftsmen and liveries for officers
and ' paill ' bearers. 7th Oct. Cleansing of the town.[1]]

4th Sept. 1579

Visitouris
maister of
the Hie Scoles
tragedies.

(The bailies and council) ordanis James Low-
soun, minister, William Littill, and Jhonne
Jhonstoun to pas to the Hie Scule of this burgh
and vesie the maister of the Hie Scoles tragedies
to be maid be the bairnis agane the Kingis heir cuming and
to repoirt.[2]

14th Sept. 1579

Villa
triumphe.

Ordanis Robert Heuisoun chirurgean, and Robert
Kar, baillie, to speik the Frencheman, vsing
William Stewart for his opinion in devyse of
the triumphe agane the Kingis heir cuming.[3]

2nd Oct. 1579

Precept
thesaurer
triumphe

Ordanis Robert Kar and Gilbert Dik, baillies,
together with Androw Stevinson, thesaurer,
and Robert Henrisoun, chirurgean, to tak
ordour with the wrychtis for vpsetting of
daillis and vther tymmer on the Nether Bow and vther
places neidfull, for the decoring of the tovne agane the
triumphe to be maid to the Kingis entres.[4]

On 4th Sept. he is granted ' thre elnis of blak ' (Vol. 1567-9, f. 59). In March
1572-3 there is a grant of £3, 10s. to ' capitane sempill to supporte him to
clay*this* ' (Vol. 1571-4, f. 117). On 20th September 1581, £13, 6s. 8d. is paid
to a Robert Semple in Dumbarton for ' outsetting of the pastyme to the
Kingis Majestie ' (*Glasgow Burgh Records, S.B.R.S.*, I, 469). There is no
evidence for the suggestion that the play to which Birrel refers was ' Philotus.'
(See *Philotus*, Bann. Club, 1835, pp. i-iv.)

[1] *E.B.R. (S.B.R.S.)*, IV, 113, 114, 115-7, 122.
[2] *Ibid.*, IV, 114.
[3] *Ibid.*, IV, 117.
[4] *Ibid.*, IV, 121.

14th Oct. 1579

Proclamatioun tapestrie — Ordanis proclamatioun to be maid be sound of tabourin throw this burgh, commanding all the inhabitantis thairof to hing thair stairis with tapestrie and ares warkis on Fryday nixt, and that nouther be nycht nor day ony fyre ballis, fyre arowis or vther ingynes of fyre be castin be ony maner of personis heirefter, and for removing of red, tymmer, swyne, and beggeris of the tovne, vnder the payne of pvnesment of thair personis at the will and discretion of the jugis.[1]

29th Oct. 1579

Precept, Adamsoun, baillie, yeir past, violeris, sangsteris. — Ordanis William Adamsoun, baillie, the yeir past to delyuer to the violeris and sangsteris at the Kingis entrie aboue the Over Bow, the sovme of thre pundis for thair dayes wages, quhairof thretty s. to the violeris and thretty s. to the sangsteris.[1]

(The following account of the entry of James VI. in 1579 is taken from *Johnston's MS. History of Scotland. Adv. Lib. Hist. MSS. 35.4.2.*)

Vol. II.

His grace com rydand in at the wast port quhair the first f. 524 wisdome of salomon as it is conteanit in the 3 buik of the Kingis the 3 chapter [2] and thair the haill honest men of ed*inburgh* wer cled in blak gownes and bure ane vaill of fyne purpo*ur* veluet wnder the quhilk his grace raid to the abay Thaireftir assendit to the overbow quhair thair was a glob out of the quhilk com ane bony boy and delyuerit to his Ma*ies*tie the keyis of the Toun Maid of fyne siluer quhair thair was melodious singing [3] At the auld tolbuith

[1] *E.B.R.* (*S.B.R.S.*), IV, 124.

[2] Cf. *The Historie of King James the Sext*, Bann. Club, 1825, 178-9. 'That port presentit unto him the wisdome of Solomon, as it is written in the thrid chapter of the first buik of the Kings : That is to say King Solomon was repre-sentit with the tua wemen that contendit for the young chylde. (New L.B. and Adv. Lib. MSS. : " and the servant that presentit the sworde to the King with the chylde," p. 412.) This done, they presented unto the King, the sworde for the one hand, and the scepter for the uther.' Cf. too *Calderwood*, III, 458-9 ; and Crawfurd, *Memoirs of the Affairs of Scotland*, 1706, 356-7.

[3] *Hist. of K. James the Sext :* 'In the streat that ascendis to the castell, thair is an ancient port, at the whilk hang a curious globe, that opnit artifi-ciallie as the King came by, wharin was a young boy that discendit craftelie. . . . During this space Dame Music and hir scollars exercesit hir art with great melodie.' *Calderwood :* 'The musicians song the xx Psalme, and others played upon the viols.' *Crawfurd :* 'A little Boy, clad like a Cupid, descended in a Machine.'

N

four ladies, peax. Justice. plentie and policie, and spak
ilkane in pair awin degrie [1] Syne past to the kirk [2] quhair
Mr James lowsoune maid ane exhortatioun quhilk endit
his maiestie beheld the storie of bachus at the croce quhairat
the spoutis The wyne ran aboundantlie [3] At the trone
(quhilk for the same effect was moveit to remayne perpetuallie to the south syd sax fute) the aff spring grie be
grie of the king quhom of he was cumeit [4] At the nether
bow the significatioun of the sewin planetis howe grie be
grie thay rang the tyme of the kingis birth as exposatour
tholomeus,[5] set furth Not forʒetand the preparatioun of the
haill forstairis with Imaidgis and fyne tapestrie [6] At the
cannon croce ane breiff fabill for abbolisching of the paip &
of the meſs with the authoritie and asisteris thairof for
evir [7] Thaireftir his grace past to the abay

[There are many entries in Vol. IX. of the MS. Council
Register from Sept. 1589 onwards relating to preparations
for the reception of Queen Anne which did not actually
take place until 19th May 1590. ' It is necessair pat all the
toun prepare and mak reddy all things concerning pe
triumph of hir said entrie and ordanis Jhonn moresoun
thesaurer to mak and deburse pe expensſs pairof vpoun pe
wallis ports croce & tronis & vper convenient places at pe
sycht of androw sclater maister of wark with all pair
payntres and vper furnitoures concerning the solemniteis
pairof and alswa to caus by and mak ane payle of veluott with
all necessairs belanging pairto with pe bybill & psalme buik

---

[1] *Calderwood :* ' When he came doun to the Old Tolbuith, the fore-face
wherof was covered with painted dailes, there he saw the crafts' standards
and pinsells sett, and foure faire young maides representing the foure cardinall
vertues, Justice, Temperance, Fortitude, and Prudence, or, as others report,
Peace, Justice, Plentie, and Policie. Everie one of them had an oration to the
King. The wheele of Fortune was burnt with powder.'

[2] *Hist. of K. James the Sext :* ' As he came towart the cheif collegiall kirk,
thare Dame Religion shew hirself, desyring his presence, whilk he then obeyit
be entring the kirk.' And cf. *Calderwood.*

[3] *Hist of K. James the Sext :* ' Bacchus with his magnifik liberalitie and
plentie, distributing of his liquor to all passingers and behalders, in sik apper-
ance as was pleasant to see.' *Calderwood :* ' Bacchus satt on a puncheon,
with his painted garment, and a flowre garland. He welcomed the King to his
owne toun. . . .'

[4] *Hist. of K. James the Sext :* ' A mercat place of salt, wharupon was payntit
the genealogie of the Kings of Scotland.' *Calderwood :* ' At the Salt Trone
was described the genealogie of the Kings of Scotland.'

[5] *Hist. of K. James the Sext :* ' And the same vivelie representit be the
assistance of King Ptolomé.'

[6] *Hist. of K. James the Sext :* ' The haill streits war spred with flowres.'
Calderwood : ' Frome the West Port to the Neather Bow, all the staires on
the High Street were covered with tapestrie, cards, and brods.'

[7] This incident is omitted in the other accounts of the entry.

and william fairly baillie to assist and tak care heirof And ỹe expensſß of the premisſß sall be allowet to ỹe said theſaurer in his compts' (f. 5). A bonfire to be 'bigget' and an honourable propine to be given (f. 6). Forty persons with halberts to await on neighbours to be appointed for bearing of the Queen's 'paill' (f. 8). 'Proclamatio. Beggaris Middings Baynefyres (f. 40).[1]]

Town
Treasurer's
Accounts,
1581-96

The compt of the expensſß maid be [2] in makine of preparatioun for the quenis entres as efter followis begyn- and ỹe first day of september 1589 ʒeiris

[Numerous details re 'daills,' spars, 'geistis,' and sand.] p. 535

Item thre grit Jeistis of fir quhair wpoun the skaffald ỹairof Is biggit vpoun at xx š ỹe pece   iij ħ.

Item for vpbringing of his haill tymer to ỹe toun
      iiij ħ. x š.

Item for fywetene laid of lyme to cast and mend ỹe nether bow   iij ħ.

Item payit to the spargeoneris [3] for spargein the nether bow
      xlij š.

[Payments for the 'armeis' at the Nether Bow and West Port.]

Item for ane dosane of pwntiouns to be skaffald   viij ħ.

Item for bringing of daillis and puntionis & staneis fra p. 536 the kirk ʒaird to the nether bow and mak skaffalding to the samyn   x š.

Item for thre doissin of walter to the lyme at ỹe nether bow
      vj š.

Item payit for careing of fourtie daillis thre grit jeistis to the west port and for wpputting of thame to the wallheid to the werkmen   xiij š iiij ₫

Item payit at command of the counsaill to the maister of ỹe sang schole for certane thingis that he haid bottit to the barneis to play   v ħ xvij š

Item mair delyuerit to the said maister aucht eħns of bukrum of cullouris to be breikis and hoidis to the barneis at aucht schillingis the eħn   iij ħ iiij š

Item payit to george doncane tailʒeour for making of thame
      xxx š

---

[1] In Documents relative to the Reception of the Kings and Queens of Scotland, 1822, 34-38, these entries have been printed.

[2] 'me' omitted in MS.

[3] Plasterers.

Item payit and delyuerit to thomas Alexander tail3eour at
command of robert hendersoun barbour to be barneis
coittis fyftene etnis of auld bukrum at aucht schillingis
ꝑe etn   summa vj ťi

p. 537   [Payments for ' gilting ' the ' armeis ' at the Nether
Bow and West Port, colouring the Cross, &c.]

Item payit be me to Johnne werkman painter for ꝑe gilting
of the tua armeis at the nether bow and for painting
of the glob [1] and for fourtene armeis and fourtene
crouneis and fourtene septouris vith certane coittis of
airmour [2] in all vas agreit vith him be the counsaill
summa xxxiij ťi vj s̄ viij đ
Item for ane doissin of hardin to cower ꝑe glob   xl s̄
Item payit to the tail3eour for cowering for his vork   xv s̄
Item payit to dauid doncane smyth for mending of the glob
and for making of ane new schyre [3] of Irne vnto   v ťi
Item delyuerit to Johne werkman painter ane doissin of
hardin to be ꝑe barneis coittis of airmour afoir writtyn
xxxvj s̄

[Payments for the unicorn for the head of the Cross.]

Item bottit at sindre tymeis of plain3our [4] naillis to the
haill skaffalding throw the toun aucht hundreth at fywe
schillingis ꝑe hundreth   summa xl s̄

p. 538 Item for careing of tua grit ruife sparis to the west port to
be standartis to ꝑe skaffald & aucht daillis   iiij s̄
Item payit to foure werkmen for helping to mak ꝑe skaffald
at the croſs and for bryning of ꝑe wnicorne from the
cannogait and for helping of it vpoun the cros and for
ane pynt of wyne to the wrichtis In all   xij s̄
Item payit to James baxter and to his ſseruandis for the
space of thre oulkis that ꝑai wer at ꝑe graithing of ꝑe
neꝑer bow west port the cros and auld tolbuithe and all
vther skaffaldis and werkis that wes to do at that tyme
and for the making of the brodis of thre airmeis
summa xiij ťi
Item for ane werkman to ſserwe ꝑem for thre oulkis at
auchtene schillingis ꝑe owlk   summa liiij s̄
Item for sawing of aucht daillis   xx s̄

---

[1] It is not clear which globe this was.   There was one at the West Port
and one at the Bow.   (Infra, 202-3.)
[2] Perhaps for the kings at the Salt Tron.
[3] Chair.
[4] MS. plain3oᵗ.

Item payit for tua pair of Irne bandis to put at ȝe west
port to the place of the glob to suddenlie discend [1]

x ȝ̃

Item the aucht day of september payit to ane boy to pas p. 542
to Dundie & feche ȝem the glob to ȝe quenis entre

summa xvj ȝ̃

Followis the materiallis quhilk ȝe compter grantis he hes p. 548
to delyuer to ȝe thesaurer present
First ane dosone of new pvnscheouns in his awin hands . . .
The glob with the chyre in Jhonn mvres & dauid duncanes
In the maister of the sang scholes hands aucht elnis of
bukrome
threttie pund pulder in Jhonn mᶜmoram thesaurer hands

Item ȝe 29 of maij 1590 payit to threscoir helbartis at ȝe p. 569
quenis entrie according to ane precept   xx ƚi
Item payit ȝe samin day to ȝe fidleris   v ƚi

ffolowis ȝe comptaris expensɾ in particular debursit at ȝe p. 571
preparatioun for ȝe quenis maiestieis entres
Item payit to alexander vddert for ix elis quarter and half
quarter of talphetie of the cord at xlv ȝ̃ ȝe ell to be hand-
seinȝeis extendis to . . .   xxj li ij ȝ̃

> [There followis a detailed account for the ' hand-
> seinȝeis ' amounting to £107. 9.]

> [Detailed account, amounting to £26. 1. 4, for the
> repairing and painting of ' the scaffald vpone ȝe
> foirsyd of the auld tolbuith ȝe xxvij aprile 1590.]

ffollowis ȝe comptaris dischairge of tymber coft be him p. 572
for scaffalding & vther neidfull provisioun at hir maiestieis
entrefɾ

> [Detailed account amounting to £72. 2. 4.]

The banefyre maid ȝe first day of maij 1590 vpon ȝe craigis
at hir maiestieis hame cuming

> [Detailed account for coals, tar barrels, &c., amount-
> ing to 47/-]

---

[1] Cf. infra, 202 and n[1].

p. 573 Heir followis the comptaris discharge of small expensſſ in
making of scaffald*is* & vtherwayis debursit be him ȝe tyme
of hir maiestie*is* entreſſ in maij 1590

Item first payit for sawing of sex dail*is* and tua garroun*is*
to ȝe salt trone   xvj ſ vj đ

Item for carying of dail*is* and vther tymber fra my close
to ȝe bow heid bow fit west port salt trone & nether
bow   xviij ſ viij đ

Item payit to nicoll gilmo*ur* wry*ch*t for making of all ȝe
scaffaldis w*ith* drink gevin ȝairto   v ħ

Item payit for blok*is* & toll*is* [1] to ȝe glob at ȝe west port
                                              xxviij ſ vj đ

Item for toll*is* to ȝe salt trone   ix ſ vj đ

Item payit to warkmen ȝ*at* helpit to mak ȝe scaffaldis
                                                      xxxvj ſ

Item I payit for nail*is* to ȝe haill scaffald*is* . . .   v ħ x ſ
[Other payments for nails.]

Item payit to ȝe warkmen for taking doune & putting vp
agane of the tua trones and carying away ȝe wecht*is* &
brod*is*   xxiiij ſ

Item payit for clengeing ȝe nether bow heid   viij ſ

Item payit to ro*bert* hendersone ȝ*at* he debursit of expensſſ
at ȝe salt trone conforme to his co*m*pt   xxviij ſ viij đ

Item payit for carying of the airmes to ȝe salt trone &
birk*is* ȝairt*o* q*uh*ilk I payit to george carkettill
                                                      xxv ſ vj đ

Item I payit for thre dosone of glaisſſ to ȝe crose [2]   iij ħ xij ſ

p. 574 Item payit for xij buist*is* scrochert*is* and co*m*fet*is* ȝat was
cassin over ȝe staig [3] of the bow ȝe day of hir entres
                                              iij ħ ij ſ viij đ

Item payit to thomas fischer for small expensſſ debursit
be him at ȝe nether bow conforme to his compt
                                                      xlj ſ iiij đ

Item payit to dauid w*illia*msone for small expensſſ debursit
be him at ȝe corſſ co*n*forme to his comptis
                                              xxix ħ viij ſ vj đ

Item payit to Jo*hn*n dauidsoneis wyfe for bucru*m* ȝat scho
payit to thomas alex*ander* for making of the nymphis
clais [4] & vther furneising furneisit be him co*n*forme to
his compt   v ħ xviij ſ vj đ

Item payit to dauid dunca*n* for Irne wark to ȝe glob &
row at ȝe west port [5]   xviij ſ

[1] Rows, ropes. Cf. *infra*, 202 and n[1].   [2] Cf. *infra*, 204.
[3] Possibly ' stair*is*.'   [4] Cf. *infra*, 203.   [5] Cf. *infra*, 202 and n[1].

Item I payit to ꝑe said dauid for ꝑe fassioun of tua gadd*is*
of Irne ꝑat was vpone ꝑe salt trone   x ſ

Item tynt vpone ꝑe wecht of the said tua gadd*is* of Irne
half ane stane wecht pryce   ix ſ

Item gevin to ꝑe menstrel*is* ꝑat playit ꝑe day of hir ma*ies*-
tie*is* entres   iij ħ

Item payit for xvij mask*is* ꝑat hing*is* in ꝑe counsall hous to
ꝑe moir*is* [1]   xxxiiij ſ

Item for painting ꝑe ȝoung men   xlij ſ

Item payit to Jo*hn*n warkma*n* for painting of sevin stalfis [2]
    xviij ſ

Item to him for painting of foure stoup*is* of ane bed at ꝑe
salt trone [3] wi*th* painting of bachus [4]   xx ſ

Item to him for painting of hercules [5] baton & rod   x ſ

Item for painting of septo*uris* [6]   x ſ
q*uh*ilk is conforme to his compt

Item gevin to foure tabareis & ane peper ꝑe day of the
muster*is* q*uh*ilk was xxiij day of aprile 1590   iij li vj ſ

Item payit for putting vp the stremar*is* vpone ꝑe stepill   p. 575
ꝑe day of hir ma*ies*tie*is* entres   x ſ

Item payit to Johne cwni*n*ghame goldsmy*th* for ꝑe tua
siluer keyis q*uh*ilk was gevin to hir ma*ies*tie for ꝑe siluer
& fassioun ꝑairof [7]   xviij ſ

Item for ane string of silk to thame & ꝑe townes seill q*uh*ilk
was prese*n*tit in ꝑe abay be ꝑe proveist   viij ſ viij đ

Item payit to ar*ch*ibal*d* geddes for tua ell*is* of quhyt talphetie ꝑat ꝑe bairne was rowin in at ꝑe west port [8]
    iiij ħ xij ſ

Item payit to paull masone for puting vp the airmes at ꝑe
west port   xiij ſ iiij đ

Item gevin to dustefit for soupeing ꝑe calsayis   iij ſ iiij đ

Item payit to ane wricht for making ꝑe bar*is* at ꝑe kirk
dur*is* ꝑe day of hir entres   xij ſ

Item for carying ꝑe dail*is* & vther tymber to ꝑame
    iij ſ iiij đ

Item payit for wodbind to set about ꝑe armes & bringing in
of it q*uh*ilk was fetche far of   xv ſ

---

[1] Cf. *infra*, 203 and n[1].
[2] Cf. *infra*, 202.
[3] Cf. *infra*, 204.
[4] Cf. *infra*, 204.
[5] He is not mentioned by name by any of the diarists.
[6] Probably for the kings at the Salt Tron.
[7] Cf. *infra*, 202 and n[1].
[8] Cf. *infra*, 202 and n[1].

Item for setting of the airmes wit*h* ꝑe wodbynd   x ſ

Item payit to (*blank*) graham ꝑe werkma*n* & vther tua
wark men ꝑ*at* weitcheit ꝑe salt trone tua ny*cht*is x ſ viij đ

Item for nail*is* to ꝑe bar*is* ꝑ*at* was maid at ꝑe kirk dur
         vij ſ vj đ

p. 576 Item for beiring in and out ꝑe kirk formes to ꝑe croſ ꝑe
day of hir entres   iij ſ iiij đ

Item payit to nicoll gylmo*ur* for taking doune of all ꝑe
scaffald*is* and for four dayis wark of him self & tua
warkmen in putting vp ꝑe q*uh*ilk is not comptit of befoir
I payit him   vj ħ

Item for drink & drinksiluer to ꝑame   xv ſ

Item for carying of all ꝑe tymber first to my clois & ꝑairefter
to ꝑe kirk   xxviij ſ

Item payit to wark men ꝑ*at* helpit to tak doune ꝑe scaffald*is*
     xxx ſ

Item payit for carying of tymber fra ꝑe tolbuith to ꝑe kirk
     viij ſ

Su*m*ma of the haill expensſ debursit in smallis ꝑe
tyme of hir ma*ie*sti*eis* entres co*n*forme to this ꝑ*ar*ticular
compt befoir writtin extend*is* comptand h'andsein3e*is*
tymber & all vtherthingis to ꝑe sowme of iij° xxxiiij ħ
j ſ ij đ q*uh*ilk is by & atto*ur* ꝑe xx ħ payit to ꝑe halbert
men alreddie comptit be prece*b*t

p. 577 ffollowis ꝑe expensſ debursit vpone ꝑe suord dance and
hieland dansſ [1]

Item ꝑe xxvj day of aprile I gaif James inglis tail3eo*ur*
     iij ħ

Item ꝑe 27 day of aprile I gaif him   v ħ

Item gevin to henrie quhyt cordiner for xij pair of quhyt
schone at x ſ ꝑe pair is   vj ħ

Item mair to ꝑat cumpanie in money   iiij ħ

Item I payit ꝑair menstrell at sindrie tymes   liij ſ iiij đ

Ite*m* mair I gaif James inglis in money   v li xiij ſ iiij đ

Item payit to alex*ande*r vddert for xij hatt*is* of flo*ur*is
     xvij ſ vj đ

Item I payit to Johne dauidsoneis wyfé for bellis furneisit
to ꝑe sword dansar*is*   v ħ j ſ

Item payit to James dalgleische for bel*is* & buccrum furneist
be him co*n*forme to his compt   x ħ vj ſ viij đ

---

[1] There is no mention of these dances in any of the contemporary descriptions of the entry.

Item gevin to dauid patersone for ꝑe warkmanship of xvij
stand of hie land menis claithis 1 s̃

Item gevin to ꝑe maister of the sang scole to interteney his
hieland danseris iij ƚi

Item to ꝑe maister of sang scoilis cumpanie conforme to ane
directioun of the counsale iij ƚi

Item payit Johne warkman for painting of xij girthis x s̃

    Suma of thir expensſ is
    Lateris li ƚi xj s̃ x đ

The money debursit be me William ff(airlie) vpon ꝑe
furnessing maid to ꝑe que(nis) entres in anno 1589

    [pp. 285 ff. Detailed list of materials for the ' paill '
and the making of it : purple velvet, lining of crimson
taffeta, gold and red fringes, ' sex beirring staiffs,' timber,
&c. Details of ' ane bybill to be gevin to ꝑe quene ' [1]
with a covering of ' ane Marokin skin,' gilt ' broddis ' and
ribbons. Payment to the goldsmith for the jewel presented to the Queen, for its black leather case, for a
' peirill hung to ꝑe Jowell ' and for five ells of ribbon
' to lat down ꝑe Jewell to ꝑe provest at ye neꝑer bow.' [2]
Payment to Henry Charterhous for ' ane psalme buke ' [3]
to the Queen and for strings to it.]

Bailies'
Accounts,
Extents,
and Unlaws,
1564-1644.

    [The most detailed account of the entry of Anne of
Denmark is given in *Papers relative to the Marriage
of James VI. of Scotland,* Bann. Club, 1828, from a
tract dated 1590.]

The Receiving of James the Sixt and his Queene at
Lyeth in Scotland the First of May Last Past.

. . . At her comming to the south side of the yardes of
the Canogit, along the parke wall, being in sight of the

p. 39

19th May.[4]

---

[1] Cf. *infra*, 202 n[1].
[2] Cf. *infra*, 204.
[3] Cf. *infra*, 202 n[1].
[4] State Papers (Scotland), Elizabeth, Vol. XLV, No. 44 (Public Record
Office). Mr Bowes to Lord Burghley. Edinburgh, 16th May 1590. ' The
Coronaĉon and th'entrie of the Q: were appointed to haue been solempnized
tomorrow in St: Giles Churche in Edenbrughe. But bicause some of the ministers thought that the pagions and devises for th'entrie should partlie prophane
the Saboth daie, therefore they perswaided that it might rather be done on
some other daie in the weke. Vpon this motion, but chefelie (as it is thought)
bicause all thinges were not fullie readie for the coronaĉon and th'entree to
haue been executed togither, the k. and counsell tooke new order to solempnize
the coronaĉon tomorrow in th'abbay Churche at holieroodhouse, and th'entrie

castle, they gave her thence a great volle of shotte, with
their banners and auncients displayed uppon the walles.
Thence shee came to the West Port, under the which her
Highnesse staied, and had an oration to welcome her to the
towne, uttered in Latine, by one Maister John Russell, who
was thereto appointed by the townshippe ; whose sonne
also being placed uppon the toppe of the Port head, and
was let downe by a deuise made in a globe, which being
come somewhat over her Maiesties heade, opened at the
toppe into foure quarters, where the childe, appearing in
the resemblance of an angell, delivered her the keyes of the
towne in silver ; [1] which done, the quarters closed, and the
globe was taken uppe agayne, so as the childe was no more
seene there.   Shee had also a canapie of purple veluet,
embrodered with gold, carried over her by sixe ancient
townesmen.   There were also three score young men of
the towne, lyke Moores, and clothed in cloth of silver, with
chaines about their neckes, and bracelets about their
armes, set with diamonds and other precious stones, very
gorgeous to the eie, who went before the chariot, betwixt
the horsemen and it, everie one with a white staffe in

in Edenbrugh on Tuesdaie next. The Prouost and Burgesses of this Towne
of Edenbrughe found themselues greatlie disapointed and greued with this
sodaine change, turning their offence to the Chancelour and the ministers
here, and laboring to procure th'order for the coronačon at the Abbay to be
reuoked. The matter for a while was something sharp & muche encombred
the k. and others. But it is now indifferentlie appeased, and yet not cleare
quenched.'
    Calderwood, V, 95 : ' The King and the Danes would have had both the
coronatioun of the queene and her entrie to Edinburgh, upon the Lord's day.
The proveist and bailliffes reviled despitefullie these ministers who laboured
in the contrare, speciallie Mr Johne Davidsone. By his perswasioun, Chanceller
Matlane laboured to have her entrie to Edinburgh upon another day nor the
Sabboth.'
    [1] *Diarey of Robert Birrel*. Dalyell's Fragments of Scottish History. 'ʒoung
boys, vith artificiall winges, at her entry, did flee touards her, and presented
her tuo siluer keyes of ʒe city.' *Moysie's Memoirs*, 83 : ' delyverie of the keyisse
as vse is.' *Johnston's MS. History*, II, f. 598, Adv. Lib. Hist. MSS. : ' quhair
ane glob was lattin, quhilk opinand ane bairne delyuerit certane keyis with
ane bybill and psalme buik.' Cf. the similar anglicised account in *Calderwood*,
V, 96-7. John Burel, *The Description of the Queenis Maiesties Maist Honorable
Entry into the Town of Edinburgh upon the* 19th *day of Maij* 1590. Quoted in
Papers Relative to the Marriage of James VI.)

> ' I haue forʒet how in a robe,
> Of clenely crispe side to his kneis
> A bony boy out of the Globe
> Gaue to hir Grace the silver Keis ;
> And how that he his harang maid,
> With countenance quhilk did not faid.'

his hande, to keepe of the throng of people ; [1] where also
rid the Prouost and Baileefes of the toune, with footeclothes
to keep the people in good order, with most of the inhabitants in their best araie to doe the like.   In this order
her Grace passed on the Bow Street, where was erected
a table, whereupon stoode a Globe of the whole Worlde,
with a Boy sitting thereby, who represented the person of
a King, and made an oration ; which done, she went up
the Bowe, when were cast forth a number of banketting
dishes as they came by ; [2] and comming to the Butter
Trone, there were placed nine maidens, brauely arraied
in cloth of silver and gold, representing the nine Muses,[3]
who sung verie sweete musicke, where a brave youth
played upon the organs, which accorded excellentlie with
the singing of their psalmes ; whereat her Maiestie staid
awhile and thence passed downe through the high gate of
Edinbrough, which was all decked with tapestry from the
top to the bottom.   At her Grace's comming to the Tolbooth, there stood on high the four Virtues, as first Justice,
with the Balance in one hand, and the Sword of Justice
in the other ; then Temperance, having in one hand a
cup of wine, and in the other hande a cup of water ;
Prudence, holding in her hand a Serpent and a Dove,
declaring, that men ought to bee as wise as the serpent,
to prevent daunger, but as simple as the dove eyther in
wrath or malice ; the last is Fortitude, who held a
broken pillar in her hand, representing the strength of a
kingdome.[4]

Thus she passed on to the Crosse, vppon the topp whereof

[1] *Johnston's MS. History :* ' 24 ʒoungkeiris, Cled with moist coistlie apparrell
some with claith of siluer wtheris with quhyt taffetie with mony precious
cheinʒeis, about ʒair airmes Legis Neckis with ringis *with visareis on thair
faces lik till Moiris.*' (Part underlined is added in another hand.) Cf. also
Calderwood. Moysie. 'xlij young men . . . and wisseouris of black cullour
on thair faces lyk Mores . . . that dancit befoir hir grace all the way.' *John
Burel* gives a detailed description of the Moors ' acoutert in an sauadage sort.'
[2] *Johnston's MS. History :* ' Thair eftir com to the throit of the over bow
quhair *maister* hercules rollok *maister* of the gramer schooll maid his Oresoun.'
Cf. *Calderwood.*
[3] Are those the 'nymphis' of the town treasurer's account (*supra*, 198) ?
Cf. the lengthy description of the 'Nymphs who supit Nectar cauld' and
their dresses, by *John Burel. Johnston* states that at the Butter Trone 'ane
bairne ('Mr Johne Craig's sonne,' according to *Calderwood*) maid ane Latine
oresoun.'
[4] *Johnston's MS. History :* ' At the tolbuith was ʒoung bairnes on ane
skaffald in wemenes cleithing representing peax plentie, polacie—Iustice
Liberalitie and temperance quhair euerie ane schew thair selffis and Naturallie
in Latyne.' Cf. *Calderwood.*

she had a psalme sung in verie good musicke, before her coming to the churche ; which done, her Maiestie came forth of her chariot, and was carried into S. Giles' Church, where she heard a sermon preached by Mr Robert Bruce. That ended, with praiers for her Highnesse, she was conveied againe to her chariot. Against her comming forth, there stood upon the top of the Crosse a table covered, whereupon stood cups of gold and silver full of wine, with the Goddesse of Corne [1] and Wine sitting thereat, and the corne in heaps by her, who, in Latin, cried that there should be plentie thereof in her time ; and on the side of the crosse sate the god Bacchus vpon a punchion of wine, winking and casting it by cups full vpon the people, besides other of the townes-men, that cast apples and nuts among them ; and the Crosse itself ranne claret wine upon the caulsway, for the loyaltie of that day.

Thence her Grace rode downe the gate to the Sault Trone, whereupon sate all the kings heertofore of Scotland, one of them lying along at their feete, as if he had been sick, whom certain souldiers seemed to awake at her Maiesties comming, whereupon he arose, and made her an oration in Latine ; [2] which ended, she passed downe to the Nether-Bow, which was beautified with a marriage of a King and his Queene, with all their nobilitie about them,[3] among whom, at her Highnes presence, there arose a youth, who applied the same to the marriage of the King and herselfe, and so blessed that marriage. Which done, there was let downe unto her, from the top of the porte, in a silke string, a box couered with purple veluet ; whereupon was embroidered A. for Anna, her Maiestie's name, set with diamonds and precious stones, esteemed at twentie thousand crownes, which the township gave for a present to her Highnes ; [4] and then, after the singing of some psalmes, with verie good musicke, her Grace departed to the Abbey for that night.

---

[1] The other accounts do not mention Ceres.

[2] *Johnston's MS. History* : ' quhair was representit the kingis grace genelageie in the forme of a trie from the bruce till himselff, quhair ane bairne at the root of the trie maid ane Oresoun in latyne discryvand the haill bairnes and brainches.' Cf. *Calderwood.*

[3] This incident is omitted in the other accounts. *Johnston :* ' And syne com to the netherbow quhair the 7 planetis war and gave the weird in Latine. All thir Oresounes was to the thanking of god and Loveing of the king and queanes grace.   And spokin in Latyne becaus the queane wnderstood na Scotis.'

[4] *Johnston* omits this, and *Calderwood* dismisses it briefly.

19th July 1598

precept
thesaurer
hie schole
play

The sam day ordanis Jhonn howesoun the*saurer* to caus bye als mekill gray as will be fyve freris weids and sum grof [1] reid clay*th* to be ꝑe weid of ane paip & his cardinells to ſſerve in ꝑe play to be playet be ꝑe principall and maist*ers* & his schollers of ꝑe hie schole Provyding ꝑat ꝑe clay*this* be at ꝑe end of ꝑe play delyuerit to ꝑe the*saurer* to be gevin to ꝑe puir at ꝑe sicht of ꝑe counsall and ꝑe expensſ heirof to be allowet to ꝑe said the*saurer* in his *compts*.[2]

play
clay*this*

Item ꝑe said 19 of Julij payit to andro creiche m*er*chant for 8 ell*is* thre quart*eris* rid freis to be gownis for ane paip and twa cardinall*is* q*uh*ilk wes playit in ꝑe comedie be ꝑe bairnis of ꝑe gramm*er* skole cost xxxv ꝸ ꝑe ell *con*form to ane precept extend*is* to ꝑe soum of   xv ħ vj ꝸ iiij ꝺ

Town Treasurer's Accounts, 1596-1612

Item to alex*ander* lyndsay for ane ell ane quarter rid freis to supplie ꝑe want of ꝑe said*is* gownis becaus Andro creiche had na mair cost liij ꝸ iiij ꝺ ꝑe ell is   iij ħ vj ꝸ viij ꝺ

1598 p. 116

Item ꝑe sam day to george huntlie tail3our for xix ell*is* & ane half of quhyt and gray clay*th* to be gownis for fyve freir*is* to ꝑe said play cost xix ꝸ ꝑe ell extend*is* to
                              xix ħ x ꝸ vj ꝺ

Item to ꝑe said george for making ꝑe said*is* gownis
                              liij ꝸ iiij ꝺ

Item ꝑe 26 of Julij 1598 for carrying of lx daill*is* fra ꝑe societie wark to ꝑe gramm*er* skole to mak ane skafald ꝑair to play ꝑe comedye & for carying of xij pu*n*schon*is*
                              xxiij ꝸ iiij ꝺ

p. 122

Item for carrying ꝑe said*is* daill*is* to ꝑe heyche tolbuit*h* and pu*n*schonis to mak ane skafald to ꝑe player*is* of ꝑe comedye & for transporting ꝑe samyn hameagain to ꝑame ꝑat lent ꝑame   xliij ꝸ

Item for ane hunder & ane half of plenscho*ur* naill*is*   xij ꝸ

Item payit to moyses skrogye wry*ch*t for his painis in making ꝑe skafald at ꝑe hie skole & skafald at ꝑe tolbuit*h*
                              xx ꝸ

Item payit to robert prestoun m*er*chant for four pu*n*schonis q*uh*ilk wes borrowit be ꝑe bairnis of ꝑe said gramm*er* skole to mak ꝑe said skaffald*is* & tint ꝑame be resoun ꝑai brak ꝑame all in stalfis & delyu*er*it ꝑame no*ch*t again
                              liij ꝸ iiij ꝺ

---

[1] Coarse.   MS. Council Register, Vol. X, f. 192.

Item to Johne m*a*kcowll offi*ciar* for ane galloun aill q*uhi*lk
ꝑe skoller*is* drank ꝑe tyme ꝑai playit ꝑe comedie in ꝑe
tolbuit*h*   x ſ̃ viij đ

<table>
<tr><td>p. 144</td><td>[In the list of ' geir ' in the ' comptar's ' hands the following items occur] :—</td></tr>
</table>

Ite*m* mair thre gownis of rid freis ꝑat wes maid for ane
paip & twa cardinall*is* to ꝑe skoller*is* ꝑat playit ꝑe
comedie

Ite*m* mair v gownis of quhyt clayt*h* and gray clayt*h* ꝑat
wes maid to fyve freir*is* in ꝑe said play

<table>
<tr><td>p. 155</td><td>[The auditors command] The *con*sal to se ꝑat ꝑe the-*saure*r resaue fra John*n* howſ ꝑe play claꝑis furneist to ꝑe scoller*is* *con*form to ꝑe *com*pt 19 July</td></tr>
</table>

<table>
<tr><td>1599-1600
p. 288</td><td>Followis the material*lis* ꝑerteni*n*g to the to*n* to be delyuerit to ꝑe *pre*se*n*t the*saure*r patrik eleis</td></tr>
</table>

First the play clayt*h*is vnderwrittin q*uhi*lk ro*bert* hereis
last the*saure*r coft

To witt foure quhyt coittis with hudeis & slewis

Ane $\frac{\text{blak}}{\text{gray}}$ coitt with ane hude

Thre reid gouns with slewis and nekis

3rd Feb. 1604

<table>
<tr><td>precept
the*saure*r
play
clayt*his*</td><td>The sam day Ordanis hector ra the*saure*r to gif to ꝑe maiste*r*s of ꝑe hospitall the play clayt*his* to be jowppis to ꝑe pure in the said hospitall and ꝑe sam to be allowet in his *com*pts [1]</td></tr>
</table>

[There are many entries relating to the visit of James VI.
in 1617 in Vol. XII. of the Council Register : Ancient
burgesses clad in black velvet to be in attendance (f. 254).
New liveries for officers. As the King has notified the
Privy Council that ' it is his will and pleſ*our* that ane
harrand and speache be maid to him at his entrie,' Mr
John Hay, Clerk Depute, is nominated to discharge that
function (f. 256). Building of the banquetting house in
the ' counsalhous yaird ' (f. 257). Propine of 10,000

----

[1] MS. Council Register, Vol. XI, f. 143.

marks (f. 258). Printing of Mr John Hay's speech (f. 259).[1]

Also in the volume of Treasurers' Accounts dated 1612-23 —*e.g.*, p. 472. Money for propine and for ' ane siluer basone o*u*rgilt ' and a purse ; also ' twa keyis of siluer.' pp. 482-3. Washing the Netherbow, cleaning and sanding and watering the streets. Repairing the banqueting house. p. 484. Making the scaffold that the Provost and Council stood on at the King's entry. p. 489. Printing the ' harrand.' p. 517. Disbursements for his Majesty's ' portraitto*u*r ' at the Netherbow. p. 519. Making scaffolds at Netherbow ' for dounetaking þe plaice q*u*ha*i*r þe portrate suld stand.' ' Waynscott ' to portrait. p. 520. Payment to the gold-smith ' for making þe scepter St andro and St george with þe ordo*u*r of þe thrissell,' &c. Books of gold for the Netherbow, &c. p. 544. ' Bottis ' to the King's picture. p. 530. ' Item to ane wyiff for sum glasſſ þe offic*iaris* tuik q*u*he*n* þe strangers danced throw þe toune. iiij ſi x ſ.']

[From 1628 onwards Charles I. was expected to visit Edinburgh. Elaborate preparations were made by the town in 1628-9. Details as to the official programme for 15th June 1633 are not to be found in the Treasurer's Accounts for that year ; but, from a comparison of the 1628-9 Account with the printed text of the 1633 pageant, there can be little doubt that the abortive preparations of 1628-9 were utilised at the later date.
Council Register, Vol. XIV., 14*th July* 1628. Letter from King announcing visit. Registers to be sought out ' anent the entrie of his Ma/ father and grandmother ' (f. 99). 17*th July* 1628. A certain number appointed ' to sett doun the haill project and forme of his Ma/ ressaite and quhat salbe doone to him at his entrie with all the pageants and vther thinges necessarie for his Royall Intertayine-ment and appointes to meit at sevin houres in the morning and at Tua houres in the efternoone ' (f. 100). 23*rd July* 1628. Council deliberated concerning the entry and ' Or-danis the same to be doone in the maist magnificent maner that can be devysit.' Money to be raised by ' extent.' Mr John Hay ' to mak the speich or harrand to his Ma/

[1] These entries from the Council Register have been printed in *Documents relative to the Reception of the Kings and Queens of Scotland*, 1822, 64-67. Cf. *The Muses' Welcome to the High and Mightie Prince James, Edinburgh*, 1618.

at his entrie at the west port.' *26th July* 1628. A 'pale'
to be carried over the King's head (f. 101). And cf. ff.
102, 110.[1]]

Treasurer's
Accounts,
1623-36

1628-9 Item to James mar wricht 4 dayes at the west port making
p. 512   ꝑe staige q*uhai*r ꝑe proveist and bail3eis sould stand
                                                    liij ß iiij đ
p. 601 Item on ꝑe xiij of december to dauid broune and thomas
       younger [2] for ane oulks wadges working in ꝑe banketthous
       at ꝑe staige of ꝑe west port   viij ŧib
       Item on ꝑe xv of december for xxx ell of hardin at vj ß
       viij đ ꝑe ell is   x ŧib
       Item to Johne smyith to paynt ꝑe toune of Edinbur*ght* [3]
       vpone ꝑe xvj of december for ij° fluiring naillis . . .
                                                    xxiiij ß
       Item on ꝑe xx of december to dauid broune and Thomas
       younger for ꝑair oulkis wadges working at ꝑe staige of
       ꝑe west port   viij ŧib
p. 602 Item thrie pais bord*is*   ix ß
       Item to m*aiste*r w*illia*m fairle for turning of twelff small
       bowllis for ꝑe peremeitheid and thrie greit bowllis for
       ꝑe heidis of ꝑe piremeit [4]
       [Loads of timber, workmen's wages, &c.]
       Item for towes and skeni3e to ꝑe paell   iiij ß
p. 603   [Other expenditure on the 'paell']
       Item on ꝑe thrid of Januarij to m*aiste*r w*illia*m fairle for
       turning four stoupes to ꝑe chyre   vj ß
       Item on ꝑe fyft of Januarij xxx ell of hardin to ꝑe staige
       of ꝑe bow at vj ß viij đ ꝑe ell is   x ŧib
       Item to Jo*h*nn Rynd ane vnce yellow silk   xxxiij ß iiij đ
       Item to alex*ande*r speir iij pund schewing gold to be ane
       frein3e to ꝑe paill weyis xxv vnce xiij drop scottis
       wecht . . .   j°xxxviij ŧib
       Item to Johne makcubeyie thrie elne and ane half blak
       and quhyt spainis taffitie to be the trumpetours
       baneris . . .   xxj ŧib

---

[1] These entries from the Council Register have been printed in *Documents
relative to the Reception of the Kings and Queens of Scotland*, 1822, p. 69 *et seq.*
Also those on p. 211, *infra*.
[2] Payments to David Brown, Thomas ·Younger, and several assistants
continue regularly up to July 1629.
[3] Cf. *infra*, 214, West Port.
[4] Cf. *infra*, 216, Salt Tron (*b*).

Item on ꝑe aucht of Januarij coft frome Adame Lambe
goldsmyith ane dowble our gilt baseine [1] . . .
ij^clviij ℔

[Taffeta bought in quantity.]

Item iij^c duir naill to ꝑe greit pilleris in ꝑe bow   xx ſ   p. 604

Item for xviij ell of claith to ꝑe paynter for ꝑe golden
letteris and ane chapter abone ꝑe west port [2] at vj ſ viij đ
ꝑe ell   vj ℔

Item for turning tua greit pilleris   xxiiij ſ

Item gewin to Johne smyith for payinting the Toune of p. 605
Edinbur*ght*   j^c ℔

Item for xv bowkes of gold to ourgilt ꝑe toune ꝑe *lettr*es
abone and ꝑe chap*tour*   xv ℔

Item for fyve pund glew to glew ꝑe toppis of ꝑe tolbuith
staige and ꝑe nether bow staige   xl ſ

Item on ꝑe nynt of februarij to george Jamesone for his
expensſ *cumming* out of aberdeine to aggrie w*ith* ꝑe
guid toune   xvij ℔ viij ſ

Item to Alex*ande*r Law for *cumming* out of falkland to p. 606
aggrie w*ith* ꝑe goodtoune   lviij ſ

[Payments for various paints, 'ane barrell of ten
gallouns of lyngit oyle with siluer and gold bookis
and plait gold bookis.']

Item to thomas and Johne stories for paynting twa
pictours   xxx ℔

Item to alex*ande*r law paynter twa dayis   xl ſ

Item coft of small claith on ꝑe xxiij of februarij lxx ell to p. 607
george Jamesone at ix ſ ꝑe ell   xxxj ℔ xj ſ

Item to m*aiste*r w*illia*m fairlie for four greit globbis
    xvj ſ

Item for turning of four pendentes   xvj ſ

Item for turneing of ꝑe thrie greit piraneittis at ꝑe tol-
buithend   vj ſ

Item to alex*ande*r law and his boy for ꝑair oulks wages [3]
    vij ℔

Item to Jo*hn*n myller paynter for fyve dayis at xiij ſ iiij đ
ilk day [4]   iij ℔ vj ſ viij đ

Item on ꝑe thrid of merche to ꝑe begynning to sett wp ꝑe
staige at ꝑe west port   xxxvj ſ

Item for twa crounis that wes maid be ane man in Leyith p. 608
wynd   lviij ſ

[1] Cf. *infra*, 215, West Port (*a*) and (*c*).
[2] Cf. *infra*, 214, West Port (*a*).
[3] This payment recurs up to August.
[4] This payment recurs.

Item for xiij piggis to ᵹe paynters for ᵹair cullouris

iiij ŝ

p. 609 Item for four qwhellis to carye ᵹe pirameit frome plaice to
plaice   xv ŝ iiij đ

p. 610 Item to maister william fairlie for turning of fyve gret
bowllis to ᵹe neᵹer bow [1]   xiiij ŝ

p. 611 Item to thomas weir for thrie stane of lead to ᵹe bottis of
ᵹe staiges . . . .   vj ƚib

Item to maister william fairle for twa reveres for ᵹe mont
at ᵹe west port twa thrissellis for ᵹe nether bow staige
and ane scheater to ᵹe pirameit altogidder   xxiiij ŝ

p. 612 Item payit to Adame Lambe deacone of ᵹe goldsmythis
for twa keyis with ᵹe cheinᵹie [2] . . .

xxxvij ƚib vj ŝ iiij đ

Item on ᵹe xviij of apryle to george Jamesone paynter

viijᶜ ƚib

p. 613 Item for turneing twa bowllis for ᵹe staige at ᵹe nether
bow   xij ŝ

Item to Robert grew calsaymaker for sewin dayis working
vpone ᵹe hie streit and about ᵹe staiges at xiij ŝ iiij đ ilk
day   iiij ƚib xiij ŝ iiij đ

Item for tackettis and wyre to ᵹe sceether   iij ŝ

Item to maister william fairlie for turning of xxj pilleris
to ᵹe nether bow   xiiij ŝ

Item to alexander law for goldsyis to lay on ᵹe gold with

iij ƚib

Item to thomas duncane for making of four crounis

x ƚib

p. 614 Item on ᵹe xix of maij for lxviij ell of lynning claith to ᵹe
kyngis staige at ix ŝ ᵹe ell   xxx ƚib xij ŝ

Item to williame broune for sewing of yelaill claithis to ᵹe
pageantis and Irneing of it   x ƚib

Item for turning of xlj pilleris to ᵹe staige of ᵹe land mercatt
callit ᵹe kyngis staige   xxvij ŝ iiij đ

Item on ᵹe fyft day of Junij coft frome alexander menteith
xviij Jeastis to mak ᵹe piramet at ᵹe salt trone [3] with
vᵹer necesŝair things ᵹairto at xxx ŝ ᵹe peice is

xxvij ƚib

p. 615 Item for lynes to mesour ᵹe pirameit   ix ŝ

p. 616 Item for saweing of sevin daillis to ᵹe covir of ᵹe bowlls
of ᵹe pirameit at ij ŝ vj đ   xvij ŝ vj đ

---

[1] Cf. infra, 217, Nether Bow (a) and (b).
[2] Cf. infra, 215, West Port (a) and (b).
[3] Cf. infra, 216, Salt Tron. (b).

Item for piggis to ꝑe paynteris for ꝑair cullo*uris*
                       vij š iiij đ

Item on ꝑe xvij day of september to george Jamesone for p. 617
   paynting of ꝑe hundrethe and sewin kyngis at ꝑe counsellis *comman*d   vjᶜlxvj ƚib xiij š iiij đ [1]

Item payit for gilting of ꝑe kyngis at ꝑe counsellis *comman*d
                        xxxiij ƚib vj š viij đ

Item to williame bannantyne for onwaytting on alex*ande*r p. 618
   law and his boy quhen he payntit the staiges . . .
                            xxix ƚib

['Summa' of pp. 601-618 is £7354, 7s. 1d.]

[On p. 717 there is 'ane nott of ꝑe perticulleris delyuerit
be ꝑe compter To Williame gray *present* thesaurer
at mertimes 1630,' which includes many of the
articles prepared for the King's entry. See, too, at
the end of the 1631-2 account.]

[*Council Register, Vol. XIV.*, 10*th Dec.* 1631. Council
have heard that the King intends to come next spring or
summer.[2] Committee appointed to make arrangements
(f. 219). 11*th Jan.* 1633. Communication from King.
Again ordained that his Majesty shall be received in the
most magnificent manner, and that the money shall be
raised by extent (f. 252). 12*th Jan.* 1633. Committee
appointed to 'conveyne at all tymes requisite and to
appoint and tak ordour for the banquett pages and all
vther thinges that may be incident to his Ma/ receptioun'
(f. 253). 14*th Feb.* 1633. Goldsmiths' and skinners' shops
above the New Tolbooth to be taken down 'and the pagin
now standing at that plaice to be sett at ꝑe end of ꝑe said
new tolbuith' (f. 256). Other details *re* raising the money,
etc. (ff. 259, 268, 270).]

[1] Cf. *infra*, 216, West end of Tolbooth. Dr Bulloch, in his *Life of George
Jamesone*, 1885, p. 68, is inclined to doubt the tradition that Jamesone painted
portraits of the Kings of Scotland from Fergus the First onwards. The above
entry leaves no room for doubt as to the extent, at least, of his painting. In
the beginning of February 1629 (*supra*, 209) Jamesone arrives in Edinburgh;
on 23rd February, £31, 11s. is expended on 70 ells 'small claith' for him;
and he apparently continues at his great task throughout the spring and summer.
He seems to have been called in to help again in 1633, when he receives a
gratuity for his 'extraordinar paynes' (*infra*, 212), and is subsequently admitted
to the freedom of the burgh (*infra*, 212). As to the fate of the portraits, see
infra, 218 (*b*).
[2] The actual date of his entry was 15th June 1633.

Council
Register,
Vol. XIV.

f. 271 *7th Aug.* 1633

Precept
The*saurer*
Tillidaff

The Quhilk day the baillies dene of gild . . . ordanis James loch thesaurer to pay to Stephañ Tilliedaff musitiañ for setting and acting of the musick at parnassus hill [1] and at his Ma/ banquett in satisfactioun of his paines Tua hundreth merkis and to Andro sinclare organist for his paines and travellis in the same ane hundreth merkis and the same salbe allowit to him in his comptes [2]

f. 272 *23rd Aug.* 1633

Precept
The*saurer*
Jamesoun

The Quhilk day the Proveist . . . ordanis the thesaurer to pay to George Jamesoun painter for his extraordiner paynes taiken be him in the Tounes effaires at his Ma/ entrie within this burgh thriescore dollo*uris* and ffyve dolo*uris* to his ſſervand in drinksiluer and the same salbe allowit to him in his comptes [3]

28th Aug. 1633

Jamiesoun
B. gild b
gratis

The same day ordanis the deane of gild to admitt george Jamesoun painter burges and gildbrother of this burgh for payment of the ordiner soumes of money and to repay the same bak againe & the said soume salbe allowit to him in his comptes [4]

f. 329 *13th March* 1635

[Consideration of the compts of James Loch, Treasurer, for the sums of money 'debursit be him towards his Ma/ entrie & receptioun, in erecting of pagins, the propyne and Banquett and vthers thinges theñ incident' extending to the sum of £41,489, 7s. . . . 'As also ꝑe counsall vnderstanding that ꝑe said the*saure*r hes sauld to Johnne fleyming conforme to ane article of the 16 pag of his compt half ane hundreth of the dailles belonging to the Toun for saxtein pundis xiij ſ̃ iiij đ As also hes sauld the actors vestures and sindrie vther thinges Thairfore ordanis the said Jams to be chairged therwith in his comptes.']

[1] Cf. *infra*, 217, n[2].   [2] Cf. *infra*, 217, Salt Tron (*b*).
[3] Cf. *supra*, 211, n[1].   [4] *Ibid.*

Treasurer's
Accounts,
1623-36

Item þe 25 Januarij To Alexander Law pynter In arles to 1631-2
attend þe penting of þe staigis   iij ƚib xij ſ p. 858

Item to thomas younger for waitting vpon þe staigis qu*hen* p. 864
we luikit for þe kingis cumyng   xlvj ſ

1633
The compter chairges himselff with the soumes of money p. 936
addebtit to the guid Toun be the Borrowis and Ressauit
be him the ȝeir of Accompt with the vther soumes borrowit
vpoun band at Witsounday 1633, for defraying his Maiesties
entrie and receptioun within this brughe—Banqueit propyne
and vther thingis as was ordeanid be the Counsall and of
the vther soumes ressauit at command of the counsall as
followes
[Two pages of details.]
The Compter dischairges himselff with the sowmes of p. 950
money debursit the ȝeir of Accompt Towardis his maiesties
entrie and receptioun within this citie in erecting of
padgines propyne banqueit and vther thingis than incident Conforme to the seuerall actis of Counsall Ordeaning
the same*n*
Item the Compter dischairges himselff with the saidis
soumes of money debursit be him in maner foirsaid Conforme to his comptis given in þairanent and ffittit be the
Auditores appoyntit be the Counsall vpoun the 12 of
Mairche 1635 and act of Counsall maid the 13 of the said
moneth Extending in the haill to the soume of
            xljᵐ iiijᶜ lxxxix ƚib vij ſ

[Payment for mending of the ' calsay ' at the Nether Bow p. 959
' that was brokine and takin away with the staiges.']

[Payment for cleaning the place that the fleshers took p. 960
' qu*hai*r the staige stuid on the landmercat.']

[£15. 4. to Alexander Baxter and Thomas Younger with
two men six days ' for putting vp the Kairtis and peices
of paynterie about the counsall and banqueit houſ.']

1634
[The Compter charges himself with £16. 13. 4 received p. 1008
from John Fleming for ' certane Dailles of the padgines ';
also with £673. 6. 8 received by him from James Naismith
' for the westuris hingingis courteines and vther Decor-

mentis vseit at his ma*ies*ties receptioun'; also with
£58. 15. for 'the hardine of the saidis paidgines' sold to
James Nairn; also with £72. 8. for 'poulder' sold to the
neighbours of the town.]

p. 1063 Ane note of the particularis delyuerit be the compter to
Dauid M^ccall present Theasurer at mertimes 1634

[The list contains various articles used in connection
with the King's entry—*e.g.*, the silver keys presented to
the King, the fringes of the 'paile,' the timber from the
stages, &c.]

[Below are summarised such details as are necessary to
throw light on the official entries in the Town Minutes and
Accounts regarding the pageants at the several stations in
1633.   These are taken from : (*a*) *The Entertainment of the
High and Mighty Monarch Charles, King of Great Britaine,
France, and Ireland, Into his auncient and royall City of
Edinburgh, the fifteenth of June* 1633.   Printed at Edin-
burgh by John Wreittoun, 1633, where the text may be
found with full details of the dresses, heraldic emblems,
mottoes, &c.   Printed also in the Scottish Text Society's
Edition of Drummond's Works, II, 113.   (*b*) Crauford's
Memoirs for a History of the University of Edinburgh.
Edin. Univ. MSS., D.C. 4, 3.   This is printed in Crauford's
History of the Edinburgh University, 1808 ; but as it is
far from being 'copied verbatim and in the original spelling,'
as the editor claims, I quote from the original manuscript.
(*c*) Spalding's *Memorialls of the Trubles in Scotland and
England, A.D.* 1624-*A.D.* 1645 (Spald. Club).   (*d*) *Rush-
worth's Collections*, II, 181.   Lond., 1680.   (*e*) Sir J. Balfour,
Historical Books, II, 196.]

A. West
Port.
(*a*) *Stage setting :* An Arch 'square with the battlements
and inmost side of the towne-wall, the face looking to
the Castle, represented a Citie situated on a rock,
which with pointed Clifts, Shrubs, Trees, Herbs, and
Verdure, *did appear in perspectiue* upon the battlements.' Names of Edinburgh and the castle and rock
inscribed, also a motto on the frieze under the town.
Paintings of 'the flood Lithus' on the one side of the
town, and of Neptune on the other. The 'Theater'
under the Arch was a mountain.

Representation : On the Mountain appeared the Genius of the town, a Nymph clad in green velvet mantle with under robe of blue tissue and blue buskins on her feet. The dressing of her head represented a castle with turrets. On her right stood Religion clad in white taffeta with a blue mantle ' seeded ' with stars and a crown of stars on her head ' to shew from whence she is.' Beneath her feet lay Superstition trampled, a blind old woman. On her left stood Justice, wearing red damask and cloth of silver and a crown of gold, trampling on Oppression, ' a person of a fierce aspect, in armes but broken all and scattered.' Each of these have scutcheons with emblems. The Mountain moved at the approach of the King, and the Nymph made a speech. Keys were delivered in a basin of silver, and the King was received under a pall of state by the Magistrates.

(*b*) ' Upon a pretty pageant, the draught of the Citie of Edinburgh and suburbs belonging thereunto, being excellently weel pourtrayed was objected to His Ma: eye and a Vale being removed the Nymph Edina accompanied with 2 other Nymphes after a short speech of congratulation to his highness delivered the keys of the Citie to be disposed of at His Ma: pleasur.'

(*c*) Spalding describes the reception by the Bailies and Council, with the speech by the Provost and presentation of gold basin.

(*a*) *Stage Setting :* An Arch. The 'frontispice' represented ' in Landskip ' a country scene with trees, beasts, mountains, and sea painted in great detail. Victories over the Romans and Picts were also portrayed realistically. Painting of dancers on the other side of the Arch. The 'Theater' was concealed by a curtain, which fell to ' discover ' the following :—   **B. West Bow.**
Representation : Speech by a Lady representing the genius of Caledonia, before whom a crown of gold hung from the Arch. Accompanying her was an American representing New Scotland, with a dress of coloured feathers and an olive-coloured mask.

(*b*) ' a statlie pageant Arched beneath for passadge haueing the Countrey of Caledonia or Scotland ' represented.

(*c*) Description of the convoy of ' gallantis ' who met the King at the Over Bow.

C West
end of
Tolbooth.

(a) *Stage setting:* An Arch, on the face of which was an 'Abacke' or square. At one side a painting of Mars surrounded by instruments of war : at the other side Minerva with the instruments of peace. Various inscriptions. 'Theater' concealed by a curtain, which was drawn at the approach of the King.

Representation: Mercury with a hundred and seven kings, whom he had brought from the Elysian fields. Latin speech by Fergus the First.

(b) 'an vast pageant arched aboue haveing on an large map the pourtraites of 109 kings of Scotland. In the Cavitie of the Arch Mercury was represented bringing up Fergus the first king of Scotland in an Convenient habite, who delivered to His Ma: a very graue speech containing many precious advices to His Royall Successor.'

(c) 'the royall pedigree of the Kingis of Scotland fra Fergus the first, delicatlie painted.'

(d) 'The Ceremony of that Pageant at the Tolbooth, there was represented in Effigie the whole Kings in order that had Reigned in Scotland since the Monarchy of that Kingdom . . .'

D. *Cross.* (a) Bacchus crowned with 'Ivie' and naked from the shoulders up bestriding a hogshead and surrounded by Silenus, Silvanus, Pomona, Venus, Ceres. The latter should have delivered a speech, but was interrupted by the Satyrs or 'Panisques.'

E. Salt
  Tron.

(a) *Stage setting:* In the middle a Mountain 'dressed for Parnassus.'

Representation: Apollo, clad in crimson and gold with a laurel wreath adorning his long gold locks and 'bowdricke' like a rainbow, surrounded by the Muses and Ancient Worthies representative of Scottish learning— Sedullius, Joannes Duns, Bishop Elphinstoun of Aberdeen, Hector Boece, Sir David Lyndsay, George Buchanan, Joannes Major, Bishop Gavin Douglas. Presentation of a book to the King by Apollo.

(b) 'the Mount Parnassus was reared up in a vast frame of Timber, the superfice representing all the varieties of rocks and vegetables which are to be seen on Mountaines. Upon the middle betuixt the two tops was erected an pyramide of great hight with an glob of

Glasse on the top therof. Out of the Cavity heerof did spring out a source of clear water, representing Hippocrene. In the belly of this Mountaine A Considerable number of Quiresters of choise singing voices, An Organist also with some other Musicians who at the Kings approaching in an sweet harmony emodulated Ane pleasant aire composed for the purpose called Caledonia and at the closing therof delivered to Him an booke of panegyriks and other poems composed be the University.[1] On the forsyde of the Mountain looking to the North sate Apollo and the nyne Muses habited conveniently The song being ended Apollo Uttered A panagyrick to the kings Ma: (who delivered the booke with the fers panegyricks to the kings Ma: haveing closed his owne).'

(c) 'Parnassus Hill wes curiouslie erectit, all grein with birkis, quhair nyne pretty boyis, representing the nyne Nymphis or Muses, wes nymphis like cled . . .'

(d) 'there were several witty Speeches in Verse . . . 2d The Song of the Muses at Parnassus.' [2]

(a) *Stage setting :* Arch on the face of which was painted the heavens with stars showing the king's ascendant, Virgo. Beneath lay the prostrate Titans with mountains over them. On the Chapter the Three Parcae. The back of the Arch had a drawing of the Three Graces. Presumably there is a curtain over the stage. F. Nether Bow.
Representation : The 'Stand' 'discovered' the seven Planets sitting on a throne, each clad to represent his particular part and bearing a scutcheon with appropriate motto. At a corner of the 'Theater' from out a 'verdant grove' came Endymion, apparelled like a shepherd, with a wreath of flowers on his head, gilt buskins on his legs, and bearing a crook. Long speeches by Endymion and each of the Planets constituted the 'actioune.'

(b) 'a statly Arch representing so much of the heavinly constellations and planetary influences as could conveniently be applyed to the purpose and from off this

---

[1] EIΣOΔIA Musarum Edinensium, &c., Edinburgh, 1633.
[2] Four five-lined stanzas are printed at the end of the *Entertainment.* The Editor of the *S.T.S.* edition of Drummond's Works, 1913 (II, 135), says that in the two early editions of 1656 and 1711 this piece was entitled 'The Song of the Muses at Parnassus,' and that in the later of these editions it was placed immediately after the verses by Caledonia.

pageant the 7 planets on after another delivered accla-
matory & congratulatory speeches . . .'

G. East
Gate.

(a) At the battlements of the East Gate stood Fame with
a Trumpet in her hand and by her Honour.

(b) ' All these pageants with the speeches were devised and
composed be Mr John Adamson primare Mr William
drumond of Hauthornden, and the Master of the high
schoole [1] joyned to an Committie of the gravest and
most understanding Citizens and Clarke, and if you
shall consider all the entries of the Mightiest princes in
Christendome for six score yeares befor that tyme and
what was done for their honour, you will find this
nothing inferiour to the most stately & magnificent
amongst them. But be an fatall neglect all were lost
in a very few yeares thereafter, scarce any vestigies
remaining, except a few pourtraites of the kings.
Whosoever was in the fault the losse was esteemed
ominous as also was this accident. In the morning
when the speakers were conveened in the lower publict
hall of the Colledge to receive their particulare directions, The primare and the rest who were to putt them
to that which they were to act being out of the rowme,
the first and last speaker falling be the ears did so teare
and deforme on anothers faces that neither of them
could be discerned, which was like in all probability
to haue marred the whole bussiness every act being
lincted to another. The primare haueing a balme of
soveragine vertue bound up their faces annoynted
therewith & keept them close. So that the kings entry
falling to be much later then was expected, no deformity
in the tyme of the acting their parts appeared in their
faces.'

(e) ' For maney ages this kingdome had not seine a more
glorious and staitly entrey, the streetts being all railled
and sanded ; the cheiffe places quher he passed wer sett
outt with staitly triumphall arches, obeliskes, pictures,
artificiall montains, adorned with choysse musicke, and
diuersse otheres costly shewes.'

[1] This testimony by Crauford, then a Professor at Edinburgh University,
as to the authorship of the pageantry is interesting.

B. *Folk Plays.*

(a) *Excerpts from MS. Guild Register,* 1487-1579.

Dec. 1492   f. 2 b
Robertus Coupland effectus est burgensis et datur Roberto
hud georgio mertyn

1494   f. 4 b
Iohannes smollet effectus est burgensis et datur gratis burgensis
georgio mertyne tamquam Roberto hud in deuorio suo

Iohannes seton filius in lege willelmi fery ad instantiam
Roberti hud

Iohannes carmure ad instantiam Andree bertram Roberti
hude gratis

149-   f. 5 a [1]
Willelmus diksoñ ad instantiam Andree bertram Roberti
hud in deuorio suo

Iacobus thompson ad instantiam Alexandri craufurd tam- f. 6 a
quam Roberti huide in deuorio suo

2nd March 1498/9
Iohannes quhite cordynare ad instantiam Alexandri car- burgensis
kettil viz Roberti hude

1498/9   f. 7 a
Iacobus strang   burgensis
    ad instantiamcapitanei castri pro georgio bron ? so . . . [2]
        abbatis de na Rent
Andreas gorge   burgensis

1500   f. 7 b
Andreas Rosß per Robertum hude duobus vltimis annis
elapsis et ea ratione

Iacobus dun per Willelmum halkston litil Iohne et ea ratione

---

[1] The date of the next two entries is uncertain. The last date is 1494 on
folio 4 ; but various folios in this volume have been misplaced, and some
may be missing. On f. 6 a there is an entry dated 1498.
[2] The edge of the page is mutilated.

(b) *Excerpts from Council Register.*

26th April 1493

(Abbot of Narent) [Anent the Abbot of Narent callit Abbat de Narentia se in the said (convict) buik, 26th Aprile 1493. Siclyk 4 Maii 1518, Ibid, quhair he is callit Robin Huid and Little Jhone.—Tr.] [1]

17th April 1518

(Dispensation from the office of Littlejohn) The quhilk (day) in presens of the president balleis counsall and communite, master Francis Boithwell producit my lord Erle of Aranis principall provestis writingis and charge till excuse him fra the office of Litiljohn, to the quhilk he was chosin for this yeir, desyrand the samyn to be obeyit, and the tenor tharof to be insertit in this instrument. The quhilk tenor of the said writting followis : President baillies and counsall of Edinburgh we greit you weill. It is vnderstand to ws that maister Frances Boithwell your nichtbour is chosin to be Litiljohn for to mak sportis and jocositeis in the toun, the quhilk is a man to be vsit hiear and gravar materis, and als is apon his viage to pas beyond sey his neidfull erandis. Quharfor we request and prayis and als chargis yow that ye hald him excusit at this tyme. And we be this our wrytingis remittis to him the vnlaw gif ony he has incurrit for nocht excepping of the said office, dischargeing yow of ony poynding of him tharfor. Subscriuit with our hand at Linlithgw the xij day of Aprile the yeir of God J^m v^c and xviij yeris (subscriptio) Youris, James Erle of Arane.

The quhilk wrytingis the said maister Frances allegit war nocht fulfillit nor obeyit, and tharefor he protestit that quhat euer was done in the contrar turn him to na preiudice, and for remeid of law tyme and place quhare it efferis.[2]

11th May 1558

The samyn day Jhonn Richertsoun saidler kyng of May And Jhonn rynde pewdrer being accusit for vp hinging of ane baner to ye cok of ye stepill / *con*fessit ye samyn / And ye said Jhonn Rynde fand maist*er* Jhonn prestoun sou*er*tie for his entrie vpoun vj ho*uris* warnyng to an*ſ*er for ye samyn [A surety found also for John Richardson].[3]

[1] *E.B.R. (S.B.R.S.),* I, 66.   [2] *Ibid.,* I, 176.
          [3] MS. Council Register, Vol. II, f. 123.

23rd April 1561

The prouest baillies and counsale vnderstanding that the prentissis and seruandis of merchanttis and craftismen and vtheris within this burgh ar of mynd vpoun Sounday nixt to mak con-vocatioun and assemblie efter the auld wikit maner of Robene Hude, nocht regarding the pvnisment thretnit in Goddis word vpoun the braikaris of the Saboth, nor having feir of the temporale pvnischment content in our Souerane actis vpoun the vsurparris of sic vane pastymes, quhairfor they all in ane voce, as cairfull fadderis our their commontie, and for eschewing of the pvnismentis and dangerris abone written, ordanis ane proclamatioun to be maid at the foure principale pairttis of this burgh, in our Souerane Ladeis and thair names dischargeing all sic con-ventionis and assemblais within this burgh and boundis of the samyn, and of all bering of armour, wappinnis, striking of suesche, sounding of trumpet, bering of baner standert or anseyne or like instrument, for sic vane besynes, certefe-ing the maister quhais seruand sall happin to be found cumand in the contrair heirof that he sall tyne his fredome of this burgh for euir, the seruand prentise or vther appre-hendit or notat to tyne the armour and abulyement appre-hendit with him and banist the toun for euer ; the lenneris of armour wappinnis and abulyement to be reput and haldin as manteinaris of the wikit inemeis to all gude ordour, and thairfor pvnist in thair personis and guddis at the will of the said prouest baillies and counsale ; and siclik that na assemblay nor convocatioun be found within this burgh with armour and wappinnis of the inhabitantis of the samyn, nor of the tounis adiacent, bot euerye man to gang and behaif him self in honest and sempill maner without multitude or gaddering, vnder the said pane of warding and pwnisment at the saidis jugis will.[1]

10th May 1561

(The Council, together with the deacons of the Furriers, Smiths, Wrights, Cordiners, Tailors, Baxters, Skinners, Barbers, Masons, being convened) maister Jhonn Spens, baillie, declarit and schew how that yisterday eftirnone, being the Saboth of the Lord, the craftismennis seruandis and prentisses enterit at the Nether Bow with displayit

[1] *E.B.R. (S.B.R.S.)*, III, 107.

baner in armour and wappinnis and passit throuch the toun to the Castill Hill, nochtwithstanding thay war chargit be the said baillie in our Soueranis name and in name and behalf of the prouest (and) baillies of this burgh ; and siclike the samyn nycht, betuix viij and ix houris at evin, enterit in the samyn maner returnyt to the Nether Port and keipit the samyn at thair plesour in manifest contempt of oure Soueranis autorite and magistratis of this burgh and thair proclamatione set furth in the contrair. . . .[1]

[Special meetings of the Council are held to decide concerning the punishment of the ' craft childer.' Deacons decide to support the Council.] [2]

[1] *E.B.R.* (*S.B.R.S.*), III, 112.
[2] Cf. *Pitcairn's Criminal Trials*, Vol. I, Pt. II, 409. ' Robin Hood—Abbot of Unreason—Lord of Inobedience. Jul. 20, 1561.—Robert Hannay, smyth ; James Cowper, tailȝeour ; Thomas Johnestone, cordiner ; Andro Hendersone, swerd-slipper ; Andro Richemanne, cuke ; William Clerk, talburnar ; James Fawsyid, talburnar ; Johne Cok, tailȝeour ; Patrik Mow, talboner ; and Alexander Bisset, taburner. The quhilk day James Cowper, tailȝeour, come in Will for arte and parte of ȝe chesing of George Durye in Robert Hude, vȝerwayis calland and nemmand him Lord of (In)obedience (Misrule) amangis ȝe Craftismen and ȝair seruandis, within ȝe burgh of Edinburgh, in ȝe moneth of Apryill last bypast, foreseand and assistand to him incontrair ȝe tennour of ȝe Act of Parliament, and for breking of ȝe said Act : Item, for breking of ȝe Proclamatioun of ȝe Provest and Bailleis of Edinburghe, maid for observing of ȝe said Act, forbiddand all ȝe Inhabitantis of ȝis burgh, ȝat nane of ȝame suld tak vpoun hand to cheise ony sic persone in Robene Hude, Abbot of Vnreasone, or ony vȝer name within ȝe said burgh : Item, for Convocatioun of our souerane ladies liegis, in cumpany with ȝe said George Durye, callit Lord of (In)obedience, to ȝe nowmer of . . . persones, bodin in feir (of weir), with ane displayit handsenȝé, halbrownis, jakkis, culveringis, morriounis, twa handit swerdis, cotis of malȝé, and vȝeris wapynnis invasive, vpone Soneday ȝe xij day of Maii last bypast, in cumpanye with certane brokin men of were, betuix thré and four houris eftir none, cumand within ȝe burghe of Edinburghe, enterand at ȝe Eist Porte ȝairof, and passed to ȝe Trone ȝairof, quhair ȝai wer met be ane parte of ȝe Bailleis, counsale, and officiaris of ȝis burghe, and chargit be ȝame to pas abak, and devyid ȝame of ȝe said burghe, for eschewing trouble and misordour in ȝe samyn : And nochtwithstanding ȝe said charge, violentlie and contempnandlie passand fordward to ȝe said Castell-hill, and returnand agane to ȝe Portis of ȝe said burghe ; vsand ȝe samyn be ische and entre, at ȝair plesour, makand plane rebellioun and inobedience aganis ȝe Magistratis of ȝe said burgh.
Thomas Johnstone, in Will for breking of ȝe said Act of Parliament and Proclamatioun maid be ȝe Magistrates, vt supra—Andro Hendirsone, in Will for breking ȝe said Act and Proclamatioune foirsaid—Item, ȝe said Andro (Hendersone) Convict of ȝe making of the said Convocatioune and rebellion aganis ȝe Magistratis, in maner foirsaid—Jhone Cok, ffylit for breking of ȝe Act of Parliament in chesing of ȝe said Lord of Inobedience and breking of ȝe Proclamatioun maid be ȝe Magistratis in maner foirsaid, alanerlie— Andro Richeman, Convict for assistence to ȝe said Lord of Inobedience and his complices, in breking of ȝe said Act and Proclamatioune ; and furnessing of ȝame of meit and drink—James Fawsyid, Patrick Mow, Alexander Bissett, Convict of ȝe breking of ȝe said Act, Proclamatioun, Convocatioun, and rebellioun foirsaid, conforme to ȝe Dittay.'
Rioting in Edinburgh—Choosing a ' Lord of Inobedience,' etc.
Aug. 8th, 1561. (Six craftsmen ' fylit ' by an assize for ' Intercommonyng

30*th April* 1562

Discharge
Robene
Hude

[Queen's letter to the Town Council] : Provest baillies counsale and dekynnis of craft of oure burgh of Edinburgh, it is notour vnto yow that be oure act of parliament it is statute and commandit that na Robene Hudis nor Litil Jhoneis suld be chosin within oure realme, nochttheles as we ar informeit ye intend to elect and cheis personis to beir sic offices this Maii approcheand, incontrair the tennour of oure said act, quha vnder colour of Robene Hudis play purpoissis to rais seditione and tumult within our said burgh, for perturbatioun of the commoun tranquilitie quhairin oure gude subjectis ar desyrous to leif ; quhairfore it is oure will, and we charge yow, that on na wys ye permit nor suffer this yeir ony sic as Robene Hude or Litil Jhonne to be chosin, nor that ony vther vnleissum gammis be vseit within oure said burgh quhilk may disquiet the communitie thairof as ye will ansuer to ws vpoun youre vtermest perell and charge in that behalf. Subscriuit with our hand, at Sanctandros, the xx of Aprile and of our regnne the xx[ti] yeir. Followis the proclamatioun maid thairefter : Quhairfore I command and charge in our said Soueranis name, and in name and behalf of my lorde provest baillies and counsale of this burgh, that na maner of persoun of quhat estait sa euir thai be, merchant craftisman or vthir, tak vpoun hand to attempt or tak vpoun thaime ony sic office or power as Robene Hude, Litil Jhonne, Abbat of Vnressoun or the like office vnder quhatsumeuir pretense or colour, to mak convocatioun or beir armour, contrair the tennour and mynde of the actis of parliament and this our Soueranis charge, as thai will ansuer vpoun thair vtermest dainger and perell for breking of the saidis actis and dissobeying of this hir maiesteis writing as said is.[1]

with George Durye, tailʒeour, vperwayis callit Lord of (In)obedience,' and his companions being our Sovereign Lady's rebels and at her horn. Seven others 'fylit' for disobedience to the Provost and Bailies at the tumult of the craftsmen on 21st July.

Cf. also the description of the tumult on 21st July given in the *Diurnal of Remarkable Occurrents*, pp. 65, 283. A cordiner, James Killone, was condemned to be hanged 'for the cuming in the toune of Edinburgh and playing with Robene Hud.' Appeals were made to the baillie and to John Knox, minister, 'quha wald doe nathing bot have him hangit.' Details of the rescue of the condemned prisoner. Cf. also *Knox*, II, 157 ff.

[1] *E.B.R. (S.B.R.S.)*, III, 134.

30th April 1562

[Alan Brown is paid 5/- for making a proclamation at the Cross for ' dischargyn of Ro^t Hude ']. [1]

1st May 1579

Proclamatio Robene Hude playes

The provest, baillies, counsall, and dekynis foirsaidis ordanis proclamatioun to be maid throw this burgh be sound of tabouryne that na inhabitant within this burgh presume to accompany any sic as ar of mynde to renew the playes of Robene Hude, or assist the defence or persute of ony catt hoillis within this burgh common mylnis or ony vther pairtis thairabout, vnder the paynis of pvneisment of thame in thair bodies and gudes at the juges discretioun.[2]

29th April 1580

Baillies to reforme the insolence on Sounday [3]

For staying of the awld superstitioun and in-solencie commounly vsit in the tyme of May, and in the somer seasoun ordanis the baillies, euery ane thair day about, fra this day furth to Lambes nixt, to gif diligent attendence at euery Sounday at evin throw the streittis of this burgh that na sic super-stitioun or insolence be done within the sam, and quhair any inormity sall happin to putt haisty remeid thairto, this ordour begynnand at the baillie of the sowth eist quarter and swa furth.[4]

26th Jan. 1581/2

Jhone Gilleis, doctour in Jhone Blakis schole, oblist himself nocht to pas in mwmschance after supper to mak playes or vse siclyke vaniteis heirafter, vnder the payne of banesing the toune.[5]

29th May 1588

[The town drummer to be warded and put in irons for ' passing on the Sondayes at his awin hand to the May playis in Kirklistoun.'] [6]

[1] *City of Edinburgh Old Accounts*, I, 367.
[2] *E.B.R. (S.B.R.S)*., IV, 106.
[3] MS. Council Register, VI, f. 39, has ' In somer.'
[4] *E.B.R. (S.B.R.S.)*, IV, 160.
[5] *Ibid.*, IV, 229.
[6] *Ibid.*, IV, 520.

C. *Excerpts from MS. Hammermen's Records.*

1494 (1st quarter)

Item to iiij men at bure þe standartis in harnes on corpus
   xis [1] day   viij š

Item to ij men at bure þe candilheddis   xxxij đ

Item to þe iiij men at bure þe iiij tortasſs   xxxij đ

Item to þe twa werlattis in brecatyniſs [2]   xvj đ

Item for mendin of þe iiij gret tortaſs & makin of iij gret
   knoppis of greñ walx to þaim & culloryne of þaim
                                         iiij š

Item to gilȝame and his marrow on corpus xis day & þat
   day viij days   v š

Item in [3] to þe processiouñ & to þe menstralis & þe beraris
   at þair disione in bred & aill oñ corpus xis day
                                      xviij đ

Item for bringin of þe poyndis fra thoñ Rais houſs   ij đ

Item for payntin of þe spere of leicht   xij đ

Item on þe viij day quheñ þai bure þe banaris & þe candill
   befor þe sacrament for ȝa gallouñ of aill at ȝed throw þe
   tovñ with þaim & a gallouñ quheñ þaj coñ In
                                      xviij đ

Item to þe furnesyng of errot & his vj knychtis at þe craftis
   command   x š

Item oñ sownday quheñ þe processiouñ was playd for þe
   king to ane menstrale   ij š

Item to þe men at bur þe banerris & þe tortasſs þat samen
   day in aill to þaim   ix đ

   [Expenses for St Eloy's day, wax, torches, etc.]

1495 (1st quarter)

Item þe secund wolk deliuerit at þe command of þe maist
   part of þe masteris of þe craft to þe abbot to pay his
   menstralis   [Sum blank in MS.]

Item to þe commoñ menstralis of þe towne þat day at our
   craft passit to sanct katerins at playt befor þe craft
                               iiij š vj đ

---

  [1] For typographical reasons, the contraction sign over this word has been omitted in this and the following pages.

  [2] So it seems to be in MS. But possibly bretacynis—*i.e.*, brotikins, brodekins buskins.

  [3] *Sic* in MS.

Item on corpuscristis day to ꝑe iiij men at bure ꝑe four
standartis in harnes   viij ŝ
   [Payments to candlehead bearers, etc.]
Item to ꝑe ij werlaitis in brecatynis [1]   xvj đ
Item to ij menstralis at ȝed with ws ꝑat day in ꝑe pro-
cessiouñ   v ŝ
Item oñ ꝑe viij day quhen ꝑe sacrament ȝeid throw ꝑe toune
to ꝑe childer at bur ꝑe banaris in drink   xij đ
Item ꝑe samen day till a menstraill befor ꝑe craft   ij ŝ

f. 10 1495 (2nd quarter)

Item in primis till a menstrale to gang with our banaris oñ
sanct geliß day   xij đ [2]

f. 13 1496 (1st quarter)

In primis quhen ꝑe craft passit to ꝑe vle well with our
abbot gevin to ꝑe menstralis at ꝑe command of ꝑe maist
part of ꝑe craft   vj ŝ
Item for flouris and threid on corpus xis day   vj đ
Item for payntin of ꝑe ij speris at buyr ꝑe candilheidis
                            iij ŝ
Item to gilliaṁ & ꝑe child at playd oñ ꝑe gret bumbart [3]
on [4] corpus x day for ꝑar playing   iiij ŝ
   [Fees, bread, and ale for the banner-bearers, etc.]
Item gevin to ꝑe' abbot of narent to furnes herod & his
knychtis   viij ŝ
Item to ꝑe ij knapis in brecatynis [1] ꝑat day   xvj đ
Item to craufurd our menstraill   ij ŝ
Item on ꝑe auchteñ day to gilȝeṁ & child   xxxij đ
Item to craufurdis man for flouris ꝑe viij day   iij 3 đ

f. 14 Item ꝑat day at we brocht hayṁ summyr with ꝑe tovne
for beryne of our twa new standartis in harnes ilk ane
of ꝑaim passand to newbottill to ꝑe ij   vj ŝ
Item to ꝑe toꝑer twa at bur ꝑe toꝑer standartis   ij ŝ
Item ꝑe samen day to craufurd menstraill for his hors &
playing   iij ŝ

[1] See *supra*, 225, n[1].
[2] Payments recur for minstrels on St Giles' Day, f. 20, f. 25, etc.
[3] Bombard, a kind of bassoon.
[4] MS. ' or.'

1497 (1st quarter)   f. 19

Item apone corpus xis day to gilȝame tauberner to play
    with ȝe bannaris   v ŝ
Item to ȝe child at playt apone ȝe gret bumbart   xij đ
    [Payments to standard bearers, etc.]
Item to ȝe twa squyeris in quhit harnes   xvj đ
Item to ȝe commone piparis of ȝe tovne ȝat day to play
    befor ȝe craft   ij ŝ iiij đ
Item for flouris & pak threid ȝe samen day to ȝe tortaſſ &
    candilhedis   vj đ
Item ȝe viij day eftir corpus xis day to gilliam to play
    throw [1] ȝe toune befor ȝe craft & his child to play of
    ȝe bumbart   iij ŝ
Item to ȝe commoñ piparis ȝe samen daye   xvj đ
Item ȝe samen day amang ȝe childer at bur ȝe banaris &
    tortasſſ in aill quhen ȝe processiouñ was done   xij đ

1498 (1st quarter)   f. 24

    [The usual payments to banner bearers (4), torch-
    bearers (4), and bearers of the candleheads (2). Also
    to Gilȝame and his child and the common pipers.]

Item to herod & his vj knychtis to ȝe processiouñ of corpis x
                                                          x ŝ

    [Payments to Gilȝame, the common pipers, banner-
    bearers, etc. for the Octave Day.]

1499 (1st quarter)   f. 29

    [The usual payments on Corpus Christi Day to banner-
    bearers, etc. Also to the 'twa knapis,' the common
    pipers, and the lad that played on the ' gret bumbart.']

Item in Iohne tayttis at ȝe on puttin of ȝar harnes on
    corpus xis day a quart ail   iiij đ
Item for ij quartis of aile & tua mayne laifis at ȝeid throw
    ȝe toune with ȝe banaris   xij đ
Item for pak threid to knyt on ȝe flouris & to ȝe candil-
    heidis   j đ

    [Also the usual payments on the Octave Day when
    the banners went with the sacrament about the town.]

                        [1] MS. ' thow.'

f. 30 **1500 (1st quarter)**

In primis ressauit fra william Raa at was gadderit throw
ye tovne to ye play furnesing be ye masteris of ye
craft   xv s̃ x đ

Item fra ed craufurd at was gadderit to ye gwñ powder
in andro muncurris ȝard   xvj đ

Item in primis at ye command of ye masteris of ye craift
expendit & deliuerit apoñ ye costis & expenſ of ye
proclamyne of ye summyr bringin haym̃ ye banaris
bering gwñ powder & vyer expenſ maid ye day of our
summyr bringin haym̃ with ye expenſ of our playe
apon ye morne as is content at mair lencht in my bill
of covnt ye sovm̃ is   ij ɫib xiiij s̃ viij đ

Item to anysle apoñ corpus xis day and apoñ ye octave
day to play befor ye banaris and ye craft yaj twa dais
                                                                      x s̃

[Payments to standbearers, etc., on Corpus Christi and
the Octave Day.]

Item to ye twa werlotis   xvj đ
Item for flouris & pak threid yat day   vj đ

f. 35 **1501 (1st quarter)**

Item for gwne powder   iiij s̃ vj đ
Item for ij horſ to ye ij men at bur ye standartis apoñ ye
sovnday forow corpus xis day befor ye craft   xvj đ
Item to ye tawbernar & fedlar oñ corpus xis day at playt
befor ye craft   iij s̃ iiij đ
[Other usual Corpus Christi payments.]

Item for a galloun of aile at ye disione [1] amang yame at
bure ye banaris candillheidis & torchis & ye menstralis or
we ȝeid furtht   xvj đ

Item apoñ ye octave day for ij quartis of aile & ij mane
bred gangand throw ye tovñ with ye processiouñ
                                                                      xvj đ

Item ye day at we brocht in summyr for iiij horſ to ye
iiij men at bur ye banaris   iiij s̃

Item yat day or ye gunnaris and ye meñ in harnes and
menstralis ȝeid furtht for a gallouñ of aile amang yaim
                                                                      xvj đ

Item for a gallouñ eftir at yaj com̃ hame amang yaim all
                                                                      xvj đ

¹ 'déjeuner.'

Item for birkis [1] till our craft at met ws apoñ ꝥe burrowmure

ij ŝ

1502 (1st quarter)   f. 40

[Usual Corpus Christi and Octave Day payments to standard bearers, minstrels, etc. Also to the 'twa verlotis.']

1502 (3rd quarter)   f. 41

Item for holingis bringin fra Roslyng at sanct loysmeß

vj đ [2]

1503 (1st quarter)   f. 44

In primis deliuerit at ꝥe command of ꝥe breꝥer of ꝥe craft till anysle ꝥe first daye at we suld haue feit him & ꝥe secund day of our Incummyn   v ŝ

Item for robert our talbernaris Iacat of al costinance fre maid tilhim   xj ŝ

Item for a pair of hoiß of red carsaye tilhim of all costinance   viij ŝ j đ

Item for vj days till robert our menstrale ilk day ij ŝ ꝥe sovm̃   xij ŝ

Item for apippane of silk to mend our banaris   iij đ

Item for iij pund of powder deliuerit to ꝥe abbot   iij ŝ

Item to ꝥe abbot at ꝥe command of ꝥe craft   xx ŝ

Item for poynttis to ꝥe hernes men to put oñ ꝥar ger with   iij đ

Item oñ corpus xis day & ꝥe octave day to gilȝame ꝥai ij dais   x ŝ

Item to clofas to play oñ ꝥe gret bumb   ij ŝ

[Usual payments to standard bearers, etc.]

Item four men in harnes oñ corpus xis day with battale axis   xxxij đ

Item on corpus xis day in ale at ꝥe processiouñ & quhen ꝥai com̃ in & in mayne breid ij gallownis & ij laiffis ꝥe price   iij ŝ

[Octave payments for ale and loaves, pack thread and 'poynttis.']

---

[1] See n[2].

[2] The feast of St Eloi (Eligius), the patron Saint of the Hammermen, fell on 1st December. Holly is the symbol of the winter festival, as birks are of the summer festival (1501, 1516).

f. 48 1504 (1st quarter)

> [Payments to Gil3ame, Robert Haye, and Clofas for playing.]

Item to herod and his ij doctour*is* [1] horß   iiij š
Item to ɥe v kny*chtis*   v š
Item for bering for ɥe four banar*is* in harnes oñ corp*us* xis day & ɥe octaue daye xvj đ ɥe ma*n*   v š iiij đ
> [Also payments to torchbearers, etc.]

Item to ɥe ij werlott*is*   xvj đ
Item on corpus xis day for aile thro*w* ɥe gait & at ɥar incu*m*myñ & bred & a q*u*art of wyñe ɥat day ij gallownis & iij q*u*art*is* of aile p*ri*ce   vj š ij đ
> [Also ale on the Octave Day and pack thread to bind the flowers on the ' tortaß.']

f. 51 1505 (1st quarter)

> [Payments to Gil3ame, Cloffas, Robin Hay, the two ' werlott*is*,' standard-bearers, etc., on Corpus Christi and the Octave Day.]

Item at the furtht passing of thai*m* at bur this geir in aill
     xvj đ
Item in wyne aill & breid one corpus x day throw ɥe gait
     xvj đ
Item one ɥe octaue day at thar Incu*m*ing in aill   xvj đ
Ite*m* ɥat same*n* day passand throw ɥe gait in aill   xij đ
Item for poynt*is* & pakthreid   viij đ
Item to herod   iiij š
Item to his twa doctour*is* [1]   ij š
Item to ɥe vj knythis [2]   vj š

f. 55 1506 (1st quarter)

Item to ɥe wricht at maid ɥe cart to ɥe danß of drinksiluer
     iiij đ
Item to ɥe ma*n* at brocht ɥe burd*is* till hi*m*   j đ
Item for nalis to ɥe same*n* cart   ix đ

> [Usual Corpus Christi expenses for banner - bearers, etc. Also for the ' twa werlot*is*,' and for wine, ale, and bread ' throw the gait ' and at the incoming.]

---

[1] Smith, *The Hammermen of Edinburgh*, **33**, reads ' dactures ' (daughters).
[2] ' Knychts ' is less likely. Smith reads ' v buythis,' and deduces the interesting fact that the play was held in five booths. (*Op. cit.*, **33**, lxvi.)

Item to ꝑe twa at bur ꝑe baneris in harneſſ at ꝑe inbringing
of sommer for twa horſſ to thaim   ij ſ̃
Item for ane horſſ to gilȝame   viij đ
Item for ane gallone aill one ꝑe octaue day gangand throw
ꝑe tovne & ane pynt wyne & ane mayne breid   ij ſ̃ ij đ
Item for ane horſſ to thome belman at ꝑe proclamyne of
sommer bringin In   viij đ

1506 (4th quarter)   f. 57

Item gevin to Iames kinpovnt of his money & expenſſ at
he laid dovne ꝑe tyme at he was abbot & maid be a
certane of ꝑe masteris to gif hym   xl ſ̃

1507 (1st quarter)   f. 59

[Payments to the various minstrels, standard-bearers,
the two varlots, etc.]

Item gevin thaim one corpuſſ xp̃i day in wyne throw ꝑe
gait & maynbreid in ꝑe processiouñ & one ꝑe octaue in
aill   xxxij đ
Item gevin for twa parchment skynnis to ꝑe bovme
     xxxij đ
Item for ane ovnce birg threid to ꝑe byndin of It   iiij đ
Item gevin for silk to mend ꝑe baneris   iiij đ
Item gevin herod   iiij ſ̃
Item to his twa doctouris   ij ſ̃
Item gevin to his fif knychtis   v ſ̃
Item to ꝑe four wiffis   iiij ſ̃
[Separate account of expenses for making of banners.] f. 62

1508 (1st quarter)   f. 63

[Usual Corpus Christi expenses, including payments to
Gilȝame and Cloffas and the two varlots.]

1509   f. 65

[Usual Corpus Christi expenses.]

Item gevin to ꝑaim at bur ꝑe four standartis at ꝑe Inbringin
of symmer to fee thaim horſſ   iiij ſ̃
Item gevin for to say mesſſ for thom wigholme eftir his
deceſſ becauſſ he feit his horſſ of his expenſſ at ꝑe Inbringin of symmer   xij đ
And all his playing one ꝑe bovme fee vnpait hym a penny
for all ꝑe tyme.

Item gevin to thaim at bur ꝧe standartis at ꝧe Inbringin
symmer eftir ꝧar hame cummyng & befor ane gallouñ
aill   xvj ꝺ
Item gevin to cudde for his sport befor ꝧe craft maid one
ꝧe octaue day   xvj ꝺ

f. 69 1510 (1st quarter)

[Usual Corpus Christi expenses, including payments to
a luter, tabernar, fiddler, and piper.]

[In the years 1512-15 the usual Corpus Christi expenses
recur, always with the two varlots, but without any mention of Herod and his company.]

f. 88 1516 (1st quarter)

Item to georg adamsoun & ade arnot for berin of ꝧe baneris
at ꝧe Inbringing of symmer   iiij ſ̃
Item for birkis ꝧe samyn day   iiij ꝺ
Item for ane horſ to ꝧe man at playit one ꝧe bovme
                                                       xij ꝺ

[Usual Corpus Christi and Octave Day payments.]

f. 89 Item to ꝧe franch menstrall for playing ꝧai twa dais
                                                       viij ſ̃
Item to herod   iiij ſ̃
Item to his twa doctouris   ij ſ̃
Item to ꝧe iiij knychtis   iiij ſ̃

f. 92 1517 (1st quarter)

[Usual Corpus Christi and Octave Day expenses.]

f. 94 1517 (4th quarter)

Item for ꝧe beriñ of ꝧe baneris throw ꝧe touñ ꝧat day ꝧe
processiouñ passit for ꝧe dolphin of france   ij ſ̃
Item to the menstralis franchmen   viij ſ̃

f. 95 1518

[Usual Corpus Christi expenses.]

Item gevin to ꝧe menstralis   xiiij ſ̃
Item to ꝧaim one corpus xp̃i day In ꝧe mornyng In ꝧe
taverouñ ane pynt of wyne & ane mayne laif   x ꝺ

Item for mending of ᵹe grene standart*is* & cuttin of ᵹai*m*

ij s̄

[Much the same entries recur in connection with the Corpus Christi and Octave Day celebrations in the years 1519-28. The two varlots drop out for the last three years. In 1522, 1524, 1525, a few pence is expended on paper to be 'ane lytill buk.' In 1524, 8/- is paid for minstrels and 2/8d. for standard - bearers for the King's entry. After 1529 the Hammermen join with the Wrights and Masons for the Corpus Christi procession.]

1529 (1st quarter)   f. 126

Item oñ corpus xp̄i day to ᵹe thre schaum*er*es for o*ur* p*ar*t

xvj s̄

Item to ᵹair disjune [1] oñ corp*us* xp̄i day to o*ur* p*ar*t   xj đ
Item for o*ur* p*ar*t to ane france child quhilk playit oñ ye
swefs   xvj đ
Item to more and his ma*n* for o*ur* p*ar*t ᵹe twa daiis

xij s̄ vj đ

Item to ᵹe ma*n* ᵹat playit oñ ᵹe new swafs [2] bait*h* ᵹe daiis
for o*ur* p*ar*t   ij s̄
Item deliuerit to sande dy at ᵹe m [3] *com*mands   x s̄
Item oñ corp*us* xp̄i day & ᵹe octo day i*n* wyne & bred to
o*ur* p*ar*t   xiiij đ
Item i*n* aile & bred for o*ur* p*ar*t   ix đ
Item to ᵹe me*n* ᵹat bure ᵹe standert*is*   ij s̄
Item i*n* bylaving*is* [4] amangis ᵹe said me*n*   xxj đ
Item for o*ur* p*ar*t of ᵹe me*n*strelis laving*is* [4] i*n* ᵹe taberoñ

ij s̄ ij đ

Item to o*ur* twa me*n* ᵹat bure ᵹe baner*is* bait*h* ᵹe daiis

iiij s̄

Item to ᵹe boiis ᵹat bure ᵹe aile & wyne to o*ur* p*ar*t

xij đ

[The following later entries may be noted : 'Item for graithing & dechtin of ᵹe harnes to o*ur* p*ar*t iij s̄' (1530). 'Item to ᵹe ma*n* ᵹat playit one ᵹe almeny quhessill one ᵹe octo day ij s̄' (1532). 'Item to ᵹe me*n* ᵹat graithit ᵹe harnefs & to ᵹe kempis vj s̄' (1534). 'Item gevin for ane monyto*ur* to gaud*er* in ᵹe sanct*is* geir *with* aw ij s̄' (1535, 3rd qr.) 'Item gevin to ᵹe twa knapis & for graithing of ᵹe

---

[1] '*déjeuner.*'   [2] drum.   [3] '*maisteris.*'   [4] fees.

harnes to ꝑe banermen vj ŝ ' (1536). 'Item gevin at ꝑe
m/[1] command for ꝑe expenſs maid ꝑe tyme ꝑe chelder maid
ꝑe Iusting in ꝑe barrois summa xxxv ŝ ' (1536, 4th qr.)
A livery to our servant, Crawfurd (1537). 'Item gevin for
birkis quhair ꝑe baneris stud to ij đ ' (1538). Expenses at
the Queen's homecoming : 'Item to ꝑe iiij men ꝑat wes
in harnes apone ꝑe tolbutht hed in drink iiij ŝ.'   'Item
gevin to ꝑe men ꝑat wes in harnes & for graithing of It
to our part ij ŝ viij đ.'   'Item gevin to henry lorymer
(drummer) at ꝑe m/[1] command xxx ŝ ' (1538). Payments
to 'Jakis ' and the two 'toddis,' minstrels ; also to ' vꝑer
ij ȝoung men quhilkis war nocht feit bot ꝑat come of gud
will.'   'Item ꝑat day quhen ꝑe kingis ȝowgest sone wes
borne to iiij men quhilk buir ꝑe baneris in processouñ
vj ŝ ' (1541). Payment to Crawfurd 'for his leveray aganis
corpus xpi day.'   Payment for the 'graithing of our swaſs
and stikkis to It '; also to ' ꝑe knaipis in harnes '; and
to 'pvnttis to ꝑe harnes.' Payment to 'todde tabroner
apone fursday ꝑe xvj day of Ianuar in ꝑe processone with
ꝑe sacrament ' (? 1543). 'Iteᵐ In ꝑe first giffin to menstralis & vꝑer deuteis betuix ws & ꝑe masonis and wrychtis
ꝑe tyme ꝑe processioun ȝeid quhen brouchty fortht wes
wyn fra ꝑe Ingles meñ to our part xviij ŝ vj đ ' (1549,
4th qr.) In the same account there are details of the
expenses of the making of two banners between the Hammermen and the Wrights and Masons. 'Iteᵐ on corpus xp̃i
day and ꝑe octaue of ꝑe samyn betuix ws ꝑe masonis &
wrychtis to menstralis waigis novnschankis disiouns and
for breyd and wyne bayth ꝑe dayis In ꝑe processiouns
and to childer ꝑat bur ꝑe samyn and to ꝑe men yat bure
ꝑe baunaris bayth ꝑe dayis & all vꝑer necessaries ꝑe
sovme of all Is xj ℔is viij ŝ iiij đ our part ꝑairof v ℔is
xiiij ŝ ij đ ' (1552). This is a typical Corpus Christi
entry for the later accounts, which do not detail the expenses of the procession. For the next few years the Hammermen's share of the Corpus Christi expenses aver-
ages about £4. 'Item gewin to robert dauesonis clathis
ꝑat he suld haue hed at Corpus christis day xl ŝ '
(1561).]

At the beginning of the Hammermen's Records there is
a list of statutes collected, 1550.

'maisteris.'

15th *May* 1538

Iteɱ the dekin & masteris for saidis hes thocht expedient
for ȝe honour of ȝis burght & ȝe craftismen of ȝe samyn
hes ordanitt ȝat na maner of ſſeruand be fund on corpus
xp̄i day nor In ȝe octaue of ȝe samyn nor in na vȝer processiouns excepad ȝai be hernest In ȝair clething eferanent
to ȝair estatis & na vȝeris ȝat is nocht be deuodit furth
of ȝair cumpany for ȝat ȝat [1] tyme bot remane in ȝair
buthis or howsſſ or on staris

Discharge for 1588-9-90

Item debursit at the conuening of the meñ to be ane gaird
to the quene in katherine stewartis in presens of thomas
millar & william symartoun x s̃

Item debursit to xij meñ that bure the halbertis at the
queneis entre in this burcht iiij ɫi

ELGIN.

[The New Spalding Club, 1903-8, has printed *The Records
of Elgin*, 1234-1800. This includes extracts from Burgh
Court Records, 1540-53, 1570-85, etc., and from Kirk
Session Records commencing 1584.]

Excerpts from Burgh Records.

12th *May* 1549

[William Hardy . . . was made freeman, and paid 5s.
which] was warit at the command of William Hay of Mayne,
provost, to Alexander Lillie, menstrall to my Lord Abbot,
and the provost and communate made assignation to the
said William of the twa auchtane partis qlk. was his umquhill
faderis and paid fourty schillingis for his entres which was
given at command of the provost to Alexander Williamson,
lord abbot, to be spendit at his pastyme.

30th *June* 1580

. . . na persone within this burgh ather freman nor onfre-
man nor that vyssis in ony tym to cum sall pretend or

[1] *Sic* in MS

caus mak ony fyris vpon the he calsay of this burgh on
Sanct Jhonis ewin or Sanct Peteris ewin in the monethis
of Junij or ryd in disagysit maner within this burgh on
Sanct Necolas day or Sanct Necolas ewin in the monethis
of December in ony tymis cuming vnder the pain of tinsall
of thair fredome that ar burgessmen and burgess vyffis
. . . [Others to be fined or put in ward.]

Excerpts from Kirk Session Records.

(a) *School Play and Abbot Play.*

21*st May* 1600

Maister of Schole—The minister and elderis inhibits the
maister of the Grammar Schole fra this furth to practeis
any comedie ather inwith the schole of this burgh or outwith the samyn without speciall licence of the Session
obtenit thairto and siclyk the maister himselff thinkis he
hes done wrang in practeizing thairoff the said comed play
so rashlie and unadvysedlie and thairfoir promesis fra hence
furth not to practeize the lyke.

23*rd May* 1600

Siclyke Thomas Mauld, maister of the Grammar Schole,
for his publict offence sall confes his fault of making a
play and comed of Tyrence in the freir kirkyaird on Tuysday
last sall stand in his awin seat on Sondaye nixt and acknow-
lege his errour by his ansuer to the minister and thair lykwayis publictlie befoir the kirk promeis nevir to commit
the lyk.

28*th May* 1600

It is appointed that the personis seikaris licence to pastyme
be tryit on Fryday nixt.

30*th May* 1600

Kay : Alex. Grant, tailyeour : Gray : Robertsone :
Stronach.—George Kaye the displaying of the taffatie on
the stepill vall quhen he vas wairdit thair with Arche
Graye, Alexander Grant, Thomas Robertsone, and William
Stronache, his complices on Monondaye last bypast for the
quhilkis and speiking presumpteous words in presens of

the Sessioun and for uther his enormiteis knawin to the
juges as for the incyting and seducing utheris his complices and collegis to cum to seik licence to haif ane Abbot
play quhairthroch ane tumult and uproar micht aryse
aganis the disciplin and commonveill of this burgh the
said George is ordenit and adiugit presentlie to be put in
the stockis to remane thairin quhill Sonday nixt and thaireftir to be adiugitt of the Sessioun. Williame Dunbar,
maisone, is becum cautioun wnder the paynis of ten pundis
that he sall not preische to vse any plays or pastymes or
wse or haunt company with the rest. [So of the others.]
John Lay, pyper inhibitt to pas throch the toun or yit
playe besyd the toun on a grytt pype under the paynes of
baneishment furth of the perroche.

Mr Schole—The maister of the Grammer Schole being
accusit be the Sessioun for transgressing of the ordour of
the disciplin of the kirk be using sic insolens and lascivious
fashiounes as mycht brangill and hurt the estait of the
commoun weill of this burgh and speciallie in the first
for conduceing a pyper to playe on the gryt pype with his
disciples to the bentt by the consent of the counsale.
2° Gif he conducit with his bairns to caus seik silver the
tym of the comed playing. 3° Gif he ves in consale of the
buying of the bellis and dansing claythis and gif thair wes
ony geir promesit to him be his skollaris to grant thame
licence to play. 4° Gif he wret the infamous bill giffin in
be the raskall soirt (grantit that) and siclyk being regrated
be the minister that he at Mr James Guthrie his desyre
and his awin past the first offens upone promeis that he
suld not commit the lyke quhilk he transgressit. [The
Session forbid him ever to do the like under penalty of
loss of his half year's fee. The master promises that neither
he nor his disciples shall commit such faults in future.]

(b) *Guising*, etc.

20th Dec. 1593

. . . all personis of quhatsumeuir degre that beis fund at
pastyme or playing on Sondaye at the tyme of preaching
ather befoir noone or efter noone sall pay xx s. ad pios
vsus.

4th Jan. 1593-4

Compeirit Tiberius Winchester quhome the minister and eldaris accusit for gysing through the toun upone the 27th day of December accompaneit with a pyper and certane utheris ryotous pepill efter nyn houris of the nicht quho denyit ony abuse in the doing thairof. [Case postponed till next day.]

5th Jan. 1593-4

[Tiberius Winchester appears and confesses his crime. Many craftsmen, tailors, cordiners, websters, fleshers, and merchants, accused of ' prophaning of the Sabbothe daye be vorking and playing.']

17th July 1594

Particular Act—James Douglas, sone naturall to William Douglas, vicar of Elgin, hes actit him self to be baneist gif euir he beis found at pastyme the tym of preaching or yit found ane common player as he haid vount.

2nd June 1596

[Three servant lasses confess to having been ' in ane dance callit gillatrype singing a foull hieland sang.']

8th Sept. 1596

All kynd of pastime during the harvest on Sondayes forbidden bot onlie a soberetie and fasting, prayers and invocatioun to be obseruit during the samyn.

15th Dec. 1596

Inhibitioun of pastyme in the Chanonrie kirkyaird. The Sessioun inhibitis all personis within this burgh to vse ony kynd of pastyme in the place callit the Chanonry kirk and zaird therof from Wedinsday nixt to the tenth day of Januarie nixt thaireftir, and all conventiounes within the samyn under pane of 40 s. to be tane up of euery housholderis geir, and euery servand 10 s. money to be applyit ad pios vsus, besyd thair publict repentance, and also

inhibitis all guysing and dancing within this toun at ony
tyme heireftir [1] . . .

22nd Dec. 1596

Scollaris—It is aggreit be the eldaris that the scollaris
quha hes tane the Grammer Schole be not molestit or put
at afoir Fridaye nixt, agane the quhilk day Thomas Hay
sall luik owt the Act maid anent the taking of the skuill,
and in the midtym that another hous be provydit to serue
the remanent of the barnis and the maister of the grammer
schole to attend and caus thame keipe guid ordour quhill
remeid be put forther thairto. [2]

15th Dec. 1598

Nycht walking and guysing forbiddin . . .

30th Dec. 1598

John Sampsoun and James Cruik accusit for dansing and
guising ondir nycht in divers houses culd not deny bot
they dansit albeit not dammaskit nor disguysit. Appointit
to stand on Sonday nixt in thair awin seattis and confess
thair offences. George Kay accusit for dansing and guysing
ondir nicht on Monunday last confessit he haid his sisters
coat upon him and the rest that were with him haid claythis
dammaskit about thame and thair faces blaikit, and they
haid a lad playand upon banis and bells with thame.
Archie Hay had a faise about his loynes and ane kerche
about his face. [Ordained to make repentance two Sundays
bare-foot and bare-legged.]

9th May 1599

[The Session approves the Monday holiday laid down by
His Majesty's statutes, [3] provided that the inhabitants
attend morning and evening before and after their ' exerceis ' and that it advises ' quhome salbe admitt gouernours

---

[1] There are many other minutes prohibiting pastimes at Yule in the Chanonrie
Kirk and Kirkyard : Dec. 14th, 1598—' specialie all conuentioun of women-
kynd is forbiddin.'   Dec. 21st, 1599—Football is excepted from the general
prohibition.   Also, Dec. 26th, 1600 ; Dec. 13th, 1601 ; Dec. 13th, 1603, etc. ;
and see *infra*, 240-242, under dates Jan. 4th, 1600, Dec. 18th, 1618.

[2] Other Minutes dealing with the scholars' play at Yule occur under the
dates Dec. 21st, 1599 ; Dec. 23rd, 1603 ; Dec. 18th, 1604, etc.

[3] *A.P.S.*, IV, 160.

in this exerceis thatt all thingis may be done decentlie
and weill.']

11th May 1599

James Law appointed to bring on Sondaye eiftir noone the
lawis of the pastyme that the samyn may be sein and considerit be the minister and eldaris.

16th May 1599

[Monday pastime-makers to attend prayers both times and
' that sic personis careis furth thair ensigneis eftir and goes
to their dansing and guysing and keipis not the prayeris
salbe puneist.']

18th May 1599

[James Kay accusit of ' displaying the ensignies ' the time
of the evening prayers.]

27th May 1599

All unlesum pastymes on Monondayes to be abolished.

2nd Jan. 1600

Alexander Smythis dauchter for guysing to be put in the
joiggis gif it be prowin that scho ves in manis claythis.

4th Jan. 1600

General Act anent Guysingis—It is appointit, statute and
ordanitt fra this furth that all sic personis as beis found
dansing, guysing and singing carrellis through the toune
or in the Chanonrie kirk and wther publict places the
tyme callit the halie dayis [to be put in the ' joiggis '] . . .
and this same act to strik on Marion Andersone for guysing
through the toun in menis claythis and to be put in the
joiggis . . .

1st Jan. 1604

Vinchister—Tyberius Winchester accusit for transgressing
the actis maid for keiping of a Christiane and decent
ordour about the tymes obseruit be sum superstitiouslie
and prophanelie for having a bedcod on his heid and ryding
thairwith throuche the toun on the tuentie sext day last

bypast of December quhilk the said Tyberius confessit, also for uttering uncomlie speaches the nycht the minister catecheized.

3rd Jan. 1604

[Two women accused for dancing and William Pattoun for ' singand hagmonayis.']

8th Jan. 1604

[Tyberius Winchester to pay £5 for ' contravening the act for inhibiting of guysing through the toun seing he confessit the having of a cod on his head through the toune.']

27th Dec. 1614

Comperit Magdalen Gray, ane guyser, dilatit Hew Kay, James Calderis man, and ane scoller playing on ane trump.

30th Dec. 1614

[Various guisers summoned before the Session.]

3rd Jan. 1615

Comperit Hew Kay and Maitland Gray delatit ane scoller of James Calder to have playit with ane trumpt. Comperit Thomas Urrall confessit he playit on the trumpt to the gwysars and that Hew Kay was with them and careit ane cott stoppit with streay wpone ane staff and dancit in Johne Bonymanis hous and Hew Kay confessit the samen and that Magdalen Gray was with them in Patrik Pettindrichs hous and therfor committit to ward. Comperit Elspet Dempster and delatit William Moreis woman, Walter Smyths woman, Alex^r. Bonymanis woman quha passit all to Thomas Hardeis hous and dancit ther with ane lad quha playit wpone ane swasche ther, contenouis till Freday to forder tryell. Siclyk comperit Cristane Sanderis and confessit scho dancit in Thomas Hardeyis hous and that scho was in John Innes hous and in William Moreis hous and that Dempster dansit with ane bonat on hir heid in Thomas Hardeis hous and that ane Andersones playit on ane swasche and that Maige Elchuner dancit with Androw Stalkeris hatt on hir heid. Comperit the

said Maige Elchuner and confessit scho was dansing with
ane hatt and that Alex[r] Bonymanis woman dansit with
ane bonat.

18th Dec. 1618

Insolenceis—It is ordenit that the superstitious obserua-
tion of auld reitis and ceremoneis expresly forbidden
during the tyme callit Yooll that they be altogidder awodit
and eschewit, viz. that na persoun within burgh or landward within this parosche pas in gwysing, dansing, singing
carallis, play at the fut ball, throch the toun, nor about
the Chanonrie kirk and kirkyeard, nather wemen to be
cled in mens apparrell nor men in womens apparrell,
casting of snaw ballis, hurling with stoollis on the streitis . . .

7th Jan. 1623

Dansers—Comperit James Tailyour for playing on ane
trumpt to ane number off lasses quha war dansing to his
playing . . .   Gwysseris — James Bonyman, Alexander
Petrie, Johne Petrie, Robert Dunbar, Archibald Law.
Theas past in ane sword dance in Paul Dunbar his closs
and in the kirkyeard with maskis and wissoris on ther
faces.   Penaltie of ilk gwysser 40 s.

22nd Jan. 1630

Gyssing: Innes, Sutherland 40 s. Innes 20 s.—Alexander
Innes, 'Doucie,' purgit himselff be his oath that he was
frie of any gyseing about Yule. William Sutherland, merchant, confessit himselff to have been gyseing in womenis
habite about the Yule tyme, ordeans him to pay 40 s.
Alexander Innes, litster, confessit gyseing with a false
beard at Yule tyme, quherfor he is ordeant to pay tuenty
shillings.[1]

---

[1] There are many other Minutes dealing with proclamations of the acts
against guising and convictions under the acts—e.g., Dec. 17th, 1619 ; Jan.
31st, 1623; Jan. 12th, 1627; Dec. 20th, 1629; Jan. 22nd, 1630; Jan. 29th,
1630, etc.

ERROL.

Excerpts from MS. 'Parochial Registers: Co. of Perth: Errol. M. 1553-1616. D. 1613-1616 ' in the custody of the Registrar-General, Edinburgh.

14th May 1592

Mayis   Discharges all bringing in off Mayes as ꝑe fascheouñ ves and pastymes on ꝑe Lordis day specially befoir ꝑe last ſſermond eftir nwn. And ordanis ꝑe vsaris heiroff to be callit and punissit.

30th Dec. 1593

carrellis   Comperit tho loony being summonit for singing off carrellis, at ꝑe thornes, and confessing his offence promisit amendement. It is ordanit ꝑat carrelleris in all tym cuming be punissit as fornicatouris.

9th Aug. 1594

Discharges all pastymes in grange vpon ꝑe sabboth and Namly till ꝑe last ſſermone be endit.

3rd Jan. 1594/5

Comperit cristein (   )sone and confessit hir singing off carellis at ꝑe thorne bot said scho knew no law aganis it. scho promissis to satisfie ꝑe kyrk as wꝑeris gilty off ꝑe said offence.

8th Feb. 1594/5

[Two men and four women confess ' ꝑair going about in ringis and carrelling vpon ꝑe day callit Ʒoull day. And allegit ꝑaj knew no command aganis it. Promising to absten in tymes cuming.']

21st Feb. 1594/5

[Pastimes in the kirkyard, especially football, etc., forbidden] [1]

[1] Similarly 8th Feb. 1601.

8th Aug. 1596

It is reportit ꝑat ꝑair is pastymes in ꝑe gra*n*ge vpo*n* ꝑe sabboth q*u*h*i*lk lattis ꝑe Meting of ꝑe pople to ꝑe preiching / And ꝑairfoir it is ordanit ꝑat befoir ꝑe last preiching be finissit ꝑair be no pastym at all.

10th May 1600

Act Maij   It is ordanit ꝑat ꝑair be No maying nor profana*tio*uñ off ꝑe sabboth be Maies in na tyme cu*m*ing vnder panis off publict repe*ntan*(ce) to euery controuenar and forder as ꝑe kyrk sall think gud.

5th Jan. 1610

[John Hay summoned for profaning the Sabbath by playing.] [1]

GLASGOW.

[*Extracts from the Records of the Burgh of Glasgow*, Vol. I., 1573-1642. Scottish Burgh Records Society, 1876. A synopsis of Glasgow Kirk Session Records is given in Wodrow's *Collections upon the Lives of the Reformers and Most Eminent Ministers of the Church of Scotland*, Maitland Club, 1848. The University Records are printed in *Munimenta Universitatis Glasguensis*, Mait. Club, 1854.]

Burgh Records.

2nd June 1599

Statute,   Item, it is statute be the provest, bailleis, and playe daye   counsale that, according to the proclamatioune and preparatione to the playe and pastyme on Thurisdaye nixt,[2] that ilk persone absent sall paye fyve lib. of penalte.[3]

15th March 1581/2

Item, gevin to Margaret Ros for ane disione gevin be hir to the bairnis, makeris of the pastyme to the Kingis Majestie,   xx ſ [4]

---

[1] Similarly 30th April 1615, 7th April 1616.
[2] *i.e.*, Corpus Christi day, which fell on June 7th this year.
[3] *Extracts*, p. 193.
[4] *Ibid.*, p. 470.

3rd June 1605

Item, to the menstrillis, officeris, and belringeris for pastyme
making that nicht the benfyris was furth   v li.[1]

Kirk Session Records.

1596, the Session appoints that a Fast be keeped both
dayes of the Communion, and that the Lord's day be not
profaned with pastimes and playes. The same renewed
8th May 1599 ; and *7th May* 1607, the Session order intimation to be made, that during the next two weeks before the
Communion weeks, no games nor playes to be used in Toun ;
and the Magistrates are ordered to be applyed to for this.[2]

24th April 1595, the drum is appointed to go throu the
Toun, discharging bickerings on Sunday, or playes, either
by young or old. *11th May* 1598, intimation that no plays
be used on the Sundays of May. This repeated, *24th Ap*ʳ
1600 . . . *19th May* 1603, That no persons go to Rugland
to see vain playes on the Sabbath. This intimation is
renewed *16th May* 1607 and *21st May* 1612.[3]

26th Dec. 1583. That such be summoned who keep the
superstitiouse day called Yuil. . . . *22nd Dec.* 1586.
Some persons, who upon the 20th of December, called St
Thomas' even, at 12 at night, went throu the Toun with
pipers etc. and laid a dead horse to the minister's yait,
are to be put in prison, without meat or drink, till tomorrow at 8 hours, and till they find caution (that) they
will appear in the Old Pillar on Sunday next. *19th Dec.*
1594, the Session make a very long act against the keeping
of Yuil ; and the observers of that day are to be punished
by the Magistrates, and to be debarred from the privilidges
of the kirk, sacraments, and marriage. *18th Dec.* 1600,
26th Dec. 1602, 20th *Dec.* 1604, this act is intimat, as also

---

[1] *Extracts*, p. 472.
[2] *Wodrow*—Life of Mr David Weems, p. 25.
[3] *Ibid.*, p. 35. Cf. *Glasgow Memorials*, Robert Renwick, 1908, p. 323 : 'May-
day celebrations are referred to in 1592. On 6th April of that year the Session
perceiving that the Sabbath was profaned by ' beggeris and youths ' bringing
in May playis, resolved that in future neither ' menis son, prenteis nor puir '
should profane the Sabbath in that way, and ordained that the fathers and
masters should pay 20s. for the first and 30s. for the second fault of their
sons and prentices respectively, and beggars were to be banished out of the
town.' [I am informed that the original manuscript of these records was
destroyed by fire recently.]

21st Dec. 1609, with this addition, that no playes, nor gysings, nor pypings, nor drinking, nor any superstitiouse exercise be used the dayes following Yuil, on the pain of censure [1]

Feb. 1605, a man is ordered to dree his repentance for putting on of women's cloathes ; and a woman for putting on of men's cloaths. Another instance of this is June 1595.

20th May 1624, the Session makes intimation that none reset commedians, juglers, etc.[2]

University Records.

2nd May 1462

Congregatione tenta ubi supra secundo die Maii anno etc. lxij. de consensu omnium magistrorum conclusum fuit perpetuis futuris temporibus observandum quod festo Translationis Sancti Nicholai nono videlicet die mensis Maii singulis annis fieret congregatio generalis decano intimante in valvis ecclesie maioris in festo precedenti ad eligendum duos discretos magistros qui providebunt necessaria et utilia pro convivio habendo in collegio facultatis artium die dominico aut festo sequenti dictum diem Translationis Sancti Nicholai prout videbitur facultati congruentius expedire et aure temperies expostulat. Pro quo quilibet magister in congregatione aut presens in civitate Glasguensi si beneficiatus fuerit dabit provisoribus tres solidos et non beneficiatus octodecim denarios. licentiati bachallarii et studentes similiter. Insuper ordinavit Facultas quod die illo statuto a Facultate conveniant omnes magistri licentiati bachallarii et studentes sub pena duorum solidorum hora octava ante meridiem in capella Sancti Thome Martiris ibique missam audiant et post illam unusquisque honeste et solenniter accipiat flores et frondes ᶠarborum quos dicti provisores expensis communibus illic afferri facient et in equis ad hoc quam honeste poterunt ordinatis procedant omnes gravi et maturo incessu processionali per stratam publicam a superiori (parte) civitatis usque ad crucem fori et sic redeundo usque ad collegium Facultatis ubi cum letitia corporalis refectionis conferant magistri de

---

[1] *Wodrow*—Life of Mr David Weems, pp. 37-8.   [2] *Ibid.*, p. 72.

illis que promovere possunt facultatem commodumque et augmentum suppositorum eius. . . . expeditoque prandio procedant omnes magistri in turma cum studentibus ad locum solatii convenientiorem ubi magistri aliqui vel studentes si interludium habeant vel aliquod tale quod iocundare potest populum matura deliberatione prehabita presertim per regentes Facultatis honeste perficiant. Et quia justum est ut qui pro honore Facultatis operas suas conferunt et expensas remuneratione digna non careant statuit insuper Facultas quod magistri et studentes qui pro honore eius talia solatia fecerint habeant speciales gratitudines et prerogativas in suis promotionibus et justis per eos a facultate petitis. . . .[1]

HADDINGTON.

[Manuscript records in Burgh archives : Council and Court Books, 1530-55, 1555-71, 1571-75, 1575-81, 1581-1602, 1603-16. There are a few stray treasurers' compts from 1554, some of which are at Register House. The earliest manuscript Presbytery records, in the custody of the Clerk to the Presbytery, date from 1587.]

Excerpts from MS. Council Records.[2]

(a) Corpus Christi Procession and Pageants.

23rd May 1532

[Dispute between the Masons and Wrights on the one side and the Baxters on the other concerning ' ᵹe plaissing of ᵹe maissonis & wrychtis in ᵹe procession on corpus ʋristis day & oᵹer tymmis quhen ᵹai ga in procession.' The Council directs the Wrights and Masons to procure a testimonial from the Common Clerk of Edinburgh stating the places allotted in the Edinburgh Corpus Christi procession.]

---

[1] *Munimenta Universitatis Glasguensis*, II, 39.
[2] Some of these excerpts were printed in the *Proceedings of the Society of Antiquaries of Scotland*, Vol. II, 1854-7.

28th May 1532

The quhilk day ɣe syſs delyueris ɣat ɣe maissonis & wrychtis sall paſs in procession on corpus cristis day & all oɣer processionis in ɣe place & compane wyth ɣe smythis & hamyrmen ane of ɣe ta craftis & ane ɣe toɣer in oixstaris as breithir & companʒonis becawſs It wes delyuerit be ane queist afor ɣat ɣai suld be placit in procession in haidinton as ɣai wer in edinburgh The said maissonis & wrychtis producit in Iugment & to ɣe syſs a actentik testimoniall onder ɣe seill of office of ɣe hamyrmen of edinburgh & subscriptionis manuell of ɣe deikyn of hammyrmen to ɣe effet abone writyn

29th May 1532

The quhilk day it wes delyueryt be ɣe consell ɣat ɣe smythis wrychtis & maissonis sall paſs to gydder in procession on corpus cristis day & all oɣer processionis eftir ɣe testimoniall of ɣe common clerk of edinburgh & ɣe prowestis beris in effet And at ɣe smythis sal paſs onder ɣe tovnis baner quhill yai maik ane of ɣair awyn quhilk salbe maid betweix ɣe daɪt heir of & ɣe nixt processione saiffand ɣe octauis of corpus cristis day & to be maid or ɣe assumpcion of our laydy nixt to cum onder ɣe pane of viij s ſs of ylk craft maister of ɣe craftis

4th June 1532

[Copy of testimonial from the Common Clerk of Edinburgh to the Wrights and Masons of Haddington.]

. . . It is ɣe loifaibill vse and ordour obſseruit & keipit wythin ɣis towne amangis craftismene in ɣair passing in processioñ one corpus cristis day ɣe octauis ɣaireftir & all oɣer generall processionis & gadderingis ɣat is to say ɣe haill breɣer of ɣe hamyrmen of all kynd of sortis to gidder witht ɣe maissonis wrychtis glasinwrychtis & paintouris pasſs all to gidder wyth ɣair bannaris nixt ɣe sacrament And nixt ɣaim & befoir passis ɣe baxtaris The threid craft befor ɣaim passis ɣe wobstaris & walkaris to gidder The feird is ɣe tailʒouris The fift place befor ɣe sacrament is ɣe cordanaris The vj place is ɣe skynnaris & furrouris The vij place befor ɣe sacrament pasſs ɣe barbouris The viij place quhilk is ɣe formast place passand befor ɣe procession is ɣe flechouris & candillmaikaris And ɣis is ɣe ordour keipit wythin ɣe towne amang ɣe craftismene in all processionis & gathringis [Dated Edinburgh, 27th May 1532].

[Copy of a testimonial from the Wrights and Masons of Edinburgh to the Wrights and Masons of Haddington.]

. . . ꝩe ordour & passag in ꝩe procession on corpus cristis day & ꝩe octauis of ꝩe samyn & all oꝩer generall processionis amangis ꝩe saidis craftis wythin ꝩe said bruche is all to gidder wyth four baneris viz twa pertenyng to ꝩe said hamyrmen & oꝩeris twa pertenyng to ꝩe said maissonis & wrychtis equale borne befor ꝩe said craftismen And ꝩe said brether of craftismen pasfs ꝩaireftir in oꝩeris oixstaris as ꝩai wor brether of ane craft And quhat expenfs ar maid in ꝩe said processionis ar equale payit ꝩe tane half be ꝩe said hamyrmen ꝩe toꝩer half be ꝩe maissonis & wrychtis [Dated Edinburgh, 26th May 1532].

21st April 1534

The quhilk day ꝩe craftis consentit of ꝩair awyn confession to play ꝩair pagis on corpus cristis day

28th May 1537

The quhilk day ꝩe syfs wyth awifs of ꝩe bailȝes contenuis ꝩe craftis to play ꝩair pagenis quhill midsomir day
The quhilk day ꝩe sifs delyueris ꝩat ꝩe baxsteris mawtmen flechouris smythis barbouris tailȝouris skynaris furiouris masonis vrychtis vobsteris cordinaris & all oꝩer craftis sall playe ꝩair pagenis ȝeirly & ꝩis ȝeir oñ midsomerday

14th June 1541

The quhilk day ꝩe baillies chargit ꝩe dekynnis of ꝩe craftis of haidynton personly present to play ꝩar piadȝanis [1] ꝩis ȝeir as ꝩai did afoir

(b) *Folk Plays : The Abbot of Unreason.*

30th Nov. 1530

The quhilk day ꝩe action betwne Iamis biris & will dowglace to assifs quhilk delyueris ꝩat will dowglace sall content & pa to Iamis biris ꝩe sovm of xiiij ş for his fee & playing to wille dowglace quhen he wes abbot & in a merciment of court for his wrang defens

[1] Or ' pradȝanis.'

28th March 1531 [1]

The quhilk day wylȝem dowglace tuk an act of cowrt ɣat
mowngo myllar faillit in his preif quhilk tuk ɣis day & ɣe
laif of his marrois to preif ɣair waigis for ɣair dansyne

5th Nov. 1532

The quhilk day ɣe syſ ordanis a officiar to pound robyn
turnor for xxij ſ vj đ for thre playe cottis becawſ It wes
assignit to hym to pa & to be Inlowit in his covnt

12th Aug. 1534

thomas dyson & Ihon ayton bailȝes maid Iamis raburn
burgis gyffyn to robyn wolson abbot of Vnresson

20th June 1535

wylȝem anderson ves maid burgis gyffyn to Ihon loigan
abbot of vnresson

8th May 1536

Memorandum ɣat Ihon ryklyntoñ Ihoñ wolsoñ & georg
rychartsoñ wes choissyñ to be abbot off wnresson ɣe
quhilk ɣai all thre forsuk & wes content ylk man to pa
xl ſ to ɣe kyrk maister & he to maik cownt ɣairof to ɣe
towñ

24th April 1537

The quhilk day ɣe syſ deliueris ɣat georg rychartsoñ sall
pa to ɣe tressurar xx ſ at witsonday nixt heir eftir & oder
xx ſ at ȝoull nixt ɣaireftir quhilk xl ſ georg ves awand ɣe
town becauſ he vald nocht be abbot of Wnressoñ

8th April 1539

[List of 25 names.]   The quhilk day ɣe baillies efter ɣe
takyn of ɣe aythis of ɣir personis abone vrytyng requirit
ɣe saidis personis quhether ɣai thocht expedient till haue
ane abbott of vnressoun ɣis ȝeir or nocht to ɣe quhilk ane
certane anſſerit & said ɣai thocht It expedient till have
ane abbot & ane vther certane quhais namis eftir followis
thocht It nocht expedient viz nicholace swynton Iohne
dowglace baxster adam volson patrik trottar Iohn dowglace
mason thomas ponton Iohn volson & dauid fowrus

[1] MS. has ' 1530.'

the quhilk day ꝩe baillies & namis aboꝰ vrytyng ꝩat thocht
expedient till have ane abbot for ꝩis ȝeir thynkis ꝩai will
gyve fowr pownd and ane burgeschip till him ꝩat ꝩe tovn
chesis abbott of vnresson for ꝩis ȝeir And all ꝩat refusis
It sall gyve fowrty ꝸ ꝩe first xl ꝸ to be gevin till him ꝩat
takis It on him and ꝩe laif to cum to ꝩe common veill of
ꝩis tovn The quhilk day thomas ponton wes chosyne abbott
of vnresson for ꝩis ȝeir & he till do ſ̈eruice vsit & vont
& faillieng of him thomas synclar and faillieing of ꝩe said
thomas synclar thomas burrell and faillieng of thomas
burrell Iohn ayton &c. &c.

14th April 1539

The quhilk day Iohn peyrson ane of ꝩe baillies in name
& behalf of ꝩe tovn askit Instrument ꝩat ꝩe baillies had
causit ꝩe covnsall to convene to ꝩe towbuyth on twysday
last bypast for chesyng of ꝩe abbot of vnresson and allegit
ꝩat ꝩe maist part of ꝩe cownsall had dissassentit till have
ane abbot as he allegit testibus communitate . . .
The quhilk day ꝩe cownsall abon vrytyng thinkis to put
ꝩe actis mayd on twisday till execution & thinkis ꝩaim
ordourlye done in ꝩe chesyng of ꝩe abbot And ordanis ꝩe
baillies till cauſ ꝩair officier till profer ꝩe horn till him ꝩat
ꝩat office Is layd on or ellis gif he takis It nocht tyll poynd
hym for xl ꝸ & ꝩe tovn & common gud till varrand & defend
ꝩe baillies gif ony pley happyn ꝩaireftir And gyf ꝩat he
ꝩat It is layd on fyrst gevis xl ꝸ to profer It to ꝩe nixt It
Is layd on & syne ꝩe thryd & syne ꝩe feyrd And all ꝩe
communite ratifijs ꝩe samyn &c.

24th April 1539

The quhilk day ꝩe covnsall delyueris ꝩat ꝩe baillies paſ
& put ꝩe actis to executioun of ꝩe abbot chesing as ꝩai will
anſer on ꝩair aythis & ꝩat Incontinent but delay &c

6th May 1539

the quhilk day dauid fowrus thesaurar grantit hym ressauit
fra Iohn badbe iiij ƚib for his burgeschyp / and als xl ꝸ
fra thomas ponton for ꝩe forsakyn of ꝩe abbotschyp &
syklyk of thomas synclar xl ꝸ

The quhilk day ꝩe assyſ delyueris ꝩat ꝩe thressarar sall
vayr ꝩe fowr pownd he gat fra thomas synclar & thomas

ponton on play coittis & ꝑa coittis to be kepit in ꝑe common
kist quhill ꝑe nixt ȝeir to ꝑe abbot & ꝑat abbot to deliuer
ꝑaim in ꝑe common kyst agane vnspwlt & sa furth ȝeirly to
ſſerue ꝑe tovn & na vꝑeris

16th *May* 1539

Eodem die villiam purwes wes maid burgeſſ for fowr pownd
gevyn to Iohne ayton abbot / & he to cum & duell within
ꝑe tovn within a moneth eftir he cum hame . . .

10th *Dec.* 1539

The quhilk day george Rechartsone wes exonerit and
maid payment of fourty ſ for the abbotschip quhilk he
refusit to tak of quhilk dauid fourroyſſ had ressauit for
ꝑis ȝeir xx ſ & philp gipson ather xx ſ

17th *Feb.* 1539/40

The quhilk day ꝑe baillies & covnsall exoneris thomas
synclar of xl ſ & for ꝑe refuſſ of his abbotschip

30th *March* 1540

The quhilk day ꝑe baillies & communite ordanis ꝑat quha
euer be maid abbot ꝑis ȝeir ꝑat he sall tak ꝑe samyn on him
vithin xxiiij houris nixt eftir ꝑai be chosin & chargit
ꝑairwith or ꝑan to refuſſ ꝑe samyn & pay ꝑair xl ſ ylk ane
eftir vther as ꝑai refuſſ & ꝑis to be obſſeruit in tyme tocum
the quhilk day Iames horne wes chosyne be ꝑe baillies &
communite abbot of vnresson for ꝑis ȝeir / & faillieng of
him patrik dowglace fleschour & faillieing of him Io dowglace mason syne philp gipson syne Robert litstar syne
Iames raburn syne Iohne dowglace baxster & george vaik

20th *July* 1540

The baillies and assyſſ will ꝑat ꝑe first burgeſſ ꝑat beis
maid except burgeſſ air be gevin to patrik dowglace for
his abbot of vnresson ꝑat he suld have & vill releve ꝑe
tovne of ꝑe band ꝑat ꝑai ar bund to him ꝑairfor /

9th *Oct* 1540

Eodem die the saidis baillies maid Iohne dawgleiſſ burgeſſ
and gevin to patrik dowglace for ꝑe burgeſſ ꝑat he suld
have for his abbot of vnresson

16*th May* 1541

The q*uhi*lk day ꝑe baillies thomas dykyson and villiam gibson maid william lourie burgeſs for ꝑe burgeschip q*uhi*lk ves gevin to gavane sanderson abbot And ꝑe said gavane held him veill content ꝑair*of* & dischargis ꝑe tovne

23*rd Dec.* 1552

The q*uhi*lk day ꝑe counsale w*ith* aduiſs of ꝑe provest and bailleis hes dischargit all abbott*is* of vnressoun in tymis cu*m*yng

Excerpts from MS. Presbytery Records.

4*th Dec.* 1588

Vol. I.
1587-96

[Under this date is registered an obligation made 14th Oct. 1583 by the Provost, Bailies and Council of Haddington. They promise to uphold the true religion and to assemble themselves, their wives, children and apprentices every Sunday forenoon and afternoon in the parish church and to prohibit any gaming, playing, buying or selling on that day.] . . . in q*uhi*lk day we sall nother p*er*mit fair m*er*ket nor *convention* of craftis nor ganging of the ruys in time of preiching or prayer*is* in any tyme heireft*ir* also to abolische and remoue the *conu*enementis of sup*er*stitious Observatio*n* of festuall dais callit of ʒule pasche witsonday and the pasche of maj plaijs of robe*n* hude litle Iohne abitis of vnresoun setting furth of banefyris singing of car-rell*is* w*ith*in or about the kirk or ellis at *c*ertane seasonis of the ʒeir togith(er) w*ith* geving of anie significatioun of the fostering ꝑair*of* in apperell or banketting but specially in dais dedicate in time of papestrie to sanctis sumtimes namit patronis invented to the dishonouring of god contempt of his trew Religio*n* & fost*er*ing of grit blindnes & erro*ur* amanges people Q*uhi*lkis papisticall sup*er*stitioni*s* rites and customes we p*ro*meis in man*er* forsaid to punische according to the act of parliament maid at ed*inburgh* the xxiiij day of october the ʒeir of god jᵐvᶜ four scoir j ʒeir schap: 6 . . .' [And because it has pleased God to establish an eldership, an undertaking is made to convene to the hearing of the word every Wednesday. 'And that nether counsell salbe haldin ye said tyme tharof nor playing *in* hauchis sands vsit nor m*er*chandis buith oppened . . .']

Aganis
pasche
playis

16th April 1589

The q*uhi*lk day ꝑe Brethrene co*n*ferring and resoni*ng* the abusis tha(t in ?) [1] creis in [2] be ouirseing ꝑe insolence of ꝑe ꝛouth in chusing robene hui(d and) v*ꝑer* *p*rophane playis vsit vpone the sabo*th* day in co*n*tempt of god and his (religion) for repressing thairof appointis alex*ander* forreste*r* M*aiste*r thomas makgy M*aiste*r w(alter) hay and Iamis gibsone to acco*m*pany M*aiste*r Iamis Carmichaell to ꝑe tou(n) of hadingtoun for to admonische thame desyri*ng* that ꝑe said*is* playis Be thair authoritie may be dischargit wit*h*in thair bound*is* Alswa ordanis M*aiste*r Iohne Ker Iamis gibsone & M*aiste*r Iohne Nimbill speik the Laird of Samelstoun for discharging of ꝑe play callit ꝑe trik [3] vsi(t) vpoune ꝑe first sounday of may As also ꝑe haill brethrene ar ordanit to admonische in eu*er*y of thair p*er*ticular kirk*is* to discharge ꝑe said*is* playis

Maister Iohne Nimbill was desyrit to seik out ꝑe extract of ꝑe actis maid at ꝑe last synodall assembly

23rd April 1589

[Patrick Scugall, piper, summoned for playing on the Sabbath day.]

The sub-
missioun
of ꝑe
ꝛouth of
hadingtoun

30th April 1589

The q*uhi*lk day compeirit nycoll aytoun alex*ander* seytoun & george thomsone wit*h* the rest of ꝑe ꝛouth of the toun of hadingtoun thair co*m*plices q*uha* gaue in thair submissioun in wrytt q*uha*irin was declairit that thay had done nathing in co*n*tempt nather wald thay co*n*tinew any pastyme q*uha*irof sould any sclande*r* or offence be geui*n* And as for thair mi*n*strallis throw the toun q*uhi*lk thay haue alreddy vsit that was callit pasche playis abbot of onresone robene houd & sic v*ꝑer* *p*rophane playis thay neuer vsit ꝑe effect*is* ꝑair*of* and gif thair said mi*n*strallis throw toun hes bene offensyue to ꝑe brethre*n* thay ar hartlie sorie for the sami*n* . . . [The Presbytery accepts the explanation for this and other offences, and lets them off with a caution.]

---

[1] The MS. here is mutilated at the edge.

[2] ' Haddingtoun ' omitted.

[3] At first I was inclined to read this as ' tuk,' or, possibly, ' cuk.' But it is indistinguishable from the ending ' trik ' of the word ' Patrik ' in a subsequent entry ; and when it re*c*urs under date 30th April (*infra*, 255), the scribe seems to have rewritten it to make the ' r ' and ' i ' clearer, and there is a distinct dot over the ' i.'

M*aister* Iamis Carmichaell being askit his diligence in conferring w*ith* ɥe Laird of samelstoun for discharging the play callit ɥe trik [2] of samelstoun vsit ʒeirlie vpone the first sounday of may anſserit that he past thither and fand not ɥe laird bot he had co*n*venit sax of the honest mene of the toun and schew thame ɥe ordina*n*ce of the assembly as also he past ɥaireftir and spak ɥe laird q*uh*a promesit thair sould na sic playis be vsit and he sould discharge ɥe sami*n* ɥe q*uh*ilk was obeyit

Diligence schawi*n* i*n* dischargit [1] of ɥe peace playis

Sept. 1589 ?

. . . [3] at ɥair be ane suit gevin to ɥe synodall assemble that ɥe synodall may . . . at ɥe *g*en*er*all & *g*en*er*all at ɥe p*ar*liame*n*t ɥat ane mair substa*n*tious act may be maid aganis peace playis robene huid etc

26*th* Oct. 1589

[Proclamation in the name of Robert Lord Seytoun, who had been granted the privilege of holding a market at Tranent. Prohibits all persons within the barony of Tranent from ' all passing to aillhousſſ gammis or playis ' in time of sermon.]

13*th June* 1593

[Appoints Mr Walter Hay to ' trawell ' with Lord Setoun in Edinburgh and James Gipson with the Presbytery of Dalkeith to desire them to send some of the brethren to the Laird of Ormiston ' and to co*m*plaine ɥat ɥai tak no*ch*t ordo*u*r w*ith* ɥe profanatioun of ɥe saboth be ɥe pladayes of prestoun and ormistoun ']

Setoun & Ormistoun

4*th July* 1593

The brethring appointit to trauell w*ith* ɥe L. setoun and Laird of ormistoun reportit ɥat ɥaj had no*ch*t only bein diligent w*ith* ɥe p*ar*teis In ɥat mater bot also ɥat ɥaj had purchasit ane chairge of his Ma*ie*ste to chairge ɥe p*ar*teis ɥairto

setoun and ormistoun

10*th May* 1598

fforsamekle as ɥair is ane greit sclaunder be ɥe prophane play maid at samelston vpon sonday last It wes ordanit

---

[1] *Sic* in MS.   [2] See *supra*, 254, n.[3].   [3] MS. mutilated at edge.

that the laird of samelston suld be chargit to compeir ƿis
day xv dayis ƿat ordour mycht be put to ƿe said mater at
leist in tyme cumming

The laird of
samelstoun

24th May 1598

The quhilk day compeirit patrik hamiltoun laird of samelston
And efter ƿat ƿe presbitrie had greitlie regraitit vnto him
ƿe profanatioun of ƿe sabboth be ane profane play at his
toun to ƿe quhilk ƿe haill countrey convenit desyring him
to mak sum resistance ƿairto at ƿe place he anſerit ƿat
vpon sonday ƿe 7 of ƿis instant quhen he vnderstuid ƿat
ƿair wes ane conveniioun of pepill he went out himself with
his servauntis and tuik ƿair sweshe & ensigne from ƿame
& stayit all his awin folkis bot culd nocht put ordour to ƿe
rest with q(uhom) he had nathing ado Promising in tyme
cumming to stay (ƿe) said abuse all ƿat he culd be resisting
ƿe people at ƿe ver(ie) place quhairwith ƿe brethren being
satisfied exhortit him (to) keipe his promise

Robert
Stewart
menstraller

23rd Aug. 1598

The presbyterie ordanis Robert Stewart menstraller to be
summonit to compeir this day aucht dayis for prophaning
ƿe sonday in west fentoun [1]

9th May 1599

[Presbytery ordains the Laird of Samuelston to be summoned for profaning of the Lord's day.]

23rd May 1599

[The Laird of Samuelston and his brother ordered to stand
up in the Kirk on Sunday and confess their fault and to
promise that they will henceforth resist the like breaking
of the Lord's day.]

11th May 1603

Anent ƿe play of Samelstoun The presbitrie ordanes the
minis(ter) of hadinton to serche out quha war the prin-
cipallis ƿairin and ordanit tham to gif in ƿair names ƿe
nixt day, And the laird to be travelit with for eschewing ƿe
lyke in tyme cumming [2]

---

[1] On 30th Aug. five 'menstrellers' within the bounds of the Presbytery are
summoned. On 8th Aug. 1599 one of the five is summoned for breaking the
Sabbath day by playing in Athelstaneford.

[2] I was unable to examine the Register further, so do not know whether
this last attempt to suppress the Samuelston play was successful.

INVERNESS.

[*Records of Inverness.* New Spalding Club, 1911. This includes excerpts from Burgh Court Books, 1556-86.]

EXCERPTS FROM BURGH RECORDS.

10*th July* 1574

Johne Robertson burges of Innernis hes actit him self of his awin fre motywe will to content and pay to Thomas Ross and his spouse the sowme of xl s. vsuall monye of this realme within xv dayis, and that for expenssis maid be thame at Witsundaye in anno lxxiij yeiris vpon the said Johne and his cumpanye at Abbot Vnresson for the tyme.

8*th June* 1575

Jonat Cuthbert comperit acclamand Johne M'Kearrois ane greit pan contenyng thrie quartis j pynt, quhilk he tuike fra hir quhen Johne Robertson was Lord Abbot, price thairof xx s. monye of this realme, quha postponis to rander the said pan nor content and pay the pricis foirsaidis without he be compellit. Comperit the said Johne and allegit he poindit hir thairof and deliuerit the samyn to the Lord Abbot, nochttheless the jugis hes decernit and ordanit the said Johne M'Fargus to rander and delywer the said pan to Jonat Cuthbert or ellis the pricis foirsaidis.

KELSO.

[Manuscript Presbytery Records, Vol. I., 1609-39, in the custody of the Clerk to the Presbytery. Only partially examined.]

EXCERPTS FROM MS. PRESBYTERY RECORDS.

26*th April* 1610   f. 6

Ordaines ro*bert* clerk to sumond geordie ker in (lintoun) [1] ꝑe guidma*n* of schairp*is* rig Iohne herone plewma*n* to (ꝑe

---

[1] Many of the pages of this manuscript are mutilated at the edge.

R

laird) of lintone geordie young in hoisla for ꝑe ma(y playis)
vsed by ꝑeme called lord or abbot of vnresso(n) . . .
*con*trair to ꝑe lawes of god & ꝑe countrie.

f. 6b **3rd May 1610**

Ordaines m*aiste*r Iohne balfour to su*m*mond publikle george
ker in lintone ꝑe guidma*n* of schairpsrig Iohne herone and
george davidsone [1] in hoisla w*it*h *cer*tification if ꝑei co*m*peir
not ꝑej sal be excommunicat for ꝑair open *con*tempt and
abuse of ꝑe sabbothe because of ꝑair no co*m*peirance being
su*m*mond and no co*m*peirand

f. 7 **10th May 1610**

[As Mr John Balfour has not summoned the above ' anent
ꝑair abuse and insolence,' they are to be summoned the
next day.] [2]

f. 7b **17th May 1610**

Compeired Iohne midelmest of schairpesrig schirreff george
davesone in hoisla littiljohne and wattie ker for ꝑe foirsaid
fault being cheiff actor*is* and author*is* of ꝑe said abuse in
respect of ꝑe rest*is* no co*m*peirance ref*eris* ꝑese to ꝑe nixt
day
george ker robene hude in lintone hob [3] herone lord plewma*n*
to ꝑe laird of lintone elder geordie young in hoisla co*m*-
peired no being su*mon*d w*it*h *cer*tificatioun ordanis ꝑe
exer*c*iser ꝑe nixt day to ent*er* in ꝑe p*ro*ces of excomunica-
tioun aganst ꝑem

The presbytrie direct*is* m*aiste*r Iohne balfo*u*r to go to
fꝉir w*illia*m crainstoun & desire him to wrge ꝑe penaltie
of ꝑe act of p*ar*liament aganst ꝑe cheiff actor*is* of ꝑe pasche
playis in lintone or a penaltie at his awin discretioun

f. 8a **24th May 1610**

M*aiste*r Iohne balfo*u*r reportit that conform*e* to the ordi-
nan(ce of) the presbitrie he had spoken S*i*r w*illia*m cranstoun for . . . had usit pashe playis that his anꝉer was
Let the (presbitre) ordane tham & he sould make tham

[1] Inserted instead of ' young,' which is erased in MS.
[2] Part of this minute is now illegible.
[3] Inserted instead of ' Iohne,' which is erased in MS.

obedient bo(th) to th(e) ordinance off the presbitre & the
actis off parliament
[Then followis an entry which is partially illegible, in
addition to the MS. being mutilated at the edges. Apparently 'first admonition' is given to George Davidson and
George Ker, and 'second admonition' is ordained.]

31st May 1610

Compeired hob herone Lord in ꝩe pasche playis in linto(n)
. . . his obedience for his former fact—As also Iohne [1] . . .
to ꝩe sammyn effect in respect the presbytrie find (ꝩe
penaltie) of ꝩe act of parliament to be ten poundis (and
ꝩairfore) ordeines ꝩe foirsaidis personis to pay ꝩe samyn
(ten) poundis and remittis ꝩe exactioun to . . . [2]

7th June 1610   f. 8b

[Sentence of excommunication intimated against George
Ker and George Davidson. 21st June. (First prayer of
excommunication.) 28th June. (Second Prayer.) 5th July. f. 9
(Third prayer not to take place until further information
obtained.)]

28th March 1611   f. 15b

In respect ꝩe former proces led aganst ꝩe perochineris of
lintone viz Iohne midilmest geo ker rob herone   [3]
Dauidsone in hoisla for ꝩair insolent behauiour in pasche
playis was found wnfourmal becaus ꝩe said proces was
led befoir ꝩe presbytre & no be ꝩe nixt adjacent minister
Ordaines maister Iohne balfour to enter and procure in ꝩe
said proces except ꝩej be obedient to ꝩe ordour of ꝩe kirk.

20th June 1611   f. 17b

Compeired Geord ker & Iohn middelmest in scharpisrig &
being vrged to satisfie our ordinance for ꝩair pashe playis
refused and appailled to ꝩe Bishope of glasgow.

7th Nov. 1611   f. 20b

The breꝩer ordaines to intimat ꝩe excommunicatioun of ꝩe
personis of lintone viz george ker in lintone Iohne midilmest

---

[1] Probably John Midelmest.
[2] The rest of the entry is illegible except for a word here and there. They
are evidently threatened with ' excommunicatioun for ꝩair dissobedience.'
[3] Blank in MS.

of schairpis rige geordie Dauidsone in hoisla rob herone
servand to ꝑe laird of lintone in everie ane of ꝑaire kirkis
within ꝑairis boundis

21st Nov. 1611

Compeiret geord davidsoun hosla excommunicat & desiret
to be relaxet from ꝑe sentence of excommunicatioun ; we
find no repentance in hem ordenis hem to repair hither
quhen god shal touch his heart vith repentance & he shal
be further ansueret.

f. 21 5th Dec. 1611

Comperit Iohn middelmest george ker george davisone &
Robert hero(ne) excomunicat for ꝑair pasche playis &
disobedience & offeris ꝑair obedience for assoil(ʒeing)
thame fra ꝑe sentence. The Brethre continewis ꝑair anſſer
till this day . . . dayis

f. 24 28th May 1612

Comperit by thair bill of supplicatioun George Ker Iohn
middelmest George davisoune & Robert heroun & desyris
to be relaxed fro ꝑe sentence of excomunica(tioun) thair
publict repentance & satisfactioun being compleitt. The
presbytere (ordanis) thame to be resaiffed the nixt sabbath
according to ordour.

f. 24b 18th June 1612

Maister Ihone Balfour reportis that he had absolvit George
ker, Ihone Midlemes, George davidsone, Robert herron
from excommunicatioun

LANARK.

[*Extracts from the Records of the Royal Burgh of Lanark*,
1893. The Guildry records are of comparatively recent
date, and no trace can be found of any of the old craft
records. *Extracts from the Presbytery Records* were printed
by the Abbotsford Club (1839).]

(a) EXCERPTS FROM THE BURGH RECORDS.

12th June 1488 [1]

Item, for the costis of the procession of Corpus Christi,
iij s iij d.[2]

1490 [3]

Item, for beryn of the dragon and mendyn of it,   viij d.
Item, for beryn of the chapel and to Sanct Mertyn, xij d.

Item, to John Watson for Corpus Christi day,   ij d.[4]

June 1503 [1]

Item, for beryn of the dragwn, viij d.

Item, to John Stenson for the futyn off the cros to Corpus
Christi play, iij d.
Item, for the beryn of the dragon at command of Sir Stein
Lokhart, viij d.
Item, for beryn of the chapell, iiij d.

29th July 1507 [1]

Item, for makyn of dragone, mending of chapel and Cristis
cors, xiiij d.
Item, for twa handis to Cristis cors, viiij d.
Item, for the dychtyn of sellat and splentis viij d., to Sanct
George.
Item, for nalis to the dragown and the chapell,   iiij d.
Item, for beryng of hym viij d ; item for thred,   iiij d.
Item, in gold fulye to Cristis pascione,   vij d.
Item, gold fulyie (to the) ladis crownis,   iiij d.
Item, the skynis to Cristis cot,   ij s.
Item, to the skynnis [5] (and) padyen,   ij s.
Item, for the makyn of it,   viij d.

---

[1] Date of audit of the account for the Martinmas and Whitsunday terms.
[2] 'The foot of the page is reached here, and the next leaf being amissing, the remainder of the " cownt " is lost.'—*Extracts*, p. 3.
[3] 'The commencement of this account is awanting.'—*Extracts*, p. 7.
[4] MS. has ' ij s.'
[5] In the MS. at Lanark only ' sky ' remains, the edge of the page being torn away. The next line commences with padȝen. This the editor of the *Extracts* glosses as ' padding.' But the earliest instance of this word cited by the *N.E.D.* is in 1828. I take it that the word is ' pageant,' but, in view of the next entry, it is doubtful how the gap ought to be filled in.

Item, for ane paer of gl(uffis) to Crist,　　　　　　iij d.

Item, ane quar of paper to bill the pla withaw,　　viij d.

Item, to Will Mader to mak the actouris [1] hattis of,
　　　　　　　　　　　　　　　　　　　　　　　viij d.
Item for fulye to the s(cermen) and the ladeis crownis and
　　other crownis to the pla and parchment,　　　xij d.

Item for nalis to the chapell and mendyn of it and nalis,
　　　　　　　　　　　　　　　　　　　　　　　xij d.

For the beryn of the dragone and the chapell,　　xvj d.
For pak threid to tham, ½d.　Item, for parchment,　vj d.
Item, for strynis [2] to Cristis cot,　　　　　　　xxx d.
Item, for ane payr of gluffis to Crist,　　　　　　iij d.
Item, for makyn of the cot,　　　　　　　　　　xij d.
Item, in paper to bill this last pla,　　　　　　iij d.
Item, the xl s. at the towne as contenuit quhill Mertimes.
　　For gold fuilyie and parchment to the Kingis of Cullane,
　　　　　　　　　　　　　　　　　　　　　　　iiij d.[3]

19th Dec. 1566

Minister
calumny
Ellesone Tayis deponit be hir grit aith that
scho hard Besse Tuodall call the minister commoun theiff ; quhay wald stoip thair bairnis
fra the plaj for him, for hie trouit that the volger wald
gef him ane fie, bot devill haif it all that hie suld get, men-
suorne theif that hie wes.

(b) EXCERPTS FROM THE PRESBYTERY RECORDS.

23rd June 1625

Jo[n] Baillie, W[m] Baillie, Jo[n] Hirschaw, Jo[n] and Thomas

---

[1] ' Player ' is the regular word in the vernacular at this period. ' Actour,' if correct here, may be used in the wider sense of one who takes part in any affair, a doer, the earliest instance of actor in the sense of stage-player or dramatic performer cited in *N.E.D.* belonging to 1581. But I question this reading of the MS. and suggest, with some diffidence, ' *trumatouris* ' (tormentors) instead of ' the actouris.'

[2] I should read ' skynnis ' in MS.

[3] Owing to the scanty and fragmentary nature of these early accounts, it is not easy to say whether two Corpus Christi plays may have fallen within the financial year in 1506-07, or whether there was another play at Martinmas or during the Yule season. If the final group of entries denotes a Corpus Christi Passion Play, the inclusion of the Kings of Cullane is interesting. This latter entry may, however, be misplaced.

Prentisses, Ro[t] Wat, pyper, prophaners of the Sabbothe in fetching hame a maypole, and dancing about the same upone pasche sonday, to be summoned with a lybelit summonds.

16th March 1626

(William Weir, 'pyper to the gysarts of Lesmahego,' summoned.)

4th Jan. 1627

Ordaines M[r] Thomas Bannatyne to summond the gysartes of Douglas, and to try out those who wer clothed in womens habit.

PEEBLES.

[Charters and Documents relating to the Burgh of Peebles, with extracts from the Records of the Burgh, S.B.R.S., 1872.]

20th April 1472

Burgess
Abbot of
unrest

The quhilk day, was mad burges John Necoll, and hys fredom gewyn to John Morchowson abbot of vnrest in that tym . . .

6th May 1555

Murro burgen.
Robene Hude

The quhilk day, Robert Murro wes creat burges and mad his aith as vse is, and fand his hand and his land to do thai thingis that concernit till his aith . . . and to pay his burges siluer to my lord Robene Hude.

PERTH.

[The regular Council sederunt books commence only in 1601. Prior to this date all that has been preserved in the way of continuous records useful for my purpose is : (1) two volumes of the 'Red Book,' 1500-42 and 1543-1684, the first of these being in a mutilated and fragmentary condition ; (2) Register of Decreets, 1547-52, 1570-72, etc. It is particularly to be deplored that the regular treasurers' accounts of the period have not survived. A few odd compts for the years 1575-6, 1577-8, 1578-9, 1579-80, 1580-2, 1627-8, etc., are to be found at Register House, Edinburgh ; but, unfortunately, with one exception, these do not give detailed extraordinary expenses. The manuscript Guild Book, in the custody of the Dean of Guild, dates from 1452 to 1631. The earliest minute book of the Glovers now in existence commences in 1593 (*Annals of the Glover Incorporation of Perth*, ed. George Wilson, 1905). The Hammermen's records were privately printed for the Craft in 1889 (*The Hammermen Book of Perth*, 1518-1568, ed. Colin Hunt). I have made careful inquiries in the hope that some other Perth Incorporations would still have their early records, with the result that I have traced three other sets of pre-Reformation minute books. The first two of these did not yield any positive results. The Book of the Incorporation of Tailors commences in 1530, but various references to the ' compt buik ' of the craft show that the accounts were kept separately in a volume of which no trace can now be found. The ' Cordinar Buik of Perth', which contains sparse entries from 1545, is likewise incomplete. The Incorporation of Wrights has the following manuscript volumes : (1) a narrow vellum bound manuscript containing entries in great confusion from 1519-1618 ; (2) a foolscap size manuscript bound in vellum containing a few stray pre-Reformation minutes dating from 1530 ; (3) a much mutilated minute book containing entries c. 1537-1641. Kirk Session minute books dating from 1577 are still in existence. Large portions of these were transcribed about the end of the eighteenth century by the Rev. James Scott of Perth, and are now among the Scott collection of manuscripts at the Advocates' Library, from which excerpts were made for the Spottiswoode Society *Miscellany*, Vol. II. For various reasons I found it advisable to make my extracts from the original manuscript volumes in the custody of the Session Clerk at Perth. Peter Baxter, in *The Drama in Perth*, 1907, does not go to the original records for his earlier material.]

Excerpts from MS. Guild Book.

p. 111   *27th April* 1485

Sepulture Robertus gallowaye Emit sepulturam suam pro xx s̃ quos soluit domino Roberto douthle capellano pro suis laboribus

et expenßis factis In processione et ludo corporis xp̃i de
mandato prepositi et consulum dicti burgi pro tempore

30th Aug. 1486

p. 115
Sepultura

Andreas berß Emit sepulturam suam pro xx s̃ quos soluit
domino Roberto douthle capellano de mandato prepositi et
consulum dicti burgi pro tempore pro suis laboribus et
expenßis factis in processione et ludo corporis xp̃i

7th March 1487/8

p. 118
sepultura

Donaldus Robertson Emit sepulturam suam pro xx s̃ quos
soluit domino Roberto douthle capellano de mandato
prepositi et consulum pro tempore pro suis laboribus et
expenßis factis in ludo corporis xp̃i

16th May 1545

p. 225
Solut.

Quo die robertus Sibbald factus est burgensis et confrater
gilde burgi de pertht admissus ad libertatem eiusdem cuius
compositio est soluta Iacobo macbrek robyñ hwyd de
mandato prepositi balliuorum consulum et confratrum gilde
et cepit saisinam per alexandrum blair balliuum Inde soluti
ij s̃

21st May 1545

Quo die Robertus meik factus est burgensis et confrater
gilde burgi de perth et admissus ad libertatem eiusdem
Cuius compositio est soluta Iacobo makbrek Robeyñ
hwde . . .

27th May 1545

Quo die Walterus oliphant filius et heres quondam oliphant
de newtouñ factus est burgenßis et confrater gilde dicti
burgi Et admissus ad libertatem eiusdem Cuius compositio
est soluta Iacobo macbrek Robene hwde . . .

30th July 1546

p. 231

Quo die Iohannes walcar alias hatmaker factus est burgensis et confrater gilde burgi de perth admissus ad libertatem eiusdem gratis . . .

We baillies counsall and decanis of craftis of ꝑe burght
of pertht haveand consideratiouñ of ꝑe surfat and gret

expen*ß* mayd be Iohne walcar al*ias* hatmaker apoñ ge*m*mys ferchis and clerk playis making and plaing i*n* tymes bigane for o*ur* pleissur and ye hail co*mun*ite herof as Is notourlie knawin / And is of gud mynd to co*n*tinew and p*er*seueir in ye samy*n* in all tymes to cum And as ȝit Is vnrewardit y*air*for be us Quharfor for causis foresaid and vther*is* movand vs gevis and grant*is* to ye said Iohne to vß and bruik ye p*re*uilege of burges and gildbruthirschip fre wit*h*out ony payme*n*t to be maid be hym to o*ur* deñ of gild And ordanis Alex*ande*r lindesay o*ur* deñ of gild to ressaue admitt and inter ye said Iohne to ye said liberte and fredom̃ grat*is* as said [1] Is quhilk salbe thankfully allowit to ȝow in ȝo*ur* nixt compt*is* ȝe keipeand yis for ȝo*ur* warand Subscriuit wi*th* o*ur* hand*is* to o*ur* said burght ye xxviij day of Iunij i*n* ye ȝeir of god j^m v^c and xl sex ȝer*is*

Excerpt from MS. Register of Decreets.

14*th* *Feb.* 1577/8

Dec*er*nit and ordanit w*illiam* lausoun deacone of the wobsteris to *con*tent and pay to Iames dauidsoun lorimer the sowme of xx s̃ and that for ane gowne of ye said Iames sonis borrowit and ressauit be ye said w*illiam* fra ye said Iames at corpus cristies play last & oñ deliu*er*it as ȝit Inco*n*tine*n*t vnder the panes of pu*n*ding or varding And that *con*forme to the said Iames aith maid heirvpon ref*er*rit y*air*to be ye baillie becaus the samyn wes ref*er*rit of befoir to the said w*illiam*is aith quha being lau*ful*lie warnit to y*at* effect recordit be [*blank*] offic*er* *com*perit no*ch*t to gif ye samy*n* lau*f*ull ty*m* of day biddiñ

Excerpts from MS. Register of Acts of Council.

I, f. 51 23rd *June* 1603

ffyff deane of gild

Ordanis the deane of gild to entir Iames fyff burges and gild bro*yer* to yis bur*ch*t frelie quhais compositione is payit to ye support of ye play to be plyit [2] on tuyd*ay* in ye playfeld

[1] MS. repeats 'said.'
[2] *Sic* in MS.

Ordanis the deane of gild to entir ony qualefeit
m^cgregor   *perso*ne q*uhom* gregor macgregor *prese*nts to
deane of   him burges & gild bro*per* to *pis* bur*cht* quhais
gild
compositione is advancit be *pe* said gregor to
pe support of *pe* said play

23rd *July* 1611   f. 277

proclamatioun   Ordanis the fyft day of august to be solemlie
anent *pe* v day keipit and *pe* p*ro*clamatio*n* to pas about *pe*
of august   tou*n* viz [Proclamation quoted] [1]

2nd *Sept.* 1611

Allowis to *pe* p*ro*uest for spyce and wyne p*ro*pynit be him
to my lord*is* of scones *fservantis pat* come to *pe* toun vpone
pe fyft day of august last for making of triumphe wit*h*in
burch for his ma*ie*stie deliuerens lviij *s* viij *d*   Ordanis the
dene of gilde to pay *pe* sami*n*

2nd *Aug.* 1613   f. 217

Ordanis the dene of gilde to pay to *pe* acto*uris* of *pis* play
the price of ane gild brotherschip frelie q*uh*ilk sall be allowit
to him in his gilde compt*is*

1*st Aug.* 1614.   f. 231

dene of   Ordanis the dene of gilde to deliuer to m*aiste*r
gild Rynde   pat*ri*k rynde xx m*erkis* for his payines tane be
him in making of ane play agane fryday nixt
pe fyft d*ay* of august instant of *pe* first due of ane gild
bretherschip q*uh*ilk sall be allowit in his gilde comptis

22nd *April* 1617   f. 314

[Missive from the Privy Council, dated 14th April 1617.]
. . . The kingis ma*ie*stie being desyrous that in *pe* spe*ci*all
burrowis of *pis* kingdome q*uh*ilk*is* his ma*ie*stie intendis
godwilling to visite the tyme of his being heir suche showes
of ornament comlines & civilitie may be sene as may gif
vnto his ma*ie*stie contentment and may mak *pe* strangeris
that ar to accompany his ma*ie*stie persawe & sie that *pis*
countrie is no*ch*t sa barrine of formalitie ordo*ur* and civilitie
as they ignorantlie apprehend His ma*ie*stie hes *pair*foir

---

[1] Similar decrees for 1605, 1606, 1608, 1612, 1614, etc.

commandit ꝩat at his first entre in ꝩe saidꙇs burrowis at
ꝩe port ꝩairof the cheiff and princꙇpall inhabitantis in
ꝩe toun in ꝩair moist comelie ciwill and formall ordour
sall attend his maꙇestie and that ane speche sall be maid
vnto his maꙇestie by some persone (nocht being of ꝩe
ministeris of ꝩe toun) in name of ꝩe haill toun congratulating
his maꙇesteis comming to ꝩat toun and making his maꙇestie
hartlie welcolme and ꝩat ꝩis speche be deliuerit in sensible
ticht and gude language as alsua ꝩat at ꝩe princꙇpall portis
of ꝩe toun quhairat his maꙇestie is to enter his maꙇesteis
armes be ingrawen & sett vp both within and without and
ꝩat thay be ourgilt in ꝩe best fassoun . . .

f. 315   [A second letter from the Privy Council, dated 17th
April 1617.]

. . . And anent ꝩe speche ꝩat is to be maid to his maꙇestie
ꝩow sall informe him whome ꝩow ar to trust with ꝩat
mater That first in name of ꝩe toun he mak his maꙇestie
welcolme and then in sensible & good language he sall sett
furth his maꙇesteis awin praiss by innumerabill confortis
& blissingis quhilkꙇs ꝩis countrey hes haid boith in kirk
& policie wnder his maꙇesteis moist happie gouernament
& last so far as modestie may permit he schall speik to
ꝩe praiſs of ꝩe toun both anent ꝩe antiquitie ꝩairof the
ſſeruices done be ꝩe same to ꝩis crowñ & estait the willing-
nes of ꝩe present inhabitantis by ꝩair best endeworis to
ſſerue his maꙇestie in all & eueriething lyand in ꝩair possi-
bilitie without ony priuat respect, . . .   This being the
substance of ꝩe speche ꝩow schall caus it be deliuerit in
ꝩe best forme ꝩat may be and remitting the same to your
awin grawe consideraꙇionis as a poynte heichlie importing
ꝩe credit of your toun . . .

Appointis euerie day heireftir befor his maꙇestie cuming
to convene immediatlie eftir ꝩe morning prayeris and
sermones

f. 319 23rd June 1617

skynneris   Ordanis the skynneris to prouyde for ane
dance   ſſword dance the baxteris ꝩe egiptiane dance
the [1] maister schole ꝩe bairnes gud dance to his
maꙇestie cuming to ꝩis burch

----

[1] MS. repeats 'the.'

deane of
gilde
skynnaris

Ordanes the deane of gilde to deliuer to ȝe
skynneris for ȝe dance before his maiestie
fourtie pund*is* in ȝe first due of ane gild ḥrether-
schip.

[Nov. 23rd 1618 : 300 marks to be given to the children
of the late John Stewart, merchant, burgess of Perth,
who made and declaimed the oration to His Majesty
on his entry into the town, in which His Majesty took
great pleasure.]

26*th April* 1624   II[1]

Scholema*ister*

The counsall thinkis meitt that m*aiste*r Joh*n*n
Durward schole maister caus ȝe bairnis gang
about ȝe toun wit*h* ȝer bowis & arrowis ilk oulk In may
ane day in the oulk according to wse and wount and mak
als many as they pleis

9*th May* 1625

The haill co*n*sall all in ane woyce ordanis the theſ*aure*r to
satisfe Patrik Pitcairne fourtie pundis mo*n*ey aduancit &
deburssit be him to the skynneris the tyme the king wes
last in ȝis cuntrie for danceing of ȝe suorde dance befoir
his ma*ie*stie q*uh*ilk sall be allowit in his theſ*aureri*s comptis
be p*r*oduceing thir p*rese*ntis for his warrand

16*th May* 1625

merschell
scole ma*iste*r

The co*n*sall all in ane woice ordanis Patrik
merschell deacone of the cordonaris to creawe
the co*n*sall and m*aiste*r Johnne Durward scole
m*aiste*r pardoun for the offence done to him & ȝe bairnis
be the deacone & trubling of ȝame in ȝair pley

mershell
wry*ch*t schole
ma*iste*r

Ordanis also gilbert merschell and Dauid wry*ch*t
to be wardit wit*h*in ȝe tolbuyt*h* of ȝis bur*ch*t
for ȝe offence done be thame in mispersoning
of ȝe m*aiste*r and bairnis in pleying of thair
playis And to remane ȝairin induring ȝe m*aiste*ris will and
q*uh*ill the m*aiste*r request for ȝame at the bailleis handis
to putt ȝame to libertie

---

[1] No foliation in this volume.

27th June 1625

[Another act ordaining the payment of the £40 to Patrick
Pitcairne ' for furnessing be him furnessit to the skynnars
for danceing of ȝe sword dance befoir ȝe king in augist
1617.']

19th April 1630

durward   The prouest bailleis & counsall ordenis Andro
wilsone deane of gilde to enter gilde brother
any qualefeit man quhom maister Johne durward scole
maister sall present and he to haue ȝe dewitie ȝat beis
gewin ȝairfoir for playis and pastyme making to ȝe bairnis
in may quhilk sall be allowit to ȝe deane of gilde in his
gilde comptis

6th May 1633

The counsall ordenis the best housȝ to be kepit for Inglis
men malt barnes for stabillis Ane sword dance on the
water of Tay

20th May 1633

[Various preparations *re* King's visit]

Ordaneis william duncane deacone of ȝe skynneris to caus
exerceiȝ ȝair men in danceing of ȝe suord dance

27th May 1633

staig   Nominatis andro wilsone baillie for frameing
wilsone   of ȝe staig for ane speache to his maiesteis
heircumyng Robert burrell for the play and
somer housȝ

            Nota ȝair wes ane suord dance dancit to his
suord dance maiestie be the skynneris foiranent the chan-
on Tay to
his maiestie cellaris ȝearde head george erll of kynnoull on
tymer on the water of Tay with ane speiche
spokin be tuo boyis andro wilsone baillie framer ȝairof [1]

---

[1] Cf. *The Chronicle of Perth* (Mercer's Chronicle), Mait. Club, 1831, p. 33.
Therefter wpone the 8 of July his majesty come to perth, and wes weill receawit
with Ten scoir of men for guard, all in quhyte doublattis, and red breikis,
with partiȝanes. Mr william bell delfuerit him a speeche. Mr william wischart
minister at leithe preichit in our kirk to his maiestie.
Thair wes ane suord dance dancit to his majestie the morne efter his cumyng,

Excerpts from MS. Hammermen Book.

[The book is dated 1584. It is ' The extract of ꝑe ham-mermeñ buik exatractit fourth of ꝑair auld buik of ꝑe dait 1518 ȝeris *constantine* arthur being dekyn for ꝑe tyme of ꝑe statutis and ordinances ꝑairin *contenit* ' and is ' The Iust copie of ꝑe auld buik . . . wreting be Iohne Andersouñ at command of ye haill craft.']

22nd April 1518   f. 2

The playaris oñ corpus christie day and quhat money sall be payt till ꝑame that is to say
Item in primis till adam vj đ and ewa—vj đ Sanct eloy —vj đ The marmadin—viij đ The devill—viij đ his

wpone ane iland maid of Tymer, wpone the water of Tay, and certaine wersis spokin to his maiestie be ane boy, representing the persone of the River of Tay and sum conference in his maiesties praise betuix Tay and another representing perth, made be Andro wilsone baillie. Various garbled tran-scripts of the minute in the *Glovers'* *Book* describing the King's visit have been published. The following transcript is made from the original manuscript at the Glovers' Hall, Perth : ' 8th July 1633 . . . Quhair at ye entrie of our South Inche port he wes receavit honorablie be the provest baillies and aldermen And be delywerie of ane speache mounting to his praise and thankisgeving for his maȝesties comming to wiseitt this our cittye quha stayit wpone horsebak and heard ye samene patientlie / and therfra con-woyit be our ȝoung men in guard with partizanes cled in rid and whyte to his ludgeing at the end of ye southgait belonging now here*tab*lie to George eirle of Kynnowll heiche chancellar of Scotland The morrow thaireftir came to our churche and in his royall seatt heard ane rewerend sermone, Immediatlie thaireftir came to his ludgeing and went doun to the gairdin thaireof. His majesties chayre being sett wpone the wall nixt the watter of Tay quhairwpone wes ane floitting staige of tymber cled about with birks Wpone the quhilk for his maȝesties welkome and entrie Threttein of our brethereine of this our calling of glovers with greine cappis silwer strings rid ribbens whyte schoes and bellis about ꝑair leggis scheiring raperis in thair handis and all wther abulȝement Dauncit our sword daunce with mony difficill knottis And alla-pallaȝesse fywe being wnder and fywe aboue wpone thair schowlderis Thrie of them daunceing thro*ch*t ꝑair feit and about them drinking wyne and breking glasſ—Quhilk (god be praisit) wes acted and done without hurt or skaithe till any. Quhilk drew ws to great chairges and expensſ amountting to the sowme of 350 merk*is* ȝit not to be remembrit Becaws graciouslie accepted be our Soueraigne and boith estaittis To our honour and great commendatioun.' The actual dress worn by one of the craftsmen on this occasion is still pre-served in a glass case in the Glovers' Hall, Perth. (It was exhibited at the Scottish Exhibition of National History, 1911, as a Morris or Moorish dancer's dress.) The white leather shoes, gloves, and rapier which accompanied the dress have also been preserved. For Scott's notes to the *Fair Maid of Perth*, the following description was supplied by a local antiquarian : ' This curious vestment is made of fawn-coloured silk, in the form of a tunic, with trap-pings of green and red satin. There accompany it two hundred and fifty-two small circular bells, formed into twenty-one sets of twelve bells each, upon pieces of leather, made to fasten to various parts of the body. What is most remarkable about these bells is the perfect intonation of each set . . .' (Cen-tenary Edition, 1887, p. 465, Note M.)

mañ—iiij đ   The angell and ꝑe clerk—vj đ   Sanct
erasimus—viij đ   The cord drawer—viij đ   The king—
xij đ   The thre tormentouris—iij s̃   The best baner—xij đ
The vꝑir—vj đ   The stule berer and ꝑe harnes—v đ   The
devillis chepmañ—viij đ   till robert hart for vestiment—
iiij đ   Item for   [1]—ij đ   Item to ꝑe menstrell—ij s̃
Subscryvit be constantine arthour dekyn

f. 2b 13th May 1518

Item to ꝑe playaris vpone corpus christie day in all thingis
xv s̃

f. 3b 13th June 1520

Item gadderit about ꝑe touñ to furneis ꝑe play affoir ꝑe
processiouñ   v s̃ viij đ

f. 5 1520 [2]

Item for sancterasmus cord   iij đ [3]

f. 7 11th June 1522

(The deliuerance this instant ꝣeir)
Item in primis deliuerit to peter currour for ane new
septour and aputtis [4]   vij đ
Item deliuerit for ꝑe mending of ꝑe dewillis cot and play
claythis   vj đ
Item for ꝑe mending of ꝑe speit and making of twa signettis [5]
iij đ

Item for bluud [6] and chars [7]   ij đ

[1] Blank in MS.
[2] The exact dating of some of the entries in this MS. is difficult.
[3] It is not always easy to decide which items in these accounts have reference to the Corpus Christi play. Thus there is a previous item : ' Item for ꝑe lowsing of ꝑe reist of ꝑe smyddie coll   xij d.'
[4] Hunt, *The Hammermen Book of Perth*, reads 'inputts.' The meaning of ' aputtis ' is not clear. I suggest that the 1584 copyist may have misread the word ' apullis,' apples.
[5] Can this be cygnets ?
[6] Perhaps ' blund,' which is equally obscure. Hunt, *op. cit.*, reads ' bluid,' which may be what the scribe intended. Blood was not likely to be used in a play which ended with the expulsion from the garden of Eden, but might conceivably have been required in connection with the martyrdom of St Erasmus (*supra*, 69), which was also played at least as late as 1520.
[7] Hunt reads ' thairn,' which is incorrect, though the end of the word is not too distinct. Various interpretations of ' char ' given by *N.E.D.* and the dialect dictionaries include (1) turn of work ; (2) car, cart, cart-load ; (3) chair ; (4) charred substance ; (5) small fish of the trout kind. Of these (5), though perhaps rather specialised, is the most attractive possibility. In a

Item for braid and drink oñ corpus christi day to ꝑe playar*is*   iij ſ̃

22nd May 1532   f. 9b

Item pay*t* apou*n* corpus cristi day and evin be dioneis caveris *com*posito*ur* in play clathis and vꝑir expensſ̃— xxxj ſ̃ v đ Swa rest*is* ꝑe said dioneis awand to sancteloy
            vij ſ̃ viij đ

7th Oct. 1534   f. 12

  (Andro dogleiſ̃ dischairg)
Item of xviij ſ̃ viij đ for corpus christ*is* play
Item of ij ſ̃ for ane speir
Item of gudstring*is* and caber*is* xij đ
Item ij đ to ꝑe tailȝeour
Item of iiij đ to ꝑame ꝑ*at* buire ꝑe banerr*is* oñ ꝑe octaus of corpus christi day
Item of i đ for takatt*is*
Item of iiij đ for peper
Item of ij ſ̃ for ane skyn [1]

8th June 1541   f. 15b

The q*uhi*lk day the dekyn and craft p*rese*nt for ꝑe tyme ar all co*n*tentit in ane voce ꝑat ane prenteschip of twa mark*is* be spendit for ꝑe honestie of ꝑe craft oñ petermes evin and corpus christi day eftir none

23rd May 1553   f. 29

Item ꝑis instant ȝeir ar chosin playaris to wit george allañ trinitie/ Andro brydie adam/ dauid horne eue/ patrik balmeñ ꝑe mekle devill/ Robert colbert ꝑe serpent/ Williame ꝑe angell/ Andro kelour ꝑe litill angell/ Williame ky*n*loch ane vꝑ*er* [2]/ Iohne allañ ꝑe devillis chepmañ/ Iohne robertsouñ sanct eloy/ Andro thorskaill marmadin/

French mediæval representation of the Creation there occurs the stage direc-
tion : ' on fait monter et saulter des poissons ' (Gustave Cohen, *Histoire de la mise en scène dans le theatre religieux français*, 1906, p. 147). Similarly in one of the Cornish mysteries, ' Let fysche of dyuers sortis apeare ' (*The Non-Cycle Mystery Plays*, E.E.T.S., 1909, p. xxxiv.)

[1] It is not clear that the subsequent items in this discharge have any bearing on the subject, though perhaps a payment of ' viij đ to f*ir* Iohne fargissoun ' should be included.

[2] Hunt, *op. cit.*, arranges these entries in an order different from the MS., with the result that William Kynloch (who follows William, the Angel) appears as ' another angel ' rather than ' another little angel.'

Iohne rogie and thome pait to beat [1] ꝑe bannerris   And
the dekyn and haill craft hes chosin ꝑir ꝑersones vnder ꝑe
pane of half ane stene of vax vnforgiffin

Excerpts from the MS. Records of the Incorporation of
Vol. (1).   *Wrights.*[2]
f. 7 **1530**

Item on corpus christeis day for thre quartis of aill   xj đ
Item for papir   j đ
Item for ꝑe mending of ꝑe play gair   vj đ
Item for Impis ꝑat I gef out of my awyñ purſ   vj đ
Item for ꝑe baner bering   xvj đ
Item to ꝑe menstrall   xvj đ

Item on thuresday eftir corpus christeis day   viij đ
Item for ane crownñ to ſſir Iohne farguson ane plak

f. 69 **[Date ?]** [3]

Item gevin for makin of ꝑe torchis   xvj đ
Item gevin for ympis   x đ
Item ane plac for drynk siluer
Item for ane row   x đ
Item gevin viij đ tyll ꝑaim ꝑat bwyr ꝑe baner eftir corpus
   cristeis day

Item gevin oñ corpus cristeis day x đ for breyd & ayll
Item gevin for menden of ꝑe castell   viij đ
Item ꝑe deykan rasauit owt of ꝑe stok on corpus cristeis day
                                                      xiiij ſ
Item xvj đ to ꝑe menstrall oñ corpus christes day
Vol. (2)
f. 1 **1530**

Baneir
bering
Ther wes spent on him ꝑat caried ꝑe baneir at
ane play of ꝑe wricht craftis William kerane
being decane sextein penneis

[The first folio of Vol. (3) opens with an account which,
except for minor orthographical variations, is practically
identical with the 1530 account in Vol. (1).   The top of the
page is torn, and the date is lost.]

[1] *Sic* in MS., but may be a mistake for ' bear,' as in Hunt, *op. cit.*
[2] For description of the MSS., see note on Perth records.
[3] First part of compt, with date torn away.   Many erasures in remainder.

Excerpts from MS. Kirk Session Minute Books.

Vol. I.
1577-86

1st July 1577

act of
corpus
christies
play

Becaws certane inhabitantis of þis town alsweill aganis þe expres commandement of þe ciuill magistratts in cown-sall as aganis þe Ministeris prohibitiouñ in pulp(itt) hes playit corpus christeis play vpon thursday þe vj of Junij last quhilk day ves vovnt to be callit (cor)pus christeis day to þe great sklander of þe kirk of god and dishonour to þis haill touñ And becaws þe said play is idolatrous super-stitiows and also sclanderows alsweill be ressoun of þe Idell day [1]

23rd Aug. 1577

practeis
off þe
act of
corpus
christies
play

Quhilk day compeirit Thomas thorskaill [2] quha desyring to (haif) his bairñ baptisit and confest him to be ane of þe nwmer of þ(aim) of corpus christeis playaris quha bwir þe ansenȝe of þe samyn off þe quhilk sklander he offeris and submittis him self to þe discipl(ine) of þe kirk with my Lordis adwyſſ And promisſſ in tyme cuming (ne)uir to mell with sik thingis again onder þe pain of þe censures (of) þe kirk In respect quhairoff and of his obediens of þe kirk þe elderis presentlie convenit viz [seven names] thinkis expedient þat þe said Thomas thorskailis barñ be baptis(it) becaws he hes offerit him self obedient to þe kirk according to þe act maid þairvpon

1st Sept. 1577

Practeis
also

Quhilk day compeirit Robert paull befoir nwñ immediatlie eftir þe sermwnd in presens of þe congregatioun quha desyring to haif his bairñ baptisit and confest him to be ane of þe nw(mber) of þam of corpus christeis playars amangis þe skinners ffor þe quhilk sklander he offeris and submittis him self to þe disciple(ne) of þe kirk And promisſſ in tymis cuming neuir to mell with sik thingis again vnder þe pane of þe censures of þe kirk In Respect quhairoff þe elderis presentlie convenit viz [five names] thinkis expedient þat þe said Robert paullis [3] be baptisit becaws he hes offerit him self obedient to þe kirk according to þe act maid þairvpon

[1] This entry breaks off at the foot of the page.
[2] An Andrew Thorskaill had played the mermaid in the Hammermen's play in 1553.
[3] 'bairn' omitted in MS.

practeis
also

2nd Sept. 1577

[Eight other men compered 'and confest ᵹam to be of corpus christeis playars.' Promise never to 'mell' with 'sik thingis' again.]

practeis
also

16th Sept. 1577

[Three other men appear and make the same confession, etc.]

Quhan ᵹe
act aganis
super-
stitioun
vas maid

16th Dec. 1577

Quhilk day ye elderis ordanis ᵹe act maid aganis superstitio(un) anno 1574 Novembris 27 to be publist on sonday nixt

Ordanis all thai personis ᵹat ves playing sancttobertis [1] play ᵹe x of (december) to be varnit to ᵹe assemblie agane ᵹis day viij dayis

Quhilk day compeirit Thomas Smyth Thomas vilso(un) James hendersoũ and Andro schang and confest ᵹam to be playaris of corpus christeis play ffor ᵹe quhilk sklander ᵹai offer and submittis ᵹam selfis to ᵹe disciplein of ᵹe

---

[1] This saint has puzzled all the local antiquarians, who generally follow Scott in referring to him as St Obert. I have compared all the entries in the MS., and am of the opinion that throughout the reading 'sanct tobert' (sanctobert, santtobert, S. tobert, etc.) is to be preferred to 'sanct cobert' and the corresponding variations. (In Jan. 1581-2, only, the reading appears to be S obert; but there is a mark before the 'o' in the MS. which may be a 't'). According to J. H. Macadam, *The Baxters' Book of St Andrews*, 1904, the patron saint of the baxters of Dundee and St Andrews was St Cuthbert, the name occurring in the St Andrews entries as St Tobert and St Cobert. The Haddington MS. Burgh Court Book has a reference to the baxters and 'sanct towbartis' (cowbartis) altar (5th March 1554); and to 'ᵹe baxter craft of sanct towbert (cowbert) and ᵹe altar of ᵹe samyn' (25th June 1555). The *Registrum Cartarum Ecclesie Sancti Egidii*, Bann. Club, 1859, alludes to the 'altare Sancti Coberti' (lxxii), and quotes (ciii) the reference from the *Edinburgh Burgh Records*, I. 15, to the 'altare of Sanct Vbertis foundit be the craft.' *The Edinburgh Burgh Records*, I. 214, Seal of Cause to the Bakers, have various references to 'St Cubert.' J. Cameron Lees in *St Giles', Edinburgh*, enumerates the altars of the Church, and gives both St Ubert and St Cuthbert, neither of which he can place. A comparison of the original MSS. might result in establishing the identical saint as patron of the baxters in Perth, Dundee, St Andrews, Haddington, and Edinburgh. 'Sanct tobert' may be a corruption of 'sanct cobert' or Saint Cuthbert. But the difficulty of accepting St Cuthbert in the case of the Perth baxters is the date of 'sanct tobertis ewin'—10th December (see entry under 20th Dec. 1577): for the festival of St Cuthbert fell on 20th March, and the dates of his first and second translation were 4th September and 30th July or 11th August. Nor does the 'Sanc Howbart' mentioned, apparently as the patron saint of the baxters, in the *Extracts from the Records of the Royal Burgh of Stirling*, I. 29 (the Town Clerk has kindly had this reading confirmed from the MS.), help us, as the festival of St Hubert fell on 3rd Nov.

kirk and promisſſ in tymis cuming neuir to mell with sik
thingis again vnder ye pane of ye censures of ye kirk

20th Dec. 1577 santtobert

Quhilk day compeirit Jhone fywie and confesſſ yat vpon
ye tenth of december instant quhilk ves callit sanct tobertis
ewin he passit throche ye touñ strikand ye druñ quhilk ves
ane of ye commone drumis of ye touñ accompaneitt with
certane vtheris sik as Jhone mᶜbaith william Jak Rydand
vpone ane hors gangand in mumschance [1] And sayis ye
said Jhone mᶜbaith delyuerit to him ye druñ ffor ye
quhilkis promisſſ he submittis him self to ye disciplein of
ye kirk And also promisſſ neuir to streik ane druñ agane
without ye command of ane magistratt vnder ye panis as
salbe layit to his charge

29th Dec. 1577

[Three other men confess themselves to be 'playars of
corpus christeis play.' For which 'sklander' they submit
themselves to the discipline of the Kirk and promise never
to 'mell with sik thingis again.']

5th Jan. 1577/8

Compeirit William Jak [2] and being demandit gif he ves
in sanc tobertis play he confest yat nochtwithstanding he
ves ane of corpus christeis playaris for the quhilk he submittit him self to ye disciplein of ye kirk promisand yat Sttobert
he vaid neuir do ye elyk ʒit he confesſſ yat he ves in sancttobertis play rydand

15th Dec. 1578

Comperitt gilbertt robertsoun and sayis thomas rollok bad
him putt on ye deuillis cott
Gilbert robertsoun william mertein thomas rollok thomas
Jak Jhone mᶜbaith confesſſ yatt yai haif transgressitt ane
actt maid In ye assembly of Minister and elderis and rate-
fiett be ye prouest and bailʒeis of bailʒeis (sic) In yatt superstitiously yai passitt aboutt ye touñ on S toberttis ewin

---

[1] The Scott MS. transcript in the Adv. Lib. gives 'a horse which went in
men's shoes,' which picturesque detail has been taken over and elaborated
by subsequent local historians. The word is, of course, 'mumchance,'
mumming.

[2] He was one of the three players who appeared on 16th Sept. 1577 before
the Session.

disagasatt In pyping and dansin and tar torchis bering for
ȝe quhilk ȝai Submitt ȝam selfis to ȝe disciplin of ȝe
kirk

2nd May 1580

Ordainis ane act to be maid be ȝe Minister concerning discharging off all passing to ȝe draggouñ holl superstitiously
and the samyn to be publist on thursday nixt out off pulpit
and ȝaireftir to be giwen to ȝe bailȝeis and proclamit at ȝe
mercat croce

Act of ȝe dragoñ holl Becaus ȝe assembly of ȝe minister and elderis vnder standis
ȝat ȝe resorting to ȝe draggoun holl [1] alsueill be ȝoung men
as vemen vyth ȝair pyping and drummes streking befoir
ȝame throcht ȝis toun hes rasit na small sclander to ȝis
congregatioun and ȝat nocht wythout suspicioun of filthines
eftir to follow ȝairupone for awoyding quhairoff in tymes
cuming ȝe said assembly vyth consent of ȝe magistratis
of ȝis toun hes statut and ordanit ȝat na persoun heireftir of
ȝis congregatioun neither man nor voman resort nor
Repair heireftir to ȝe said draggoun holl as thay haue
done in tymes bygane namly in ȝe moneth of may nether
paſs throcht ȝe toun vyth pyping streking of drummeis as
heirtofoir thay haue done vnder ȝe pane of tuenty schillingis
to ȝe puir to Euery persone alsueill men as vemen ȝat
salbe conuict heirof and alsua to mak ȝair publict Repentance vpon ane sabboth day in presens of ȝe peipill and
ȝis ordinance to be publist at ȝe mercatt croce vpoun
satterday nixt, as also in ȝe pulpit be ȝe Minister on thursday
and sonday nixt to cum that nan heireftir pretend ignorance
heiroff

> This act vaſs publist ȝe saxt off maij at ȝe mercat croce
> as also in ȝe pulpit

George Mᶜgregor *9th May* 1580

Ordanis ȝe act maid of ȝe draggouñ holl to strek wpoun
dauid rollok becaus he is conuict off braking of ȝe samyn and
he hes fund his decan cautiouñ for satisfactioun of ȝe said
act vnder ȝe pane of ten poundis to ȝe puir

---

[1] A large cave in the rock of Kinnoull Hill.

10*th April* 1581

The holl assembly of ꝑe Elders vyt*h* awyſs of ꝑe Magis-trat*is* ratifies ꝑe formar act co*n*cer*n*ing ꝑe dragouñ holl

17*th April* 1581

Ordanes no pastyme to be vsit thro*ch*t ꝑe touñ vpo*n* ꝑe sabbot*h* In speciall in ꝑe tyme of Maj

25*th Dec.* 1581

Quhilk day the Minister and eldaris *pre*sentlie co*n*uenit co*n*siddering the Idolatrus pastyme off sindrie insolent young me*n* in playing off Stobertis play to ꝑe gret greif off ꝑe co*n*science off the faithfull and infamous sklander off the haill co*n*gregatioun throughout the haill cuntrie hes ordenit for *pre*se*n*t punischment off ꝑe same And siclyk Idolatrus pastyme in tymes cu*mm*ing that walter [name obliterated] Henrie hall Jhone me*r*tyne James fargesoun Robert farge [1] Andro carmichell vith all the Rest to be putt in ward theirin to remaine wnreleifit quhill Euerie ane off thame haif payit xx ſ to ꝑe puire forder to *pre*se*n*t thame self in the seat off Repentance thair to Remaine the sab-bothe day in tyme off ſsermond And attoure to find Catioun wnder the paine off x lib and dubling off the formar punisch-ment sa aft as euer thei offend ꝑai*r*in neuer to do ꝑe lyk in tyme cu*mm*ing And giff ony off the foirsaidis be nott responsable for ꝑe twentie schillingis to stand in the Irinnis on the croſs heid twa houris on ane me*r*ket day for ꝑat pairt And this act to be extendit wpon all syclyk Idolatrus players and obſseruers off syclyk supe*r*stitious dayis in tymes to cu*m* without exceptiouñ

Act Aganis Sanctober-tis me*n*

22*nd Jan.* 1581/2

[Six men, players ' of S*t*(t)obertis play hes in all poyntis satisfiet ꝑe kyrk for ꝑe foirsaid supe*r*stitious pastyme and hes *p*romisit neuer to do ꝑe lyk.']

29*th Jan.* 1581/2

Ordanes ꝑe same act to be vsit aganes sanctobertis me*n* qu*h*ilk is maid aganes dioniſs blakwod

---

[1] Perhaps ' fargesoun.' The edge of the page is discoloured.

5th Feb. 1581/2

Ordanes ꝑe ordinance of befoir mentionat towart dionyſß blakwod and sanctobertis men

12th Feb. 1581/2

Ordanis the ordinance concerning dioniſß blackat [*sic*] and Sᵗtobertis men to be Ratifiet ꝑat is ꝑay be wardit quhill thay obey the Iniunctiounis off the kirk

19th Feb. 1581/2

[Continues the former act against Dionysius Blackwood to be put in execution.]

Vol. II.
1587-97

Baxteris play
S tobertis play

11th Dec. 1587

Ordanis ꝑes baxteris ꝑat on saturday last at ewin playit Sanctobertis play to be vairdit quhaireuer ꝑai be apprehendit ay and quhill ꝑai giff ꝑair obedience for satisfactioñ off kirk and congregatioñ

Act for sanctobert-is playes

5th April 1588

[The minister and elders ' considdering ꝑe Idolatrouſß pastyme off sindrye insolent young men in playing off sanc tobertis play to ꝑe greite greife off ꝑe conscience off ꝑe faythfull and infamous sklander off ꝑe haill congregatioñ throchout ꝑis haill countrie hes ordanit for present punis-ment off ꝑe same and siclyk Idolatrouſß pastyme in tymes cuming ' that six men shall be put in ward until they pay 20/- each and present themselves in the seat of repentance on Sunday, etc., as in act of 25th Dec. 1581.]

The baxters craftis act anent sanctobert

30th Jan. 1587/8

Quhilk day ꝑe deakin oif ꝑe baxters off ꝑe burght off perth vith ꝑe haill breꝑerne off ꝑe samyn craft being conwenit for ꝑe tyme To tak ordour for amendment off ꝑe blasphemus and ethnick playes off sanc tobertis pastyme and to repreſß ꝑe insolencie off sick as sall heireftir presume or mint to do ꝑe lyke And finding ꝑat ꝑe playing off ꝑe same ꝑis ȝeir hes ingenerat without ꝑis haill cuntrie greit sklander off ꝑe gospell euill reporting off ꝑe toñ and disdaine off ꝑe craft Ordanis ꝑat william schairpe valter symesoñ williame mal-

come thomas dawnye dauid Randye and James Malloche
sall attour and vith ꝑe punisment inionit to ꝑame be ꝑe
bail3es and counsell submitt ꝑem selfe in ꝑe Minster and
elderis villis to satisfe ꝑe kirk in all poyntis for remofing
off ꝑe said sklander Also giff ꝑai or ony off ꝑame or 3it ony
vꝑer off ꝑe said craft be found heireftir to uſs ꝑe elyk
Idolatrouse pastyme ꝑai sall be debarrit frome all ꝑe
liberties off ꝑe craft neuer to haue entres to ꝑe same agane
and to be banist ꝑe toñ for euer Also giff ony off ꝑe said
craft be found to procwir for siclyke offending heireftir
ꝑai sall be reput as menteners off ꝑe said Idolatrouſs pastyme
and incur ꝑe penaltie abone specefeit [Signed by George
Jak, deacon of the Baxters, etc.] [1]

22nd March 1587/8

Ordanis ꝑes ꝑat vas ꝑe players off sanctobertis play on
sonday nixt to enter in ꝑe seat of repentance and ꝑair to
humbill ꝑem selffis and declair ꝑair repentance to ꝑe
exempill off vꝑers to do ꝑe elyk in tymes cuming [2]

3rd June 1589

Licence
off ye play

The Minister and Elders gewis licence to play ꝑe play vith
conditiouns ꝑat naꝑer swering banning nor nane skurrilitie
be in it to be ane offence to our religioun quhilk ve profest
and ane euill exempill to vꝑers and incaice ony be in ꝑe
samyn or ony persoñ ad ony off ꝑe samyn by ꝑe register
off play it selff ordanis him to be vairdit and mak his publick
repentance

3rd May 1591

Ordanis all ongodly pastyme to be dischairgit ꝑat is vsit
on sonday at ewin eftir preitsching throch ꝑe hie streitis
off ꝑe town especially filthy and wngodly singing about ꝑe
Mayis And giff ony persoñ beis found contraweninge ꝑe
same to stand on ꝑe keikstwl and repentance stwle ꝑair
to declair ꝑair offence and schew ꝑair repentance for ꝑe
same This same to be intimat fra ꝑe pulpit

28th June 1591

This day ꝑe haill towñ being occupiet in ꝑair preparatioñ

---

[1] This notarial instrument was apparently forwarded to the Kirk Session.
[2] This entry seems to be misplaced in the Register.

for ꝑe quens maiesteis entres in the towñ ꝑe assemblie vas nocht haldin

22nd May 1592 [1]

[Injunction to William Kinloch at Brig Tay Port]

Ᵽat nane off ꝑe burght be sufferit to go out on ꝑe saboth afoir nor eftir preitsching to ꝑe pastyme off scone and incaiſs ony will wiolently go furth he to report thair names wnder ꝑe pane foirsaid

Cargill

21st July 1595

Ordenis Thomas Cargill to declair his publick repentance befoir his mariage : becaus ꝑat thir ȝeiris bypast he gawe him self owt for a full [2] and prophane sporter walking in a foolische garment and playing the counterfet man quhilk is sklanderous

Later Volumes

Jhonesowne cuninghame Jaksone stobie hynd

13th Feb. 1609

Compeired Andrew Jhonestowne and Jonet Cuninghame his spous James Jaksone and Stobie [3] his spous dauid Jaksone and helene hynd all warnit to ꝑis day and being inquyrit quhy thay went all disgysed about ꝑe towne on tuysday last wes at ten and ellewin houris at ewin with suordis and stawis trowbling and molesting thair nicht- bouris on ꝑe streitis quhom thay met anſserit that eftir thay had all sowpit togidder thay had resolwit to go about ꝑe towne of no ewill purpoſs or intentione bot of mirrines and denyit that thay molestit any   Thay being remowit it wes certenly found that thay wer disgysed namly andrew Jhonestownes wyf hawing hir hair hinging downe and ane blak hat wpon hir head hir husband androw Jhonestowne with ane suord into his hand dauid Jaksone hawing ane curch wpon his head and ane womanis gowne as Constantine Malice balȝie and sindrie wtheris declairit and that thay hurt and molestit sindry personis   The sessione findis thair deyd to be sklanderous prophane & dangerous and that becaus the pestilence ȝit continewis amangis vs and all thir persones laitly come in from ꝑe feildis quhar the boch

---

[1] After this date I did not make such a detailed examination of the Register.
[2] Perhaps 'fuill.'
[3] Christian name omitted in MS.

& boyll wes on thair persones. [They are to put in ward, to appear next Sunday in linen clothes in Church at the place of repentance and to be rebuked as dissolute and licentious persons in presence of the whole congregation.]

14th Jan. 1634   gy*feris*

[Henry Merser and his associates ordered to appear upon the repentance stool next Sunday ' for thair prophane gysing throw the toun and for thair contempt in going efter they were prohibite to do.']

19th Jan. 1634   gy*feris*

Q*uhi*lk day compeirit the p*er*sounes gyseris wpone the stule of repentance for declaratioun of thair contritioun for thair prophanatioñ afoirwreittin, promeissing nocht to do the elyk heireftir

ST ANDREWS.

[With the exception of a Burgh Court Book, 1589-92, all the early continuous Burgh records have been lost. There are no treasurers' accounts before 1611. Various Craft books are still preserved in the University Library. Of these, the Hammermen's Book, with spasmodic entries from c. 1542, and the earliest Baxter Book, ed. J. H. Macadam, 1904, date back to pre-Reformation times. The Minutes of the Faculty of Arts, which date from 1413, are preserved in a manuscript volume in the University Library, entitled *Liber conclusionum vniversitatis sanctiandree.* For the *Statutes of the Faculty of Arts,* see *St And. Univ. Publications,* No. VII. The *St Andrews Kirk Session Records,* edited for the Scottish History Society, 1889-90, by Dr Hay Fleming, date from 1559.]

Excerpts from the MS. Liber Conclusionum Universitatis Sanctiandree.[1]

26th Nov. 1414   f. 1b.

Item fuit conclusum quod sollemnitas quam faciunt grammatici in festo Sancti Nicholai transferatur ad festum

---

[1] These excerpts were made originally from a transcript of the Minutes, kindly lent to me by Dr Maitland Anderson. They have been collated with the original manuscript.

translationis ejusdem, quod accidit in aestate et quodam-
modo cum episcopo suo non transeant ad exigendum nec
ad recipiendum pecunias de domo ad domum de castro
ad monasterium nec econtra. Verum tamen placuit eis
pro isto anno duntaxat tollerare residuum sollemnitatis
consuetae in festo principali, quod est jam in hieme absque
omni exactione et receptione pecuniae.

f. 15 21*st Nov.* 1432

Item prohibemus modum quem annis preteritis habuerunt
magistri nostri et scolares importando mayum seu estatem
vz in habitibus dissimulatis mutuo procuratis a militibus
et dominis in equis in armis in insigneis regalibus symeando
reges et presides seu imperatores nec tantum prohibemus
tanquam inutilem infructuosum et periculosum sed etiam
vel tam magistris quam scolaribus dampnablem reprobamus
et condempnamus statuentes si causa recreacionis velint
adire campos ad capiendum ayerem quod vadant omnes
simul si voluerint vel scorsum et separatim secundum
domos et scolares inhabitantes in vestibus propriis suo
gradui statui et honori condecentibus et simul audiant
missam in regressu ad villam omnibus aliis superfluitatibus
postpositis et vanitatibus pretermissis.   Simile modo
statuimus de festo regum eundem eundo ad ecclesiam et
redeundo cum rege ffabe quod magistri et scolares incedant
in habitibus propriis hoc solo excepto quod liceat regi
portare habitum dissimulatum aliqualiter statui regali
congruentem.

f. 48 8*th April* 1460

[The Congregation discusses the great loss which the
University is suffering ' per scholarium die ac nocte totidem
discursum in publico vico et platea magistros suos non
formidantes sed otio ludis et spectaculis vacantes quia
sciunt se peccare impune ab altero magistrorum semper
nequint defensi timore transferendi se ad alium magistrum
dum puniuntur.']

f. 137 8*th May* 1514

In qua congregacione propter scurrillitates et infamationes
que nonnunquam fiunt in ludis et proclamationibus ipsorum
ad supplicacionem decani decretum erat quod de cetero
ludi et proclamatoria examinarentur per regentes loci ad

quem spectat ludus. Ita quod nullomodo fiant scurrillitates
aut speciales notationes quaruncunque personarum in
particulari que possunt veresimiliter ledere eorum famam.
Quare si aliqid horum ut absit contigerit corrigantur regentes qui de hoc debent habere curam ad arbitrium decani
et facultatis artium.

13th May 1517   f. 141b

Insuper conclusum erat vt ordo processionis regalis solita
fieri in pedagio in festo Sancti Johannis evangeliste deinceps
fiat secundum arbitrium et discressionem principalis magistri
dicti pedagogii et reliquorum regentium eiusdem . . .[1]

Excerpts from Kirk Session Records.

21st July 1574

Nota. Anent
the comede
askit to be
playit be M.
Patrik
Authinlek
upon Sunday
the first of
August nixt
to cum.

The said day, anent the supplicatioun gevin be
Maister Patrick Authinlek for procuring licence
to play the comede mentionat in Sanct Lucas
Euuangel of the forlorn sone, upon Sunday the
first day of August nixt to cum, the seat hes
decernit first the play to be revisit be my Lord
Rectour, Minister, M. Johnne Rutherfur(d)
Provost of Sanct Saluatour Colleage, and Mr
James Wilke Principal of San(ct) Leonardis Colleage, and
gyf they find na falt thairintill the sam to be play(it) upon
the said Sunday the first of August, swa that playing thairof
be nocht occasioun to wythtdraw the pepil fra heryng of
the preaching, at the howre appointed alsweil eftir nune
as befoir nune.[2]

---

[1] There are other references to the feast of the Faculty of Arts on St John's
day :—3rd April 1465, two ' magistri ' elected to collect ' pecunias et sumptus
festi Sancti Johannis evangeliste ' ; 27th March 1534, the feast of St John to be
postponed this year—' Ita tamen quod missa publice in capella cum nota solita
celebretur processio solita in die Sancti Johannis et alie solemnitates solite
fieri eo die fiant et obseruentur.' No further details are given of the method
of celebrating this feast, but it is probable that the minute quoted above under
8th May 1514 concerning scurrilous plays had special reference to the feast
of St John the Evangelist, which had been celebrated two days previously
on 6th May.

[2] See Dr Hay Fleming's note, I. 396, and the various references cited. I
quote some of the Minutes in extenso. The Booke of the Universall Kirk of
Scotland, Maitland Club, 1839-45, I. 312, Aug. 1574 : ' Anent the answers
reported from Mr Robert Hamilton, Minister of Sanct Andrews, direct to
the Moderator present, to the bill direct from the Assembly to him for his
compearance before them to answer super inquirendis, excusing him be the
business of the Colledge, and be the Superintendent of Stratherne who declared

2nd March 1574/5

Nota
Forbidding
of the
play of
Roben Hwid

The said day, the seat ordenis the minister, on Sunday nixt to cum, or uthirwayis as he sal be chargit and warnit, in the name of the eternal God, to command and chairge all and quhat-sumevir personis indwellaris in this citie and spetialy yowng men in general, and als in spetial as he salbe informit, That nane of them presume nor tak upon hand to violat the Sabbat day, be using of playis and gemmis publiclie as they war wont to do, contrafating the playis of Robein Huid, expres defendit and forbiddin be Act of Parliament, undir all hiest pane that the seat may injone to them.

1st March 1595/6

The quhilk day, Jhone Ros, maister of the sang scole, maist humlie, with all reverence on his kneis befoir the sessioun, askit God mercy and the kirk forgifnes for his negligens, and for his using and playing of ane part of the comode and play in St Leonardis College, tyme of the last baichelar act, by advys of the kirk ; as also Mr Jhone

to him that the Assembly was to dissolve incontinent : The Generall Assembly of the Kirk giveth commission to Mr John Spotswood, Superintendent of Lothian, Mr Robert Pont, Provost of the Trinity Colledge, Mr David Lind-say, Minister at Leith, John Brand and the Kirk of Edenburgh, with any three of the fornamed persons, conjunctly to summon the Ministers, Elders and Deacons of Sanct Andrews to compear before them and to try the cause, why the Fast was not keeped among them according to the Act of the said Assembly ; and of the violation of the Sabbath day by profane playes, and such other things as they shall inquire of them at their coming ; and what beis done by them hereinto, to certify the brethren in their nixt Assembly.' *The Book of the General Kirk of Edinburgh,* cited in Lee's Lectures on the History of the Church of Scotland, I. 313 : The Commissioners met on 17th Feb. 1574/5, and ordained a precept of summons to be sent to the minister, elders, and deacons of St Andrews. 24th Feb. 1574/5 : ' The s[d] day compeirit Mr Robert Hamilton, minister, for himself, and . . . desyrit the heids qlk yai wald inquire of him to be pendit yrefter, delyverit to him, to gif ans[r] yrto, of ye qlk heidis the tennor followis, etc. Item, imprimis to enquir Mr Robert Hamilton, min[r] of Sanctandr[s] quhairfoir ye Act of ye General Assemblie was not keipit anent ye fasting . . . Item, to inquir quhat is ye caus yt at that tyme Robin Huidis playis wes sufferit to be playit, and thair throw prophanand ye fasting . . . To inquier gif ane Clark play was playit at ye tyme of ye preching, at ye marrage of Mr Tho[s] Balfouris dochter, &c. . . . Qlk heidis being deliverit to him, ye said Mr Robert producit his ans[r] yairto . . . As to ye 2d (question) concerning ye suffering of Robin Huids pl(ayis) certane servands and young children plaid ym certane days,   alwayis ye kirk bay[t] prevatlie in thair assemble, and I publiclie in tyme of preching, dischargeit ye samen, as it is notorious knawn, and desyrit ye magistrattis to tak ordour thairwith. 3 Ane Clark play wes plaid be ye scollo[r]is of ye grammar scull, bot not at ye tyme of preching, and ʒit for causes moving us we dischargeit ye mais(*ter*) to play ye samin &c. . . . Sic Subscr. Mr R. H.'

For subsequent legislation by the General Assembly, see *supra*, 93 n[2].

Heklein, regent to the baitchelaris, and Mr Jhone Dow-
glas, pedegog to my Lord Bucheane, confessis, in presens
of the sessioun, that it wes aganis thair willis that the
samyn play wes playit ; and promissis heireftir to stay
and withstand all sic thingis at thair power, and nevir to
do the lyke in tyme cuming. And thairfor the sessioun
ordanis Jhone Rosis humiliatioun, and thair declaratioun
and promis, to be publisit to the pepill Sonday nixttocum.

1st Oct. 1598 (Sunday)

Staige play
inhibite

The quhilk day, ane Jnglishman haveing desyrit
libertie of the session to mak ane publik play
in this citie, it wes voted and concludit that he
suld nocht be permitted to do the samin.

Excerpt from Pitscottie's Croniclis of Scotland, S.T.S.,
1899-1911, I, pp. 378-9.

[Landing of Mary of Loraine on the Fife coast. At St June 1538
Andrews she was received by the King and nobles ' witht
great honouris and mirienes, witht great treumph and
blythnes of phrassis and playis maid to hir at hir hame
comming. And first scho was ressawit at the New Abbay
zeit. Wpoun the eist syde thair was maid to hir ane
trieumphant frais* be Schir Dawid Lyndsay of the Mont,
lyoun harrot, quhilk caussit ane great clude come out of
the heavins done abone the zeit quhair the quene come in,
and oppin in two halffis instantlie and thair appeirit ane
fair lady most lyke ane angell havand the keyis of haill
Scotland in hir handis deliuerand thame into the quens
grace in signe and taikin that all the heartis of Scottland
was opnit to the ressawing of hir grace ; witht certane
wriesouns and exortatiouns maid by the said Schir Dawid
Lyndsay into the quens grace instructioun quhilk teichit
hir to serue her god, obey hir husband, and keep hir body
clene according to godis will and commandement. This
beand done, the quen was ressawit into hir palice and
ludging quhilk was callit the New Innes . . .' Next day
' the king ressawit the quen in his palice to the denner
quhair thair was great mirth schallmes draught trumpattis
and weir trumpatis witht playing and phrassis efter denner.']

*[MS. I has ' pheirs ' . . . Ed.]

Excerpts from the Diary of Mr James Melvill, Wod. Soc.,
1842.

p. 27 (This yeir in the monethe of July, Mr Jhone Davidsone,
1571 an of our Regents, maid a play at the mariage of Mr Jhone
Colvin, quhilk I saw playit in Mr Knox presence ; wherin,
according to Mr Knox doctrin, the Castle of Edinbruche
was beseiged, takin, and the Captan, with an or twa with
him, hangit in effigie.)

p. 28 That yeir we haid our Bachelar art, according to the solem-
1573 nities then used of declamations, banqueting, and playes.

p. 81 That yeir was the King's first progress and promene athort
1580 his countrey, with solemnities of entress in manie of his
Hienes' brouches ; and amangs the rest of St Androis . . .
Whar, on a day, the gentilmen of the countrey about haid
a gyse and farce [1] to play befor the King ; His Majestie
was in the new Innes of the Abay, befor the windowes
wharof the schow was to be maid. Grait confluence of
peiple conveined, and the place read with a fear circuit ;
It continowed void for the space of a lang houre, wither
that his Majestie was nocht readie to behauld, or the
playars to present tham selves, I can nocht tell, bot whill
all ar gasing and langing for the play, in stappes Schipper
Lindsay, a knawin frenetic man, and paesses upe and
down in the circuit with a grait gravetie . . . Wherat
first the peiple maid a noyse with lauching ; bot when
he began to speak he movit sic attention as it haid bein
to a preatcher . . . I market the Erle (*of Morton*), standing just fornent him, mikle movit with this first interlude,
as ernest and nocht play ; sa, that during all the sportes
that followed, he altered never the gravitie of his counte-
nance.

STIRLING.

[*Extracts from the Records of the Royal Burgh of Stirling,*
A.D. 1519-1666, were printed for the Glasgow Stirlingshire
Society, 1887. MS. Presbytery Records, Vol. I., 1581-9,
are in the custody of the Clerk to the Presbytery.]

---

[1] *Calderwood*, III, 462, ' guise or fence.' If ' fence ' is meant for ' ferce '
—*i.e.*, ' farce,' the mistake occurs in the original MS.—British Museum, Add.
MSS. 4737, f. 316b.

Excerpts from MS. Presbytery Records.

7th May 1583

Breking of the Sabbothe day

The brethrein wndirstandand ỹat on sonday last thair was ane drum strwkin in ỹe brugh of stirling be ane certane of servand men & boyis & Maij playis vsit quhairby the sabbothe day was prophainit and ỹe kirk sclanderit Thairfor ỹe brethrein ordaniᵴ ỹe minster of stirling to command the bailleis of ỹe touñ in name of ỹe kirk to tak ordur with the saidiᵴ personis prophanairiᵴ of ỹe sabboth day & pwneis ỹame in exampill of vỹeriᵴ & nocht to suffir the lyk in tymis cuming wndir ỹe paine of ỹe censuriᵴ of ỹe kirk to be execute againiᵴ ỹame

21st May 1583

Iohnne wod
Iohnne brouñ

The quhilk day ane summondiᵴ beand producit lauchfullie execute and indorsit vpone Iohnne wod & Iohnne brouñ schulmaistiriᵴ at ỹe kirkiᵴ of mwthill & strogayth chairgeing ỹame to compeir ỹe said day to anſer at ỹe instance of ỹe kirk for playing of clark playis oñ ỹe sabboth day ỹairby abvsing [1] ỹe samin for minstratioun of baptisme & Mariage without lauchfull admissiouñ as at mair lynthe is conteinit in ỹe said summondiᵴ Compeirit the said Iohnne wod / and being accwsit be ỹe moderatour for abwsing of ỹe sabboth day in playing of clark playis ỹairon The said Iohnne confessit ỹe same & is penitent ỹairfoir and offeriᵴ himself in ỹe will of ỹe kirk ỹairfoir Qwha is ordeinit to mak publict repentence ỹairfoir in ỹe kirk of Mwthill & confeſs his fault in presens of ỹe congregatioun immediatlie eftir ỹe sermond And ordaniᵴ the brethrein of Dunblane to try his habilitie for teiching of ane schulle / and ỹaireftir to report it to ỹe brethrein
The said Iohnne brouñ being oft tymis callit compeirit nocht Thairfor ordaniᵴ him to be summond of new to ỹe effect foirsaid vndir ỹe paine of excommwnicatioun

28th May 1583

Iohnne brouñ

The quhilk day ỹair was ane summondiᵴ producit befoir ws dewlie execute & Indorsit vpone Iohnne brouñ scholmaistir at stragaithe chairgeing him to compeir befoir ws the said day to anſer at ỹe instance of ỹe

---

[1] Perhaps ' awsing ' in MS.

T

kirk as at mair lynthe is conteinit in ꝩe said sum*mondis*
Compeirit ꝩe said Iohnne brouñ p*er*sonallie / And being
accwsit for disobeying ane admonitiouñ gevin to him be
Mr al*exander* chisholme mi*n*ster in p*r*ophani*n*g of ꝩe sabbot*h*
day in playing of clark playis ꝩai*r*on with*d*rawing ꝩai*r*by
sindrie of ꝩe pepill fra ꝩe preiching eftir the said admonitiouñ was gevin to him The said Iohnne denyit ꝩe sami*n* /
Bot confessit gif ony play was playit oñ ꝩe sabbot*h* day /
It was playit be ꝩe bairn*is* by his avyſ . . . The brethrein
being advysit wit*h* his anſ*seris* ordan*is* & decern*is* him to
produce the register of ꝩe clark play (playit be his bairn*is*
as he allegis) befoir ꝩe brethrein oñ ꝩe xj day of Iunij
nixt to be sein & considerit be ꝩame And to heir & se
farther tryell tane ane*n*t his accusa*ti*onis wnd*er* ꝩe paine
of disobedience the said Ioh*n*ne warnit ꝩai*r*to apu*d* acta

11*th* *June* 1583

Iohnne brouñ The q*uh*ilk day being asſ*seru*it to Iohnne brouñ
scholmaistir at Stragayt*h* to p*r*oduce the Register
of ane clark play playit be his bairn*is* (as he allegis) Compeirit ꝩe said Iohnne brouñ and p*r*oducit the Register of
ꝩe said play / ffor veseing of ꝩe q*uh*ilk bwik the brethrein
appoint*is* the brethrein in striuiling to vesie ꝩe same & to
report ꝩai*r* Iugeme*ntis* ꝩai*r*of to ꝩe brethrein on ꝩe ij day
of Iulij nixt The said Ioh*n*ne warnit ꝩai*r*to & to anſ*er* to
vꝩir accusa*ti*onis apu*d* acta wndir ꝩe paine of disobedience

The sami*n* day the brethrein appoint*is* to ꝩe said Ioh*n*ne
brouñ this thesis viz Is it lesum to play clark playis oñ
ꝩe sabbot*h* day or no*ch*t And qwethir gif it be lesu*m* or
no*ch*t to mak clark playis oñ ony p*a*rt of ꝩe scriptur
Q*uh*ilk thesis the said Iohnne is ordeinit to put in latein
And to vse sic probabt̄e argwme*ntis* as he can / for preving
of bayt*h* ꝩe p*a*rtt*is* of ꝩe said thesis & to p*r*oduce ꝩe sami*n*
in wret befoir ꝩe brethrein oñ ꝩe ij day of Iulij nixt wndir
ꝩe paine of disobedience

2*nd* *July* 1583

Iohnne brounis play In ꝩe t*er*me asſ*seru*it to ꝩe brethrein of striuiling
appointit to vesie the register of ꝩe clark play
playit be ꝩe bairn*is* of Iohnne brouñ scholmaistir at Stragayt*h* to report ꝩai*r* Iugeme*ntis*
anent ꝩe same / The said brethrein reportit ꝩaj hade fund
oft tymis ꝩai*r*in mekill ba*n*ing & swering su*m* badrie and

filthie ba*n*ing / the said Io*hn*ne brouñ beand p*r*es*en*t quha
denyit no*ch*t ᵹe sam

Io*hn*ne brouñ In the te*r*me asſ*er*uit to Iohnne brouñ to
produce declama*tion*is oñ the thesis ressauit
be him fra ᵹe brethir Compeirit ᵹe said Io*hn*ne & p*r*oducit
declama*tion*is oñ the said thesis in proiſſ & verſſ as ᵹaj
beir in ᵹame selffis w*it*h ᵹe q*uh*ilk*is* the brethir twik to
advyſſ

[Unfortunately the report of the Brethren on John
Brown's thesis, 6th August 1583, is concerned only with
his proficiency ' in ᵹe grund*is* of ᵹe latein gra*m*mir.'
There is not a word as to the matter of the thesis.]

Excerpt from Knox, I, 62.

c. 1535. ' Ane Black freir, called Frear Kyllour, sett
furth the Historye of Christis Passioun in forme
of a play, quhilk he boith preached and practised opinlie
in Striveling, the King him salf being present, upoun a
Good Friday in the mornyng : In the which, all thingis
war so levely expressed, that the verray sempill people
understood and confessed, that as the Preastis and obstinat
Pharisyes persuaded the people to refuise Christ Jesus, and
caused Pilat to condampne him ; so did the Bischoppes,
and men called Religious, blynd the people and perswaid
Princes and Judgeis to persecute sick as professis Jesus
Christ his blessed Evangell.

This plane speaking so enflammed the hartes of all that
bare the beastis mark, that thei ceassed nott, till that the
said Frear Kyllour, and with him Frear Beverage . . .
(and others) who all togetther war cruelly murthered in one
fyre, the last day of Februar in the zeir of (God) 1538.'

APPENDIX II.

STROLLING MINSTRELS AND TRAVELLING COMPANIES OF PLAYERS.

STROLLING MINSTRELS AND TRAVELLING
COMPANIES OF PLAYERS.

Acts against Unlicensed Minstrels.

(a) ' Histriones, ludiones, mimi et reliquum ociosorum
nebulonum genus, nisi regis peculiari gratia ita permittantur, ad aliquod artificium agendum coguntur :
quod si recusent, nisi inepti aegritudine aut mutilatione
fuerint, iumentorum more ad aratrum aut plaustrum
trahendum adiguntur.'—Macbeth's Laws, *Boethius :
Scotorum Historiæ*, 1574, f. 251.

> (Bellenden translates : ' Fulis, menstralis, bardis,
> and al othir sic idil pepil, bot gif thay be specially
> licent be the king, sal be compellit to seik sum craft
> to win thair leving : gif thay refuse, thay sal be
> drawin lik hors, in the pluch and harrowis.'—*Works*,
> 1821, II, 262.)

(b) ' Vetuit quoque saluberrimo exemplo, nullos vlla
regione histriones, vagos et nusquam certas habentes
sedes, aut ludicras artes exercentes in urbes recipi,
extra tibicines, tubicinesque peritos, nec nisi victum
artificio praeterea alio quaeritantes.'—Earl Thomas
Randal's [1] Laws, *Boethius : Scotorum Historiæ*, 1574,
f. 310.

> (Bellenden translates : ' Attoure that virtew suld be
> autorist in this realme, he commandit na vagabound
> nor idill pepill to be ressavit in ony town, without
> thay had sum craft to debait thair leving. Be this
> way, he purgit the realme of mony idill limmaris.'—
> *Works*, 1821, II, 411.)

(c) ' ITEM It is ordanit for þe away putting of sornaris
ouřlyaris & masterful beggaris with horſ hundis or

---

[1] Randolph, Earl of Moray, Regent after the death of Robert I. It is not,
of course, claimed that these excerpts from Boece are strictly accurate historically. Cf. *supra*, 36.

vthir gudis ꝥat al officiaris batħ schereffis baronis
alderman & balȝeis als wele within burgh as vtwitħ
tak ane inquisicione at ilk court ꝥat ꝥai hald of ꝥe
forsaid thingis ande gif ony sic be fundyn ꝥat ꝥar
horſs hundis & vthir gudis be eschet to ꝥe king & ꝥair
personis put in the kingis warde quhil ꝥe king haf said
his wil to ꝥaim Ande alsua at ꝥe said scheref balȝeis &
officiaris inqueř at ilk courte gif ꝥar be ony ꝥat makis
ꝥaim fūlis ꝥat ar nocht bardis or sic lik vꝥeris rynnaris
aboute Ande gif ony sic be fundyn ꝥat ꝥai be put in
the kingis warde or in his yrnis for ꝥar trespaſs als
lang as ꝥai haf ony gudis of ꝥar awin to leve apoñ
And fra ꝥai haf nocht to lefe apoñ ꝥat ꝥar eris be nalyt
to ꝥe trone or to ane vthir tre and cuttit of and bannyst
ꝥe cuntre Ande gif ꝥareftir ꝥai be fundyn again at ꝥai
be hangit.'   (A.P.S., 1449, c. 9, II, 36.) [1]

(d) ' ITEM the lordis thinkis speidfull ꝥat in all Justice
ayris the Kingis Justice ger tak Inquisicione of sornaris
bardis maisterfull beggaris or fenȝeit fulys and oꝥer
bannyſs ꝥame ꝥe cuntre or sende ꝥame to ꝥe Kingis
presone.' (A.P.S., 1457, c. 26, II, 51.)

(e)   ' Anent the pvnisement of strang and ydle beggaris
           and prouisioun for sustentatioun of the puyr and
           impotent.'
' FORSAMEKILL as thair is sindry lovabill actis of parliament maid be our souerane lordis maist nobill progenitouris for the stanching of maisterfull ydill beggaris
awayputting of sornaris and prouisioun for the puyr
Bearing that nane salbe tholit to beg nowther to burgh
nor to land betuix xiiij and lxx ȝeiris That sic as
makis thame selffis fwlis and ar bairdis or vꝥeris siclyke
rynnaris about being apprehendit salbe put in the kingis
ward or Irnis als lang as thay haue ony gudis of thair
awin to leif on . . . (etc., as in 1449 Act). And that it
may be knawin quhat maner of personis ar meanit to be
ydill and strang beggaris and vagaboundis and worthy
of the pvnisement befoir specifiit It is declarit that all
ydill personis gaying about in ony cuntre of this realme
vsing subtile crafty and vnlauchfull playis As iuglerie
fast and lowiſs and sic vtheris The ydill people calling

─────────────
[1] In this and the following Acts of Parliament I have expanded the con-
tractions as printed in A.P.S.

thame selffis egiptianis Or ony vther that fenȝeis thame
to haue knawlege in physnomie palmestre or vtheris
abused sciencis quhairby thay perswade the people
that thay can tell thair weardis deathis and fortunes
and sic vther fantasticall ymaginationis . . . And all
menstrallis sangstaris and taill tellaris not avowit in
speciall service be sum of the lordis of parliament or
greit barronis or be the heid burrowis and citeis for
ɏair commoun menstrallis, . . . All vagaboundis scollaris of the vniuersiteis of sanctandrois glasgow and
abirdene not licencit be the rector and Dene of facultie
of the vniversitie to ask almous . . . And that na
Irische and hieland bairdis and beggaris be brocht
and ressauit in the lawland be boittis or vtherwayis
vnder the pane of xx ɫi. of the bringaris . . .'   (*A.P.S.*,
1574, App. III, 86-9.) [1]

(*f*) ' The commoun corruptiouns of all Estates within this
realme. . . . Ane great number of idle persons without
lawfull calling, as pypers, fidlers, sangsters, sorners,
pleasants, strang beggers, living in harlotrie, and
having thair children vnbaptizit, without all' kynd of
repairing to the word.'   (1596, *B.U.K.*, III, 873.)

The following local Acts may also be cited :—

Aberdeen (*g*) See App. I, s.v. *Aberdeen* (C) for the Act *re* ' lusores
malorum ludorum,' Jan. 1444/5.

Dumfries (*h*) ' Item it is fundin be ɏe secrete *con*sale of ɏis burgh
ɏat ɏe *con*ventioun of sundry mynstralis maister*full*
begarris hais oftymes gen*er*it discord amang*is* our
souɏrane ladyis legeis wi*th*in ɏe fredome of ɏis bur*ght*
hairfor was statuit and ordanit be ɏe said *con*sale ɏat
na mynstrale be rasawit at feast*is* bainkittis nor *con*-
ventionis wi*th*in ɏis burgh bot alan*er*ly ɏe (mynstra)le
of ɏe burgh chosin be ɏe *con*sale ɏair*of* & ɏat he be
ansuerit . . . conforme to ɏe rite & *con*suetude of
burgh.'   (This occurs in a collection of burgh laws not
later than 1548 in Dumfries MS. Burgh Court Book.)

' Mynstralis awaye
The qu*hi*lk day ɏe Inquest decernis & ordanis the
bailȝeis to discharge all mynstralis and resettar*is* of

---

[1] Re-enacted in 1579, *A.P.S.*, c. 12, III, 139-142.

ɥam at feist*is* & vthir tymes ilk resawer wit*h*in ɥis
bur*g*ht vnd*er* pane of viij s of vnlaw vn forgevin to be
tane wit*h*out at all rigo*ur* becauſ it is fundin ɥat ɥai
ar maist*er*full begar*is* no*ch*t lesum to resawe admytit
or treitt as the act*is* of ɥ*ar*liame*n*t beris ' (*Ibid*, 3rd Oct.
1561.)

(*i*) ' The q*uh*ilk day the baileis Intemaittis to Jhone Dundee
Magrego*ur* fidlair that gif he forbeir no*ch*t playing
vpoun ɥe fiddel in tyme cu*m*ing & draw him to ane
vɥer occupat*i*one ɥat ɥai vil tak ordo*ur* wit*h* him
*c*onforme to ɥe act of parliame*n*t ' (13th May 1580,
Dundee MS. Burgh Court Book).

(*j*) ' Item it is statute & ordanet that na vagabunds evill Edinburgh
steilleris sturdy beggares nor idill ɥ*er*sounis havand na
maister nor honest occupatioun and ɥat na nicht-
walkeris dyssers or cairteris na singeris of vngodlie
sangs pypers fydlers commoun menstralles ɥat hes
no*ch*t ɥe privelege of the acts of p*ar*liame*n*t Remayne
wit*h*in this bur*g*ht . . . ' (22nd Oct. 1589, Edinburgh
MS. Council Register.)

(*k*) ' Item, it is statute and ordanit that na pyparis, fidleris, Glasgow
Pipers, menstrales, or ony wther vagabundis, re-
fiddlers, mane in this toun fra this tyme furtht
minstrels, during the tyme of the pest but speciall
vagabonds. leif of the prouest or vnder the pane of
scurgeyng and banisment.' (29th Oct. 1574, Extracts
from the Records of the Burgh of Glasgow, I, 29.)

Additional Cases of Vagrant ' Scenici.' [1]

26*th* *May* 1598

Item ɥe 26 of Maij to henrye nisbet ɥroveist q*uh*ilk he gave
to ɥe Inglis man ɥat playit wit*h* ɥe hors in ɥe abay ȝairdi*s*
v ħ [2]

10*th* *July* 1598

The 10 of Julij, ane man, sume callit him a juglar, playit
sic sowple tricks upone ane tow, q*lk* wes festinit betwix

---

[1] For other cases, see App. III, Excerpts from *L.H.T.A.*
[2] For other instances of performing animals, see App. III, *L.H.T.A.*, Aug.
1503 and April 1508. The above case is taken from Edinburgh MS. Burgh
Treasurers' Accounts.

the tope of St Geills kirk steiple and ane stair beneathe the crosse, callit Josias close heid, the lyk wes nevir sene in Ꝩis countrie, as he raid doune the tow and playit sa maney pavies on it.[1]

11th July 1598

Tow man

The presbyterie hawing takin an offence at Ꝩe spectacle sene ȝisterday in ed*inburgh* of a man cum*ing* down a tow of Ꝩe stipill heid to Ꝩe cassay hes ordanit thair brether the minister*is* of ed*inburgh* to rebuke Ꝩe ma*gistrattis* for suffering sic spectacles in Ꝩair citie.[2]

12th July 1598

Stewart m^r of actiuitie

Item Ꝩe said 12 of Julij payit to robert stewart callit m*aister* of activitie for his playing vpoun ane coird betuixt Ꝩe steiple and Ꝩe corß *con*forme to ane precept   vj li xiij ß iiij đ [3]

Sept. 1598

Item be his hienes speciall command to ane Inglis sport*our* that come doun vpoun ane Tow fra the cok of the stepill of ed*inburgh*   xx ħ

Item Lykwayis to dauid weir sport*our* be command
         vj ħ xiij ß 4 đ [4]

1600

(At that tyme, being in Falkland, I saw a funambulus, a Frenchman, play strang and incredible prattiks upon stented takell in the Palace-clos befor the King, Quein, and haill court. This was politiklie done to mitigat the Quein and peiple for Gowrie's slauchter. Even then was Hendersone tryed befor us, and Gowrie's pedagog, wha haid bein buted.) [5]

[1] *The Diarey of Robert Birrel*, p. 47, in Dalyell's Fragments of Scottish History, 1798.
[2] Edinburgh MS. Presbytery Records.
[3] Edinburgh MS. Burgh Treasurers' Accounts.
[4] MS. Accounts of the Lord High Treasurer. And cf. the *Diary of Mr James Melvill*, Wod. Soc., 1842, p. 487 n.
[5] *Diary of Mr James Melvill*, p. 487. The editor cites the following entry from the MS. Accounts of the Lord High Treasurer, Aug. 1600 : 'Item, be command of his Majestie's Precept, to Peter Bramhill, Frenche pavier ; as the said Precept, with his acquittance, producet upoun compt proportis, iij^c xxxiij li. vj s. viij d.'

Travelling English Companies.[1]

20th Sept. 1589

(Letter from Henry le Scrope, ninth Baron Scrope of Bolton, Governor of Carlisle and Warden of the West Marches, to William Ashby, English Ambassador at the court of James VI.)

' After my verie hartie comendacions : vpon a letter receyved from Mr Roger Asheton, signifying vnto me that yt was the kinges earnest desire for to have her Majesties players for to repayer into Scotland to his grace ; I dyd furthwith dispatche a servant of my owen vnto them wheir they were in the furthest parte of Langkeshire, whervpon they made their returne heather to Carliell, wher they are, and haue stayed for the space of ten dayes, wherof I thought good to gyve yow notice in respect of the great desyre that the kyng had to have the same to come vnto his grace ; And withall to praye yow to gyve knowledg therof to his Majestie. So for the present, I bydd yow right hartelie farewell. Carlisle the xxth of September, 1589,

Your verie assured loving frend,

H. SCROPE.' [2]

Feb. 1593/4

£333, 6s. 7d. paid to certain English comedians by the King's command.[3]

22nd March 1594/5

' The k. hathe hard that ffletcher the player that was here is hanged for his cause And in mirry word*es* told Roger and me thereof as not beliueing it, sayenge very pleasantlie that if it were so he wold hange vs.' [4]

1st Oct. 1598

(See App. I, 287, s.v. *St Andrews*—Kirk Session Records.)

---

[1] The more important notices have already been printed by J. C. Dibdin, *Annals of the Edinburgh Stage*, 1888, pp. 20-5 ; J. Tucker Murray, *English Dramatic Companies*, 1910, II, 195, 267 ff. ; Chambers, *Elizabethan Stage*, II, 265-70. I add some notes and a few fresh excerpts from manuscript sources.

[2] E. J. L. Scott, *Athenæum*, 21st Jan. 1882. See Chambers, *Elizabethan Stage*, II, 266.

[3] Dibdin, *op. cit.*, 20, from MS. Lord High Treasurers' Accounts. (8d. in MS.)

[4] MS. State Papers (Scotland) : Elizabeth, P.R.O., Vol. LV, No. 59. Abstract in Thorpe's *Calendar of State Papers*, II, 676.

Oct. 1599

£43, 6s. 8d. to be given by the King to the English comedians.[1]

Nov. 1599

' Some English Comedians came to this countrey in the month of October. After they had acted sundry Comedies in presence of the King, they purchased at last a warrant or precept of [2] the Bailies of Edinburgh, to get them an house within the Toun.

Upon Munday the 12 of November,[3] they gave warning be trumpets and drums, through the streets of Edinburgh, to all that pleased to come to Blackfriers Wynd to see the acting of their Comedies.

The Ministers of Edinburgh fearing the profanity that was to ensue, specially the profanation of the Sabbath day, convocated their four Sessions of the Kirk.[4] An act was made be common consent, that none should resort to these profane Comedies, for eschewing offence of God, and for evil example to others : and an ordinance was made, that every Minister should intimat this act in their own several pulpits. They had indeed committed several abuses, specialy upon the Sabbath at night before.

The King taketh the act in ill part, as if made purposely to cross his warrant, and caused summon the Ministers and four Sessions super inquirendis before the Secret Counsell.

They sent doun some in Commission to the King, and desired the matter might be tryed privatly, and offered, if they had offended, to repair the offence at his own sight ; and alledged, they had the warrant of the Synod presently sitting in the Town.[5]

The King would have the matter to come in publick. When they went doun, none was called on, but Mr Peter

---

[1] *Dibdin*, 22, from MS. Lord High Treasurers' Accounts.

[2] *Calderwood*, V, 765, has ' to.' In November £40 is given by the King's direction to the English comedians to buy timber for the preparation of a house to their pastime.—*Dibdin*, 22, from MS. Lord High Treasurers' Accounts. I can find no trace of the warrant for the pastime house, either in the MS. Register of the Privy Seal or in the collection of Royal Warrants at Register House, or in the Council Register, Register of Deeds, Burgh Court Book, or Protocol Book, covering this date, in the Burgh archives.

[3] This date must be corrected to ? 7th Nov. from the Register of the Privy Council. See below, p. 302 n.

[4] The Book of the General Kirk of Edinburgh for this date has not survived.

[5] Unfortunately there is a gap in the Minutes of the Synod of Lothian, 1596-1640.

Hewat and Mr Henrie Nisbet. After that they were heard,
the sentence was given out against all the rest unheard ;
and charge given to the Ministers and four Sessions to
conveen within three hours after, and to rescind their
former ordinance ; and to the Ministers to intimate the
contrair of that which they had intimated before. They
craved to be heard. Loath was the King, yet the Council
moved him to hear them.

Mr John Hall was appointed to be their mouth. Wee
are summoned, Sir, said Mr John, and craue to understand,
to what end. Its true, said the King, ye ar summoned, and
I have decerned already. Mr John made no reply. Mr
Robert Bruce said, If it might stand with your pleasure,
wee wold know, wherefore this hard sentence is past against
us. For contraveening of my warrant, said the King.
Wee haue fulfilled your warrant, said Mr Robert, for
your warrant craved no more but an house to them, which
they haue gotten.[1] To what end, I pray you, sought I an
house, said the King, but only that the people might
resort to their Comedies. Your warrant bears not that end,
said Mr Robert, and we have good reason to stay them from
their playes evin be your own acts of Parliament. The
King answered, Ye are not the interpreters of my lawes.
And farther, the warrant was intimat but to one or two,
said Mr Robert, and therefore desired the King to retract
the sentence. The King wold answer [2] nothing. At the
least then, said Mr Robert, let the paine strike upon us,
and exeem our people. The King bade him make away.
So in departing, Mr Robert turned and said, Sir, please
you, nixt the regard wee owe to God, wee had a reverent
respect to your Majesties royal person, and person of
your Queen ; for wee heard, that the Comedians in their
playes, checked your royal person with secret and indirect
taunts and checks ; [3] and there is not a man of honour

---

[1] See above, p. 300 n[2].

[2] *Calderwood*, V, 766, ' alter.'

[3] Cf. MS. State Papers (Scotland), Elizabeth, Vol. LXII, No. 19 (Public
Record Office) : Nicholson to Lord Burghley, 15th April 1598. ' It is regrated
to me in quiet sorte, that the Commediens of London shoulde in their play
scorne the k. and people of this lande, and wished that it may be spedely
amended and staied ; lest the worst sort gitting vnderstandinge thereof should
stir the k. and Contry to anger thereat. A matter w*hich* beinge thus honestly
and quietly deliured vnto me by m[r] struett sometyme Prouost of this Towne
and a very substantious honest man, I haue thought mete to commend to
your Lord*es* good consideracion, for pre*sent* stay of suche courses.' An abstract
is given in *Thorpe*, II, 749.

in England wold give such fellows so much as their counte-
nance. So they departed.

They were charged at two hours, be sound of trumpet,
the next day following, at the publick Cross, about ten
hours to conveen themselves, and rescind the act, or else
to pass to the horn immediately after.[1]

The four Sessions conveen in the East Kirk. They
asked the Ministers advice. The Ministers willed them
to advise with some Advocats, seeing the matter touched
their estate so near. Mr William Oliphant and Mr John
Sharp, Advocats, came to the four Sessions. The charge
was read. The Advocats gave them counsel to rescind
the act, be reasone the Kings charge did not allow slanderous
and undecent Comedies ; and further shewed them, that
the Sessions could do nothing without their Ministers,
seeing they were charged as well as the Sessions, and the
matter could not pass in voting, but the Moderator and
they being present. They were called in, and after reasoning
they come to voting. Mr Robert Bruce being first asked
at, answered, His Majestie is not minded to allow any
slanderous and offensive Comedies ; but so it is, that their
Comedies are slanderous and offensive : Therefore the
King in effect ratifieth our acts. The rest of the Ministers
voted after the same manner. The Elders, partly for fear
of their estates, partly upon information of the Advocats,
voted to the rescinding of the act. It was voted next,
Whither the Ministers should intimat the rescinding of the
act. The most part voted, They should. The Ministers
assured them, they would not.

Henrie Nisbet, Archibald Johnstoun, Alexander Lindsay
and some others, took upon them to purchase an exemption

---

[1] Cf. *Register of the Privy Council*, VI, 39. 8th Nov. 1599. The Council,
considering the ' lait contempt and indignitie ' done to the King by the Four
Sessions, ordain an officer to pass to the Market Cross and command the said
Four Sessions to convene and annul the act, ' and with that to gif ane speciall
ordinance and directioun to thair haill ministeris that thay, eftir thair sermonis
upoun the nixt Sonday, publischlie admonische thair awne flockis to reverence
and obay his Majestie, and to declair to thame that thay will not restreane
nor censure ony of thair flokis that sall repair to the saidis commedeis and
playis, considering his Majestie is not of purpois or intentioun to authorize,
allow, or command onything quhilk is prophane or may cary ony offence or
sclander with it ; and to charge thame heirto, under the pane of rebellioun
and putting of thame to the horne ; and to charge the saidis ministeris that
thay, eftir thair saidis sermonis, conforme thameselffis to the directioun and
ordinance . . .' In the Lord High Treasurers' Accounts there is a payment
entered of 10s. 8d. to the messenger for passing to the Market Cross with letters
charging the Four Sessions to annul their act made for the discharge of certain
English comedians.—*Dibdin*, 23.

to the Ministers. They returned with this answer, That
his Majestie was content that the matter sould be past
over lightly ; but he would have some mention made of
the annulling of the act. They refuse.

Their Commissioners went the second tyme to the King,
and returned with this answer, Let them neither speak
good nor evil in that matter, but leave it as dead.

The Ministers conveened apart to consult. Mr Robert
Bruce said, It behoved them either to justify the thing
they had done or else they could not goe to a pulpit. Some
others said the lyke. Others said, Leave it to God to
doe as God sall direct their hearts. So they departed.

Mr Robert and others that were of his mind justified it
the day following in some smal measure, and yet were not
quarrelled.[1]

12th Nov. 1599

[Edinburgh, George Nicholson to Sir Robert Cecil.]

' The 4 Sessions of this towne (without touche by name
of *our* Inglishe players fletcher and mertyn [2] with their
company and not knowing the *kinges* ordenance for them
to play and be hard) enacted, and the preachers exhorted
their flok*es* to forbeare and not to come to or haunt prophane games sportes or playes now when they aught rather
to make their recourse to god by praier and fasting to
prevent the displeasure of God hanging over them and
threatning them by the sword now by reason of cruell
slaughters amonge them, by the late plagues here and the
great famyne of late and appearance of it in no lesse measure
this yeare. The k. hearing of this and that this should be

---

[1] *B.U.K.*, IV, 1002. Cf. *Calderwood*, V, 765-7. The passage from Calderwood is printed in Chambers, *Elizabethan Stage*, II, 267-8. The victory of the
King is minuted in the *Register of the Privy Council*, VI, 41. 10th Nov. 1599 :
The minute recapitulates the stages in the dispute which arose ' upoun some
sinister and wrangous reporte maid to the foure Sessionis of the Kirk of Edinburgh be certane malicious and restles bodyis quha, upoun everie licht occasioun,
misconstrowes his Majesteis haill doingis and misinterpreitis his Hienes gude
intentionis quhatsumevir.' The Act of the Four Sessions has now been annulled
' sua that now not onely may the saidis commedianis friely injoy the benefite
of his Majesteis libertie and warrand grantit to thame, bot all his Majesteis
subjectis . . . may friely at thair awne plesour repair to the saidis commedeis and playis without ony pane, skaith, censureing, reproche or sclander
to be incurrit be thame thairthrow.' The Treasurers' Accounts show a payment for proclaiming at the Market Cross His Majesty's pleasure to all his
lieges that the said comedians might use their plays in Edinburgh.—*Dibdin*,
p. 23, from MS. Lord High Treasurers' Accounts.

[2] Laurence Fletcher and Martin Slater. Cf. Chambers, *Elizabethan Stage*,
Vol. II, Chap. XV, Actors, s.v. Fletcher, Slater.

don (as it was not) to countermaund him, somoned by a merser the said sessions to compere before him and his Cownsell the last Thursday, when he threatned them, and in end concluded as by the proclamacion which was proclamed will appeare to your honour. The ministers vtterly refused to countermaund anything they had sayde, and to endure thextremyty ; yet honest Counselloures especially the prouest brought the k. from his hard resolucion, with conclusion that the chardge should cease towardes the mynisters, and the ministers lett the matter ly and be dead on bothe sides : So as yesterday in their preachinges they vsed very gentle exhortacions (as they do ever with great respect) to forbeare all prophanes, in sorte as the wise might know their constancy, and none nevertheles touche them for the same with reason. The k. this day by proclamacion with sound of Trumpett hathe commaunded the players libertie to play, and forbidden their hinder or impeachment therein. The bellowes-blowferes will and do say they are sent in by vs to suow contencion betwene the k. and kirke. Thus this matter standes over, with an increase of dislike betwene the parties .k. and kirke . . .' [1]

[A copy of the proclamation dated 8th Nov. is enclosed.]

But there was a final attempt on the part of the Kirk to prohibit the plays.

13th Nov. 1599

inglisch playis	The presbyterie all in ane voce findis thir playis made be the inglischmen come in ȝe countrej unlauchtfull and sclanderouß. [2]

---

[1] MS. State Papers (Scotland), Elizabeth, Vol. LXV, No. 64 (P.R.O.). An abstract is given in *Thorpe*, II, 777, and a fuller summary is Sir Sidney Lee's *Life of Shakespeare*, 1922, p. 83. Cf. *Calendar of Border Papers*, II, 631. 23rd Nov. 1599, Sir John Carey to Cecil. . . . ' Ther hathe of lat byn sume littyll stear betwen the Kynge of Scotland and his minesters about sertayen Inglishe players that ar in Scotland ; whoe the Kerke have forbedden to playe and have preached agayenst them withe verey vehement reprehensiones ; and the Kynge hathe commanded they shall playe, and that none shalbe prehibetyd comminge to them. Wherat the Kerke is muche displesed, and muche trubeles it had like to wraighte.' Also *Spottiswoode*, Hist. of the Church of Scotland, III, 81.

[2] Edinburgh MS. Presbytery Records.

27th Nov. 1599

Inglisch
playeri*s*
Ordanis thair brether M*aister* patrik galloway
Johnn brand and the moderato*ur* To ga to ꝑe
king*is* ma*ie*stie and to ressone *with* his ma*ie*stie
That ꝑe Inglische players may be dischargit and to returne
his ma*ie*stie anſ*s*er ꝑe iiij of de*cem*ber nixt.[1]

4th Dec. 1599

Inglisch
playeri*s*
Anent the *commission* gewin to m*aister* patrik
galloway and *cer*tan vther breꝑer *with* him The
xxvij of no*vem*ber last to ga to ꝑe king*is* ma*ie*stie
According heirvnto the said brether declari*ng* that thej
had spokin his ma*ie*stie, and efter *con*ference ꝑj resauit na
vther anſ*s*er nor the *commission*ari*s* direct fra ꝑe last Synod
ressauit wiz, his ma*ie*stie [2] suld cauſ*s* ꝑair playis [3] and gif
ony fault wer in thame his ma*ie*stie suld cauſ*s* reform
thame.[1]

[£333, 6s. 8d. granted in Dec. by King to English comedians.[4] The only other notices of the company relate
to their travels in the North in the autumn of 1601.]

8th August 1601   Dundee.

To the Inglischmen that playit in the tolbuith
£33 ℔ 6 ſ 8 đ.[5]

9th Oct. 1601   Aberdeen.

Ordinance
to the
dean of
gild
The Samen day The prouest Bailleis and counsall Ordanis the some of threttie tua m*er*ki*s*
to be gevin to the kingis ſ*s*erva*nd*is presentlie
in this bur*gh*t quha Playes comedies and staige
playes Be reasoun thay ar recommendit be his ma*ie*sties
speciall letter and hes played sum of thair comedies in
this bur*gh*t / and ordanis the said soume to be payit to
tha*m* be ꝑe dean of gild q*uhi*lk salbe allowit in his *com*ptis [6]

23rd Oct. 1601

[On this date Sir Francis Hospitall of Haulʒie, Frenchman,

---

[1] Edinburgh MS. Presbytery Records.
[2] MS. repeats ' his maiestie.'
[3] ? ' be examinit ' omitted.
[4] *Dibdin*, 24, from MS. Lord High Treasurers' Accounts.
[5] Dundee MS. Burgh Treasurer's Accounts.
[6] Aberdeen MS. Council Register, Vol. XL, 210 ; *Extracts from the Council Register of Aberdeen*, II, 222.

who had been recommended by His Majesty to the Burgh of Aberdeen ' to be favorablie Interteneit with the gentilmen his maiesties ßervandis ' was made a burgess along with various gentlemen who accompanied him. Among those mentioned is ' Laurence fletcher comediane ßerviture to his maiestie.'] [1]

[In the Book of Guildry Accounts of Aberdeen, 1453-1650, the following items appear in the discharge for 1601-2 : ' Item to ye stageplayaris inglischemen xxij ħib . . . Item for the stageplayaris suppouris [2] yat nicht thaye plaid to ye towne iij ħib.' In the Treasurer's Account for 1601-2, a sum of £126, 3s. 6d. is entered ' for the expensß maid on the Interenement (sic) of Monsieur de halȝie frensche-mane and the gentilmen his maiesties servandis quho com to this burght with him in october 1601/ And for defraying of thair haill chargis during thair remaning in this burght conforme to ane ordinance of consall maid yairanent.' [3] It was, presumably, on their return from Aberdeen that the grant of £400 was made by the King's precept.] [4]

[1] MS. Council Register, Vol. XL, 229. Cf. *Extracts from the Council Register of Aberdeen*, II, xxii, where ' ferviture ' is omitted.
[2] Not ' support,' as in *Extracts from the Council Register*, II, xxi, and *Spalding Club Miscellany*, V, 73.
[3] Printed also in *Extracts from Council Register*, II, xxi.
[4] *Dibdin*, 24, from MS. Accounts of the Lord High Treasurer. The persistent tradition that Shakespeare was one of the company who visited Aberdeen on this occasion (fostered by Knight, *Life of Shakespeare*, 1843, p. 41, and Fleay, *History of the Stage*, 135-6) has been disposed of by Lee, *Life of Shakespeare*, 1922, pp. 83-4 ; J. Tucker Murray, *English Dramatic Companies*, I, 104 ; Chambers, *Elizabethan Stage*, II, 269-70.

APPENDIX III.

COURT RECORDS.

COURT RECORDS.

Excerpts from the Exchequer Rolls of Scotland. (*E.R.*)

I, 2.	1263-6	Item, Henrico fatuo, Brelmano, Patricio janitori macellorum . . . iij celdras, vj bollas.
127.	1327/8-9	Item, in expensis hominum transeuncium cum Patricio stulto, veniente de Anglia vsque le Tarbart, xviij đ.
141.	1328-8/9	Et ministrallis ad festum Natale Domini lxvjv š. viij đ.
210.		Et ministrallis ad nupcias de Berwic,[1] lxvj ħ. xv š. iiij đ. Et ministrallis domini regis Anglie apud Donbretan, iiij ħ.
398.	1330/1-1	Et per solucionem factam ministrallis tempore coronacionis dicti domini regis, . . . xx ħ.
II, 173.	1363-4	Et magistro Gilberto Armestrang, ad soluendum ystrionibus apud Inchemurthach [2] x ħ.
551.	1376/7-7/8	Et ministrallis, de mandato regis, xiij š. iiij đ.
586.	1377-7/8	Et Thome Acarsane,[3] ministrallo regis, percipienti per annum pro tempore vite sue, pro suo seruicio, decem libras, . . . v ħ.
III, 345.	1392/3-4	Et duobus ministrallis regis, pro foedis suis, anni hujus compoti [4] . . . vj ħ. xiij š. iiij đ.
431.	1396-7	Et Fulop,[5] minstrallo, de gracia auditorum ad presens, xiij š. iiij đ.

[1] *i.e*, at the marriage of David, Earl of Carrick, afterwards David II.
[2] The episcopal manor of Inchmorthach. See *E.R.*, I, cxviii.
[3] Also II, 605 ; III, 32.
[4] Also III, 459, 538 (tempore scaccarii).
[5] Also III, 403, 563 (tempore scaccarii, ex gracia auditorum ad presens), 588, 611 (servienti tempore scaccarii) ; IV, 21.

1398-9 Et Bergus,[1] ministrallo, ex consideracione audi- 484.
torum, x s̃.
Et aliis mimis, ex consideracione auditorum,
xx s̃.

1433-4 Et per solucionem factam histrionibus regis . . . IV, 603.
v ƚi. xviij đ.

1429/30- Et tribus mimis conductis per computantem 678.
36 et transmissis in Scociam, et preparando se
ad mare, sub periculo computantis,
xviij ƚi. gr.
Et quatuor aliis mimis secunda vice conductis
versus Scociam pro servicio domini regis per
compotantem, ad parandum se ad iter, ut
patet per literas domini regis sub signeto de
precepto et cujusdem Martini Vanartyne,
unius dictorum mimorum, sub sigillo suo de
recepto, ostensas super compotum,
xxxij ƚi. gr.

Et compotat transmisisse domino regi in nave 680.
vocata Skippare Henry, cum Willelmo Wik, in
vestimentis mimorum, et argento dicta bullioun
pro eisdem vestimentis, et duobus mantellis
pellium martrix dicti sabill, scripto particulariter
examinato et remanente ut supra, sub periculo
compotantis, xxxiij ƚi. vj s̃. gr.

1436-7 Et Martino, mimo, et sociis ejusdem, tempore v, 35.
coronacionis regis, de mandato regine et consilii
. . . viij ƚi. x s̃.[2]

1441-2 Et allocate computantibus per solucionem factam 116.
Roberto Macye et fratri suo ac Ade Rede, histrionibus domini regis, in denariis et denariatis,
in partem solucionis feodorum suorum de anno
computi, x ƚi. xv s̃. vj đ.[2]

1444 Et per solucionem factam Roberto Macgye pro 150.
feodo suo, . . . iiij ƚi. xij đ.[2]

[1] Also III, 512.
[2] Account of the Custumars of Edinburgh.

263. 1446-7   Et per solucionem factam Roberto Makgye,
Marco Trumpate, et Ade Rede, servitoribus et
joculatoribus regis, percipientibus annuatim viginti libras pro suis feodis de magna custuma dicti
burgi . . .   xx łi.[1]
Et per solucionem factam mimis et histrionibus
regis videlicet, Ade Rede, Roberto M'Gy, et
Marco Trumpate, in complementum feodorum
suorum anni, etc. quadragesimi sexti,   viij łi

266.   Et allocate compotantibus pro octo duodenis panni
albi lanei emptis per compotantes de mandato
regis pro vestibus lusoribus coram rege in Natali
Domini coaptandis, . . .   vij łi. xiij ś. viij đ [2]

274.   Et pro expensis Roberti M'Gy, mimi regis et
servitoris, tempore sue infirmitatis in Edinburgh . . .   xxvij ś.[3]

302. 1447-8   (To Robert Makgy, Mark Trumpat and Adam
Rede, King's servants and jesters, as p. 263, £20.) [4]

318.   Et pro instrumentis musicis pro mimis, et re-
paracionibus eorundem necessariis, de novo emptis
per compotantes,   iiij łi. xvij ś.[5]

Et allocate compotantibus pro expensis factis
circa ornamenta joculancium et ludencium coram
domino rege in sua camera in festo Nativitatis
Dominice, tam in empcione quam tinctura vestium lanearum et linearum diversorum colorum,
                                xj łi. xvij ś j đ.[5]

339. 1448-9   Et per solucionem factam Roberto M'Gy, Marco
Trumpat, et Ade Rede, histrionibus sive joculatoribus regis (as p. 263) Roberto M'Gy fatente
receptum super compotum,   xx łi.[4]

378. 1449-50 Et per solucionem factam Roberto Magy, Ade
Rede, et Marco Trumpet, histrionibus domini
regis . . .   x łi.[4]

---

[1] Account of the Custumars of Perth.
[2] Account of the Custumars of Stirling.
[3] Account of the Custumars of Edinburgh.
[4] Account of the Custumars of Perth.
[5] Account of the Custumars of Stirling.

Et per solucionem factam domino regi et regine, 396.
et eorum servitoribus, de eorum mandatis, in
pecuniis, pannis laneis, lineis, canubio, foderaturis,
auro et argento, ad ludos et disportus suos per
tempus computi . . .   ix^clxxj ħ. vj š. vij đ.

1452-3   Et in peccuniis deliberatis domine regi in ludis 607.
et disportis suis et pro naulo et diversis expensis
factis per compotantem tempore transitus domini
regis versus Sanctumandream ad baptismum
principis . . .   j^clxxxxv ħi. ix š. v đ.

1460-2   [Payment of £3, 6s. 8d. to Ade Rede ' mimo.']   VII, 144.

1465-6   Et eidem, pro xxxix ulnis de tartir, tribus stekis 423.
de bukrame, duobus libris auri, et aliis picturis
emptis per computantem et liberatis Johanni
Rate, pictori, pro le mumre regis erga Natale, de
mandato ejusdem . . .   xxv ħi. v š. x đ.[1]

1466-7   Et pro certis necessariis liberatis Johanni Rate, 501.
pictori, ad le mumre grathe in yeme elapsa, de
eodem mandato,   lvij ħi.[1]

1475-6   Et per solucionem factam Patricio Johnesone [2] VIII, 333.
de mandato domini regis pro suis ludis tempore
Natalis et Carnisprivii et expensis desuper
factis, . . .   vj ħi.[3]

1477   Et per solucionem factam dicto Patricio (Johnne- 404.
sone) pro certis joccis et ludis factis coram rege . . .
vj ħi.[3]

---

[1] Account of the Custumars of Edinburgh.
[2] See also *E.R.*, VII, 534 (Compotum Patricii Johnesone, receptoris firmarum domini nostri regis infra Lithqwschire).   VII, 628 ; VIII, 61, 65.   VIII, 305 (payment of £6).   333 (payment of xx s. ' pro feodo suo, ex gracia regis '). VII, 538 (' Et eidem Patricio de firmis terrarum de Kingisfelde sibi ad vitam concessis, . . . xx s.'   Footnote gives the charter under the Privy Seal conceding ' dilecto familiari servitori nostro Patricio Johneson, pro suo fideli servicio nobis impenso et impendendo terras nostras de Kingisfeld,' etc., 5th Nov. 1467).   VIII, 64, 153, 213, 305, 404, 604 ; IX, 16, 106, 172, 243, 400, 466, 641 ; X, 33, 177, 276, 330, 408, 495 (Acct. of Chamberlain of Linlithgow, 1494-5, ' Et eidem de firmis terrarum de Kingisfeld, concessis per dominum regem quondam Patricio Johnson, extendencium in anno ad viginti solidos de quinque terminis elapsis ante obitum dicti quondam Patricii ').   And see below under Excerpts from *L.H.T.A.*
[3] Account of the Chamberlain of Linlithgowshire.

512.   1477-8   Et eidem, per liberacionem factam dicto Patricio
                Johnsone pro certis ludis et interludiis factis
                tempore Natalis Domini in camera et palacio
                regis, . . .   vj ħi.[1]

XI, 260.   1498-   Et abbati de Narent pro suis expensis in Strive-
         1499/1500 ling,   xl š.

XIII, 123.   1508   Et histrionibus in scaccario,   xl š.

XIV, 8.   1513-4   Et histrionibus Italicis [2] in octo libris et octo
                   solidis in eorum feodis . . .

107.   1514-5   [Payment of £89, 16s. to ' sex histrionibus et
               tubicinis.']

220.   1516   [Payment of £35 to ' sex histrionibus Ytilis
             domini gubernatoris ' ' per preceptum domini
             gubernatoris.']

285.   1516-7   [Payment of £60, 16s. to ' decem le halbertaris et
               duobus histrionibus.'   Also £60 ' quatuor his-
               trionibus Ytalis in recessu ipsorum pro bene-
               volentia de mandato dicti domini gubernatoris.']

300.   1517-8   [Payment to ' Juliano Drummond, Vincenti Pais,
               Sebastiano Drummond, Georgio Forest, et Juliano
               Rokkett, tubicinis et histrionibus Italicis et
               Scotis.']

459.   1518-22   [Payment to ' decem lie herberteris et duobus
                histrionibus.']

XV, 102.   1522-4   Et officiariis ac histrionibus ministrantibus in
                   dicto scaccario per dictum tempus [3]
                                                   xiij ħi. vj s. viij đ.

---

[1] Account of the Chamberlain of Linlithgowshire.
[2] See subsequent entries. Also E.R., XV, 220 (1522-6 Acct. of feu-farmer
of Garvioch.   ' Que firme et devorie dicti dominii assignantur sex tubicinis
Italicis et Scotis in partem solutionis feodorum et gagiarum ipsorum . . .
Juliano Drummond, Georgeo Forrest, Vincencio Pais, Baptista Drummond,
et Henrico Rudman ' (five names only)), 494.   Payments from fermes of
Kintore, 30, 156, 245, 312. 682 (At the Audit held at Edinburgh, 28th July
1529, the Chamberlain of Garvioch is ordered ' to ceis fra ony forther payment
of ony feis or dewiteis of the lordschip of Gariauch to the Italiane ministralis '),
495 (1529 payments not to be made to the Italian and Scots ' tubicinis ' from
the fermes of Kintore and Garvioch without express command of the King).
[3] Similarly E.R., XV, 389, 467, et passim, up to about 1560.

*Excerpts from the Accounts of the Lord High Treasurer
of Scotland. (L.H.T.A.)*

1473   Item gevin at the Kingis commande, iij⁰ Septem- I, 43.
bris, to Johnne Broune lutare, at his passage oure
sey to lere his craft,   v ƚi.

1474   Item gevin to Andro Balfoure, iiijᵗᵒ Septembris, 60.
to by claythis to the Kingis litill lutare that he
send to Bruges,   xxiiij ŝ.

1473   Item [1] gevin to Maister William Sevas, and pait 68.
again to him be the Thesaurare, that he gafe to
ij Sanct Nicholais bischop of the Abbay and the
towne,   xlviij ŝ.
Item to thare ij deblatis,[2] the sammyn tyme, be
the said Maister William, and pait again to him
be the thesaurar,   xx ŝ.

1488   Item, to a fwle,[3] the saim day at the Kingis 91.
commande,   xviij ŝ.

Item, to Patrik Johnson [4] and the playaris of
Lythgow that playt to the King,[5]   v ƚi.

Item,[6] in Lannerik, to dansaris and gysaris,   93.
                              xxxvj ŝ.

Item, to Inglis Johne the fwle, at the Kingis 95.
commande, thre royse nobillis,   v ƚi. viij ŝ.

Item, to the clerkis of the Chapell, for thare 102.
seruice at ȝwle. . . .   xxxᵗⁱ ƚi.[7]

---

[1] At Yule.

[2] Var. of dablet, little devil, imp.

[3] Cf. *L.H.T.A.*, II, 354 (' Joke fule in Dunde ') ; II, 460 (' Wallas the fule '
in St Andrews) ; III, 205 (a coat to a fool in Linlithgow) ; 168 (9 s. for a mantle
for ' Johne, fule of Abirdene '). Are these ' fools ' talented local performers
or vagrant ' scenici ' or simply beggars of weak intellect ?

[4] For payments to Patrick Johnson ' to the censs ' at Epiphany, 1489/90
and 1490/1, see *L.H.T.A.*, I, 128, 174. See also above in Excerpts from *E.R.*,
p. 311 and n².

[5] 5th August.

[6] About the end of August.

[7] Payments occur regularly at Yule and Pasche to the Clerks of the Chapel
Royal ; also to the six ' childir ' or ' barnis.'

118.   1489   Item,[1] to Patrick Johnson and his fallowis that
               playt a play to the King in Lythqow,
                                          iij ħi. xij š.

119.   Item, the saim da,[2] to Gentil Johne the Inglis
               fule that brocht japis to the King, . . .   x ħi.

127. 1489/90 Item, to the King of Bene, the saim da,[3] xviij š.

170.   1490   Item, on Fryda, the xxiij° Julij, in Dunde, to
               the King to gif the Fransche men that playt,
               xx[ti] vnicornis,   xviij ħi.

174.   1490/1 Item, for ij elne grene cayrsay and iij elne cotton
               quhyt to Sande fwle til a coyt, and the makin
               of it,   xix š.

176.   1491   Item to Blind Hary,[4]   xviij š.
               Item, to Bennat,   xviij š.
               Item, til a harper,   xviij š.
               Item, to Wallass that tellis the geistis to the
               King,[5]   xviij š.

179.   Item, the saim day,[6] to the Spanʒeartis that
               dansyt before the King on the cawsay of Edin-
               burgh before the Thesauraris lwgeing . . .
                                                        xxvij ħi.

183.   Item, the v° Decembris, in Edinburgh, to Sanct
               Nycholas bisschop, at the Kingis command, be
               Master James Olyfant, iiij vnicornis
                                               iij ħi. xij š.

184.   Item, to gysaris that dansyt to the King the
               saim (da),[7]   (sum defaced in MS.)

---

[1] End of August. See p. 313 n[4].
[2] About 3rd Sept.
[3] Uphaly Day.
[4] See also L.H.T.A., I, xcix, c, civ, 133, 174, 181, 184. The payment quoted
above was made on 5th April at Linlithgow.
[5] Also L.H.T.A., I, 183 (' Wallass that tellis the tayllis '), 274 (' Wallas the
tale tellar ').
[6] 16th July.
[7] St John's Day at Linlithgow.

1491/2   Item, on Monnunda the ij° Januar, to Schir
Thomas Galbretht, Jok Goldsmyth and Crafurd,[1]
for the singyn of a ballat to the King in the
mornyng, . . .   ij ħ. xiiij š.

Item (on Uphaly day), to Pryngill, king of bene,
xxxvj š.

1494   Item,[2] gevin to Pringill, be a precept of the 232.
Kingis, for a liffray to mak a dans again Vphaly
day, iiij ellis of taftays ; price of the ellen
xviij š. ; summa iij ħ. xij š.

Item,[3] gevin to tua Sanct Nicholas bischoppis, 239.
at the Kingis command,   xxxvj š.
Item, to thare deblatis,   xviij š.

1496   Item, to Jhonne Goldsmyth, be a precept, for 270.
his expens quhen he was King of Beyne,   v ħ.

Item, to Gilberte Brade, be ane precept of the
Kingis, for spilling of his hous in Striuiling be the
Abbot of Vnresoun,   x ħ.

Item,[3] in Linlithquho, to Sanct Nycholas beschope, 307.
xxviij š.

Item, that samyn nycht [4] to Widderspune the
foulare, that tald talis and brocht foules to the
King,[5]   vj š. viij đ.

Item, the xij day (of December) to Watschod [6]
the tale tellare and Widderspune the tale tellare
togidder,   xviij š.

Item, that samyn nycht,[7] giffin to the gysaris in 308.
Melros,   xxxvj š.

---

[1] Clerks of the Chapel Royal.
[2] About the end of April.
[3] 6th Dec.
[4] 9th Dec.
[5] Also *L.H.T.A.*, I, 330 ('for fowlis and tales telling ') ; II, 102 (' fithelar
and tellar of tales ') ; *et passim.*
[6] Also *L.H.T.A.*, I, 378.
[7] St John's Day.

309.   1496/7 Item (the fift day of Januar was Vphaly day),
                in Edinburgh that nycht to the gysaris, at the
                Kingis command,   ij ħi. xiiij š.

322.   Item, that samyn day, in Striuelin, giffin to the
                tawbronar that playit to the King, and the
                spelare [1] with him,   xxvij š.

326-7. 1497   Item, (the xxviij day of March), to thir menstralis,
                giffin for thair Pasche reward : in the first, to
                Thome Pringil and his brodir trumpatouris,
                                                   xxviij š.
                Item, to Will Carrik and Pete Johne, trumpatouris,
                xxviij š.   Item, to Adam Boyd, fithelar, and
                Mylsone the harpare, xxviij š.   Item, Bennet,
                fithelar, and Fowlis the harpar, xxviij š.
                Item, to Jacob, lutar, at the Kingis command,
                xxviij š.   Item, to Guilliame and Pais, taw-
                bronaris, and ane spelare with thaim,   xxxvj š.
                Item, to Widderspune, that brocht wild fowlis to
                the King, xiiij š.   Item, to Pate, harpare,   ix š.
                Item, to Lundoris the lutare,   ix š.
                Item, to Ansle the tawbronare,   ix š.

327.   Item, the last day of March, gevin to the Abbot
                of Vnresone, for his reward, . . .   v ħib. viij š.

330.   Item, that samyn day, giffin to tua fithelaris
                that sang Graysteil to the King,   ix š.

370.   Item, the sext day of December, giffin to Sanct
                Nycholas beschop,   xl š.

375.   1497/8 Item, to the singaris that nycht,[2] that brocht
                the cens in to the King,   xxxj š.

                Item,[3] . . . to the King of Bene . . .   iij li.
                                                  (xvij š. vj đ.)

II, 55. 1501   Item, for ane maid cote of carsay, blew and
                grene, maid to the spelair, and for ane sark and
                schone to him,   xiiij š. v đ.[4]

                ----

[1] See p. 39 n[2].   [2] Epiphany.
[3] 7th Jan.   [4] In list of ' Vestimenta pro servitoribus.'

1502   Item, the xvij day of Aprile, for vj½ elne damas 57.
      to be ane cote to the spelair, ilk elne xxj s̃ ;
      summa   vj ħi. xvj s̃. vj đ.¹

1501   Item, to Petir de Luca and Francis de Luca, 96.
      spelair, in part of thair pensioun of l ħi. xx Franch
      crounis ;   summa xiiij ħi.²

      [Long list of April pensions to various kinds of 102.
      minstrels, including the two ' common pipers ' of
      Edinburgh.]³

      Item,⁴ to the Abbot of Unresone of Linlithqw, 111.
      quhen he dansit to the King, be the Kingis
      command,   xliij s̃. vj đ.

      Item, the xxiij day of Junij, to the gysaris that 112.
      dansit, . . .   xxviij s̃.

      Item, . . . to tua Heland bardis,   v s̃.   119.

      Item, the xviij day of October, . . . to ane 122.
      spelar,   vij ħi.

      Item, the xviij day of November, to the Thayn 126.
      of Caldoris harper, . . .⁵   xiiij s̃.

      Item, to the madinnis of Forres that com to
      Ternway and sang, . . .   ix s̃.⁶

      Item, the viij day of December, be the Kingis 128.
      command, to Sanct Nicholais beschop of Coupir
      in Fiff,   xlij s̃.

¹ In list of ' Vestimenta pro servitoribus.'
² See *Reg. Sec. Sig.*, I, No. 849. ' Apud . . . 3 Jul. A letter made to
Peter de Luca and Francess de Luca, Italianis, for thair service done and to
be done . . .,—of the gift of the soume of fifty lib. to be pait to thaim zerlie
enduring our soveran lordis will . . . etc.'
³ Rewards to common minstrels of Edinburgh and Canongate, II, 131 ;
Aberdeen, II, 124 ; Perth, III, 416.
⁴ 13th June.
⁵ Cf. *L.H.T.A.*, II, 125 (' Lard of Balnagounis harpare ') ; 145 (' Lord
Setounis menstrale ').
⁶ Similarly, *L.H.T.A.*, II, 401 (' the madinnis that daunsit to the King '
at ? Dingwall) ; 463 (' the madinnis of Forres that dansit to the King ' . . .
' the madinnis of Dernway that dansit at Elgin siclike ' . . . ' the madinnis that dansit
at Dernway ') ; III, 166 (' the madinnis that sang to the King at Spinie) ;
170 (' the madinnis of Dernway that sang to the King ' . . . ' the madinnis
in Invernes that sang ') ; 345 (' the maddinis in Dernway that sang to the
King ' . . . ' the wemen that sang at the Kirk of Logy ' . . . ' in Elgin, to
the wemen that sang to the King ').

Item, to the deblatis that wes with Sanct Nicholais
beschop, xiiij š.

131. 1501/2 Item,[1] to Johne Goldsmyth, King of Beyne, for
furnissing of his graith, . . .
iij ħ. xvij š. vj đ.

Item, the samyn nycht,[1] to the gysaris that
playit to the King, . . .   iiij ħ. iiij š.

132. Item, the samyn nycht,[2] to the gysaris, . . .
lvj š.

Item, to the bard wif in the Canonegait, . . .
xiiij š.

Item,[3] to the spelair that ȝeid on the cord, . . .
vij ħ.
Item, to his man, . . .   lvj š.

135. Item, the viij day of Februar, to the men that
brocht in the morice dance, and to thair menstrales, in Strivelin, . . .   xlij š.

139. Item, to the spelair, . . .   xlij š.

143. 1502 Item, to the spelair for to pas (his) way, . . .
xiiij ħ.

145. Item, . . . to the spelar boy callit Francis de
Luca, . . .   xiiij ħ.

151. Item, the said day, to the spelaris in Strivelin,
xiiij š.

153. Item, . . . to Petir de Luca, the spelaris master,
xlij š.

334. Item, to the spelair, his quartar pensioun
xij ħ. x š.
335. 1502/3 Item, to the spelaris maister, his quartar payment
of this terme of Candilmes bipast,
xij ħ. x š.

---

[1] 2nd Jan.   [2] 6th Jan.   [3] 11th Jan.

1502   Item,[1] be the Kingis command to Sanct Nicholais 349.
beschop, . . .   xlij š.
Item, to the deblatis and ruffyis,[2]   vij š.   350.

Item, . . . to Curry and his man, for to haf him 351.
to Arbroth agane ȝule,[3]   vij š.

1502/3 Item,[4] to four trumpetis, thre lutaris, four har- 353.
paris, tua taubronaris, thre fithelaris, in Arbroth ;
         ilk ane xiiij š ; summa, xj ħ. iiij š.
Item, that samyn nycht, to the gysaris in Arbroth,
. . .   iiij ħ. iiij š.

Item,[5] to the King of Bene, . . .   iij ħ. xvij š.   354.

Item, the last day of Januar, . . . to gysaris in 356.
Edinburgh . . .   lvj š.

1503   Item, (the vj day of Junij), payit to Andro Wod 374.
he laid doun be the Kingis command to the
Abbot of Unresonis menstrales, . . .   lvj š.

Item, (the vij day of Junij), for iij unce sewing 229.
silk blak, to be pointis to the capricht agane the
Kingis passing to the Corpus Christi play, . . .
                        x š. vj đ.

Item, (the xxvj day of Junij), to Robin Hude of 377.
Perth, . . .   lvj š.

Item, the xxix day of Junij, payit to Robert
Colvile that he gaif to the spelar, be the Kingis
command, that day he spelit,   xxviij š.

Item, to viij Inglis menstrales, . . . xxviij ħ.[6]   387.
Item, to the Inglis spelair, that playit the super-
salt, . . .   iij ħ. x š.

[1] 6th Dec.
[2] Ruffy, variant of ruffin, ruffian, a devil or fiend.
[3] Cf. II, 103, ' the lityll fithelar callit Curryis.'
[4] 1st Jan.
[5] 6th Jan.
[6] This entry, with those immediately following, relates to the marriage of James IV. with Margaret, August 1503. There are also payments to the Queen's four minstrels, the three minstrels of Berwick, the Earl of Oxford's two minstrels, and the ' five lowd menstrels ' (II, 387).

Item, to the bere ledair of Ingland . . .

v ħi. xij š.

Item, to the thre gysaris that playit the play,[1] . . .

xxj ħi.

389. Item, the xxiiij day of August, to the spelair, for to pas his way,[2]   xiij ħi.

395. Item, . . . to the Italien las that dansit, . . .

xxj ħi.

Item, to the four Italien menstrales, to fee thaim hors to Linlithqw, and to red thaim of the toun . . .

lvj š.

409. Item,[3] . . . to Sanct Nicholas beschop, . . .

iiij ħi. iiij š.

---

[1] Probably John English and his companions. See Leland, *Collectanea*, IV, pp. 299, 300. 'After Soupper, the Kynge and the Qwene being togeder in hyr grett Chamber, John Inglish and hys Companyons playd, and then ichon went his way ' (11th August). 'After Dynnar, a Moralite was played by the said Master Inglishe and hys Companyons, in the Presence of the Kyng and Qwene, and then Daunces war daunced ' (13th August).

[2] This may have been the 'Inglis spelair ' mentioned in previous entry, but cf. Leland, *op. cit.*, IV, 297 : 'After Dynnar a young man, an Italyen, played before the King on a Corde varey well.' Other entertainments included dancing and jousts, *ibid.*, 291, 296 300. *L.H.T.A.*, II, 388, 389, mentions payments for jousting spears, swords, etc., at the marriage. See, too, App. I, s.v. Edinburgh, for an account of the municipal pageants on this occasion. It is not clear whether the tournament described by John Younge (Leland, *op. cit.*, IV, 288) was arranged by the Court or the Burgh authorities : 'Halfe a Mylle ny to that, within a Medewe was a Pavillon, wherof cam owt a Knyght on Horsbak, armed at all Peces, havyng hys Lady Paramour that barre his Horne. And by Avantur, ther cam an other also armed, that cam to hym, and robbed from hym hys sayd Lady, and at the absenting blew the said Horne, wherby the said Knyght understude hym, and tourned after hym and said to hym, wherfor hast thou thys doon ? He answerd hym, what will yous ay therto ? I say, that I will pryve apon thee, that thou hast doon Owtrage to me. The tother demaunded hym if he was armed ? He said ye. Well then, said th'other, preve the a Man, and doo thy Devoir.

'In such Manere they departed, and went to take their Sperys and renne without stryking of the same. After the Course they retourned with their Swerdes in their Haunds, and maid a varey fayr Torney : And the Caller caused the Swerd for to fall of the Defender. Notwithstanding, the Caller caused to gyffe hym ageyn his Swerd, and begon ageyn the said Torney of more fayre Manere ; and they did well ther Devor, tyll that the Kynge cam hymselfe, the Qwene behynd hym, crying Paix, and caused them for to be departed. After this the King called them before hym and demaunded them the Cause of ther Difference. The Caller sayd, Syre, he hath taken from me my Lady Paramour, whereof I was insurte of hyr by Faith. The 'Defender answered, Syre, I schall defend me ageynst hym apon thys cas : Then sayd the Kynge to the sayd Defender, brynge youre Frends, and ye schall be appoynted a Day for to agre you. Wheroff they thaunked hym and so euery Man departed them for to drawe toward the said Towne. The Names of thos war Sir Patryk Hamilton, Brother of the said Lord abouffe said, and Patryk Synklar, Esquyre : and ther was com grett Multitude of People for to se thys.'

[3] 6th Dec.

Item, to the deblatis with Sanct Nicholas beschop, . . . xiiij s̃.

Item,[1] in Linlithqw, to Sanct Nicholas beschop,
xxviij s̃.

Item, the xiij day of December, to Sanct Nicholas
beschop in Strivelin, . . . xxviij s̃.
Item, to thair deblatis with thaim thare, vij s̃. 410.

1503/4 Item,[2] to Thomas Bosuell and Pate Sinclair [3] to 413.
by thaim daunsing gere, . . . xxviij s̃.

Item,[4] to Maister Johne,[5] to by beltis for the 414.
Moris dans, xxviij s̃.
Item, that samyn nycht, to the gysaris of the
toun of Edinburgh, . . . v ℔. xij s̃.

Item,[6] that samyn nycht, to Colin Campbell and
his marowis that brocht in the Moris dauns, for
thair expens maid tharon, . . . xiiij ℔.

Item, the vij day of Januar, payit to Johne
Francis for xxj elne taffeti, rede and blew, quhilk
wes sex daunsing cotis in Maister Johnis dans,
ilk elne xiiij s̃., summa xiiij ℔. xiiij s̃.
Item, for v elne blew taffeti to the womanis goun
in the said dance, . . . iij ℔. x s̃.
Item, for vij elne quhit to lyne the samyn, . . .
viij s̃. ij đ.
Item for making of the samyn, iij s̃.
Item, for xxvij elne iij quartaris taffeti, blew,
rede, and variant, deliverit to Franch Maister
Johne for the said daunsaris hede gere, . . .
xix ℔. viij s̃. vj đ.
Item, to the said Maister Johne that he spendit
on this gere for the dance, xx s̃.

---

[1] 12th Dec.
[2] 3rd Jan.
[3] Master of the King's Wardrobe.
[4] 5th Jan.
[5] The French leech, John Damian, afterwards Abbot of Tungland.
[6] 6th Jan.

X

418,   Item (the thrid day of Februar), to the gysaris
            of Edinburgh that daunsit in the Abbay, . . .
                                          iij ħi. x ß.

320. 1504 Item,[1] for iij½ elne Franch tanne to Alexander
            Kers, cuke, . . . xlix ß.; quhen he wes Abbot
            of Unreson.

430.   Item,[2] to the Abbot of Unresoun of the pynouris
            of Leith, . . .   v ß.

431.   Item, the ix day of Maij, to the barbour helit
            Paules hed quhen he wes hurt with the Abbot of
            Unresoun,   xiiij ß.

438.   Item, payit to James Dog, that he laid doun
            for girs on Corpus Christi day, at the play, to
            the Kingis and Quenis chamires,   iij ß. iiij đ.

476. 1504/5 Item,[3] to the gisaris that dansit to the King and
            the Quene, . . .   iiij ħi. xviij ß.

477.   Item, for xij cotis and xij pair hos half Scottis
            blak half quhit to xij dansaris be the More
            taubronaris devis agane Fasteringis Evin, . . .
                                       xiij ħi. ij ß. x đ.[4]

III. 127.   Item, the xxiij day of Februar, to Alexander
            Kers, to lous the Kingis stope quhilk wes tane
            quhen he wes Abbot of Unresoun,
                                     vj ħi. xiij ß. iiij đ.

141. 1505 Item,[5] to gysaris dansit (in) the Kingis chamir . . .
                                          iiij ħi. x ß.
            Item, to the men that justit in the botes of
            Leith, . . .   xlij ß.

146.   Item, for ane carsay cote, in Air, to Swaggar,
            Schir William Murrayis fule, . . . ˙
                                          xxxj ß. vj đ.

─────────────────────────
[1] Beginning of April.
[2] 27th April.
[3] 2nd Feb.
[4] There are expenses also for tournaying. See, too, L.H.T.A., II, 386, 479;
III, 182.
[5] 25th May.

Item, the xxviij day of November, to ane jes- 173.
tour, . . .   xiiij ŝ.

Item, the vij day of December, to Sanct Nicholas 175.
beschop,   xlij ŝ.
Item, to the deblatis with him,   vij ŝ.

Item,[1] to Sanct Nicholas beschop in Linlithqw, 176.
                                               xlij ŝ.
Item, to his deblatis thare,   vij ŝ.

1505/6 Item, to ane jestour in Sanctandrois, . . . 180.
                                               ix ŝ.

1506   Item,[2] to ane Quene of Maij at the Abbay ȝet, . . . 195.
                                               xiiij ŝ.

Item, the first day of Junij, to ane Quene of 197.
Maij on the gait as the King passit to the Abbot
of Halyrudhous garding,   v ŝ.

Item,[3] to the Quene of Maij in Air,   v ŝ. 332.
Item, the ferd day of September, to ane pur bard 339
fallo,   iij ŝ.
Item, the thrid day of November, for ix elne 301.
rede carsay, to be ane doctour goun and ane hude
and ane pair of hos to Johne Bute,[4] . . .
                                               xlv ŝ.

Item,[5] that nycht in Linlithqw, to Sanct Nicholas 356.
beschop,   xx ŝ.

Item, the xxviij day of December, Sanct Inno- 285.
centis day, to the Kingis offerand to Sanct Innocentis beschop,   xxviij ŝ.

[1] 13th Dec.
[2] About 13th May.
[3] August.
[4] One of the Court fools. Cf. Dunbar, *Poems*, II, 199, S.T.S., 1893, ' Of a
dance in the Quenis Chalmer.'   For a detailed description of John Bute's
doctor's hood and the dress of his ' man ' Spark, see *L.H.T.A.*, III, 308.   Sir
Thomas Nornee is another jester much in evidence. *L.H.T.A.*, III, lvj, xcij,
and Dunbar, *Poems*, II, 194-5 :—
                    ' Quhairfoir ever at Pasche and ȝull,
                    I cry him Lord of everie fuill,
                    That in this regioun dwellis.'

[5] 11th Dec.

313.   Item, the penult day of December, for xxxvj
                elne grene sey to be five dansing cotis, v doublatis,
                and v pair of hos and ane kirtill for ane woman
                for dansing ; . . .   iiij ℔. iiij ŝ.
                Item, for v elne cammes for the said hos and
                kirtill ; . . .   vij ŝ. vj đ.
                Item, for xv goldin skinnis to stomois [1] for thaim,
                and schakaris [2] and bordouris to the tailes, of
                sindri prices,   iij ℔. xviij đ.
                Item, for making of the five cotis, v pair of hos,
                and the womannis kirtill,   xxiij ŝ.
                Item, for vj pairis caffunʒeis [3] to thaim ; . . .
                                                     iiij ŝ.

                Item, vij daunsing cotis, j kirtill maid to Thomas
                Bosuel and his complicis and sex doublatis of
                Robert Bertons taffeti.   (*Sum blank*)
                Item, for xxx elne blak gray to lyne the samyn,
                                                     xxxv ŝ.
                Item, for vj elne smal cammes to lyne the doub-
                latis bodyis and stumpes of the cotis ; . . .
                                                     ix ŝ.
                Item, for making of the vij cotis and sex doublatis,
                                                     xxxiij ŝ.
359.   Item, the last day of December, for xxx dosan
                of bellis for dansaris deliverit to Thomas Bosuell,
                                                     iiij ℔. xij ŝ.

360.   1506/7   Item,[4] giffin to divers menstrales, schawmeris,
                trumpetis, taubronaris, fithelaris, lutaris, harparis,
                clarscharis, piparis, extending to lxix persons, . . .
                                                     xlj ℔. xj ŝ.

361.   Item,[5] to Thomas Edʒaris childir, in drinksilvir
                at the play cotis making,   xiiij ŝ.
                Item, to Thomas Bosuell he laid doun for tua
                gold skinnis to the play cotis,   v . . .

249.   Item, the ferd day of Januar, for vij elne Rowan
                gray to be ane mummyng goun to the King ; . . .
                                                     iiij ℔. xj ŝ.
                Item, for woll to the schulderis of it,   xvj đ.

---

[1] stomachers.   [2] thin plates of metal hanging down.
[3] ? gaiters.   [4] 1st Jan.   [5] 3rd Jan.

Item, for bordouring of it with toddis, xxiiij š.
Item, for x elne blak gray to lyne it,
xj š. viij đ.

Item,[1] for vij½ elne broun to be ane other mum- 250.
myng goun ; . . . vij ħi. x š.

Item, the xv day of Januar, to Colin Campbell, 362.
. . . in recompensatioun of ane dans maid be
him, . . . v ħi. xij š.

Item,[2] to Guilliam, taubronar, for making of ane 371.
dans the tyme of the Princis birth,
iiij ħi. iiij š.

Item, to Wantones and hir tua marowis that 372.
sang with hir, xiiij š.[3]

1507   Item,[4] for vj pair legharnes for daunsaris, 381.
xviij š.

Item, the xxvj day of August, for xxv elne Franch 323.
tanne to John Francis five Franch menstrales ; [5]
. . . xvj ħi. xiij š. iiij đ.

[Many details are given concerning the equipment for The Tour-
the great Tournament of *June* 1507 : Flanders taffeta for nament of
the ' chair triumphale ' for the Black Lady ; canvas for 1507.
lining it and ' variant ' and red taffeta for ornamentation ;
white coats for the squires to the Black Lady ; gold cloth
for the doublets for the lackeys to the Wild Knight ; (258) :
yellow and black hose and ' bonetis ' for the lackeys ;
coats for Thomas Boswell, Patrick Sinclair, and James
Stewart, ' squires for the barres ' ; gold-flowered ' dames '
with borderings of green and yellow taffeta for a gown to
the Black Lady ; also black sleeves and black leather
gloves ; green and yellow taffeta for gowns to her two

---

[1] 6th Jan.
[2] 28th Feb.
[3] See also *L.H.T.A.*, III, IV, *passim*.
[4] 13th April.
[5] See also *L.H.T.A.*, III, 328, 406 ; IV, 402, *et passim*. Bountas (Bontanis,
Bontais) is prominent amongst the French minstrels. At New Year 1538/9
there are gifts to ' twa menstralis of the Quene of Frauncis,' and to ' twa
menstralis of Monsieur de Guize.'

ladies ; canvas, ropes, etc., for the small and ' gret heich '
pailȝouns for the field ; (259) : taffeta for banners to the
minstrels, etc. ; clothes for the King ; (260-1) : ' tua quaris
gold to illummyn the articules send in France for the
justing of the wild knycht for the blak lady ' (365) : ' hert
hornes and gayt skinnis for the wildmen cotis for the
barres ' (386) : payments to six trumpeters and four
' schawmeris ' ; six books of gold to Sir Thomas Galbreth
and Piers, the painter, for banners, standarts, coat armours
for heralds, minstrels, the field and pavilions ; (393) :
goat skins and other material for the wild men's coats ;
targets ; 37 pears for the ' tree of esperance ' ; 200 ' platis '
to be leaves to the tree ; payment for making 18 dozen
leaves and 6 dozen flowers and for wire and nails to attach
them to the tree ; ' ij Estland burdis to be weyngis to the
bestis,' ' iij dosan viij cammes to Alexander Chawmir,
payntour, for the battering (*i.e.*, stiffening) of the best
hedis for the feild ' ; payment to the said Alexander for
making the beasts ; preparation of spears and bows ;
(394) : preparation of artillery, fire balls, etc. (395) : payment to Thomas Burn ' for tagging and bukkilling of the
sadilles of the bestis and renȝeis to the samyn and grathing
of thaim ' (397) : payment for ' iiij hors hyre the day of
justing quhilk tursit the bestis to the castell and the barres '
(400) : ' xxx gaitskinnis for the wildmen cotis agane the
justing ' (410). [1]

IV, 87.   1507   Item, the v day of December, to Sanct Nicholas,
                    beschop of the Canongait,   xxviij s̃.
                    Item, to his ruffyis,   vij s̃.

---

[1] See *L.H.T.A.*, III, xlvij-lij. I cite more fully the reference noted in Marc
de Vulson, *Le vray Theatre d'Honneur*, from the 1648 Edn., XX, 271-2, concerning the ' Emprise du Cheualier Sauuage a la Dame Noire.' La troisiesme
Emprise . . . est celle du Cheualier Sauuage à la Dame noire, et de deux autres
Cheualiers ses Aydes, qui tous trois ensemble firent publier par tout les articles
de leur Emprise, par permission du Roy d'Escosse, contre tous Venans, Gentils-
hommes de nom & d'armes, par l'espace de cinq semaines, à combattre à pied
et à cheual pour l'amour des Dames. . . . Le premier article de cette Emprise
est si galant, que le curieux ne trouuera pas mauuais que ie le descriue tout
au long. ' Ces armes se feront en cedit Royaume & ville d'Edimbourg dedans
le champ de Souuenir, lequel sera entre le Chasteau, nommé des Pucelles, & le
Pavillon secret, & dedans ledit Champ sera l'arbe d'Esperance, lequel croist au
jardin de Patience, portant feuilles de Plaisance, la fleur de Noblesse, & le fruit
d'Honneur . . .' *La Science Heroique*, Paris, 1644, xliii, 456, adds, ' Item, seront
tenus les venants, venir droit audit Arbre le premier iour d'Aoust, que les armes
commenceront & toucheront audit Escu blanc gardé de la Dame Noire, accom-
pagnée de Sauuages, trompettes, et tous instruments,' etc. There is some
confusion in Marc de Vulson as to the date of the Tournament.

Item, the viij day of December, to Sanct Nicholais, beschop of the hie toun of Edinburgh,

xxviij s̃.

Item, to his ruffyis, ix s̃.

Item,[1] to the Sanct Nicholas beschop of Linlithqw, 88.

xxviij s̃.

Item, to the ruffyis thare, ix s̃. 89.

Item, the xxviij day of December, to Sanct 91. Innocentis beschop, xlij s̃.

1507/8 Item, to ane jestour, v s̃. 96.

Item, for vj pair caffunȝeis for dansaris that 100. dansit at ȝule bipast : . . . iiij s̃.

Item, the v day of March, to the Franch men- 104. strales that made ane dans in the Abbay, . . .

viij ƚi. viij s̃.

Item, for thair dansing cotis to the said dans,

v ƚi.

Item, the xx day of March, to the jestour of 107. Cambuskinneth, vij s̃.

1508 Item, the last day of Aprile, in Dunfermlyn, for 21. ane callit Mure for ane hors quhilk ran up the staris of the cors, xxvj ƚi. xiij s. iiij đ.

[There are various entries relating to the Tournament May 1508. of 1508 : Details of the dresses of the Black Lady and her two 'madinnis' (64) ; of the lackeys to the Wild Knight (63) ; payment to the 'xiiij men that bure the blak lady fra the Castell to the barres and syne to the Abbay' (119) ; 'xij dosan of leifis for the tree of esper- ance,' 'five dosan of flouris' for the said tree (120) ; pay- ment for 'mending of iiij dosan iiij leiffis to the tree,' also to the 'buklar makar' for making 'xlix peris for the said tree of esperance . . . and for leffis to hyng thaim' (121) ; for 'tagging, grathing and bukkilling of the wild bestis' (129).] [2]

---

[1] 13th Dec.

[2] Cf. *L.H.T.A.*, IV, lxxxiij. See also *Pitscottie*, I, 242-4, who gives the date incorrectly as 1505, and says that the tournament lasted for forty days.

64.   1508   Item, the xxv day of Maij for xx½ elne of Birge satin, rede and ȝallo, to be v daunsing cotis agane the bancat ; . . .   x ℔. v ŝ.

Item, for v pair hos, blak and ȝallo, to thaim, . . .
l ŝ.

Item, iiij elne of taffetj to be sleffis to the fulis cote and hude and taggis to the samyn ; . . .
xlv ŝ.

Item, to the samyn j elne half quartar and ane naill of ȝallo taffetj that restit of the Kingis courtingis.

Item, for iiij elne ȝallo taffetj to be ane goun to Martin the Spanȝart for the bancat ; . . .
lvj ŝ.

65.   Item, for ij pair hos, ȝallo and blak, to ij Franch menstrales agane the bancat,   xx ŝ.

Item, to the samyn tua menstrales iij elne taffetj, rede and ȝallo, to thair doublatis ; . . .   xlv ŝ.

125.   Item, payit to Schir Johne Ramsay quhilk he laid doun for stuf at the bancat for the dans . . .
xxj ℔. xj ŝ. vj đ.

Item, for cod lases, Racland gold fulȝee, v dosan small bellis, vj dosan gret bellis, lattoun, wyre, xij½ elne blew bukram, xx elne j quartar frenȝeis, xx fawdoum small toll [1] to the bancat and for the play and dans of the samyn, of sindry pricis,
v ℔. vij ŝ. viij đ.

126.   Item, to William Raa, cultellar, for viij armyng suordis and ane knyf to the men of armes that brocht ane gys [2] to the King at the bancat,
lvj ŝ.

129.   Item, for bukkilling and grathing of Martin and the blak lady agane the bancat   xiiij ŝ.[3]

---

[1] tow, rope.

[2] 'Guise' ? The editor L.H.T.A. glosses 'goose,' which may be correct. Cf. IV, 124, where the meaning is certainly 'goose.' In any case some kind of pageantry is indicated.

[3] According to Pitscottie, loc. cit., at the end of the tournament there was a great 'triumphe and bancat' at Holyrood, which lasted for three days, beginning at nine hours in the morning and lasting till nine hours in the evening, and 'betuix everie seruice thair was ane phairs or ane play sum be speikin sum be craft of Igramancie quhilk causit men to sie thingis aper quhilk was nocht. And so at the hennest bancat pheirs and play vpone the thrid day thair come ane clwdd out of the rwffe of the hall as appeirit to men and opnit and cleikkit vp the blak lady in presence of thame all that scho was no moir seine bot this was done be the art of Igramancie for the kingis pleasour (by) ane callit Bischope Androw forman quha was ane Igramanciar and seruit the king at sic tymes for his pastyme and plesour.'

1511   Item, the xij day of October, fra Maister Johne 313.
of Murray, ij½ elnis blew taffatis and vj quartaris
ȝallow taffatis to be ane play coit to David
Lindesay for the play playt in the King and
Quenis presence in the Abbay, price elne xvj s̃ ;
summa iij ƚi. iiij s̃.

Item, the vj day of December, for offerand in 179.
Sanct Nicholace chapele of Leith,   xiiij s̃.
Item, to Sanct Nicholace bischop of Leith, . . .
xlij s̃.
Item, to the ruffenis of Leith,   v. s̃.
Item, to Sanct Nicholace bischop of Edinburgh,
for the King, v Franch crounis, and for the
Quene iij Franch crounis, eftir thair commandes
and the auld bukis ;   summa v ƚi. xij s̃.

Item, at ewin to the ruffenis of Edinburgh,   180.
xxviij s̃.

Item,[1] to Sanct Innocentis bischops, . . .   181.
xlij s̃.

Item,[2] deliverit to Schir James Inglis, to be 321.
hyme and his collegis play cotis, xij elnis taffatis ;
price elne xiiij s̃ ;   summa viij ƚi. viij s̃.
Item, for the sam cotis xij elnis canves ; price
elne xiiij đ ;   summa xiiij s̃.

Item, the xx day of December, to James Stewart, 322.
young Lard of Argowane, to by him ane covering
of ane jak because the King schure his jak in
playaing,   iij ƚi. x s̃.

---

[1] Between 26th and 29th Dec.

[2] There is some uncertainty here as to dates, but apparently Feb. 1511-12.
There are many references to Sir James Inglis in the *Accounts of the Lord High
Treasurer* : IV, 441 (' chapellane to the Prince '), *et passim ;* V, 310 (' chancellar of the Kingis chapell ') ; 325-8 (Master of Works) ; lxx (Abbot of Culross) ; *et passim.* But there must have been another Sir James Inglis at this
time, and there has been some confusion of the two names. The Sir James
Inglis mentioned, *L.H.T.A.*, IV, 443, continues to sing at Cambuskenneth
for years after the Abbot of Culross was murdered in March 1531. Cf. VI,
102 (1533), 357 (1537), 447 (1538). See, too, *D.N.B.*, *Sir James Inglis*, and
Pitcairn's *Criminal Trials*, I, 151. Mackenzie, who is, however, notoriously
unreliable, inventories his works, the first item being : ' Poems, consisting
of Songs, Ballads, Plays, and Farces, in MS.' (*Lives of Eminent Writers*,
1708-22).

330.   1511-12   Item,[1] to Gilleam, tabernar, for ane fars play to the King and Quenis Gracis in the Abbay, vj Franch crounis,   iiij ℔. iiij s̃.

331.   Item, the xxj day of Februar, to Gilleam, tabernar, for ane dans to the King and Quene, and for necessaris thairto, comptit be Maister Johne of Murray, . . .   xj ℔. iiij s̃.

333.   Item, the last day of Februar, to Cudde, fule, at evinsange, to by hyme ane coit,   xiiij s̃.

338.   1512   Item, to foure scolaris menstralez, to by thame instrumentis in Flandris, vij ℔. gret, ansuerand in Scottis money to xxj ℔, and help thair expens and fraucht, lvj s̃., and thairefter, because thai plenȝeit thai gat our litill expens and fraucht, deliverit uthir lvj s̃ ;   summa xxvj ℔. xij s̃.

399.   Item,[2] payt to Monsure Lamote servitouris, that dansit ane moris to the King, . . .   ix ℔.

400.   Item, the xvj day of December, to Monsur Lamotis servitouris, that dansit ane uthir moris to the King and Quene,   v ℔. viij s̃.

V, 254.   1525-6   Item,[3] that samyn nycht eftir suppir in mummyn,   xx ℔.

316.   1526   Item, to Schir James Inglis [4] to by play coitis agane ȝule, be the Kingis precept,   xl ℔.

379.   1529   Item, to the Egiptianis that dansit before the King in Halyrudhous,   xl s̃.

432.   1531   [A livery granted to ' the King's Robin Hood.'] Item, the v day of Aprile, for vj quarteris gray taffatis of Jeynes to be ane parte of the Kingis Robene Hudis baner, . . .   xxij s̃. vj d̃.

Item, for vj quartaris ȝallow taffaty to the said baner, . . .   xix s̃. vj d̃.

433.   Item, for ane quarter quhite taffatis to be corsis to the said baner, . . .   iij s̃. iiij d̃.

---

[1] 10th Feb.   [2] 5th Dec.
[3] New Year's day.   [4] *Supra*, p. 329 and n[2].

[Livery granted to ' Christian Rae, Queen of the ^{VI, 37.} Bean.']

1533/4   Item,[1] deliverit to Johne Murray, to be ane play ^{186.} coit to the Kingis son, ij elnis taphety of the cord reid and ӡallow, price thairof   xl ŝ.
Item, for reid and ӡallow bukrame to lyne the samyn   vj ŝ.

1535   Item,[2] to be certane play gounis to the Kingis ^{255.} grace to pas in maskrie, xxiiij elnis Scottis quhyte, price thairof   vŧi. xviij ŝ vj đ.
Item, to be the tothir half of the saidis gounis, xiiij½ elnis Scottis blak . . .   xj ŧi. xvj ŝ.
Item, to Robert Spittall for makyng of the saidis gounis   iij ŧi.

1538   [Payments for a green satin gown and yellow ^{435.} satin kirtle for ' the Quenis fule.']

1538/9   Item, deliverit to ane tailӡeour iij elnis ½ elne of ^{VII, 150.} reid and ӡallow to be ane cote to James Atkinsoun, jugleour, price of the elne of the dymmegrane,[3] xxiiij ŝ and of the ӡallow xx ŝ ;   summa   iij ŧi. xvij ŝ.
[Also red hose ' drawn' with yellow, red and yellow satin doublet, and a red ' bonet.']

1539/40   Item, the thrid day of Januar deliverit to Thomas ^{276.} Arthur to be iij play cotis agane uphalyday, vij elnis half elne reid and vij elnis half elne ӡallow taffites of cord . . .   xiij ŧi x ŝ.
Item, deliverit to him to be ane syde cape to ane of the playaris, vj elnis purpur taffites of corde and ane elne of reid taffites to be ane hude, . . .   vj ŧi. vj ŝ.
Item, deliverit to him to draw the talis of the ^{277.} saidis play cotis, twa elnis reid and ӡallow taffites of twa threid, . . .   xviij ŝ.
Item, gevin for xv elnis bukrem to lyne the saidis play cotis with,   xxx ŝ.

---

[1] 30th Jan.
[2] 28th Dec.
[3] A kind of scarlet cloth.

Item, deliverit to Thomas Arthur for making of the saidis play cotis and cape,   xx s.[1]

VIII, 282.   1544   Item, the xxvj day of Apprile, to Robert Hude in Edinburght,   xliiij s.

386.   1545   Item, at his command, to ane baird fallo callit Hercules,   ij s.

466.   1546   Item, to ane baird husse in Dumbertane,   v s.

IX, 73.   1547   Item,[2] to certane menstrallis of the toun, and thair Robert Hude,   xliiij . . .

74.   Item, xiiij^to Maij, at oure returnyng to Edinburght, at his graces commande, to Robert Hude of Edinburght,   iiij ti. viij s.

282.   1548/9   Item, to Williame Lauder for making of his play and expensis maid thairupoun,   xj ti. v s.[3]

316.   1549   Item,[4] to Jhonne Arthure, Robene Hude of Edinburght, in iiij crounis of the sone,   iiij ti. x s.

393.   1550   Item [5] to Robert Hude in Edinburgh,   iij ti. ix s.

X, 167.   1553   Item,[6] be commande of the saides lordes, to Jaques the Jouglar,[7]   iij ti.

---

[1] These entries occur under ' Expensis debursit upoun the King and Quenis personis the said moneth.'

[2] May, at Dumbarton.

[3] The play was for Lady Barbara Hamilton's wedding.

[4] June.

[5] End of April.

[6] During a circuit court held at Dundee.

[7] Cf. the *Buke of the Howlat*, Scottish Alliterative Poems, *S.T.S.*, II, 73 :—

' In com japand the Ia, as a juglour,
With castis and with cawtelis, a quaynt caryar.
He gart thaim se, as it semyt, in the samyn hour,
Hunting at herdis in holtis so hair ;
Sound saland on the se schippis of towr ;
Bernes batalland on burde, brym as a bair ;
He couth cary the cowpe of the kingis dess,
Syne leve in the sted
Bot a blak bunwed ;
He couth of a hennis hed
Make a mane mess.'

The repertoire of the mediæval juggler is further developed in the next stanza.

1561/2   Item, the last day of Januar, to Jaques Foulis, XI, 103. tailʒeour, xxxviij elnis of reid and quhite taffeteis to be maskin claithis of divers prices,

xx ƚi. xvj s̃. iiij d̃.

1564/5   Item, to the painter for the mask on Fastronis 347. evin to Marie Levingstonis mariage   xij ƚi.

1565   Item,[1] vj maskis, the pece xx s̃ ;   summa vj ƚi.   358.

Item,[2] to Johnie Ramsay, passand of Edinburght 359. to Striviling witht certane merchandice concernyng the furnetour of the Quenis grace for the Maij plais . . .   xl s̃.

[Payment for red and yellow to James Geddie, 405. fool.] [3]

Excerpts from MS. Accounts of the Lord High Treasurer.

Vol. 1566-7.

Dec. 1566   Item the thrid day of december be ꝩe quenis f. 15⁴ grace precept to bastiane paigeir xl elnis of taffeteis of Cord to be sovm preparatenis for ꝩe baptisme [5] ꝩe elne xxvj s̃ *summa* as ꝩe said precept to gidder *with* ꝩe acquittance of ressait schawin vpoun̄ Compt beris   lij ƚi

---

[1] 12th April.
[2] End of April.
[3] There were female fools also at the Court of Mary, Queen of Scots : *L.H.T.A.*, XI, xxvii, xxviii, 420, 473, *et passim*, Nicholas la Jardiniere ; 159, Jonat Musche.
[4] The foliation is not always continuous in these MS. volumes.
[5] *Memoirs of his own Life*, by Sir James Melville of Halhill, Mait. Club, 1833, p. 171 : ' During ther being in Stirling, ther wes daily banketing, dancing, and triumphe ; and at the principall banket ther fell out ane gret eylest and gruge amang the Englis men : for a Frenchman callit Bastien deuysed a nomber of men formed lyk sattyres, with lang tailes and whippis in ther handis, runnyng befoir the meit, quhilk wes brocht throw the gret hall vpon ane trym engyn, marching as apperit it alain, with musiciens clothed lyk maidins, playing vpon all sortis of instrumentis and singing of musick. Bot the sattiers wer not content only to red rown, bot pat ther handis behind them to their tailes, quhilkis they waggit with ther handis, in sic sort as the Englismen supponit it had bene deuysed and done in derision of them, daftly apprehending that quhilk they suld not seam to haue vnderstand. For Mester Hattoun, Mester Ligniche, and the maist part of the gentilmen desyred to sowp before the Quen and gret banket, that they mycht se the better the haill ordour and cerimonies of the triumphe ; bot sa schone as they saw the sattires waging ther tailes or romples, they all set down vpon the bair flure behind the bak of the burd that they suld not see them selues scornit as they thocht . . .'

f. 37 May 1567 Item be ꝑe quenis *grace* precept to James
geddie fule to be him ane abuleȝement ij elnis
j quarter of braid Inglis ȝallow to be Cote
and breikis, ꝑe elne l s̃ *summa*   v℔ xij s̃ vj đ
Item for lynyng and making of ꝑame   xxv s̃
Item to ꝑe said James geddie for iij quarteris
of quhite to be ane pair of schort hoifs and
ane pair of schone   xij s̃

f. 43 June 1567 Item deliverit to Johnne cheisholme comp-
Onerand*us* trollar of ꝑe artailȝerie in compleit payment of
est chesholme ꝑe expensfs of ꝑe fire werk maid be him ꝑe
tyme of ꝑe baptisme of ꝑe kingis grace maiestie
As ꝑe said Johnne p*art*icular Compt maid ꝑairupoun Subscriuit wit*h* his hand producit vpoun
Compt proportis j^clxxxx ℔ xvij s̃ v đ ob.[1]

Vol.1569-71
f. 38 Aug. 1570 Item ꝑe first day of august be ꝑe regentis /g/
speciale co*m*mand to nichola ꝑe fuile to mak
hir expensis and fraucht to france   xv ℔

Vol.1579-81
              Dec. 1580 Item be the kingis ma*ie*steis precept to williame
hudsoun his hienes balladine as for his extraor-
diner panis taikin in teitcheing of his grace
to dance . . .   j^cj ℔

f. 35 Jan. 1580/1 Item aucht e℔n of quhyit sating to be ane slip
to his ma*ie*sties masking claithis the tyme of
the erle of m*ur*rayes mariage price of the e℔n
sex pund Inde   xlviij ℔
Item four e℔n of laun theirto price of ꝑe e℔n
iiij ℔ Inde   xvj ℔
Item fo*ur* elnis of ca*m*merage to the said vse
at iiij ℔ x s̃ the e℔n   Inde   xviij ℔

f. 36   Item thre e℔nis of stiff buckrum to lyne the
heidis of the saidis play claithis at viij s̃ the
e℔n Inde   xxiiij s̃
Item ane bolt of silkin rybbennis to his hienes
masking claithis conteni*n*g lxviij elnis
                                     viij ℔ x s̃
Item fo*ur* vnce of quhyit silk to the saidis
claithis at xviij s̃ the vnce   Inde
                                     iij ℔ xij s̃

[1] Cf. *infra*, 339ff.

Feb. 1581/2 Item be his maiesties precept to thomas hutsoun f. 96
for furnessing of necesſſair apparrell and wappinnis to a mask danſſ as is requisite As the
said precept & his acquittance producit vpoun
compt beris   lxvj ħ xiij ſ iiij đ

Item to James huntare glaissinwrycht for the f. 97
furnessing of glaſſ making and mending of
glaissin windois in the dansing chalmer
[etc.]   xliiij ħ. j ſ iiij đ [1]

Vol. 1593-5

Aug. 1594 [Payments for clothes to the ' keiper of the f. 120
lyouñ ' and his boy.]
Item be his maiesties speciall command and
directioun for transporting of the lyoun fra
haliruid houſſ to striueling and ȝairfra bak
agane And for ȝe expensſſ of men and horsſſ
appoynted to ȝat effect . . .
ij c lvij ħ xvj ſ iij đ [2]

Vol. 1600-1

1600   Item ane quarter of satin to be ane mask to f. 50
hir face at ix ħ ye eln   Inde   xlv ſ [3]

Vol. 1601-4

Feb. 1603   Item be his maiesteis speciall command direc- f. 235
tioun delyuerit to Mr cobler and vthir thrie
commendianis to be ilk ane of ȝame coit and
breikis viij elnis skarlot claith at nyne pund
x ſ ȝe ell   Inde   lxxvj ħ
Item aucht elnis ȝallow veluote to be bordis
ȝairto at xiij ħ vj ſ viij đ ȝe ell   Inde
jc vj ħ xiij ſ iiij đ
Item aucht vnces cramasie silk to steik on ȝe
saidis bordis vpone ȝair claithis at xl ſ ȝe
vnce   xvj ħ

---

[1] In the MS. Accounts of the Master of Works (Portfolio I.), 1579, for repairs
at Holyrood, there is a payment to a slater ' for poynting and bettement of
. . . ye dansing hous.'
[2] For an account of the revels at Stirling for which the lion was required,
cf. *supra*, 50.
[3] This occurs in a list of clothes for Princess Elizabeth.

Excerpts from Inventaires de la Royne Descosse Douairiere
de France, *ed. J. Robertson, Bannatyne Club,* 1863.
(See Preface, lxxii-lxxxix.)

125.   Memoire de tout ce qui a este distribue des draps de soye
et aultres chozes depuis le larriuee de la Royne en Ecosse
commençant au premier jour de Septembre 1561 jusque au
premier jour de Januier 1564 auant Pasques.   Le tout
deliure par moy Seruais de Condez vallet de chambre de
ladicte Dame et le tout deliure a laune de France :—

127.   Plus je deliure a Michelet et a Mernard [1] vj aulnes de toille
Oct. 1561 pour doubler leur habillement de masque.

128.   Plus je deliure au tailleur de Monsieur Danuille [2] xvj
Oct. 1561 aulnes de toille pour doubler des habillementz de masque.

133.   Je deliure a Jacques le tailleur sept aulnes de satin noir
Aug. 1562 pour faire vne cotte pour la Royne aussi deux touretz de
nez deux cornettes et deux masques.

136.   Plus vne aulne et demie de damas blanc pour faire six gibe-
Jan.   sieres de bergers pour des masques au nopces de Monsieur
1562/3 de Sainct Cosme.[3]
        Plus jay deliure a Jacques le tailleur deux manteaux de
masque faictz de taffeta blanc pour faire daultre sorte
dhabillementz a ceux qui jouoient du lut pour lesdicts
masques.   [*Deleted in MS.*]
        Efface pour ce quil est escript en vng aultre endroict.

138.   Il a este rompu trois habillementz de taffetas blanc borde
July 1563 de rouge lesquelz seruirent a abiller des joueurs aux nopces
de Monsieur de Sainct Cosme.

139.   Plus je deliure a Jacques le tailleur deux chanteaux de
Sept.   damas gris broche dor pour faire une robbe a vne poupine.
1563   Plus je deliure a Jacques le tailleur trois quartz et demi de
toille dargent et de soye blanche pour faire vne cotte et
aultre chose a des poupines.

---

[1] Valets of the Queen's Chamber.
[2] Son of the Duke of Montmorency.
[3] The Commendator of St Colm's Inch, who married the sister of the Earl
of Argyll.

Je rompu vng soye de velours bleu pour faire trois grands 141.
bonnetz a la Souisse pour faire des masques.   Dec. 1563

Je delliure a Jehan de Conpiengne [1] troy rest de taffetas 144.
orangie chengent contenant xxviij aulnes demy cart qui Feb.
furt enploye pour les masque qui fit la Royne le jour de son 1563/4
bonque.[2]

Plus je delliure a vng coutellier iij quartier de veloux 162.
noyr pour fairre viij fourreaux a des dacques dEcosse.[3] Jan.
Plus je delliure a Jehan de Conpiengne iij aulnes et demye 1565/6
de toylle dor plainne pour fairre des flanbe sur vj abillement de masque pour des famme le tout en viij morseaux.

Plus audict tapissier je delliure lv aulnes de petitte frange 167.
dor qui fut deffet de dessus des abillement de masque Sept.
laquelz frange a estez mise sur des vieux rideaux de damas 1566
rouge qui seruent au lictz de veloux cramoysi a simple
pantes.

The Inventareis off the Buikis / Ornamentis / and Maskyn 185-7.
Cleiss ressauit be Maister Jhone Wod and James Murray 1569
vpoun the xv day of November the yeir of God j^m v^c lxix
yeiris frome Serues Franchmane.

The Inventarie of the Maskyne Cleise.
Item ane coit of blew satyn with starnis of toig.
Item thre leauche coitis of crammasie satyn pyrnit with
    quheit.
Item tua of the same dowblit with variand tauffateis.
Item thre coitis of greine veluat raynit with yellow · with
    bodeis and slewis of yallow satyn.
Item tua coitis of yallow satyne champit with greine with
    bodeis and slewis of the same.
Item tua coitis of the same champit with blew · the ane
    thairof the bodeis and slewis of yallow satyne.
Item tua coitis of quheit tauffateis figurit with blew with
    bodeis and slewis of quheit.

[1] Queen's tailor.
[2] Bain and Boyd, *Calendar*, II, 47 ; *Keith*, II, 220.
[3] Cf. *Diurnal of Remarkable Occurrents*, 87 : ' And vpoun the ellevint day of
the said moneth . . . at evin our soueranis maid the maskrie and mumschance,
in the quhilk the quenis grace, and all hir Maries and ladies wer all cled in
men's apperrell ; and everie ane of thame presentit ane quhingar, bravelie
and maist artificiallie made and embroiderit with gold, to the said ambassatour
and his gentilmen, euerie ane of thame according to his estate.'

Item tua coitis the ane of reid and the vther of blak ['satyne' *deleted in MS.*] champlet.

Item vj leauche coittis of yellow satyne lynit with sum toige of siluer.

Item ane coit of reid satyne with bodeis and slewis of quheit begareit in the bodeis with toige.

Item ane vthir coit of quheit satyn with bodie and slewes of the same.

Item ane coit of quheit reid and blew tauffateis hingand full of schakaris.

Item ane coit of quheit armesing tauffateis hingand full of schakaris.

Item vj coitis begareit with quheit and reid satyne and dropit with cleith of gold.

Item ane howd of blew reid and quheit tauffateis with schakaris.

Item four bodeis tua aprounis the ane of yallow satyne and the vthir of greine tauffateis.

Item tua pair of slewes of yellow satyne.

Seruees of Condy / ye sall deliuer to our seruitouris James Murray and M[r] Jhone Wod · the haill stuiffe and buikis heir aboue expremit etc. . . . (Signed) James Regent.[1]

Excerpts from A Collection of Inventories and other Records of the Royal Wardrobe and Jewelhouse, etc., 1488-1606. *T. Thomson,* 1815.

Inventory of Jewels, etc., in Edinburgh Castle belonging to James VI. and his Mother. 1578.

229. Tua scheiphirdis kirtillis of quheit canves.

237. Schrynis cofferis buistis caissis pippennis fantaseis fedderis masking claithis pictures cairtis and veschellis of glass.
In the first ane cais with fedderis of divers hewis
Fyve masking garmentis of crammosie satine freinyeit with gold & bandit with claith of gold
Sex maskenis of the same pairt of thame uncompleit
Tuentie foure scheildis of claith of gold for bak and foir

---

[1] Cf. Report on the Muniments of the Rt. Hon. the Earl of Murray, *Hist. MSS. Commission, 6th Report,* p. 672 : 'Maskeine cleis ressauit be James Murray frome Serue the Frencheman, vpoun the xv day of Nouember, 1569.' The list varies only in unimportant details from that quoted above.

Tuelf heid peces of clath of silver claith of gold and crammosie satine.

Ellevin pair of slevis of craip of silver bandit with claith
of gold

Thre Egiptianis hattis of reid and yallow taffeteis

Sum uther bladdis of silver claith and uther geir meit for
maskene

Fyve masking quaiffis for the hind heid

Fyve litle crownis for the foirheid

Ane creill with sum bulyettis of tymmer and pippennis 238.
Ane coffer quhairin is contenit certane pictouris of wemen
callit pippennis being in nomber fourtene mekle and litle,
fyftene vardingaill for thame, nyntene gownis kirtillis and
vaskenis for thame, ane packet of sairkis slevis and hois
for thame, thair pantonis, ane packet with ane furnist bed,
ane uther packett of litle consaittis and triffillis of bittis of
crisp and utheris, tua dussane and ane half of masking
visouris.

Ane uther litle buist grene paintit on the cover with nyn- 240.
tene portratouris of men on horsbak and utheris fantaseis
of evir bane & woid.

Fireworks.

Excerpts from *Manuscript* in the *Royal Household
Papers*, Queen Mary, 1542-67, at Register House.

Expensis maid be Johnne chisholme comptrollar of the
artailȝerye wpouñ certane nummer of fyreworkis Ordanit
be the Quenes maiesties to be maid and put to executiouñ
at the baptisme of hir hienes darrest sone in stiruiling
The said expensis beginning the xix day of Nouembere
1566 And ending the xxij day of decembere nixt eftire
following As at maire lenth is contenit in euery article of
this present compt [1]

[There are many entries relating to the composition of the
fireworks : barrels of powder and brimstone, ' oyle petrole,'
gum of Araby, turpentine, silver, camphor, Lombard
paper, canvas, tar, tallow, lead, packthread, wire, nails,
fish oil, and other ingredients occur. Numerous ' piggis '

---

[1] There are eight folios in the Account, two of them blank.

and pots are required for making the fireworks, also ' twa
peices of treis to mak fyre pompis,' ' xvij plaittis of quhit
yron quhairof was maid fywe flambrant*is*,' ' nyne littill
girthis quhairof was maid balles coverit wi*th* canevas,' one
dozen ' lang fedd*er*it arrowis,' ' four new fyre pa*n*nis togidd*er* wi*th* ane fork of yron to schaw ly*ch*t in the ny*ch*t,'
' thre tuyme pu*n*cheouns quhairin was pakkit the maist
pairt of the small fyrework*is* & tourtrant*is* send out of
Ley*th* to sti*r*uiling.']

Ite*m* for thre dosone of daillis quhairwi*th* was maid the
closing of the forth haldin in sti*r*uiling aganis the men of
warre/ price of the dosone iij ℔ vj š   Su*m*ma   ix ℔ xviij š

Ite*m* for ane dosone & aucht double fir spars to serue for
vpstanders to ᵹe said closing of daillis & als for gibettis
to hing the fyre cransis [1] on / schawing ly*ch*t in the forth
price of the dosone xviij š   Su*m*ma   xxx š

Ite*m* for aucht littill peices of aykin ty*m*mer alsua ſſeruing
for vphald to ᵹe said*is* daillis qu*h*ilk*is* closit the forth in
sindry places price of the peice iij š   Su*m*ma   xxiiij š

Ite*m* for twe*n*ty aucht gaitt sky*n*nis quhairof was maid
four hieland wyld mens cleithing*is* fro*m* heid to fute . . .
                                                         v ℔ xij š

Ite*m* for twe*n*ty aucht ellis thre quarters of bougrem cou*l*-
lo*uris* reid blew blak & quhit . . .   vj ℔ ix š iiij ₫ ob[us]

Ite*m* for four ellis & ane half of vᵹ*er* bougre*m* . . .
                                                    xxij š vj ₫

Ite*m* mair for auchtein ellis of vᵹ*er* bougre*m* being of the
said*is* coullo*uris* . . .   iij ℔ xviij š

All this bougre*m* abone writtin maid in fyftein cleithing*is*
to wit for four lanskny*ch*t*is*, four for morres, four for horſ
men & thre for contrefait dewillis qu*h*ilk*is* cleithing*is* war
distributit to fyftein soldio*uris* of the *com*panyes quha
combattit wi*th*in & wi*th*out the forth togidd*er* wi*th* the
foirsaid*is* hieland men having the executiou*n* of the fyre
work*is* in thair hand*is*

---

[1] Wreath, garland.

Item for thre lamis skynnis quhairof was maid four bon-
netis or fals hair to the saidis mores . . . vj s̃

Item payit for litting of ane pairt of the said bougrem̃
quhilk was blew Into blak for parfitting of the saidis
cleithingis dewlie iij s̃

Item for hardin quhilk was stuffing to ane pairt of the
saidis cleithingis quhair It was necessare ix s̃ iij d̃

Item payit for the making of the saidis fyftein stand of
cleithingis togidder with the four hieland cleithingis of
gait skynnis making in the haill xix stand . . .
vij ł xij s̃

Item payit in drinksiluer to ȝe boyis ȝat helpit to mak the
saidis cleithingis v s̃

Item payit for the cariaige of the haill cleithingis abone
writtin from̃ Edinburght to stiruiling x s̃

Item payit for the len of ane pik pot xv dayis quhairin
was maid the tourtrantis [1] ij s̃

Item for bearing of ane barrell of pik fra the place It was
coft in to ȝe houß quhair the fyre work was maid iij d̃

Item to ane man for fetching afeild & bearing haym̃ of ane
borrowit tar trough quhairin was tarrit the cransis
iiij d̃ obus

Item payit for stray to ȝe pakking of the small fyre workis
alswele within the puncheouns as In the boit ij s̃

[Various payments for bringing of pots, lanterns, ropes,
and munitions from Edinburgh Castle to Leith ; to the
Leith tailor for making ' pokkis ' and for ' making &
sewing of the fyre cransis ' ; to a couper for girthing
puncheons and barrels of fireworks and munitions ; to
various gunners and wrights for making the fireworks ;
for the freight of a boat from Leith to Stirling 'laidin
hayllie with the fyreworkis preparit for the baptisme.']

[1] I have not been able to trace this word.

Iteṁ payit to Johnne Lamy & henry scherar marinellis for thair labouring during the space of four dayis endit the foirsaid xiij day In heitting pik & tare oppinning out towis & dipping of nummer of tourtrantis & cransis . . .

xvj ś

Iteṁ for sawing of twa dosone of the foirsaidis daillis quhairwith the forth was closit . . . xxviij ś

Iteṁ payit for twa horś feis of Edinburght to stiruiling the xiiij day of december quhairon raid the said James hector & charles bourdeouś quha war send to ꝫe said touñ for gydding & principall handilling of the fyre workis & asseiging of the forth xxxij ś

Iteṁ payit to twelf men for Ilk ane ane bourding of fyre-work borne In the nycht for feir of knawlege ꝫairof froṁ the place the boit lay in to ꝫe touñ of stiruiling . . . vj ś

Iteṁ to carters of the said touñ for ten drauchtis of the foirsaid fyrework & munitiouñ vpoun thair cartis froṁ the boit to the touñ x ś

Iteṁ payit to sax workmen quha helpit to loiś ane grit pairt of all that was in the said boit als Labourit at the buylding of the forth carying of tymmer to ꝫe same & bearing chalmeris of gunnis & all vꝫer munitiouns necessare to ꝫe said forth & ꝫat be the space of ane day & ane half . . .

xviij ś

Iteṁ for collis to ꝫe fyre in the forth xxiij đ

Iteṁ for having doun of twa faulcons furth of the castell to ꝫe asseigeing of the forth and taking of thame vp agane

xv ś

Iteṁ payit to twa tailꝫeouris in stiruiling quha helpit the tailꝫeoure ꝫat maid the play claythis to translate thame & augment quhair It was necessare togidder with the helping on of thame vpouñ the souldiouris the tyme of the asseig-ing of the said forth & that be the space of twa dayis

xvj ś

Item for carying doun out of the touñ of stiruiling to the boit of the rest of the munitionis ꝑat ware left eftire the forth asseiging as chalmeris of gunnis & sindry vꝑer munitiouns alswele vpoun cartis as be men bearing   vij s̃

Item payit to ane man in Recompance of his ȝaird dyk cassin douñ at the horsmarcat quhair the Q. maiestie & Embassadouris stuid   iij s̃

Item payit to Cloux helyot, Johnne smyth / James roknow, Robert murray/ Johnne hunyman/ Robert bikertouñ & Johnne mylne ordinar gunnaris for ten dayis endit the xxij day of december foirsaid for thair passing of Edinburght and awaitting in stiruiling during the said space vpouñ the executiouñ of the forth asseigeing & handilling of fyrework Ilk ane on the day iij s̃ iiij d̃   Summa
           xj l̃ xiij s̃ iiij d̃

Item mair payit to James reid wrycht for his awaitting & ſeruing of wrycht craft during the foirsaid space of ten dayis at the constructiouñ of the said forth & vꝑer labouring Ilk day iij s̃   Summa   xxx s̃

Item alsua payit to the said James hector & Charles bourdeouſ principall ordinaris for thair expensis awaitting in stiruiling vpouñ the said ſeruice . . .   v l̃

    [Horse to James Hector going home. Freight of munitions, etc., from Stirling to Leith.]

Item maire payit to Johnne chisholme comptrollare of the said artailȝerye for his awaitting and extraordinare ſeruice makin In the dressing & ouirseing & causing to mak this triomphe of fyrework abone speciffyit be the space of fourtye dayis to wit xxx dayis in leyth And ten day in stiruiling for his panis & extraordinare waigis Ilk day vj s̃ viij d̃   Summa xiij l̃ vj s̃ viij d̃

    Summa quhaironto extendis this haill compt Is jᶜ iiijˣˣx l̃ xvij s̃ v d̃ obᵘˢ

                 Johnne chisholme

Excerpts from *MS. Master of Works Accounts* at Register
House.   Vol. 15, 1616-9, *Edinburgh Castle*, etc.

[From April to June there are weekly wage lists detailing
payments to John Pratt and some half-dozen assistants
for ' *the expenses maid vpoun the fyirwark(is) within the
Castell of Edinburght and in the vtter cloiſ of the palace
of halyruidhous* 19 *June* 1(617) ' ;   also for ' prouisionis,
including canvas, resin, bowstrings, pasteboard, brimstone,
paper, oil, vinegar, ' aquavitye ' sheep skins, dart heads,
wire, and other materials for making the fireworks.   Some
of the more interesting entries are quoted below.]

f. 55. for sex lynis to haill the dragoun and Sanct george with
                                                              x ħ xvj ſ
To Ralf ralinsone carver for making the dragoñ & Sanct
george   xij ħ
To him for making muldis to the plaisterers   x ħ
To a tailȝeour & wrycht that wrocht with him 3 dayes
                                                          iij ħ xij ſ
for a pair of gloves to Sanct george   viij ſ
f. 58. To thomas haddowy tailȝeour for making of the fyir wark-
mens clothis   lvj ſ
To wm wallace for a pund and a half of tyn to be a horne
to the vnicorne and for making of it   xxiiij ſ
f. 60. Item for making of Sanct George his spere at the fyir
warkis to him   xij ſ
f. 68. for transporting of the saidis sevin fyrework men fra
Bervick to Edinburgh haifing 8 horsſ   xxx ħ
for tua great reames quheillis   xl ſ
for tua litle reames quheillis   xxxvj ſ
Item for transporting of Elias prat fra Bervick to Edinburgh
with horſ hyre   iiij ħ
for careing the hobby horſ & the boy fra Bervick to
Edinburgh   iiij ħ iiij ſ
f. 69. for tackettis to the hobbie horſ   iij ſ
for v pair of bellis at 18 s pair   iiij ħ xij ſ
for 8 pair of bellis at 8 s pair   iij ħ iiij ſ
for 24 pair bellis at 6 s pair   vij ħ iiij ſ
f. 70. To Ralf dryden for his hobbie horſ   iiij ħ
for a wissoren [1]   xxx ſ

[1] Visor, mask.

for a bowett [1] & cam*m*le [2] to the hill   xij š

for sex torches   iiij ħ

for j^{cj} xl wavers to the hielandmen   iiij ħ vj š

for tuyges [3]   xxx š

for a pair of schone to the Cap*tain* of Envie   xl š   f. 71.

To the Earle of Abircornes tabern*our* & quhisler for attending the youthes at the Moreiſs dance the ny*cht* of the fyrwark*is*   viij ħ xij š

To the fyrewarkmen to drink   vj ħ xiij š iiij đ

for the fyrewarkmenis beddis 15 ny*chtis* haifing 16 s ilk ny*cht* Inde   xij ħ

To John*n* pratt & sevin wi*th* him for transporting them wi*th ʋair* horſs hyre fra Ed*inburgh* to Bervick and for *ʋair* charges   j^{cj} 1 ħb

Sum*m*a of the haill expensſs debursit in fyrewarkis according to this preceiding compt extendis to ane thousand fourtene pundis fourtene schillingis sex đ.

---

[1] Lantern.

[2] A piece of wood used for hanging anything on.

[3] Teug, rope.

APPENDIX IV.

PAGEANTS AND PLAYFIELDS.

PAGEANTS AND PLAYFIELDS.[1]

A. Pageants.

The following forms of the word appear in MS. Records :
Aberdeen—Pageant (1505/6 *et passim*), badgeandis (1515/6),
pagganis (1530), pageane (1531), pan3eanys (1531), pagane
(1532, 1534, 1546), pangeaniſs (1533), peggane (1538),
baganis (1551), paganis (1551), pegane (1554) ; *Lanark*—
pad3en (1507) ; *Haddington*—pagis (1534), pagenis (1537),
piad3anis (1541) ; *Edinburgh*—pageants (1628), pages,
pagin (1633), padgines (1633, 1634), paidgines (1634).

At Aberdeen, whereas, on the one hand, in several
cases the representation is clearly indicated (1505/6, the
first time ; 1526 ; 1531, the second time), on the other,
in the majority of cases, the interpretation cannot be
determined with certainty. It has generally been assumed
that the 1505/6 statute commanding ' tua of ilke craft to
paſs *with* ȝe pageant ȝat ȝai furnys to keip thar*e* geir*e* ' on
Candlemas Day points to moving stages of the type associated with the English cyclical mysteries. The fact that in
this same minute the term is used definitely in the other
sense need not discredit this view ; which does not, however, fit in with the suggested interpretation of the Candlemas play (*supra*, 67) unless the pageants are to be regarded
merely as ' convoy carts,' with, perhaps, an appropriate
grouping of the characters for the purpose of a preliminary
spectacular display. This may also be the correct interpretation of the 1554 entry, when the Wrights and Masons
and Coopers protest against having ' ane honest baner and
pegane of ȝair awin ' whereas they had always gone with
the smiths ' vnder ane baner and pegane.'

In England the respective crafts were charged with the
upkeep of these ' edifizi ambulanti.' The records of the
Hammermen of Edinburgh, which alone among surviving

---

[1] Where authorities are not specified, see under respective sections of
Appendix I.

craft records are sufficiently detailed,[1] reveal no such item
of expenditure. In short, there is no absolutely clear
instance in Scotland of either the use of the term ' pageant '
to denote a movable stage, or, if we except the ' cart to ᵹe
danſs ' made for the Edinburgh Hammermen (1506), of the
actual existence of such a vehicle under another name.
(The ' convoy cart ' of the 1558 play at Edinburgh seems
to have fulfilled the secondary function of bringing the
players to fixed scaffolds. Note, too, the part played by
the ' cart with certane bairnes ' in the 1561 ' entry.') But
here, again, the records are so meagre as to render any
reliable conclusion impossible. Later, in connection with
the 1633 entertainment at Edinburgh, the word ' pageant '
is used repeatedly both in the official records and by contemporary writers to represent the fixed scaffolds on which
the representations were staged.

B. Playfields.

Playfields are found attached to various burghs. The
term ' play ' here, as elsewhere, cannot be resolved with
certainty. There is, however, evidence to show that the
playfields, at any rate at (1) Aberdeen, (2) Dundee, (3)
Edinburgh, (4) Perth, were utilised at some time or other
for dramatic performances.

(1) Aberdeen.

The Haliblude play was performed at ' ly wyndmylhill ' in 1440 and 1445.

8th July 1559 : ' The said day malcum moreis wes
maid freman & burgis of gild for ᵹe compositioune of
tene merkis quhilk wes consignit be ᵹe consell to
help to ᵹe makyng of ᵹe play feild & sua ᵹe den of
gild to be dischargit ᵹairof In his nixt compt.'[2]
This, presumably, was the playfield at the Spa Well,
which was subsequently leased by the Town Council
to George Jamesone, the painter. 13th May 1635 :
The Council being convened ' anent the petitioun
gewin in to thame be George Jamesoun, indweller

---

[1] Even the Perth Hammermen's accounts are far from complete.
[2] MS. Council Register, xxiii, 186.

in the said burght, makand mentioun, that for
sameikle as a greate pairt of the playfeild belongeing
to the toune whair comedies were wont to be actit
of auld besyde the well of Spa, is spoilled, brockin,
and cariet away be speat and inundation of watter
. . . so that unles some course be taikin to withstand suche speattis and invndatiounes, the whole
playfeild, within a short space of tyme will alluiterlie
decay, and serwe for no wse . . .'   The Council
agree ' to giwe, grant, and sett to the said George
Jamesoun a lease and tack of the said plott of ground
callit the Playfeild during all the dayes of his lyftyme
allanerlie . . . with full power, libertie, and priuiledge
to him to build and mack sic policie and planting in
and about the said plott of ground in all pairts . . .
as he sall think most convenient.' [1]

(2) *Dundee.*

' Item the commoun play feild with the boundis
thairof Limitat as followis To witt the dyik of ꝑe
barne daill and ꝑe grey sisteris dyikis at ꝑe west
The commune burn or wattergang at ꝑe north The
Townis wall on ꝑe east And ꝑe commune gaittis oñ
ꝑe south pairtis.' [2]

Calderwood, I, 142, refers to the ' Historie of Dyonisius
the Tyranne ' having been acted in the playfield.   ' John
the Baptist ' may have been performed there too ; for the
playfield lay just outside the West Port.

In 1553 the Council Records have a reference to ' the
play at the westfield.' [3]

21*st June* 1593 : ' The quhilk day It is statute and ordanit
that the haill commoun boundis about ꝑe playfeild of
this burght betwix the commoun burñ at ꝑe north the
acre occupeit be patrik andersouñ & Robert myln at ꝑe
west & ꝑe tenementis direct north fra ergyillis port at
ꝑe eist pairtis sal be keipit in all tyme cumming haill
& vnbrokine or cassine in ony sort for ſserving to ꝑe

[1] *Extracts from the Records of Aberdeen*, 1625-42, pp. 74-6.
[2] Rental list in the ' Lokkit Book,' f. 2.
[3] MS. Burgh Court Register.

commoun vse of ҏe Inhabitantis of this bur*gh*t and
Incaiſs ony persoun be apprehendit braking or casting
ony p*art* ҏ*air*of w*ith*in the bound*is* foir said To pay fyve
lib for ilk tyme for ҏe contraventioun . . .' [1]

(3) *Edinburgh*.

In 1456 King James the Second granted a charter
under the Great Seal to the Burgh of Edinburgh
of the land known as the Greenside ' pro tournamentis
jocis et justis actibus bellicis ibidem, ad nostri et
nostrorum successorum complacenciam, faciendis et
peragendis.' [2].

7th Oct. 1552. James Henderson approached the Town
Council with a proposal for a new playfield. ' And
quhair as your commoun landis and pastour groundis is
analit and put away be ane till help ane wther that
was gevin you be kingis for nurssing of the pepill and
bringing of thame vp in lesum pastymes meit for deffence
of the realme and tovne, insamekle that thair is no wther
place left to play interludis in to draw pepill till the
toune, nor pastyme ground for the induellaris, quhair-
throuch thai ar compellit till greit chargis to seik thair
plesour in wther tovnes ; in remeyd quhairof gif ye sall
grant vnto me and my said pertynaris bot the lytill
groundis that lyis betuix the Gray Freyr porte and the
Kirk of Field, with ane penny of ilk hand bow, corsbow,
and culvering, bowlis and wther pastymes, we sall big
the said groundis for all sic necessaris and plesouris.' [3]

This proposal, apparently, did not materialise ; for,
two years later, the Burgh records show items of expenditure for constructing a playfield on the original
site of the Greenside. *27th June* 1554 : The Council
' ordanis the thesaurar Robert Grahame to content and
pay to the maister of wark of the makar of the playing
place the sowme of xxiiij li. for compleiting thairof.' [4]
20th July 1554 : The Council ordains the Treasurer to pay
to the Master of Work £42, 13s. 4d. 'makand in the hale

[1] MS. Burgh Court Register.
[2] *Charters relating to the City of Edinburgh,* No. 36 (*S.B.R.S.*) ; also *Edinburgh Council Records*, I, 327 (*S.B.R.S.*)
[3] *Edinburgh Burgh Records* (*S.B.R.S.*), II, 172.
[4] *Ibid.*, II, 195.

the sowm of ane hundreth merkis and that to complete the play field now biggand in the Grenesid.'[1] The Treasurer's account for 1553-4 has, ' Item, payit to the warkmen that compleitit the playfeild, be ane precept datit the xvij day of August xxxiiij li.'[2] For plays acted at the Greenside in 1554, see App. I., *s.v. Edinburgh*. The Treasurer's account for 1555-6 details expenses made for ' cutting and outlatting of the walter in the Play-field,' and to ' the calsay maker to flag it.'[3] 1*st Nov.* 1588 : John Hill, tenant of the ' lands of the rwid of the Grenesyde ' is discharged from ' ony teilling and ryving of ony pairt of the playfeyld.'[4]

(4) *Perth.*

23*rd June* 1603 : there is a reference in the Council minutes to ' ye play to be plyit on tuyday in ye playfeld.'[5] The playfield, which still survives by name in the sasine register, was situated at the end of the High Street. There was also the ' amphi-theter of St Johnstone,' in which the Satyre of the Thrie Estaitis is said to have been acted.[6]

The following places also had playfields, but there is no actual record of their being used for dramatic perform-ances :—

(1) *Glasgow.*

' After the sale of the Greenhead lots in 1588-9, the Old Green, extending from the River Clyde on the south to St Enoch's Croft on the north, and from the Stockwell tenements on the east to St Enoch's Burn on the west, remained almost intact for another hundred years. Used as a place of public resort, it is referred to in 1558 as the playground of Glasgow (*palestram de Glasgw lusoriam*) . . .'[7]

---

[1] *Edinburgh Burgh Records (S.B.R.S.),* II, 196.
[2] *City of Edinburgh Old Accounts,* I, 106.
[3] *Ibid.,* I, 178.
[4] *Edinburgh Burgh Records,* IV, 532.
[5] App. I, 266, *s.v. Perth.*
[6] John Row's *Historie of the Kirk of Scotland,* Mait. Club, 1842, II, 312.
[7] Robert Renwick, *Glasgow Memorials,* 1908, pp. 73-4. Cites reference to Glasg. Prot. No. 469.

(2) *Haddington.*

7th May 1610 : ' ꝥe cairt throw ꝥe playfeild '—
Council statute to prevent ' ꝥe playfeild in ꝥe sandis '
being used as a thoroughfare for carts.[1]

(3) *Markinch.*

A piece of land there is still known locally as the
Playfield.

(4) *Stirling.*

Charter under the Great Seal—' Apud Castrum de
Striviling, 28 Sept. (1578) Rex—pro diligenti servitio
sibi quotidie impenso—cum avisamento secreti con-
cilii ad feudifirmam dimisit Thome Ritchie et Jonete
Meclum ejus sponse, heredibus,. eorum subscript. et
assignatis—peciam terre vocatam the Auld- playfeild, jacentem prope castrum de Striviling ex boreali
latere ejusdem . . .' *etc.*[2]

I have not found any trace of a regular playfield at
Cupar, Fife, but we know that the Satyre of the Thrie
Estaitis was acted on the Castlehill.

[1] Haddington MS. Burgh Court Books.
[2] *Reg. Mag. Sig.,* 1546-80, No. 2800, cited in Stirling Natural History and
Archæological Society Transactions, 1897-8. A plan of the old playfield is
given in the *Stirling Antiquary,* Vol. II.

INDEX.